S0-ADI-217

PAUL AXELROD is a member of the Division of Social Science at York University.

Propelled by buoyant economic conditions, favoured by free-spending politicians, and buttressed by wide-spread public support, higher education during the 1960s became one of Ontario's major growth industries. But less than a decade later, in a dramatic reversal of spending priorities, funding policies threatened to squeeze the very life out of the provincial university system.

In this wide-ranging study, Axelrod explores the impact of economic changes on Ontario universities since the Second World War. He addresses the questions of how universities were perceived by the public, why they were supported during the period of expansion, how they set out to fulfil their prescribed functions, and how they were affected by the diminished opportunities and cooler economic climate of the 1970s.

This volume touches on such diverse issues as business-university relations, student financial assistance, manpower planning, and faculty unionization. It examines the internal dynamics of university life against the background of the social and economic conditions which directly affected Ontario universities but over which they had virtually no control. How could they plan for an economy that valued having no plan?

The author concludes that not only did the universities prove to be imperfect instruments of economic development, but the efforts expended in the task compromised their vital roles as islands of culture and critical thought in a materialistic society.

PAUL AXELROD

Scholars and Dollars: Politics, Economics, and the Universities of Ontario
1945-1980

UNIVERSITY OF TORONTO PRESS

Toronto Buffalo London

© University of Toronto Press 1982
Toronto Buffalo London
Printed in Canada

ISBN 0-8020-5609-1 (bound). – ISBN 0-8020-6492-2 (pbk.)

Canadian Cataloguing in Publication Data
Axelrod, Paul Douglas.
Scholars and dollars

Originally presented as the author's thesis (Ph.D.),
York University, under title: The economy, government
and the universities of Ontario, 1945–1973.
Includes index.
ISBN 0-8020-5609-1 (bound). – ISBN 0-8020-6492-2 (pbk.)

1. Universities and colleges – Ontario – History – 20th century.
2. Higher education and state – Ontario.
I. Title.

LA418.06A95   378.713   C82-094715-6

TO MY PARENTS

RUTHE AND MORRIS AXELROD

Preface

This book began as a doctoral dissertation in the Department of History at York University. I would like to thank the members of my thesis supervisory committee whose advice, criticism, and encouragement were sought, proffered, and valued: Michael Katz, Peter Oliver, Viv Nelles, and David Bell.

Others who commented helpfully on all or parts of the manuscript at various stages of its preparation include Alison Prentice, Paul Craven, Fred Gibson, Jack Granatstein, Brian McKillop, Tom Traves, Susan Houston, Ed DesRosiers, Gerry Tulchinsky, and Roger Graham. Not all of the readers will be pleased with the way in which I responded to their suggestions; none, therefore, bears responsibility for any of this book's deficiencies.

Among the many archivists who provided valuable assistance, David Hughes of York University deserves special mention for his genuine interest and his exemplary expertise.

Rik Davidson at the University of Toronto Press provided editorial guidance in a manner that made my association with the publisher a smooth and happy one.

I am grateful to the journals, *Interchange* and the *Canadian Historical Review*, which have previously published abridged versions of chapters 2 and 3 respectively.

This book has been published with the help of a grant from the Social Science Federation of Canada, using funds provided by the Social Sciences and Humanities Research Council of Canada, and of a grant to the University of Toronto Press from the Andrew W. Mellon Foundation. A doctoral fellowship from the Canada Council supported much of the research for the book, and a Queen's University Research Award helped offset typing expenses.

My deepest debt is to Karen Levine. Her contribution cannot be described; it can only be treasured.

P.A.

Contents

INTRODUCTION 3

One
Education, Utilitarianism, and the Acquisitive Society 7

Two
Corporate Aid to Higher Education 34

Three
Private Power and Public Institutions 54

Four
Provincial Planning 1945–67 77

Five
The Curriculum, Professionalism, and the Market Economy 100

Six
More Scholar for the Dollar 1968–73 141

Seven
Students, Staff, and the State: The Politics of Scarcity 1974–80 179

CONCLUSION 214
NOTES 221
NOTES ON SOURCES 255
STATISTICAL APPENDIX 257
INDEX 261

Abbreviations

ACAP Advisory Committee on Academic Planning
AUCC Association of Universities and Colleges of Canada
CAUT Canadian Association of University Teachers
COPSE Commission on Post-Secondary Education in Ontario
COU Council of Ontario Universities
CPUO Committee of Presidents of the (Provincially Assisted) Universities of Ontario
CUA (Advisory) Committee on University Affairs
CUASA Carleton University Academic Staff Association
CUF Canadian Universities Foundation
CUS Canadian Union of Students
DUA Department of University Affairs
HRC Humanities Research Council
IFE Industrial Foundation on Education
MCU Ministry of Colleges and Universities
NCCU National Conference of Canadian Universities
NRC National Research Council
OCUA Ontario Council on University Affairs
OCUFA Ontario Confederation of University Faculty Associations
OFS Ontario Federation of Students
OISE Ontario Institute for Studies in Education
OSAP Ontario Student Awards (Assistance) Program
RG-2 Record Group 2, Education Department Records, Provincial Archives of Ontario
RG-32 Record Group 32, Committee on University Affairs Records, Provincial Archives of Ontario

SCHOLARS AND DOLLARS

The two distinct objects of university education are mental culture and practical utility. In recent years the latter has steadily gained upon the former owing to the utilitarian character of the age and the increased expenditures have doubtless been chiefly responsible for the development of this branch of instruction.

Report of the Royal Commission on the University of Toronto, 1906

Our true wealth resides in an educated citizenry. Our shrewdest and most profitable investment rests in the education of our people.

John Robarts, Premier of Ontario, 1965

There will be cries of alarm from here and there when the first step makes it clear to the university community and everyone in Ontario that we insist on more scholar per dollar from this point on.

John White, Ontario Minister of University Affairs, 1971

Introduction

In the fall of 1981, amid a flurry of publicity, the federal government rediscovered Canada's universities. Long the silent partner who paid half the bills and asked few questions, Ottawa seemed intent on reversing this process by slashing its grants and tightening the strings. It floated plans to reduce dramatically its support of higher education through the Established Programs Financing arrangement and to redirect its funds towards university programs designed to serve the country's economic needs.[1] The extent of the cuts and the nature of the conditions remained unclear, even after the federal budget of 12 November. None the less, the episode effectively crystallized the central dilemma of Canadian universities in this century: what is their role in society and how should they fulfil it?

Most historians of higher education have addressed these questions in an unrestrained spirit of optimism and idealism.[2] They celebrate the universities' contribution to culture, their provision of educational opportunity to ever-increasing numbers of students, and their civilizing role in preserving intellectual freedom and pursuing truth. Through such accounts, universities are personified – and the 'biographies' almost always detail heroic epics of struggle, commitment, survival, and success. Furthermore, they are mostly 'whiggish' or progressivist in their assumptions and themes: the past is treated as an extended and continuing voyage to the best educational world yet – that of the present. The massive expansion of education facilities in the 1960s, of course, represents the most glorious voyage to date. All this progress reflects positively on society at large – a society that would encourage, cherish, and pay for such valuable endeavours.

Undoubtedly, there is an element of truth in this perception. But if it is a totally accurate insight into our history, then how does one explain the present? Why, in 1981, was Ottawa threatening to squeeze the life out of these cherished institutions, and why, during the 1970s, did the Ontario government practically succeed in doing the same?

Was there a sudden shift in values about the importance of higher education? This study argues that there was not. The assumptions that accompanied the expansion of the universities in the 1960s were remarkably similar to those that combined with the spending restraints of the 1970s. Higher education was valued *not* for its ideals, but primarily for its products – skilled professionals who would contribute to economic prosperity. So long as they seemed to be fulfilling this function, universities remained an important social priority. But once they produced surplus manpower, redundant programs, and a burdensome addition to the public debt, they no longer appeared to be such profitable social investments. Hence, the federal government's evident desire to be more selective – and pragmatic – in those programs it intends to support.

This process can be fully understood only if the historian places the development of higher education in a context broader, less idealistic, and more critical than that of the traditional historiography. The present study makes no effort to explore the detailed history of every university in Ontario, nor does it address every important facet of post-secondary education. Instead, it attempts to cut across institutional lines by focusing on certain dominant themes in the relationship of university to society since the Second World War. It addresses the questions of how universities were perceived by the public, why they were supported during the expansion of the late 1950s and mid-60s, how they set out to fulfil their prescribed functions, and how they were affected by the diminished opportunities and cooler economic climate of the 1970s. Through a contextual approach, the book touches on issues as diverse as business-university relations, student financial assistance, manpower planning, and faculty unionization. Thus it examines the internal dynamics of university life against the background of social and economic conditions which directly affected Ontario universities but over which they had virtually no control. In short, this book is presented as a study in the political economy of higher education and as a chapter in the political culture of the province of Ontario.

This, of course, is not the first attempt to explore the development of universities from a critical perspective. Other writers have examined the function of higher education within sustained critiques of the role of the state in modern society.[3] Largely Marxist or neo-Marxist in orientation, such authors contend that universities are a vital economic and political instrument through which the dominant classes have asserted their authority over less powerful groups in evolving capitalist societies. They argue that wealthy businessmen have established the direction and determined the priorities of universities by securing the majority of positions on university boards of governors; that higher education provides the skilled manpower to manage and direct private corporations; that in classrooms students are socialized to accept the values of a capitalist political economy; and that, in their failure to ensure adequate access for students from lower-income classes, universities have perpetuated social and economic disparity in Canada. All of this, it is claimed, has been done primarily with public funds so that, while the rich and powerful were not compelled to pay the piper, they have unmistakably called the tune.

Some of these conclusions will be confirmed in the essay that follows. But while my own views derive from similar concerns about the uneven distribution of power in society and while my major interest is also the relationship between the economy, the state, and higher education, I am convinced that the above interpretations (in their present form) suffer from certain deficiencies. Higher education has seldom received in such accounts extensive or penetrating treatments. Discussions of universities and colleges usually constitute only a single chapter or a few paragraphs of studies on the role of the state in modern capitalist societies. The dominant role of businessmen in the university is assumed, proven with selective evidence, or not proven at all. Without more intensive analysis, many questions about the relationship between the corporate, government, and university worlds remain unresolved within current Marxist writings.

First, if members of the corporate sector (who undeniably control the boards of non-denominational universities) have sought to administer these institutions in their own collective interest, then how can one reconcile this with the fact that boards of governors, both by law and practice, have generally had little control over the development of university curricula, which has been the prerogative of academic authorities on university senates? In fact, the precise role played by businessmen in the expansion of individual universities has not been adequately investigated. Furthermore, if the primary function of higher education is seen as an economic one, then how can one explain the establishment of 'impractical' arts courses, interdisciplinary programs, and non-professional subjects which grew as rapidly during the 1960s as professional courses, graduate programs, and vocational studies? Even with regard to these latter areas, no one has satisfactorily explored the *process* through which specific economic goals were in fact achieved. For that matter, the frequent *failure* of universities to respond adequately and consistently to the demands of the market remains unexamined. And exactly what part did the universities' major benefactor – the government itself – play in creating initiatives and co-ordinating the massive expansion of higher education in the post-war period?

In addition, if universities were intended primarily to serve the specific needs of business and the professions, then how should the deep-rooted and far-reaching support in other areas of the community for the expansion of higher education be interpreted? What did the people of Ontario hope to gain by endorsing the massive extension of university facilities and what relationship did their attitudes towards post-secondary education have to other social and economic concerns in post-war Canada? Finally, why was this enthusiasm eroded so suddenly and so deeply in the past decade? What is missing, then, are answers to such questions – studies which explore in depth the rationale behind and the process through which universities became instruments of economic growth in the 1950s and 60s and objects of economic restraint in the 1970s.

Thus this book, which focuses on the province of Ontario, probes two central problems. It documents the vulnerability of higher education to shifting perceptions of its economic importance; and it discusses the continuous difficulty universities faced in attempting to achieve economic goals. The study concludes with the observation that, although the universities proved to be imperfect instruments of economic development, the very efforts they devoted to this function badly compromised their vital role as islands of culture and critical thought in a materialistic society. At no time was this more evident than in the economic recession of the 1970s.

ONE

Education, Utilitarianism, and the Acquisitive Society

The enormous progress made in the development of Canadian education in the past century has been the object of high praise by politicians, educators, and various writers in Canada. One author attributes this admittedly impressive advancement to society's 'never-ending effort to develop an organizational structure which encourages every individual ... to realize his fullest potentiality'.[1] Too often, however, historians of educational change in Canada and elsewhere have carried out their work within narrow and uncritical intellectual parameters. The result, as Bernard Bailyn notes in *Education in the Forming of American Society*, has been the 'wrenching of events from historical context.' In these accounts the history of education has come to mean the history of institutions, administrations, and pedagogy in isolation from other social, cultural, and economic events. The most polemical and enthusiastic studies of this type have recounted, in Michael Katz's sardonic words, 'tale[s] of sacrifice and triumph through which the contemporary public school came into existence as the great achievement of Western political culture.'[2]

In response to such deep-rooted historiographical traditions, there has evolved in Europe, the United States, and Canada a revisionist approach to the study of educational history. Less sanguine than their predecessors about the strengths and accomplishments of 'western political culture,' revisionists have exposed the ways in which schools have reinforced the class prejudices, the political values, and the economic interests of ruling elites.[3]

Though revisionist educational history in Canada is still in its infancy, two distinct (but related) themes recur in the literature that has been produced. On the one hand, school systems have been treated as vital instruments of political and cultural socialization throughout the history of Canada. On the other hand, schools have been portrayed as essential elements in the process of economic growth. While these two ingredients have coexisted as the dominant purposes of education, the emphasis has shifted from one to the other at different times and at different levels of the educational system. As we shall see, the economic imperative was clearly pushing its way up the educational ladder in the years preceding the Second World War.

In the 1870s elementary education became a basic and permanent feature of children's lives in Ontario. There, as in several other provinces, laws were passed ensuring that schooling was both compulsory and free for children up to the age of 12. According to Alison Prentice, educators and politicians who supported these causes in Upper Canada were interested far less in spreading the rich rewards of educational opportunity than in imbuing youth with the values of thrift, discipline, patriotism, and class identification.[4] In the words of Ontario's high school inspectors in 1873, the main function of elementary education was 'to provide for every child of sound mind and body the means of obtaining a minimum of knowledge and mental training,'[5] or, as the chief superintendent of education in New Brunswick phrased it, 'to prepare the child to discharge the duties and meet the obligations of coming manhood, including his relations to the family, society and the state.'[6]

Egerton Ryerson, the chief superintendent of Ontario schools, had tried to inject a more practical formula into the school curriculum by introducing courses in commerce, agriculture, and practical science in 1871, but for the most part students interested in becoming craftsmen and tradesmen did so by apprenticing with masters outside the schools themselves. Those able to afford the costs of becoming professionals went on to high school and possibly university where it was 'presumed that the leading men of the next generation, its clergymen, its lawyers, its doctors, its editors, the men who will make farming a science, its engineers and machinists, its prominent manufacturers and its teachers would be trained.' Students at the higher levels of the educational system were privileged as well by being exposed more deeply to the elements of a 'liberal culture.' While the public schools 'exist[ed] to sow intelligence widely, the High Schools [were designed] to plough deeply a small portion of mental soil.'[7] Apart from the tiny élite who profited from post-elementary training during the period preceding the industrial revolution, students attended schools that had not yet been integrated into the economic mainstream of Canadian life. In the classroom students were immersed in the cultural values of their elders, but they were not yet being trained for specific vocational pursuits.

Between 1870 and 1900, the economy of Ontario made slow but steady progress as the roots of the modern industrial age were firmly implanted. While 78 per cent of the population had lived on farms in 1871, thirty years later 57 per cent lived in rural areas and 43 per cent in the cities. Between 1881 and 1891, the number of industrial establishments in Toronto increased from 932 to 2401.[8] Spurred to new heights by the National Policy of 1879, the manufacturing sector in Ontario increased its productive capacities significantly in subsequent years as the province began exporting stoves, farm machinery, steam engines, and clothing to the Maritimes and abroad. This shift was marked as well by an increasing trend towards the concentration of industry. In industries associated with the major resource sectors such as agricultural implements, furniture, and brewing, the number of companies actually declined between 1871 and 1891, but their output increased enormously.[9]

The impact of these developments on the educational system was considerable. Educators and employers realized that the traditional method of training students to work in industry – the apprenticeship system – was increasingly unworkable. The rise of the mechanized factory system, the increasing division of labour on the factory floor, and the disappearance of small business establishments owned and operated by single proprietors seriously eroded the position of independent craftsmen and tradesmen as major producers of finished goods. Their role as teachers of apprentices diminished accordingly. The need evolved, then, not only to teach young people the skills required of specific vocations but to familiarize them with the industrial process as a whole. As one employer told the commission investigating the relations between labour and capital in the 1880s:

I believe that the proper place for the training of the hand is in the lower classes in school, where all are attending. What I urge is manual training or industrial training, such as the training of the hand to make it expert, and the training of the head to make it clear and definite in controlling the hand, together with some slight training in use of tools, which should be done without teaching any particular trade.

Another industrialist testified to the inquiry investigating the mills and factories of Canada in 1882: 'Employers are seriously inconvenienced by this lack of education in those applying for work, necessitating the importation of educated labour when our own people should be trained for these positions.'[10]

Those stressing more practical forms of education were supported as well by liberal educators who called upon schools to abandon anachronistic programs and methods of study:

Dissatisfaction with the narrow range of Victorian education was not confined to critics outside the school. On the inside, educators were becoming increasingly impatient with the formalistic, academic mould that had hardened around much of Victorian education ... Th[e] new theory raised relevance to an educational virtue, and allowed educators to promote the new 'practical' subjects and methods with enthusiasm and conviction ... Everyone it seemed – manufacturers, workmen, and many educators – agreed that the public schools as instruments of the state should assume a larger responsibility in preparing people for occupations more appropriate to the new economy.[11]

Against this background, a number of important changes were introduced into the school program. In 1891 the Toronto Technical School was opened for the purpose of offering theoretical and laboratory instruction in such subjects as physical science, mechanical construction, architecture, and building. In 1899 manual training was introduced into the elementary schools of Ontario. As both a 'practical and cultural subject, it could be taught in the elementary school where most people completed their education but where it was agreed specialized training had no place.' The process of exposing students in a general way to the scientific and technical developments of the era was enhanced by the offering of such subjects as chemistry, physics, botany, and zoology which had all gained an entrenched place in most Ontario high schools by the end of the century.

Yet according to some industrial leaders, the type of educational training available was not yet specific and practical enough. Elementary and secondary school students were now lectured more regularly on subjects related to science and technology, but employers were still not satisfied with the quality and scope of educational training. Bluntly, *Industrial Canada*, the journal of the Canadian Manufacturers Association, asked in 1905:

Where, then, is the training ground from which we are to recruit our department foremen, our factory superintendents, and the men who are to guide and direct the practical side of our national industries ...? The skilled help problem is rapidly becoming the most serious problem which the manufacturer is called upon to contend with.

Not until the first decade of the twentieth century, when prominent industrial and business organizations initiated a campaign for technical and industrial education, were fundamental changes introduced into the school curriculum. Gathering support from educators, labour unions, and the media, the campaign culminated in 1910 with the publication of a report called *Education for Industrial Purposes*, prepared by John Seath, the superintendent of education in Ontario. He argued that industrial education was vital if the province were to meet the demands of 'national commercial rivalry' and if it were to reverse the 'imperfect provision of skilled labour due to the decline of the apprenticeship system.'[12]

Three months after the report was published the Industrial Education Act (1911) was passed in the province. A number of new institutions and programs were created. General industrial schools were established in order to offer training in the basic trades as well as in subjects considered essential for a good general education. Special schools were created for the purpose of providing theoretical and practical instruction in specific trades practised in local communities. Within high schools, technical departments were developed throughout the province. And for those already working in industry, co-operative industrial schools and evening courses were designed to provide practical and theoretical instruction in specific occupations. In response to these changes, noted commentators, such as the editor of the *Canadian Annual Review*, were unrestrained in their enthusiasm over the economic value of educational training:

Parents have felt that Canada can no longer lag behind in a matter of such paramount importance as education. No public money is more wisely spent and none brings richer returns to the state than that spend on schools. The expansion of Canada in material things would be of little worth if a decline in educational enthusiasm were to accompany it. Fortunately, the contrary spirit has asserted itself.[13]

While preserving its loftier academic function, then, secondary education had broadened its vocational parameters and superseded the public schools as the dominant arena for practical training. Universities, on the other hand, retained their function of schooling the tiny and privileged élite who would occupy society's leading profesions. Yet higher education was not immune to the pervasive impact of the industrial revolution. While no pretense was made that universities should abandon their élitist character by admitting more than a small fraction of Canadian youth, their own professional programs were expanded in key areas at the turn of the century. Reflecting the growth of the major resource sectors in the economy, Queen's University opened a school of mining in 1893 and an engineering faculty in 1905. The University of Toronto established a school of forestry in 1907. The Royal Commission on the University of Toronto acknowledged the growing emphasis on economic themes when it commented in 1906:

The two distinct objects of university education are mental culture and practical utility. In recent years the latter has steadily gained upon the former owing to the utilitarian character of the age and the increased expenditure have doubtless been chiefly responsible for the development of this branch of instruction.[14]

Furthermore, as the industrialization of Canada proceeded at a rapid pace, the limitations of denominationally controlled universities became ever more apparent, and a number of institutions severed their sectarian connections in order to meet the demands of an increasingly secular era. The University of Western Ontario and Queen's University became independent of Anglican and Presbyterian control in 1908 and 1912 respectively. (The University of Toronto had become independent in 1849 as a solution to the competing religious demands of Anglicans and their opponents.) Impelled as well by a provincial government which had, since 1868, refused to finance universities controlled by denominational organizations, Ontario institutes of higher learning were thus forced to divest themselves of their clerical ties in order to receive sufficient funding for their 'practical' and professional programs.[15]

Finally, the universities became more business-like in structure and operation in accordance with the concern over efficiency among 'progressives' of the day.[16] The reorganization of the University of Toronto in which a board of governors, consisting largely of wealthy businessmen, was given financial control over the university, became the governing model for Canadian universities of the future.[17] This structural reorganization reinforced the image of Toronto ('the provincial university') as an important element in the economic future of the country. As the royal commission on the university noted in 1906:

It is in the interest of the state to devote a generous share of the public funds to the development of an institution so intimately associated with the material interests of the country. Canada must train her own sons to be her captains of industry. The agricultural, mineral and forest wealth and the water power of this Province call for a practical capacity and a specialized knowledge which only a modern university can supply, not only to sustain the moral influence that comes from higher education but to contribute to national prosperity by adequate votes of money for the training of youth.

Impressed with the recent administrative and academic improvements at the University of Toronto the *Globe* claimed in 1913 that 'the provincial university is quite the most vital of all the responsibilities of the Government and the Legislature of Ontario.'[18]

The First World War interrupted this steady 'progress' in the educational system. Most Canadians, including those in the academic world, recognized that while domestic needs such as public education had legitimate demands upon limited government funds, financing the war overseas was the top priority. If anything, however, the war's end increased public awareness of the need for sophisticated advances in the industrial sector. Technological progress during the war and post-war eras dictated that unless Canada moved ahead in these fields as well, she would slip further behind her international rivals in the search for new markets.[19] This situation convinced the federal government to introduce its long-delayed Technical Education Act in 1919 for the explicit purpose of investing more heavily in vocational training across the country. The thrust of educational change evident in Ontario before the war deepened as a result of the Act and was applied to other regions of the country.

It helped break the 'academic' monopoly of the high schools and collegiate institutes; schools in the larger centres now found themselves dealing with students bound for jobs in industry as well as for places in university. By the time of the Act's original expiry date in 1929, the number of technical education students and classes in Canada had more than doubled.[20]

But the perceived economic value of post-elementary training was not restricted to the role played by vocational and technical education programs. An important development of the 1920s and 30s was the recognition that, even for the academically oriented students, higher levels of secondary education would produce increasingly worthwhile economic rewards. In 1925, in reference to university-bound high school students, *Maclean's* magazine noted that 'each day in high school adds $25.00 to a [a student's] life earnings.' And in 1930 the Toronto Board of Education echoed these sentiments when it suggested that academic subjects such as English and History were a 'real asset to the students in whatever business he may become engaged.'[21] The fact that Ontario raised the compulsory school-leaving age to 16 in 1921, that tuition fees were virtually abolished in secondary schools throughout the province, and that the secondary school population quadrupled during the 1920s (while the population as a whole increased by only 17 per cent) all indicated that high schools had indeed replaced elementary schools as the 'universities of the people.'[22]

High schools also played a vital role in transmitting to students the values of good citizenship, patriotism, and moral strength, reflecting both the legacy of the war and parental fears of undisciplined behaviour in an era when the automobile and alcohol were considered dangerous social vices in the hands of young people.[23]

Although many students stayed out of school in order to assist financially burdened families during the Depression, high school enrolments increased significantly. The explanation for this apparent paradox could be found in the special social and economic role schools played during a period of economic crisis. Unable to find employment with limited schooling, 'many young people are out of work and are returning to school, increasing enrolments at the grade 11 and 12 levels.' Furthermore, many parents hoped that schools would serve as agents of both idealism and social control during the difficult Depression years. 'While the period is a time of storm and stress for all youth,' noted the Ontario minister of education in 1936, 'it is also a seed time for ideals. These ideals depend largely upon the influence of the environment and the environment of the school room forms one of the most important factors of such influence.'

Thus, in response to changing social and economic conditions, secondary education undertook an increasingly comprehensive role, both as a public custodian and as an instrument of economic growth in the three decades preceding the Second World War. An observation by an Alberta Department of Education official in 1924 applied to Ontario, and even more so in the context of the late 1930s:

A generation ago a public school education was considered adequate for all except those who proposed to enter upon the learned professions. But new standards have been set up for admission to the professions, business and the skilled trades. At least partial high school training is essential today to success in any occupation.[24]

In the face of a renewed materialistic surge during the quarter century following the war, higher education in turn would supersede secondary training as the vital link between vocational preparation and economic progress.

The fate of the universities throughout the Depression was indicative of the rather low priority they held both in government circles and the community at large. Restricted still to the sons and daughters of the upper classes, their perceived social importance was severely limited. While the problems of the Depression inspired many academics to act as consultants and advisers to governments throughout the country, this did not translate into significant financial support for the universities themselves. Renowned for his personal hostility to academics and intellectuals, Mitchell Hepburn, the premier of Ontario from 1934 to 1943, aggravated the situation by forcing the universities to languish in economic despair throughout his years in office. As late as 1939, when the worst of the Depression had passed, Hepburn incited student demonstrations in London and Toronto when he actually reduced the funding of the province's three non-denominational universities.[25] According to an official at Queen's, 'nowhere were university endowments high enough to make up for rising university deficits.'[26]

The Second World War, which disrupted and transformed so many facets of Canadian life, was instrumental in altering public perceptions about the respectability and value of higher education. The *actual* changes in the post-secondary system in Ontario between 1945 and 1960, however, were not profound. For one thing, public spending was still restrained by a frugal government more interested in highway building than higher learning.[27] Furthermore, primary and secondary education continued to occupy more of the government's immediate attention since these sectors were the first to feel the profound demographic effects of the baby boom. None the less, throughout this period, interest in higher education, stimulated by the war, grew steadily until it reached a crescendo in the early 60s. Post-secondary learning was to be thrust to the forefront of public attention for the first time in the twentieth century.

Mobilization for war is generally a wrenching experience for the people of any society, especially a people weaned on the principles of liberty and limited government involvement in their personal affairs. Freedom of movement, enterprise, and choice are suddenly replaced by sweeping economic and political controls, forced military service, and sacrifice. But if independent writers, speakers, and institutions subscribe to these ends, then the task of mobilization becomes less difficult since government actions are then buttressed by popular approval.

During the Second World War, politicians, editors, businessmen, and academics played just such a role as they forcefully urged their respective audiences to come to the defence of the nation. Teachers and university professors were especially well placed to perform an influential role. Above all, argued Duncan McArthur, the minister of education in Ontario, students must be informed of the reasons for the war itself. Democratic parliamentary government was in peril, he felt, unless prospective voters and leaders appreciated its value and were prepared to defend it against dictatorial challenges. For the moment, at least, exhorted the minister, the student's pursuit of individual fulfilment in school must be supplanted by the teaching of 'community responsibility.'[28]

Yet those who supported the development of higher education, such as the editors of the adult education journal, *Food for Thought*, saw no need to underplay 'individualism' even in wartime. Fostering personal growth – the traditional goal of universities in a democratic society – was itself a powerful weapon against tyranny: 'the spread of higher education is encouraged in a democracy as likely to produce citizens who will be individuals, self-reliant, and adaptable ... Dictators would rather have citizens who are obedient than citizens who think for themselves.'[29] In late 1940, ministerial representatives of departments of education from across Canada met at a conference on Education for Citizenship and resolved to 'stimulate in the minds of all Canadians a greater appreciation of democracy as a way of life to the end that they may better understand the present struggle and thereby make the maximum contribution to the war effort of the nation.'[30]

Enlisting the classroom as an agent of pro-war socialization, then, was one important function of schools during the hostilities overseas. Given their centralized organization, primary and secondary schools could carry out this task more easily than universities, where the traditions of institutional autonomy and academic freedom had generally kept government out of the lecture halls and laboratories of the nation. It is all the more significant that, because its spokesmen readily committed themselves to the patriotic cause, the university began to be perceived as having a role in the prosecution of the war effort as vital as that of any institution in society.

While their main efforts were devoted to the production of skilled manpower and scientific research, the universities, like the high schools, lectured their students on the justice of the paramount struggle in which the Allies were engaged. In his annual report of 1941, H.J. Cody, the president of the University of Toronto, noted that: 'In all the relevant developments, special efforts have been made to teach the fundamental issues at stake in the present struggle and to emphasize those spiritual values which make democracy possible and desirable, and make human life liveable.' And 'with other universities,' Queen's claimed 'to share the responsibility of demonstrating to the world that universities are an essential factor in upholding, maintaining, and strengthening our democratic way of life.'[31]

To realize these ends, every Canadian university imposed compulsory military training on all males over 18 in the Officers' Training Corps or in the Training Centre Battalion. All young men received at least six hours a week in military drills and lectures. Female students, as well, were required to play their part, by engaging in war-related work such as the Red Cross or auxiliary service training. In 1942, in an admirable fit of patriotic fervour, hundreds of male students from eastern universities responded to the federal government's plea for aid to Saskatchewan wheat harvesters. For those returning to university late as a result of this project, the beginning of the academic year was delayed.

The Second World War produced not only expressions of patriotism but sophisticated forms of organizing for the war itself. The federal government was far better prepared than it was in the First World War to face the challenges at hand, and with remarkable facility and speed mobilized its citizens through institutions created for specific wartime functions and through those that were already in place.[32] It was in this latter context that the universities were enlisted to serve the nation in very concrete terms. Indeed, noted Sherwood Fox, the president of the University of Western Ontario, 'with regret we must face the stern fact that exigencies of war have compelled all universities of the allied nations temporarily to relegate many basic principles of education to second place.'[33]

The National Conference of Canadian Universities (NCCU), the administrative umbrella organization of universities across Canada, co-ordinated much of this effort by responding to government initiatives for the production of trained technicians and professionals capable of turning their skills to the pressing national need. So imperative was the universities' role that an annual report of the Wartime Bureau of Technical Personnel exclaimed: 'It was evident in all their dealings with the Department of Labour [that] the universities' attitude was one of simple readiness to carry out any task which they might be called upon by government to undertake.'

Among a number of projects, the federal government set aside $300,000 for the purpose of attracting high school students into engineering and science, the graduates then being designated by the National Selective Service to various posts, with the army having first choice. At the 1942 NCCU conference, while some academics expressed fears that the universities might become mere trade schools as a result of the special tasks they were called upon to perform in the war, the delegates nonetheless passed the following resolution: 'The Universities' Conference should see to it that our war potential does not fall short of maximum realization for lack of full use of technical facilities.'[34]

In line with this purpose, some unprecedented steps were taken by the universities in the organization of their curriculum requirements. In Ontario, the minister of education, working in close collaboration with the federal minister of defence, solicited and received from the presidents of the province's five universities a commitment to revise their entrance requirements so that the Defence Training Course, taught in all high schools, could be substituted for other less 'practical' credits upon the student's application to university. Queen's University's Faculty of Medicine accepted the Defence Training Course as a credit 'in lieu of the language other than Latin for Junior Matriculation requirements.' In the Faculty of Applied Science, Queen's accepted it for History or a language other than English; and in the Faculty of Arts, for any subject other than English. Western permitted the Defence Training Course credit to be substituted as an option for Shop work, Commercial work, Home economics, Music, Art, Geography, or a language not otherwise counted. In courses not considered essential to the immediate national interest (mainly those in the arts and humanities), by federal decree only the members of the upper half of such classes were allowed to remain at university until graduation. No student was permitted to proceed to graduate work or to transfer from one faculty to another without the approval of the National Selective Service.[35]

Some academics, led by F. Cyril James, the principal of McGill University, and R.C. Wallace, the principal of Queen's, were so enthusiastic about the practical role the universities were capable of playing that in late 1942 they recommended to the federal government that all teaching in Commerce, Arts, Law, and Education be suspended for the duration of the war. This astounding proposal was supported in a *Globe and Mail* editorial.[36] Only after an emergency meeting called by another group of professors, headed by J. Watson Kirkconnell and Harold Innis, in which a brief was drawn up and presented to Ottawa defending the teaching of humanities even in time of war, was the implementation of this recommendation prevented.[37]

As a result of such initiatives, student enrolment across the country in the 'practical' courses increased dramatically during the war. Among the 1943 crop of graduating students, there were 50 per cent more doctors and dentists than there were in 1939, 20 per cent more engineers, and 15 per cent more bachelors of science.[38]

Aside from the training of manpower, the universities performed another valuable and highly acclaimed wartime function: scientific and military research. One observer went so far as to claim that, during the war, the 'laboratory became the first line of defence and the scientist, the indispendable warrior.'[39]

A good deal of the responsibility for this effort went to the National Research Council, whose output in the Second World War was far more impressive than it had been in the First. As well as running its own laboratories with extensive federal support, the NRC drew upon the resources of every Canadian university by engaging the research talents of Canadian scientists.

The NRC was turned from a peace-time operation into a war machine, and enlarged from a body of three hundred persons to an institution of thirteen hundred smoothly operating full-time personnel (and many hundreds more in the advisory structure), without faltering or missing a step. Through the forty-three associate committees and their seventy-three subcommittees, every relevant Canadian scientific establishment and laboratory in government, industry and university, was welded into a single, smoothly functioning implement of war.[40]

Among the accomplishments of Canadian scientists, working both for the NRC and in the universities, were the adaptation of radar for land, sea, and air use; the establishment of the first Canadian optical glass industry; the development of new processes for producing metallic magnesium (thereby ending dependence on imports); improvements in pressure suits and other advances in aviation medicine; degaussing and other defences against a variety of destructive German mines; the invention of temporary refrigeration for carrying foodstuffs to Britain; and much defensive work on war gases and on ballistics. The principal of Queen's University highlighted these efforts when he reported proudly in 1941 that scientists at his university were engaged in top-secret research.[41]

Such achievements did not go unnoticed by the Canadian public. Typical of the great tribute paid to the universities during the war was a two-page pictorial essay in *Saturday Night* magazine which claimed that scientists and technicians enhanced both the value of the universities and the reputation of Canada abroad through their contributions to the war effort.[42] Aside from lauding a number of the projects mentioned above, the article praised universities such as Saskatchewan for having adapted the jeep as an alternative to the tractor; Queen's was commended for its research in the reproduction of fish in order to increase their stock for commercial purposes; the University of British Columbia was acclaimed for experimenting with vitamin diets to increase the output of poultry farms. It was noted that penicillin, which reduced death from war wounds by as much as 90 per cent, had, of course, been pioneered in a university laboratory.

As a selling point in their solicitation for private funds, universities boasted of their own patriotic activities during the war. In a campaign pamphlet, for example, McMaster University noted that not only had the university's own contingent of the Canadian Officer Training Corps and the University Naval Training Division trained a large number of officers, but many of the university's faculty were on leave 'serving in the armed forces and in special capacities in various sectors of the Civil Service.'[43]

In the immediate post-war period, higher education proved itself to be of impressive practical value in one additional area. Canadian universities attracted much public attention by agreeing to educate, in a type of emergency program, thousands of post-war veterans, many of whom had interrupted their schooling to fight overseas. Although the federal government had undertaken a veterans' educational program towards the end of the First World War, the earlier plan had been severely limited both in its aspirations and its accomplishments. But at the behest of the universities themselves, the government effected a far more comprehensive scheme at the end of the Second World War. Each student received living stipends in addition to a fully subsidized tuition payment. The veterans' program injected new life into the country's universities: enrolment jumped from 38,000 in 1944–45 to just over 80,000 by 1947–48.[44]

After years of unrelieved poverty, then, it appeared that the universities had finally achieved the public prominence and financial security to which they felt entitled. Certainly the Ontario treasurer and future premier, Leslie Frost, seemed far more impressed than the leader of the previous government with the importance of higher education. His 1944 budget was intended 'to free the universities from the burden of debt which was hampering their efforts' and 'additionally,' he claimed, 'grants should be made to them which permit them now in time of war to organize for peace.'[45] Accordingly, $816,000 was allotted to the University of Toronto; $250,000 each went to Queen's and Western; and special aid was provided for programs in child study and medicine.

But alas, such financial security was illusory. Universities received very little funding for building projects; and operating support was intended primarily to address the immediate needs of the veterans. Thus while the universities had been revered, revived, and renourished during and immediately after the War, they were not financially stable. The special aid that the universities received had been tied to their very positive and practical role during the war. Once the war ended, and after the last of the veterans had passed through the system, the universities faced the dismal prospect of returning to the earlier state of genteel poverty. One authoritative source lamented in 1950 that, 'our universities are facing a financial crisis so great as to threaten their future usefulness.'[46]

The universities received a short-term reprieve in 1951 following the publication of the Report of the Royal Commission on the National Development of the Arts, Letters and Sciences. Reflecting the growing mood in post-war Canada over the need to preserve and nourish indigenous culture, the Massey report recommended, among other things, that the federal government provide direct financial support to Canadian universities. The vital service they had performed in the war, the role they played in training professionals and civil servants, and their importance as cultural outlets, especially in small communities, had earned the country's universities, according to the Massey commission, the right to economic security.

Although the federal government rejected the commission's proposal for a series of national scholarships for Canadian students, and delayed for six years the creation of the Canada Council (also recommended by the commission), Ottawa did allot over seven million dollars in direct aid to higher education, to which the struggling universities expressed a collective and gratified sigh of relief.[47] They had been rescued from imminent financial disaster, but the piecemeal nature of even this support would become shockingly evident in a few short years.

Only the romantic and naive would attribute the massive expansion of educational facilities in post-war Canada to a sudden burst of renaissance-type enlightenment among the Canadian public and its leaders. Even the most cursory appraisal reveals that the basic motives were undeniably utilitarian. As they had on rare occasions in the past, Canadians invested heavily in higher education in the hope of realizing concrete, profitable returns.

The war's conclusion left Canadian society in a peculiar and perhaps paradoxical state of smugness and uncertainty. Canadians were justifiably proud of their contributions made and sacrifices incurred in checking the cancerous spread of European fascism, in preserving traditional institutions, and in upholding the 'democratic way of life.'[48] Yet as their compulsive interest in overseas politics receded, they seemed unprepared to restore domestic life to its pre-war condition. The miseries of the Depression were deeply embedded in the country's collective memory and Canadians were grimly determined to extend the material security that the war had provided well beyond V-Day.

As the war wound down, there were numerous signs of this new social priority, as well as some whispered fears that economic prosperity might not be maintained. The remarkable political progress made by the democratic socialist CCF in Ontario and Saskatchewan in 1943 and 1944 on the strength of a comprehensive program for social reform, the attempted shedding of its reactionary image by the Conservative party of Canada which in 1942 embraced welfare state policies and added the prefix 'Progressive' to its title, the introduction of family allowances by the Liberal government in 1944 and its proposed New Social Order in the 1945 federal election campaign, the equally progressive thrust of George Drew's '22 Point Program' in the 1943 Ontario election – all pointed to the interest of Canadian politicians in addressing the felt needs of a people seeking just rewards for incomparable personal sacrifices.

But privately federal ministers during the war talked of ominous economic realities once the war machinery was dismantled. They feared that the type of massive economic dislocation which occurred after the first World War would once again develop unless a comprehensive social and economic program could be quickly fashioned.[49] The Canadian people were not unaware of the dangers ahead, as a 1944 Gallup poll revealed. Asked which soldiers should be demobilized first, the largest respondent group chose those who had employment awaiting them on their return. And a 1945 poll indicated that the achievement of full employment was the main concern of 40 per cent of the Canadian public.[50]

The Canadian economy did not collapse after the war, even after the abandonment of wartime controls. Through the selective application of Keynesian economic principles, in which the private sector was sustained and encouraged by government initiatives, the recession, which Canada suffered in 1945 and 1946, was followed by a decade of unprecedented economic growth.[51]

Aside from initial steps taken in the provision of social security for Canadians, the bulk of government activity in the 1950s involved the allocation of funds for economic development. Highway construction, oil pipelines, the St Lawrence seaway, railway subsidies, public transportation, direct grants to business, and hydro-electric power facilities, consumed the energy and expertise of government economists and private corporations.[52] Continuing immigration to Canada and migration from rural to urban centres raised the prominence and multiplied the budgets of provincial and local governments. Despite their solid commitment to free enterprise, Canadians demanded such publicly funded essential services as sewage facilities, street cleaning, snow removal, and garbage collection. Newspaper reports hailed the increasing productivity of the Canadian economy, the growth in employment opportunities, and the country's envied standard of living.[53] The message was economic growth; the medium was government and business; the public spirit was one of unbridled optimism.

Throughout the 1950s, the Gallup polls continually revealed the depth of this feeling. When, in 1951, the conspicuously consuming public identified the high cost of living as the country's basic problem (39 per cent), in the same year 53 per cent of Canadians praised as 'sound' the economic development of the country. One year later, in a poll whose very question – 'What do you plan to buy in the coming year?' – reflected, as much as did the responses to it, the values of an acquisitive society, the vast majority of Canadians expressed their intention to purchase at least one expensive household item. In 1956, an impressive 79 per cent of Canadians from all social classes in all parts of the country, predicted that the 'good times' would continue.[54]

The tranquillity, apathy, and political quiescence that has characterized images of the 1950s should not overshadow the reality of a people hard at work, seizing upon opportunities that had been vanquished by the Depression and delayed by the war. The enormous success of the post-war veterans' educational program was one indication of this determined spirit. The educational system as a whole was swept up in this surge of optimism as Canadian parents sought to achieve vicariously through their children what had slipped away from their own generation in nearly two decades of economic and military turmoil.

The post-war baby boom, from which were derived the hordes of students who would fill the schools and universities in the 50s and 60s, can itself be viewed as the product of delayed marriages and confidence for the coming years. While this event deserves greater examination, most scholars attribute such population surges to a popular belief that the future will be better than the past.[55]

As early as 1947 a national Gallup poll pointed to the tendency among Canadians to tie educational training to pragmatic ends. Sixty per cent of those sampled felt that schools should teach 'more practical subjects.' That education itself was treated with great deference – a result, at least in part, of the positive role the schools had played in the war – was suggested in a poll in which 60 per cent of Canadians claimed to be satisfied with school facilities and an equivalent number believed teachers to be as capable as they should be. In 1954, the largest minority of men surveyed (17 per cent) and women (11 per cent) said that their decision to leave school early was their greatest mistake in life. A few years later, once the desperate shortage of educational facilities had become apparent, 51 per cent of Canadians said teachers should be paid more and 58 per cent agreed that taxes should be raised in order to alleviate the problem. In Ontario, the nation's most heavily populated and industrialized province, 62 per cent favoured raising taxes. That educational training in the mind of the public was linked to the goals of personal security and industrial progress was indicated in a 1957 poll in which the largest minority of Canadian men questioned said they would choose a career in engineering over any other.[56]

If any date can be isolated as a pivotal point in raising to unprecedented levels public consciousness over the value of education, especially over the increasing importance of higher education, 1956 would surely qualify. In the previous year, Edward Sheffield, a federal government consultant, released a study to the National Conference on Canadian Universities projecting that, through demographic pressure alone, university enrolment would double to over 120,000 by 1965.[57] The report sparked a period of frenetic activity among educators and businessmen. The NCCU sponsored a special conference in the fall of 1956 entitled 'Canada's Crisis in Higher Education' in which the very survival of the country was pinned to the expansion of educational facilities. Papers, speeches, and conference resolutions from some of Canada's most prominent academic figures underlined the crisis. To reach the nation's information nerve centres, the NCCU struck a committee under Claude Bissell, the president of Carleton University, which employed an 'effective and simple device' of sending a one-page letter to the editors of all the newspapers in Canada, presenting the statistical case of the Sheffield report and 'underlining that in ten years we would have a doubling of our university population.'[58] In the same year a conference of renowned educators, businessmen, and scientists was convened at St Andrew's, New Brunswick, where similar statements thickened the air and received wide publicity.[59] The conference established a private business-run organization called the Industrial Foundation on Education whose expressed purpose was to promote the cause of and raise money for higher education in Canada.[60] In 1957, the Report of the Royal Commission on Canada's Economic Prospects drew these threads together, reinforcing the link between Canada's educational development and the country's economic fate. Universities, asserted the Commission, 'are the source of the most highly skilled workers whose knowledge is essential in all branches of industry ... It is incredible that we would allow their services to society ... to lapse or lag.'[61]

Virtually every aspect of education was explored in scores of publications during this period, but for public consumption certain prominent themes stood out. The quietude of the 1950s had been regularly disturbed by lurid accounts of Soviet political ambitions, coldly and at times hysterically documented in the nation's media. Indeed, aside from the public preoccupation with economic growth and material security, the simmering cold war constituted the other major issue that absorbed the attention of North Americans in the post-war period. In 1951, one opinion poll identified the fear of war as the major concern of Canadians (53 per cent). Following the sensational American espionage trial and executions of Julius and Ethel Rosenberg in 1953, 62 per cent of Canadians were prepared to deny communists freedom of speech; only 26 per cent of the public favoured upholding such a fundamental democratic right. And in 1961, while 42 per cent of Canadians felt that the 'free world' could live peacefully with the Russians, fully 48 per cent predicted a new world war.[62]

How did this issue relate to the incessant demands for improved educational facilities? Soviet progress had been generated by a remarkably sophisticated technology, if not equalling, then at least approaching that of the United States. For North Americans, the successful launching of the Sputnik satellite in 1957 underscored these extraordinary developments in a frightening way. Such advances were based on the speedy training of technologists, engineers, and scientists, financed by the government and trained in universities. One researcher, citing Allen Dulles, the director of the Central Intelligence Agency, reported that the Soviet Union would graduate 1,200,000 students in pure science during the 1950s, while the United States would graduate only 990,000.[63] A statement to the St Andrew's Conference by James Duncan, former president of Massey Ferguson, chairman of Ontario Hydro, and a member of the Industrial Foundation on Education, suggested that the connection between the economy, the cold war, and higher education was apparent to many:

In my opinion we are in danger of losing the cold war unless we do something very drastic about it and education is very close to the core of our problem. Science and engineering have made such remarkable progress in recent decades that the nation which holds the lead in these fields holds the initiative in world affairs.

The conference concurred and passed the following resolution:

The representatives of the universities express their considered opinion that it is their urgent duty to warn the people of Canada that the problem of the universities has become an emergency of grave national concern to the certain disadvantage of our progress as a nation, and can only be solved by energetic and immediate assistance and cooperation of all governments in Canada, of business and industry and of private benefactors.[64]

Without this type of commitment, echoed the Royal Commission on Canada's Economic Prospects, Canada, along with other non-communist nations, risked falling victim to Soviet 'ecumenical ambitions.'[65] In his 1956 budget statement, the treasurer of Ontario also felt compelled to remind his listeners of the incredible advances that the Soviets had made 'in various branches of science and applied technology'; he then went on to increase the funding for university development.[66]

On the heels of the Sputnik launching, the minister of education in Ontario called a meeting of the province's university presidents, and told them: 'it is essential that we do everything we can to reassure those of the public who are anxious about present conditions that everything is being done and will be done to strengthen and to support the services rendered by the Ontario Universities.'[67] In demonstrating from an academic perspective that the cold war raised questions about the state of the national culture as much as it did about the condition of technology, Claude Bissell, now president of the University of Toronto, published an article in *Maclean's* magazine in April 1958, entitled, 'Universities Must Answer Sputnik with Higher Standards.' The NCCU brief to the Royal Commission on Canada's Economic Prospects claimed that the humanities and arts, 'from which the soul of man is fed, and through which the heritage of civilized communities is passed to mortal generations,' also deserved greater financial support.[68] Senator Donald Cameron, the director of Banff School of Fine Arts, cited Robert Hutchins of the University of Chicago on the same theme. 'It seems useless to hope that democracy can survive unless all people are educated for freedom. Mass stupidity can now mean mass suicide.'[69]

But the appeals of the academics were, for the most part, as intensely practical as those of the business community and underscored the utilitarian impulses of highly practical people. According to the NCCU, 'The demand for expert persons, for intelligent persons, with background and perspective, increases with every increase in the population, with every increase in the gross national product, with every requirement for increased investment.'[70] No one, in fact, disputed the Ontario government's claim that educational investment was necessary for Canada to become a 'modern industrial power.'[71]

The task ahead entailed not merely waging ideological war against the nation's potential enemies but of securing as well Canada's competitive advantage over the country's economic rivals. The Industrial Foundation on Education both marvelled and panicked at the incredible progress Germany and Japan had made since the war: 'In 1945 Western Germany lay in ruins and a starving people wandered through the rubble of her devastated cities. Today Germany competes successfully in foreign markets with finished products incorporating the latest technology. The weakness of Canada's educational training facilities was demonstrated by her heavy reliance on skilled immigrants and refugees from other countries. In the first nine months of 1957, disclosed the IFE, Canada brought in nearly 2,150 engineers. For the whole year this would prove to be some 3,600 'which is over twice as many as graduated from all Canadian universities in 1957.'[72] According to the president of Polymer Corporation, 'over the next 25 years we will need as a minimum three to four times as many engineers and scientists as now employed and ten times as many technicians.'[73]

Indeed, Canada was so far behind her rivals that she spent proportionately one-third of funds allotted in the United States to industrial and scientific research and only three-fifths of those in the United Kingdom.[74] In a survey which revealed in direct terms the perceived relationship of educational training to corporate performance, the Department of Labour reported that:

The shortage of professional personnel is evident and is not a matter of conjecture. 50 per cent of Canadian employers of professional personnel are experiencing difficulty finding staff. Of the companies surveyed, 47 per cent reported a curtailment of production and expansion plans, 33 per cent a curtailment of planning and research, 21 per cent overloading of present personnel, 14 per cent inability to offer adequate training, and 11 per cent a potential shortage of future executives. In 1955 twice as many engineering vacancies were registered by employers with the National Employment Service as there were persons applying for these positions.[75]

On a personal basis, the message cut deeply and effectively, as economists were able to prove in simple and compelling terms that Canadians who were well educated would earn more money than those who were not. 'Estimates have shown,' noted the Economic Council of Canada, 'that better education appears to have raised labour earnings per man by about 30 per cent from 1911-1961.'[76] In a 1963 poll, the public revealed how completely it had absorbed such information over the years: 60 per cent of Canadians agreed that a boy should not leave school at age 16 even if he wanted to, while only 30 per cent said he should be permitted to do so. As if to convince by example, 39 per cent of Canadians in a 1965 poll confessed that leaving school too early had been their greatest mistake in life.[77]

The dimensions of the 'national emergency' appeared so profound that in a 1963 television poll, CTV reported that of 1,000 people questioned 72.5 per cent believed that education should be the responsibility of the federal government, despite the constitutional prerogative historically held in this area by the provinces.[78] In 1965, 89 per cent of Canadians agreed that more money for education would be needed in the next few years; only 7 per cent disagreed. (Ninety-two per cent of sales and office workers favoured increased funding. Also, in the Gallup poll cited in the last paragraph, working-class men and women showed a slightly higher appreciation for the value of staying in school than professionals.)[79]

One further set of events demonstrates the priority that parents placed on advancing the careers of their children in the popular and lucrative professions. From the end of the war well into the next decade, dozens of solicitations were made by Ontario constituents to their members of the legislature on behalf of students seeking admission to the professional faculties of the province's universities.

Since entrance standards were relatively high, the competition for admission was particularly fierce. Some twenty letters were written to the minister of education in 1947-48 from parents of aspiring doctors, lawyers, teachers, and engineers seeking his assistance in ensuring their children's admission. For the most part the minister responded politely, but firmly, that he had no intention of interfering in the enrolment procedures of Ontario's 'autonomous universities.'

But in 1955, one Conservative caucus member revealed that admission to professional schools could play a useful role in paying off election debts. After reviewing the career ambitions of a constituent, he wrote to the minister:

I have much more than a passing interest in this case since [the student's] father was until last fall's by-election a strong and active supporter of our opponents. He has supported us since then. He tells me he asked the defeated candidates in the last Dominion election for assistance in this matter, and received none. If we can do anything at this time, it will be a very good thing for the future.

In this instance too, the minister responded in no uncertain terms that he could do nothing for the student. 'Any interference on my part [at the university] would mean swift rejection.' But on at least three other occasions, the minister either promised to do what he could to assist the families in question, or to gain information that might improve the students' chances for admission. In the case of one student seeking entry to the University of Toronto medical school, the minister told a fellow cabinet member, 'certainly I shall try to do whatever I can on behalf of Miss J.E.'[80] Amid this competitive environment where professional education held such a high priority for Ontario's families, its value as a political tool was not lost on at least some politicians and their supporters.

Even when economic conditions worsened, as they did in the recession of 1960, public faith in education was not dislodged. It was indeed reinforced. Since society had become increasingly automated in recent decades, higher levels of unemployment could be explained, in part, by the gradual disappearance of unskilled jobs. As the trade journal *Canadian Office* pointed out: 'It is increasingly difficult for a young fellow to pick up a factory job after he figures he's had enough school.'[81] Only the best trained Canadians could be assured of staying employed. Both the Canadian Labour Congress and the Ontario Farmers Union recognized the seriousness of this situation and its bearing on the educational system. At its 1962 conference the CLC announced the creation of a labour college in Quebec as one potential solution to the problem, and the members called upon the federal government to invest heavily in technical and vocational training.[82] In a brief to the Ontario minister of education, the Ontario Farmers Union supported such views. 'Our education system continues to increase in importance each year. Increased technology demands continually higher educational standards for workers. Agriculture continues to supply other industries with highly skilled and educated young people.'[83]

John Deutsch, a well-known economist and the first chairman of the Economic Council of Canada, argued for greater investment in scientific research to facilitate more innovation 'in order to develop Canadian technology.'[84] The problems were serious enough for the Senate Committee on Manpower and Unemployment to lament that 'creeping unemployment became an imbedded feature in the Canadian economy during the 1950's.'[85] Indeed, the scope of this dilemma was so evident that the federal government, constitutional barriers and all, forged ahead in 1961 with a massive program to upgrade and retrain the Canadian labour force.[86]

That the message had got through to the Ontario government, which characteristically saw such problems (and its own role) in national (if not global) terms, was reflected in a statement of the Minister of Education, William Davis, in 1963: 'Today as never before in our history, our very survival, our future development and prosperity as a nation depend on the proper education of our youth and a section of our adult population as well.'[87]

While support for the expansion of higher education was shaped by broadly based economic demands, the system felt as well the impact of pressures to 'democratize' access to Canadian universities. Indeed the post-war veterans program, which provided opportunities to thousands who would otherwise never have attended university, underlined the humanitarian dimensions and democratic potential of educational development in Canada. The 'equality of opportunity' argument, heard increasingly in the late 1950s, became almost an article of faith among liberally minded citizens and politicians in the 1960s. And in 1972, the Report of the Commission on Post-Secondary Education in Ontario reiterated this commitment: 'The guiding principle of the province's policy of financing post-secondary education should continue to be universal access to appropriate educational services for all who wish and are able to benefit from them.'[88]

Indeed the democratization theme accounts, in part, for the ability of university promoters to solicit the support of those with different interests and competing political persuasions around the central goal of expanding the university system, and it would be foolish to deny its import. But in a period when all investment in higher education was viewed as inevitably profitable, it was unnecesary for official spokesmen to distinguish between the democratic and economic benefits of post-secondary education. For the middle and upper classes, universities were the vehicles to professional status. For the less privileged, they held out the promise of upward social mobility. Both of these goals could be rationalized as worthwhile investments in the future of a country starved for highly trained and locally educated professionals. In the context of the over-all economic value of higher education to society at large, student aid schemes, as we shall see, were themselves considered investments worthy of public support.

There was, however, considerable debate over the form student assistance programs should take. Despite their increasing interest in the question of equal opportunity, the governments of Canada imposed severe limitations on the types of student aid plans that were introduced. Conceived and implemented within the context of a capitalist culture, the programs themselves reflected and reinforced the utilitarian objects and the ideological corollaries of a free-enterprise society.

During the 1950s, educators and parents expressed considerable concern about the academic performance of students at all levels of the school system. In a society so conscious of the importance of education to the country's economic future, it was considered vital for schools to encourage students both to continue their education for as long as possible and to perform at the highest possible level of achievement. Student retention rates increased steadily throughout the 1950s and, when the drop-out rate showed signs of rising, educators were quick to draw attention to the problem. For example, in 1954 and again in 1959, increased failure rates in first-year courses at the universities of Toronto and McMaster did not escape notice.[89]

Indeed, one businessman was so concerned about the 'lack of student motivation' among Canadian young people, that he asked the disturbing question: 'Are we raising a generation of failures?'[90] He explained the phenomenon in (unproven) sociological terms by suggesting that Canadian society was becoming so prosperous that students, on the example of their parents, were unwilling to work hard for minimal immediate rewards; just as parents demanded higher wages, so too many students were unprepared to bear the drudgery of homework and self-discipline. Similarly, the Industrial Foundation on Education noted that while Canadians spent several billion dollars a year on consumer items such as toilet preparations, alcohol, movies, and new cars, they apportioned only $115 million to industrial and scientific research. This compared unfavourably and dangerously with the situation in the Soviet Union where a very different spirit prevailed: 'We are competing with an ideology whose principals believe in it with a religious fervour. The question we must answer deals with whether or not we can combat this system with lukewarm attitudes toward our own beliefs.' While no one recommended emulating the methods used by the Soviet Union to achieve its ends, there was, even among certain business spokesmen, a curious respect for the enormous educational accomplishments of that nation. Unlike Canada, Russia seemed free of 'laggards' and 'intellectual duffers' in the educational system.

In light of these perceptions, the main problem became one of encouraging the best students to pursue their education. In a confidential report submitted to the Ontario minister of education, the Industrial Foundation on Education documented the extremely high 'casualty rates' among students in several Ontario communities. In one city, 35 per cent of those students with an IQ level above 110 had no intention of going to university. Only 23.9 per cent of all Ontario students planned to obtain a higher education. In fact, only 7 per cent of grade 13 students actually did. Once in university, over 40 per cent of students were found to drop out before completing their degrees. According to the IFE, through a combination of financial problems and lack of motivation, Canadian students were simply not performing to the best of their abilities.[91] This attitude and these conditions could hardly be tolerated by the achieving society.

In order to search out the competent from all social classes, commentators talked increasingly of the need to improve the ability of lower-income families to send their children to university. If universities maintained high standards, and if the poor were given financial assistance, then society would be well served by those traditionally unable to afford, but qualified enough to partake in, post-secondary education. When financial pressures forced universities across the country to raise tuition fees in 1951, many presidents lamented the deleterious effect this would have on students from low-income families.[92] The fact that the student's share of educational costs had increased intolerably and compared unfavourably with that of Britain and the US provided a potent argument for increasing public aid to higher education.[93]

In a well-written brief, the National Federation of Canadian University Students argued in 1960 that, since the role of the state had increased in other areas of health and welfare, it was logical for similar aid to be extended to such a valuable social service as higher education. In fact, the student organizations argued, as they would with increasing vigour throughout the 1960s, that higher education should be tuition-free, both on principle and as a practical vehicle for raising the participation rates of lower-income students in institutions of higher learning. This view was endorsed, if in less insistent and more qualified terms, by spokesmen for the Canadian labour movement. At successive biennial conferences, the Canadian Labour Congress recommended 'free university education for all students who are qualified and who maintain suitable standards of achievement.'[94]

With one brief exception, however, no provincial government or university ever adopted a policy of free tuition,[95] although every politician paid deference to the need for democratizing access to higher education. The argument against such a radical step in the late 1960s was largely based on the problem of prohibitive cost.[96] By that time it was simply too expensive a proposition. But in the late 50s and early 60s, when the elimination of fees would not have been so financially burdensome, the argument was rationalized in very different terms. Despite the enormous growth of the public sector, Canada remained fundamentally a free-enterprise society. 'Rugged individualism' was still the cultural staple of the system and thus the need for students to learn the value of individual responsibility by paying their way through university was proclaimed consistently.

The statements of both Canadian businessmen and spokesmen for the Ontario government were a revealing insight into this state of mind. That higher education was recognized by corporate leaders as a valuable social investment has already been established (and will be explored more fully in the next chapter). Furthermore, as if to prove their commitment, many companies in the late 1950s donated large sums of money to universities through direct grants and scholarship programs. Though the motives of individual business leaders might have varied widely, they appeared in their public statements less impressed with the moral import of the democratization and accessibility arguments than with the very pragmatic contention that increasing the participation rates of the brightest Canadian students was an absolute necessity in light of the prevailing 'national emergency.' While students, social democratic politicians, and labour leaders talked about the need to eliminate income disparities through increased educational opportunities, businessmen believed that financial barriers to postsecondary education should be reduced for the essential purpose of training as many Canadians as possible. But higher education must never be free. As Stanley Deeks of the Industrial Foundation on Education exhorted: 'In a free country such as ours, motivation must be provided through incentive only.'[97] By eliminating fees, the universities would only be increasing 'our trend toward becoming a soft society, and our propensity to expect to obtain something without making the effort to earn it.'[98] Leaving the private family unit with the prime responsibility for financing university education, yet buttressing this support with material incentives for the best students, was perfectly consistent with the free-enterprise view that the most competent, competitive, and ambitious students would succeed in the outside world. Premier John Robarts articulated a similar justification in 1963 for refusing to abolish tuition fees.[99] Unlike the student groups and labour spokesmen, businessmen and Conservative politicians were not interested in eliminating the class system; for them the market would judiciously weed out the strong from the weak. They favoured a meritocracy, not equality.

Student aid programs which evolved in the late 50s and early 60s reflected this mix of cultural and political ideologies. After persistent opposition pressure, the Ontario government introduced a program in 1958 providing $500 loans, interest-free until graduation, for all needy students with at least a third-class standing. Premier Leslie Frost defended the program in this way: 'I think that no person in this country who has the potential to make good in the university world and the things that lead from the university should be denied that education.'[100] The democratic thrust of this statement, however, was somewhat undermined in a different speech by Frost in the same year. In it he exposed the over-riding importance of economic considerations behind government funding policies.

The policy of the Ontario government towards higher education has always been the same. The policy has been to expand and improve the facilities for higher education in this Province. I must admit, that although this policy was motivated to a great extent by our desire to assist young people to develop their intellectual potential and to develop into well informed citizens, it was motivated by our early realization that if this Province was to advance, it would need more than will, it would need brain power – and this perhaps is the world's most scarce resource.[101]

While the 1958 student aid program was an important step forward for the province, it was subject to considerable criticism for the financial debts it would impose upon the recipients of the loans. It was attacked further for offering insufficient funds to each student. While the Minister of Education claimed in the House that he was sure the $500 loans would cover a needy student's educational costs, he appeared overly sanguine on this score. In retrospect, one observer has noted: 'Such a view seems astonishing in view of the fact that tuition alone at any provincial university would have taken the major part of the maximum loan. It seems clear that there was no real intention of making attendance at the university possible unless the student had private resources or was able to secure satisfactory employment during the summer.'[102]

Further provision for student aid was made by the federal government in 1964, when $1,000 loans were extended to students meeting minimum university entrance requirements. While critics continued to call for a program with more generous terms, the minister of finance, Walter Gordon, was convinced that the student loan plan was both morally acceptable and practically justified. His statement demonstrated once again the vital relationship between the democratic and utilitarian themes:

A university education or its vocational equivalent is the highest achievement of our educational system and it should be within the financial grasp of every young Canadian who is capable of making good use of it. If we do not provide the means whereby all children with necessary abilities can share the privilege of higher education, then we are doing them a great injustice and denying our country a source of economic and intellectual benefit which we can ill afford to sacrifice.[103]

Sceptics persisted in their protests that an aid program based solely on loans was usurious and self-defeating and would do little to facilitate the entry of lower-income students into the post-secondary system.[104] To address these concerns, the Ontario government made further changes in the student aid scheme in 1966 and established the rudiments of the present system. Student assistance would be allocated through a formula combining loans and grants, the amount of the latter based on a student's financial need. In 1967, a ceiling of $600 was placed on the amount any student would have to borrow, the remainder of the award being distributed in the form of a non-repayable grant.

Despite these obvious improvements, tuition fees were still not abolished. The program also retained the immovable principle that the family was primarily responsible for financing the student's education, and the qualifications a student had to fill in order to be considered independent from his or her parents were damned by critics as excessively stringent. Finally, the debt factor still loomed large for the poor since they had first to commit themselves to sizeable loans in order to qualify for grants. All of this produced a complex student aid scheme, mirroring the values of a mixed economy in a prosperous age – in which the government, driven partially by moral pressures but mainly by practical imperatives – would provide limited financial assistance to students leaving them then exposed to the debts, rigours, and uncertainties of the market place.

Not surprisingly, in a society awed by the prospect of endless economic growth, the demand for more students, more money, more professors, and more buildings, expressed in starkly statistical terms, was the final approach used by university spokesmen in their appeals for more public support. From briefs to the Massey Commission and to the Royal Commission on Canada's Economic Prospects, through conferences and presidential speeches, the academic community and its supporters painted a grim picture of the plight of post-secondary education.[105] Since the end of the war, they claimed, professors' salaries had remained humiliatingly low; public funding of higher education in Canada compared poorly with that of other countries; the students paid too much, business and government contributed too little. In pragmatic terms that an acquisitive society could readily understand, university spokesmen delivered their important message and elicited results that exceeded their expectations. By 1965, amid the euphoria over the value of higher education, Premier Robarts expressed his firm conviction, the national consensus, and his government's policy in a business-like analogy that was much more than a mere metaphor:

Our true wealth resides in an educated citizenry. Our shrewdest and most profitable investment rests in the education of our people.[106]

Corporate Aid to Higher Education

The attitudes of Canadian businessmen towards higher education throughout
the late 1950s and early 60s did not differ significantly from those of other
groups in Canadian society. The crucial relationship of educational training to
the economic development of Canada, reflected in speeches, conferences, editor-
ials, and polls, was established with powerful, unceasing, even tedious consistency. If ever there was unanimous consent over any issue in Canadian history
that cut across class lines and regional barriers, the faith of Canadians in the
economic value of higher education was surely it. But if the main link between
education and society was perceived to be an economic one, and if business was
the heart and pulse of the nation's economic life, then the corporate sector
should have had a special interest in seeing the educational system perform its
work adequately. How was this task perceived by the business community itself,
and what precise role did business leaders play in this process? These are the
concerns of the following two chapters.

Ever since the publication of Adam Smith's *The Wealth of Nations*, the most
enthusiastic supporters of free enterprise have perpetuated a powerful myth
about the nature of capitalism, namely, that the system functions best when
unfettered by government interference. Only through the free play of market
forces, composed of competent and competitive businessmen, and propelled by
the dynamic of supply and demand, is the free-enterprise system perceived by its
vociferous advocates to work with greatest efficiency. That governments, however, have always intervened in the free market, by regulating tariffs, encouraging immigration, hindering and then facilitating union development, building
transportation and electric power systems, and subsidizing industry indirectly
through tax relief and directly through outright grants, is as undeniable a feature

of capitalist development as is the unencumbered interplay of private corporations.[1]

In the most recent phases of their economic histories, capitalist countries have encountered a phenomenal increase in government activity. In Canada, for example, the proportion of the gross national product accounted for by all government spending increased from 3 per cent in 1867 to 32 per cent in 1967. In 1960 Ottawa spent $7 billion; in 1972 it spent $22 billion. From 1944 to 1964, the number of civil servants in the government of Ontario alone increased from 7,712 to 41,074.[2]

The most common explanation of this phenomenon derives from the wide recognition that 'free enterprise' failed to prevent the devastating Depression of the 1930s; nor could it be credited with rescuing the western nations from economic despair – that was the achievement of the Second World War.[3] At the very least, a centrally run currency system, a co-ordinated monetary and fiscal policy, and a publicly funded welfare program are essential tools still used by governments in capitalist countries to moderate the vagaries of the market economies. Accompanied by a host of other activities ranging from the provision of cheap electric power to capital depreciation allowances, governments have performed services from which major companies have consistently derived benefit, even if the state, as an economic institution, has earned only the faintest praise.[4]

In Canada especially, a country rich in resources and poor in population, the government has always played a prominent role in enhancing private industry's ability to produce wealth and earn profits. Whether the private sector has been uncommonly weak, as some theorists have recently argued, whether the historical desire of the Canadian people for government activity has been uncommonly strong, as others have surmised, or whether inspired by the endless problems of regional disparity and national unity, Canadian governments have played a vital role in buttressing, stimulating, and stabilizing the free-enterprise economy.[5]

The situation of higher education provides a clear example of this phenomenon and explains a good deal about the attitude of business towards university development in its expansion phase. In the late 1950s, unlike the United States, Canada found itself singularly lacking in large, privately financed institutions capable of absorbing the massive inflow of students arising from the baby boom. Both in Ontario and in the country at large, universities with rich private endowments were the exception, whereas in the US they were far more prevalent.[6] This is not to suggest that the degree of public resources ultimately devoted to educational expansion in the United States was less impressive than in Canada, only that this country began from a position of considerable disadvantage, a weakness alluded to by many observers.[7]

As this chapter will later demonstrate, the business community devoted some effort to filling this financial gap, but it could neither afford, nor was it prepared, to shoulder the burden of educational costs. Once the dimensions of the educational 'emergency' were apparent, business, in unison, called upon the government to seize the initiative and meet the national crisis.

Through articles and speeches recorded in the country's major trade journals, business leaders argued in no uncertain terms that the primary responsibility for financing higher education lay in the hands of government. Supported by statistical evidence, the Bank of Montreal *Business Review* took pains to establish the point that the state must be the key financier of post-secondary education. Contending that students should continue to pay at least part of the cost of their education, the editors admitted that students 'can't provide more than a fraction of the increased income that will be required.'[8] Similarly, as the president of Falconbridge Nickel of Canada argued, corporations were equally handicapped in their ability to pay:

The financial problem is entirely beyond the means of philanthropic individuals or corporations. It must be remembered that corporations handle the funds of individual investors and have the duty and responsibility of using these funds only for the proper purposes of the business and in the best interests of the shareholders ... Our educational problem is a national problem.[9]

The educational needs of Canada were so outstanding, said the Industrial Foundation on Education, that industry required government not only to fund universities, but to provide direct 'subsidies' to business itself in order to pay the cost of industrial and scientific research. Indeed, noted the IFE, 'government policy is largely responsible for the success or failure of Canada's educational progress.'[10]

Lest their corporate brethren were unconvinced by the Gallup polls, the politicians' speeches, or the academic lobbyists, prominent company spokesmen argued the case of higher education in starkly practical terms, which all businessmen could readily understand and would ignore only at their peril. An editorial in *Trade and Commerce* claimed that 'in supporting higher education business is to a certain extent just buttering its own bread ... Graduates of engineering and science faculties are being channelled directly into the service of business so that universities actually are saving the businessmen considerable expenses that might be encountered in on-the-job training.'[11] 'It is out of the universities,' emphasized A.A. Cumming, the president of Union Carbide Canada, that 'we shall get the professional engineers, geologists, research scientists and others who can lead us forward in the search for technological excellence. They are also the place from which will come the economists, the accountants, the investment people and others for whom a professional economic training is essential.'[12]

Apart from the 'products' it turned out in the form of skilled employees, educational investment was itself seen by *Canadian Business* as a fabulous boon to the construction industry: 'If the [educational] industry had not increased its investment in construction from 1961–63 by some $211 million, or a gain of nearly 70 per cent above 1961 levels, our $6 billion construction industry would have shown only about half the gain it made during the past two years.'[13]

Such perceptions were rooted in a strong conviction that higher education involved a profitable form of public investment both for the nation as a whole and for individual companies. Framed in this light, educational spending elicited especially strong support from the private sector. The Ontario Chamber of Commerce posed the question: 'what is this money on educational spending buying?' It then passed favourable judgement on what it found in manpower training, training for the unemployed, provincial institutes of technology and trade, advanced technical evening courses, apprenticeship training, and vocational guidance.[14] Significantly, one company president argued that if higher education were viewed as a national priority, then the costs would not be prohibitive and could be successfully defended. 'We can easily afford the cost of a superb educational system,' he contended, 'if we can convince voters and politicians of the need for such a programme, and of its vital national importance as compared with some of our politically popular welfare expenditures.'[15]

Public spending on education, then, like railway building and hydro-electric power construction before it, was viewed as a solid investment in the nation's future, from which business would profit handsomely. Unlike welfare, as the previous speaker implied, it involved no mere handouts to questionable recipients. According to business spokesmen themselves, there was little need either to resist or rationalize such public spending, since heavy government funding of education posed no practical or ideological threat to the business community's collective interest.

The issue, however, did not end there. Having established the principle that government should incur the bulk of educational expenses, business freely admitted that the private sector still had an important financial role to play. Indeed, the campaign undertaken by the Industrial Foundation on Education was based, in part, upon the realization that private contributions to Canadian universities had seriously declined in recent decades. In 1920–21, private endowment income accounted for 16.5 per cent of Canadian university operating costs; by 1955–56, less than 6 per cent was covered by private donations.[16]

On the premise that a proper corporate contribution to higher education involved 1 per cent of pre-tax profits, the IFE campaigned strenuously in the corporate community for greater financial assistance. A later section of this chapter will record the success that the IFE and the universities had in this field. But in theory, business writers agreed, even if they differed on the actual amount, that greater private contributions to higher education were, in fact, essential. As Herbert Lank, president of Dupont Company of Canada, argued in 1956, 'business gifts to education should be regarded by the donors not as charitable donations but as an essential cost of doing business and staying in business.'[17]

Not surprisingly, the supporting arguments for business contributions were framed in ideological terms that businessmen would be unlikely to dispute. If university income was buttressed by healthy private donations, then total government control over higher education could be successfully resisted. The autonomy of the university, which all academics cherished, was thus equated with the freedom of the corporation from government intervention. Crucially, it was argued that, even while government paid the bulk of university expenses, the institutions themselves should be free to plan their own priorities. Private aid would help preserve this precious independence.

Perhaps the most significant reason for corporate aid to universities is that the autonomy of our higher educational institutions must be protected and preserved. It is stated that free enterprise in education is a natural corollary of free enterprise in industry and commerce and that the greatest insurance of its preservation is to provide university income from as many sources as possible.[18]

Furthermore, in such a diverse, pluralistic society, a national consensus could more easily be moulded if a large number of groups lent support to important social causes. Thus, the initiatives taken by the private sector, such as those by the Bank of Montreal which gave money through a number of projects to several areas of higher education, would have an exemplary effect, noted the journal *Trade and Commerce*; this could only strengthen the 'fibre supporting democracy.'[19] If private sector funding would never replace, it could at least supplement government support of Canadian universities and help raise the respectability of higher education across the country.

Before exploring the dimensions and actual details of corporate contributions to Canadian universities, it would be useful to broaden our perspective on this issue by noting how 'corporate giving' reflected the attempts by business enterprises to plan their goals and activities in an increasingly sophisticated manner. In the past, charitable donations, like business activity itself, had been subject to the whims of individualistic entrepreneurs who responded, largely in *ad hoc* terms, to the pressures and vicissitudes of the market place. But with the emergence of various forms of long-term planning, based on such corporate practices as vertical integration, manpower forecasting, and extensive advertising, large companies especially strove to eliminate uncertainty in the traditionally unpredictable business world.[20] This tendency was characteristic even of such relatively unimportant corporate activities as charitable donations.

That corporate giving had become an increasingly integral part of planned corporate activity was revealed in a 1962 survey of 222 companies which gave to philanthropic causes in Canada. Seventy-nine per cent actually budgeted for charitable causes.[21] In 1951, it had been estimated that only one-third of Canadian companies allotted charitable contributions in this manner. At that time most relied on the unpredictable responses of company presidents and executives to public and private appeals for financial aid.[22]

There were other important changes that suggested a more carefully formulated corporate strategy in this area. John A. Pollard, a writer for the *Harvard Business Review*, found that in 1960 corporations had progressed from 'spontaneous' forms of corporate giving to 'planned investment.' Usually through a management committee, and always under the aegis of at least one full-time executive person (who usually possessed a background in education), 'corporate giving' strategy was mapped out. 'These new management people [usually young men, not elder statesmen about to retire] begin with a study of the company, its educational activities to date and possible additional opportunities. They develop a sound philosophy of giving, and work out a policy with appropriate organization and program.'

According to *Chemistry in Canada*, these executive groups sought to achieve 'continuity, flexibility and ingenuity in the program and to maintain a balance between kinds of institutions and causes aided.' In all cases, it was found necessary for those doing the staff work to have 'access to the highest levels at which the major management decisions are made.'

An example of this approach was described at CIL (Canadian Industries Limited), a major corporation in the chemical and chemical processes industry. Dr John Tomecko, a former university and high school teacher, was assigned the responsibility of determining the corporate giving strategy for CIL: 'He is responsible for planning what the company should be doing for education in the future. He recommends what action the company should take on all requests for financial aid to education in addition to studying and reporting on various educational matters such as teaching and science forums.'[23] Tomecko's work was always co-ordinated with the company's various divisions and departments and was then adjusted to general company policy. He was responsible for maintaining liaison with universities and other science-related institutions, especially with reference to their capital needs and fellowship requirements.

Some companies, especially those providing large donations, went so far as to create separate foundations devoted exclusively to philanthropic causes. As in the case of Shell Oil, a foundation would permit the company 'to maintain its contributions despite ups and downs in earnings, to improve the administration of corporate giving and to discover and apply the best means of using available resources equitably in all program areas.'[24]

With such a healthy allotment of management resources to the area of philanthropic aid, companies were anything but indiscriminate in their distribution policies. They generally insisted on a series of satisfactory responses to specific questions put to the appealing agency. What were the organization's aims and objectives, its operating record and current status, its financial situation, the details of its current fund-raising campaign, its capital needs, and other requirements?

Some companies used actual 'yardsticks' in creating a formula for the amount of aid to be given. For example, the formula might be based on a percentage of the campaign goal or on a fixed amount per company employee. Some paid out a flat sum per unit of population in the local community, or a ratio of company employment to the total community employment multiplied by the campaign goal. Other corporations might take a day's payroll, add to it 1 per cent of annual profits before taxes, and then divide by two. Interestingly, most companies appeared unwilling to provide aid in the form of company goods, for as one executive said, to provide free what the company produces 'is to cheapen the produce.'

A number of separate surveys based on interviews and/or questionnaires submitted to corporations produced a variety of responses as to why individual companies gave to specific projects. On the whole, however, they leaned heavily to the conclusion that corporations were as pragmatic as possible in their aid distribution policies. Some did give, or at least said they gave, out of purely philanthropic and benevolent motives: 'There is a straightforward and humanitarian element that is not reducible to calculated advantage but is analogous to disinterested personal charity.' But even in those cases where the direct benefit to the company was not easily calculable, there was a tendency for the corporations to contribute in a way that would be, at least in broad terms, consistent with the company's self-interest. One corporation reported: 'It shall be the policy of this company to contribute to worthy aims, charitable, educational and religious, where these are deemed to be of benefit directly or indirectly, to a substantial number of the company's employees.' Another company placed the priority on the benefits that would accrue to its own shareholders, and went on: 'It recognizes those [causes] particularly in those communities in which the business of the company is concentrated, where it owns property, and where it has a large number of employees.'

Since all companies were subject to pressures from their clients and customers, they often found themselves forced to aid charities as a method for ensuring the loyalty of their most influential buyers. 'Important customers with whom we have two- or three-year contracts subject to renewal have pet charities and are constantly after the company to assist them with the projects. We find no alternative but to help since we cannot afford to lose their business.'[25] Where the immediate self-interest of the corporation could not be exploited, fund-raisers usually emphasized the long-term economic and political value of supporting 'charitable causes.' According to the president of a large retail firm:

Philanthropy rests squarely on the shoulders of big business. We use that as a weapon to try to force business to give. We tell them that if they want the system of free enterprise to continue, they *must* continue to give ... Most of those interviewed claimed that they looked on private philanthropy as an important bulwark of the system of free enterprise for, if charity became the prerogative of government, it would mean the welfare state or socialism.[26]

Another survey in 1967 of eighty-one prominent Canadian firms revealed that over the decade the motives had not changed substantially. In the 'national interest,' corporations found it necessary to contribute in order to uphold the principle of good corporate citizenship, though one university development officer noted that there, too, a company's motives were largely of a practical nature. 'Most companies,' he observed, 'seem to have a PR component in their motivation.'[27]

In the 'company interest,' corporations were drawn to projects such as building a hospital wing or a university arts complex, projects 'that would bolster their image directly.'[28] Aid to universities was found, significantly, the easiest to justify, both for philanthropic and pragmatic reasons. For in this case, as we have noted throughout, there was no perceived distinction between the corporation's practical needs and the wider national interest regarding the importance of higher education.

Industry's growing response to the needs of universities is explained by its acknowledged interest in recruiting well educated people as well as highly trained specialists, and more broadly as investment in the future of our society as a whole. Concern over manpower needs is seen, for example, in paper companies' support of forestry; in insurance companies' interest in advanced mathematics; and in the chemical companies' grants in aid of chemical research or fellowships in this field of study.[29]

Indeed the practical reasons for corporate support to universities were so convincing that two university-trained consultants, writing in *Business Quarterly*, recommended that companies be intensely selective in their corporate giving policies.

We agree that pure philanthropy has no part in business. The reasons for donations should be purely economic, but such economic reasoning should be broadly and imaginatively conceived and consistently and effectively put into action. Thus support for higher education – at specific universities that contribute to the type of manpower needed – can logically be justified by the reasoning that educated people make better employees, education provides higher incomes and a higher standard of living and thus company sales are increased ... We maintain that business has a responsibility to society and we support the concept of business donations that are rationally conceived, carefully disbursed, consistent with the economic goals of business and distinct from the basic welfare contributions allocated by the state.[30]

While it would be difficult to determine with precision the effect that the Industrial Foundation of Education had on enlisting support for higher education across Canada, it is certainly due to the efforts of this organization that historians can now gain insight into the patterns of corporate giving to Canadian universities from 1956 to 1961. Founded in 1956 at a special conference in St Andrew's, New Brunswick, on engineering, scientific, and technical manpower on the initiative of Crawford Gordon, president of A.V. Roe Canada Limited,[31] the foundation secured on its board of directors a dozen of the most prominent names in the Canadian business community and gained the backing of an equally impressive list of corporate sponsors (see tables 1 and 2).

The foundation perceived itself as a 'permanent fact-finding and executive organization, to be financed entirely by industry, performing broad functions on behalf of industry in the field of education, as related specifically to the needs and acknowledged responsibility of industry.'[32] The atmosphere within which the organization was established was recalled by Sidney Smith when he was president of the University of Toronto:

I believe that as far as universities are concerned it is not the generosity of business that we should appeal to, but simply their common sense. Industry needs educated people; universities need money to educate them. Indeed last autumn, I was elated by the far sighted ideas and resolutions that were expressed at conferences where this subject was discussed. With characteristic realism businessmen surveyed the financial needs of universities, and it was said that a concerted plan of action would be developed under which Canadian business would do its share toward meeting these needs.[33]

In order to accomplish these ends, the foundation employed two staff members – Stanley Deeks and Ray Woodfield (both former employees of Gordon's A.V. Roe Company) – and published fourteen booklets in six years on various aspects of corporate aid to higher education. By conducting its own surveys and by drawing together the disparate information of the Dominion Bureau of Statistics on the issue of private aid to higher education, the foundation provided a wealth of information on this important subject. Its main purpose was to measure, through a variety of criteria, the performance of companies in donating money to Canadian universities. Once the results were known, the foundation would circulate the information in published form, through the media and often through speeches delivered by Stanley Deeks.[34] Aside from six booklets entitled *The Case for Corporate Giving to Higher Education*, which reported annually on the level of direct industrial and commercial aid to Canadian universities, the publications also examined the scholarship and bursary programs of business and industry, the problem of student motivation in schools and universities, and the 'internal matching grant' programs of the private sector. The reports (some of whose contents have already been revealed in Chapter One) are important not merely for the information they provide but as a testimony to the wide interest in and discussion about higher education within the Canadian business community.

During its first full year of operation, 1957, the foundation reported, in what would prove to be its most glowing account, that the contributions of business to Canadian universities had reached unprecedented and unexpected heights. Recovering from its rather meagre contributions of 1956 (which had been consistent with the history of corporate giving over the previous several decades), business and industry had raised their level of aid from $2.7 million to $11.6 million in 1957 – an increase of 450 per cent, and two to three times higher than had been anticipated even by the optimistic IFE. From a pre-tax profit contribution rate of only .083 per cent in 1956, the private sector had pushed its donations to .384 per cent in 1957.[35]

Accounting for this success by the novelty of the campaign undertaken by the foundation, by the widely publicized success in 1956 of both the St Andrew's Conference and the NCCU conference on Canada's Crisis in Higher Education,[36] by the concern over the Soviet launching of Sputnik in the autumn of 1957, and by the fact that a number of universities in Quebec had undertaken their own special fund-raising projects, the IFE looked for even greater accomplishments in

TABLE 1

Industrial Foundation on Education

BOARD OF DIRECTORS

D.W. Ambridge, president and general manager, Abitibi Power and Paper Co. Ltd.
J.B. Barrington, president and managing director, Ventures Ltd.
J.R. Bradfield, president, Noranda Mines Ltd.
S.H. Deeks, executive director, Industrial Foundation on Education
E.J. Durnin, past president, Canadian Council of Professional Engineers
James S. Duncan, chairman, Hydro-Electric Power Commission of Ontario
A.E. Grauer, chairman and president, British Columbia Power Corporation
Crawford Gordon, president, A.V. Roe Canada Ltd.
Dr R.R. Hearn, consultant, Hydro Electric Power Commission of Ontario
Dr O.M. Solandt, vice-president, Research and Development, Canadian National Railway
H.M. Turner, chairman of the board, Canadian General Electric Co. Ltd.
E.H. Walker, president and general manager, General Motors Products of Canada Ltd.
J.R. White, president, Imperial Oil Ltd.
A.R. Williams, assistant to the president, A.V. Roe Canada Ltd.
H.S. Wingate, president, International Nickel Company of Canada Ltd.
A.H. Zimmerman, chairman, Defence Research Board

EXECUTIVE COMMITTEE

R.J. Askin, vice-president, Developing and Engineering, Abitibi Power and Paper Co. Ltd.
J.N. Kelly, manager, public relations, Cockfield, Brown and Co. Ltd.
W.H. Evans, president and general manager, Honeywell Controls Ltd.
C.B.C. Scott, assistant general manager, personnel, Hydro Electric Power Commission of Ontario
A.R. Williams, assistant to the president, A.V. Roe Canada Ltd.

the years ahead. It cautioned its readers that, in spite of the recent achievements, the need for private funds was still critical and it urged the corporate sector to raise its contributions, for universities and colleges alone, to a full 1 per cent of pre-tax profits.[37]

Against the background of such lofty expectations, the business contributions of 1958 were a palpable disappointment. The total raised was $10.4 million, down $1.2 million from the previous year. Some consolation was derived from the fact that this decline was due in large measure to the decreasing level of foundation grants to Canadian universities, an area to which the IFE devoted less attention than that of direct aid from individual companies. The level of the latter remained what it had been in the previous year, approximately $8.8 million, but the over-all corporate contribution as a percentage of pre-tax profits declined by .016 per cent to .368 per cent.[38] Conspicuous by their absence in the 1959 report were the superlative acclamations about the great contributions of Canadian business that had riddled the 1958 issue of *The Case for Corporate*

TABLE 2

SUPPORTERS AND MEMBERS

Industrial Foundation on Education

Abitibi Power & Paper Company Ltd.
Algoma Steel Corporation
Aluminum Company of Canada Ltd.
Anaconda American Brass Ltd.
Anglo-Canadian Oils Ltd.
Anglo-Canadian Pulp and Paper Mills
The Anthes-Imperial Co. Ltd.
Asbestos Corporation Ltd.
Babcock-Wilcox & Goldie-McCulloch Ltd.
The Bank of Nova Scotia
Bathurst Power and Paper Co. Ltd.
Bell Telephone Company of Canada
British American Oil Co. Ltd.
Building Products Limited
Campbell Soup Company Ltd.
Canada Iron Foundries Ltd.
Canada Valve and Hydrant Co. Ltd.
Canada Wire and Cable Co. Ltd.
Canada International Paper Co.
Canadian Kodak Company Limited
Canadian Manufacturers' Association
Canadian Oil Companies Ltd.
Canadian Pratt & Whitney Aircraft Co. Ltd.
Canadian Westinghouse Co. Ltd.
Chrysler Corporation of Canada Ltd.
Community Relations Consultants
William E. Coutts Co. Ltd.
The De Havilland Aircraft of Canada Ltd.
Distillers Corporation Ltd.
Dominion Electrohome Industries Ltd.
Dominion Foundries and Steel Ltd.
Dominion Rubber Co. Ltd.
Dominion Textile Co. Ltd.
Dow Brewery ltd.
Dow Chemicals of Canada, Limited
Du Pont of Canada Limited
Eldorado Mining and Refining Ltd.
Ethyl Corporation of Canada Ltd.
Ole Evinrude Foundation (Canada)
Falconbridge Nickel Mines Ltd.
Federation des Colleges Classiques
Federation of Women Teachers' Associations
  of Ontario
General Foods Ltd.
General Motors of Canada Limited
Goodyear Tire and Rubber Co. of Canad Ltd.

Great-West Life Assurance Company
Harris and Partners Ltd.
Hawker-Sidley Canada Ltd.
H.J. Heinz Co. of Canada Ltd.
Honeywell Controls Limited
Household Finance Corporation of Canada
Imperial Oil Limited
Imperial Tobacco Co. of Canada Ltd.
Industrial Acceptance Corporation Ltd.
International Business Machines Co. Ltd.
International Nickel Co. of Canada Ltd.
Interprovincial Pipe Line Co.
S.C. Johnson & Son Ltd.
Kerr-Addison Gold Mines Ltd.
Lamaque Mining Co. Ltd.
Liquid Carbonic Canadian Corp. Ltd.
Massey-Ferguson Ltd.
National Trust Co. Ltd.
Noranda Mines Limited
North American Life Assurance Co.
Northern Electric Company Limited
O'Keefe Brewing Company Limited
Ontario Paper Company
Pfizer Corporation
Placer Development Ltd.
The Proctor & Gamble Co. of Canada Ltd.
Remington Rand Ltd.
Rolland Paper Co. Ltd.
The Royal Trust Company
Schering Corporation Ltd.
Security Freehold Petroleums Ltd.
Shawinigan Chemicals Ltd.
Shawinigan Water and Power Co.
Shell Oil Co. of Canada, Ltd.
Socony Mobil Oil of Canada Ltd.
The Southam Company Ltd.
Spencer & McMullen Ltd.
The Steel Company of Canada Ltd.
Steep Rock Iron Mines Limited
Texaco Canada Ltd.
Time International of Canada Ltd.
Trans-Mountain Oil Pipe Line Co.
Union Carbide Canada Limited
Ventures Limited
Victoria College (B.C.)
Western Plywood Co. Ltd.
Anonymous

Giving to Higher Education. The new report was much drier in tone, reflecting no doubt the restrained enthusiasm of the IFE research staff.

This deteriorating trend continued over the next three years. In 1959, pre-tax profit contributions fell to .364 per cent. And more seriously, if foundation grants in 1959 were excluded, the direct contributions of business and industry were down to $7.3 million, and the pre-tax profit rate of non-foundation aid was only .253 per cent. Donations slipped further in 1960 to $11.4 million and the over-all pre-tax rate fell to .356 per cent. Finally, in 1961, the last year for which the IFE produced statistics, they showed that both in absolute and percentage terms, corporate aid suffered its most serious decline – down half a million dollars to $10.9 million, and to only .317 per cent of pre-tax profits.[39]

Apparently the novelty of corporate giving to higher education had begun to wear thin. The situation was reinforced by the fact that the government portion of university support had continued to climb steadily throughout this period. By 1960-61, public funds accounted for 63.5 per cent of university income across Canada, compared to 56.6 per cent in 1957-58. The percentage of university income derived from corporate and foundation support over the same period slipped from 6.7 to 4.7.[40]

In subsequent years, the situation, as confirmed by other independent researchers, changed very little. In a survey done for the year 1965 on behalf of the National Industrial Conference Board (later renamed the Conference Board), it was shown that, while corporations donated to universities and colleges an increasing amount of their total contributions to all charities, such aid still accounted for only .322 per cent of their pre-tax profits.[41]

Throughout the 1960s, business journals reported on these patterns of support. Writers noted that those companies which did contribute to culture and the arts had refined their corporate giving techniques, but they bemoaned the relatively poor showing of the private sector as a whole. One went so far as to ask: 'Do Companies Care for Culture?'[42]

Before exploring the broader implications of this situation, it would be instructive to note in greater detail certain characteristic trends in corporate support among those companies that did contribute to higher education in Canada.

The overwhelming proportion of corporate aid went consistently and increasingly to the capital or building budgets of Canadian universities: some 60 per cent in 1957 and 1958 and 63 per cent in 1965. Conversely, the tendency to fund the universities' operating budgets showed a marked decline over the same period, never climbing above 7 per cent of the total corporate donation. Over this period as well, corporations contributed a steady but decreasing portion of their funds to research projects.[43] And their support for scholarship and bursary programs, while highly publicized where it did exist, barely kept up with the increasing enrolment trends and the heavier educational costs for Canadian students. As the Industrial Foundation noted:

Despite the increase in student support of some 40 per cent from 1957 to 1961, it is interesting to note that the total awards available in 1960 in relation to the estimated total aggregate costs of student fees and living expenses has increased only approximately one-half of one per cent over that of 1957. In other words it is apparent that the availability of scholarships and bursaries had done little more than keep pace with the larger number of students registered at Canadian universities.[44]

How can these patterns be explained? Corporations were most receptive to the appeals for special building projects designed to expand the facilities of existing institutions or launch the development of new universities. 'A predominance of business aid has been channelled into capital expansion largely because well planned campaigns have provided a sound understanding of the need. It is evident that when the need is well demonstrated the response of business is good.' That capital support was indeed the preference of Canadian corporate donors was borne out by an IFE study which showed that many companies, even those which gave substantially in one year, failed to follow through in the next. In other words, while the edifice itself was of great interest to the individual company, whether a school of architecture, business, medicine, or engineering, the responsibility for funding the subsequent maintenance and operating costs was deemed to lie elsewhere. Over half of the companies who contributed to universities in 1958 did not do so in 1959.[45]

For the most part, companies had little interest in the details of university administrators' plans, but they insisted that their donations be put to good use in a carefully rationalized expansion program:

Building campaigns by well known hospitals and universities command confidence on the strength of the public reputation, so that contributing companies have no desire as a rule to look into the administration. But as a condition of many commitments in such cases, some donors say they would wish to know whether any given drive represents part of a phased program and if so whether the program is supported by the institution's record of long term growth.[46]

Furthermore, capital grants enabled companies to plan their own financial priorities more effectively than did on-going operating, maintenance, or student aid programs: 'A company is able to hand out a share of fair weather profits to the capital campaign of a university, for example, and still roll with the punches of a business downturn by cutting back on contributions the next time around.[47]

Thus corporations were disciplined to tie capital grants to tight strings and sought, above all, security in the knowledge that the money would be spent on a specific need in a responsible fashion. Interestingly, Henry Borden, vice-chairman of the University of Toronto Board of Governors, discovered during his university's fund-raising campaign that one condition upon which a number of companies would give money was that the projects be 'government approved.'[48] Some individuals undoubtedly had a 'bricks and mortar' bias because of the favourable publicity that would come their way if a building were named after them. Capital projects, then, because they served a visible need, because they were easier to campaign for, and because they implied a beginning and an end to an individual corporate obligation, were more popular than other forms of aid – especially operating costs – where the need was on-going, unpredictable, and therefore not viewed as a permanent responsibility of the private sector. Faculty salaries, maintenance and repair work, electricity, and grounds keeping were obviously considered to be the sole responsibility of government agencies.

While business depended on the universities to establish sensible priorities and upon the government to approve building plans, corporations could play a direct and influential role in the area of university research. In this field the potential for direct business influence in university life was most apparent. Although universities preferred to receive unconditional and unrestricted grants that would be distributed according to internally determined priorities, very few research grants were in fact allotted in this manner. In 1957, 80 per cent of all research grants from business and industry were categorized as 'restricted.' In 1958, that figure climbed to 90 per cent. In 1961, over 98 per cent of all such grants were restricted.[49]

Through such forms of support, the immediate needs of particular industries could be served directly by the universities. The resource sector and the chemical industries, for example, which were among the largest corporate supporters of restricted research, would finance studies in metallurgy or other fields of scientific inquiry.[50] Through contract research as well, consultants could be hired to carry out specific corporate studies. In an economy where specialized knowledge could be translated into corporate power, the universities could play a useful role in enhancing business productivity and profitability.

Nonetheless, this type of aid was given only by the largest companies, and as late as 1965 constituted only 5.5 per cent of the total corporate contribution to Canadian higher education. Even in the chemical and allied products field, which donated more than any other sector to the category of restricted research, the latter consumed less than 18 per cent of the industry's grants to higher education.[51] To the degree that universities were treated as the direct servants of business, they were construed to be so in general, rather than specific, terms.

The broader question of which business sectors contributed most heavily to higher education is itself an interesting insight into the nature of the Canadian economy during the impressive expansion phase. The patterns changed very little from 1958 to 1965, and revealed that the dominant industrial and commercial sectors in the country were also the heaviest contributors to higher education. A 1958 survey by the IFE showed that the chemical industries, the resource sector, the banking sector, the merchandising sector, and the food and beverage industries were the major private contributors to higher education in Canada. In 1962, nine corporate sectors incorporating industries in these areas accounted for 67 per cent of all company donations, with the chemical and allied products industries and the pulp and paper companies at the top of the list. A 1965 survey of 127 companies by the National Industrial Conference Board confirmed these patterns, with the primary metals and the banking, financial, and insurance businesses leading the way.[52]

The fact that Canada's richest industries were dominated by a small number of large companies was also reflected in the patterns of corporate giving to higher education. For while the resource and banking sectors contributed the greatest amount of money to higher education, as the previous account demonstrates, they were not so high on the list in terms of the number of companies in each sector which donated. Far and away, the sector with the largest number of actual donor companies was the merchandising group (wholesale and retail) which comprised 19.3 per cent of all individual corporate givers in 1961. But in terms of actual dollar donations, this sector contributed only 7.2 per cent of the total.[53] In second place was the professional services sector, accounting for 8.3 per cent of the total individual donors, but for only 1 per cent of the total actually collected. Conversely, while the chemical and allied products industries contributed over 10 per cent of all business funds to higher education, they constituted only 6.5 per cent of all companies that donated in 1961. More impressive still was the banking industry, which in 1961 supplied 7.3 per cent of all the funds raised, but comprised only 0.3 per cent of all individual companies that contributed.

The IFE explained these patterns by pointing out that while the resource industries, the chemical and allied products sector, and the banks consisted in the main of companies with assets over one million dollars, the merchandising industries and the professional services sector did not. The task of raising funds for higher education in Canada was hampered by the high degree of dependence on a small number of large companies for, although a large number of small corporations contributed impressively, the amounts they could raise were not substantial.

This structural imperative accounted in large part for the declining level of funds raised after 1958. The number of large donors (companies with assets above one million dollars) declined from 1,000 in 1958 to 850 in 1959, accounting for 16 per cent of all contributions realised in 1958 and only 13 per cent in 1959. Furthermore, it was reported that of the 500 companies who contributed over $1,000 in 1958, 'the smaller companies contributed two and a half times as much on a percentage of profits basis as large companies.' In 1961, the number of large companies donating to higher education increased to 900, up 50 from the previous two years, but their over-all performance still compared unfavourably with that of small companies. The former contributed only 0.15 per cent of their pre-tax profits to universities, while the latter gave 0.85 per cent of their pre-tax profits. Still, the high dependence of universities on large companies was apparent, since only 6 per cent of all companies which contributed to higher education in 1961 provided over 70 per cent of all the funds raised.[54]

All of this was a microcosm of an economy whose strength lay in the resource-related industries, whose lifeblood was fed by a small number of large financial institutions, and whose business was conducted by importers and exporters, by wholesalers and retailers, and by professionals in the service industries.

The ability of Canadian universities to raise money in the private sector was limited by one other overwhelming reality of the Canadian economy – its domination by foreign-controlled businesses. As all conscious Canadians became aware in the late 1960s, the largest and richest industries in Canada were owned and / or controlled outside Canada. In a survey of selected industries, the Gray Report on Foreign Direct Investment in Canada reported that, in 1967, non-resident control of Canadian manufacturing industries over-all was 57 per cent, which included 80 per cent foreign control of the rubber, transportation equipment, tobacco, and chemical industries. Seventy-four per cent of the petroleum and natural gas industries was foreign-controlled, as was 65 per cent of the mining and smelting industries. By contrast, Canadian ownership was shown to be strongest in furniture, printing and publishing, leather products, wood, food and beverage, textiles, clothing, and non-metallic minerals. In the commercial sector, including banks and insurance companies, Canadian ownership and control were particularly high.[55]

This situation was reflected in the area of corporate donations to Canadian universities. What reduced the ability of Canadian universities to raise money was the tendency of American corporations to contribute fewer of their funds to the capital and operating costs of Canadian universities than did Canadian companies. In 1957, only 30 per cent of the total came from American corporations while 65.8 per cent came from Canadian. This trend accelerated in 1958 with only 22.8 per cent of all funds coming from companies controlled outside Canada (of which virtually all were located in the US) and 70 per cent coming from Canadian companies.[56]

American corporations, on the other hand, contributed a far higher proportion of their total funds to student aid than did Canadian companies. In 1957, 67.1 per cent of scholarship and bursary funds came from foreign companies, while 32.9 per cent came from Canadian businesses. The explanation for this distinction is not easy to find. It is possible that the philanthropic priorities of American head offices lay in their own communities (much as they did among Canadian parent companies).[57] Operating in a society where private universities were able to accumulate huge endowment funds over the decades, and through their investments generate their own funds for capital expansion, American companies were often besieged less for capital funds than for research support. Traditionally, the number (and proportion) of research foundations in the United States has far exceeded that in Canada.[58]

Furthermore, the charitable donations policies of branch plants were rigidly controlled by American head offices. Only minor donations could be contributed by a subsidiary without the parent company's approval.[59] Since it has been found by other studies, including the Gray report, that Canada's industrial and scientific research capacity has always been limited in relation to that of the United States, precisely because American corporations prefer to finance research in the United States instead of Canada, perhaps this attitude prevailed as well in the area of corporate support for the capital expansion of Canadian universities. Those foreign companies which did contribute substantially to Canadian higher education (such as Imperial Oil) might have been fulfilling their duties as good corporate citizens, but this responsibility was by no means perceived in the same way by the majority of non-Canadian companies. As the president of Carleton University noted, his institution 'had no greater success than other Canadian universities in persuading corporations with head offices in the United States to respond to its appeal.'[60] Whatever the cause, the result was serious. The ability of Canadian universities to raise private funds was severely restricted by the inherent weaknesses of the dependent Canadian economy.

It is not a little surprising then that, despite these relatively unimpressive demonstrations, despite the admonishments of Canadian business writers, Canadian universities (with some notable exceptions) achieved their fund-raising objectives during this period. From 1940 to 60, $94,930,245 had been raised against an over-all aspiration of $98,729,106. Ontario and Quebec universities were especially successful in reaching their goals, and in some cases they obtained more than they sought. By contrast, universities in the Maritimes and, to a lesser extent, those in western Canada, were less successful. The former were pledged or received only $8 million of the $13 million sought from 1940 to 1960, while the latter raised $14 million out of a goal of $16 million.[61]

As we will show in the next chapter, the success of university campaigns might well have hinged on the sophisticated use of professional fund-raisers. There is at least some evidence that universities themselves might have limited their demands on the realization that to be too lofty in their expectations was to be foolishly optimistic.[62] Furthermore, the envied reputation of established universities placed them at a great advantage over the smaller, less renowned, or affiliated institutions. Indeed, statistics showed, time and again, that the latter failed to achieve their fund-raising objectives, despite the relatively high percentage of Canadian students that they served. In 1957,

The smaller, affiliated institutions continued to receive a relatively small amount of the total business and industry grants (5 per cent) despite the fact that these institutions accounted for approximately 25 per cent of the total enrolment in Canadian universities and colleges ... In 1961 aid to these institutions dropped to .5 million dollars from $1.2 million in 1960.[63]

The disparity in corporate support between central Canada and the Maritimes was so great that the explanation probably lies in the greater priority placed by corporations on the importance of Ontario and the St Lawrence Valley regions in the national economy. This, too, reflected the structural biases and business prejudices of Canadian economic life.[64]

In aggregate terms, to conclude, the performance of the private sector in Canada was not overly impressive. In 1958, only 2.8 per cent of all tax-paying corporations contributed anything to Canadian universities, a situation that evidently changed little over the next several years.[65] But as this study has thus far argued, this should not imply that the expansion of higher education was considered by business merely a frivolous venture. The pattern suggests that by the early 1960s Canadian corporations, while favouring the rapid improvement of higher educational facilities, held the government primarily responsible for ensuring this growth. Once the initial forms of public and private lobbying had been accomplished through such forums as the St Andrew's Conference, the NCCU campaign, and the activities of the Industrial Foundation on Education, business was aware that, whatever its efforts, higher education would indeed be well served in the future by government funds.

The money donated by business was considered essential by the universities themselves, however, because it provided them with a 'margin of freedom' to engage in special academic projects, to quicken the pace of expansion, and to enhance the prestige of their own board of governors and campaign committees with prominent business personalities who would undoubtedly be noticed by government decision-makers. But in Canada, business assistance to higher education was complementary to government support, a situation consistent with traditions in Canadian business history, and determined, to a great extent, by the structural exigencies of the Canadian economy.

THREE

Private Power and Public Institutions

Businessmen involved themselves in the expansion of higher education in two basic ways. In the first instance, as we have seen, a number of companies provided universities with financial support from their private and corporate resources. The second method involved those who, at the behest of university organizers and administrators, became directly involved in the organization, planning, and governing of Canadian universities. But if corporate donations provided only a small portion of a university's total budget, then why was the participation of prominent corporate leaders considered to be so vital in institutions that were essentially publicly funded? The answer to this question is the central concern of this chapter. It traces by way of example the role played by businessmen in founding new universities in Ontario and in expanding the facilities of established institutions.

Completing the analysis in this chapter of the interaction between the corporate and university communities in the late 1950s and early 60s is a case study of the path followed by one particular institution through its inception, establishment, and first fund-raising campaign. York University, in the north of Metropolitan Toronto, is a particularly fitting example for such an investigation. Founded in the midst of the euphoria over the increasing importance of higher education, it provides a good measurement of business attitudes towards a new university. Located close to the industrial heartland of Ontario, it is neither the province's largest nor smallest university and thus lacks both the special status of the University of Toronto as well as the regional character of some of Ontario's less populated institutions. The pages that follow will provide an insight into the activities of business leaders who became directly involved in the administrative affairs of the modern university and, in so doing, made the institution's cause their own.

The process through which individual universities expanded their facilities in Ontario occurred in a variety of ways.[1] First, established institutions such as the University of Toronto, Western, and Queen's all undertook to increase their enrolments substantially throughout the 1960s. Second, denominational institutions in Ottawa, Hamilton, Windsor, Kitchener, and Sudbury were involved in a process of partial or complete secularization which led to government funding and then rapid expansion. Third, universities such as Lakehead and Guelph arose from the roots of existing institutes of post-secondary training. Finally, schools such as Brock and Trent developed from the activities of local community groups and evolved into chartered universities free of any formal association with other institutions of higher learning. York University can be viewed as a hybrid of the third and fourth approaches.

Common to all of these approaches, however, was the vital role ultimately played by national and local business interests in the creation or expansion of each university. Despite its recognition of the need to expand educational facilities, the government of Ontario took a *laissez-faire* and, on occasion, negative position on the issue of building new institutions. Indeed, in the late 1950s, Premier Frost and his minister of education expressed the view that, instead of constructing new universities, the necessary expansion should be undertaken by existing schools. None the less, in the absence of government initiatives,[2] Frost and his successor, John Robarts, were ultimately responsive to those communities which seized the opportunity, lobbied persistently, and demonstrated their own financial commitment to the institutions they sought to build. While clearly exaggerating the situation, Leslie Rowntree, a Conservative MPP from Toronto, contended that 'any community that felt it should have a college or university could organize one just as public spirited citizens were proposing at York.'[3]

Those communities taking the member at his word were soon to discover that sincerity and 'public spirit' were necessary, but not sufficient, ingredients in the campaign for a new university. The key element of a successful undertaking was the amount of support, financial and otherwise, that influential business interests extended to such projects. In her study on 'Organized Philanthropy in an Urban Community,' Aileen Ross found that in every city, there is an 'inner circle' in whose hands the success of a fund-raising campaign lies. One corporate leader interviewed by Ross noted: 'There are fifty or sixty people around here who can make or break a campaign. If they don't participate in it one way or another, such as even having their names on the letter-head, the campaign won't go over.'[4] In the eyes of university administrators, fund-raising specialists, and the government itself, this was a basic and powerful truth.

The experience of Brock University clearly reflected this situation. The campaign for a post-secondary institution in Welland and Lincoln counties was initiated by the Allenburg Women's Institute in 1957. After passing a resolution calling for the establishment of a university in the Niagara peninsula, the association received support for its efforts from the Welland District Women's Institute.[5] When the minister of education, William Dunlop, was presented with the proposal, however, he was unreceptive. He felt that the province required expansion in the area of the professions – medicine, engineering, and forestry – and the Niagara community could not demonstrate sufficient resources to move ahead in these fields. The fact that McMaster University, in nearby Hamilton, had already undertaken to extend its program in the sciences did not augur well for the proponents of the new institution.

None the less, the community pressed ahead. In October 1958, a Niagara Peninsula Joint Committee on Higher Education was established with representatives from the surrounding area. A population survey was completed and the impressive demographic projections it contained convinced the committee that a new minister might be more receptive to local appeals than was the conservative Dunlop.[6] The survey showed that while the population of Canada had increased by 27 per cent from 1949 to 1958, the population of Lincoln and Welland counties had risen by 45 per cent over the same period. Similar increases were documented in the university-aged population and foreseen in the decade ahead.

Over the next three years, while discussions continued, there was little tangible progress made on the project. McMaster University was especially critical of the prospect of competition from a neighbouring university, though its president noted that if a new university were created in the Niagara area, it should be affiliated with McMaster in order to avoid duplication of facilities.[7] Not until the citizens' committee was re-established with an array of prominent corporate sponsors did the efforts of the campaigners begin to bear fruit.

In April of 1962, M.A. Chown, a St Catharines alderman and a member of the joint committee, invited Stanley Deeks, the executive director of the Industrial Foundation on Education and a former participant in organizing activities for York University, to attend a meeting to discuss the project. After agreeing to use his influence in raising support for a new university, Deeks discussed the fundamental need for the community to form an 'influential citizens' committee' to carry on the campaign. As a result, the committee contacted D.G. Willmot, the president of Anthes-Imperial Limited of St Catharines, who agreed to participate.

On Willmot's advice, Arthur Schmon, chairman of the board of Ontario Paper Company Limited (Thorold) – considered to be the 'leading citizen of the area'

– was invited, and agreed, to become the chairman of the new Founders' Committee of the proposed Brock University. As constituted in 1962, the new committee included nineteen of the most influential business and political figures in the Niagara region. It contained representatives from companies of both national and local prominence such as Gunning Oil, Niagara Falls; Union Carbide, Welland; Anthes-Imperial Ltd.; McKinnon Industries, St Catharines; the *St Catharines Standard*; Canadian Ohio Brass, Niagara Falls; International Nickel, Port Colborne; Provincial Gas, Thorold; Page Hersey Tubes, Welland; A. Newman and Co., St Catharines; Atlas Steel, Welland; Cyanamid of Canada, Niagara Falls; and a representative of the United Steel Workers of America.[8]

The importance attached to attracting the interest of the corporate concerns was revealed in the discussions surrounding the participation of International Nickel. The company was the largest employer in Port Colborne, but when the president, Ralph Parker, was invited to join the Founders' Committee, he initially declined on the grounds that he was heavily involved in the newly created Laurentian University in Sudbury – the home of the company's head office. According to Arthur Schmon: 'We know that Port Colborne is not happy about the fact that it is not represented [on the Founders' Committee] and we are not happy because we cannot persuade the principal industry there to join us in our important project. It leaves a great question mark in the minds of the public and especially insofar as outsiders are concerned.'[9] But after a further conference between top officials of International Nickel and the Founders' Committee, Parker changed his mind and agreed to participate. Though the president did not personally join the committee, he appointed a representative who brought to the project the benefit of the company's prestigious name.

The rationale for creating a board of governors with such a prominent membership was explained by Deeks in a report prepared for the chairman of the Founders' Committee. According to Deeks, Brock was merely following the rewarding route taken by other universities both in Ontario and the United States. The consensus of university planners was that, while boards of governors should reflect a variety of interests in the community including municipal groups, 'a representative of labour,' a 'Jewish representative,' and 'at least two members of the Roman Catholic faith,' they should primarily consist of 'top businessmen, professionals with an influence in the community and Canadian society.' In slightly more blunt fashion, one of the Founders' Committee members, and a subsequent member of the Brock Board of Governors, indicated his concurrence with Deeks:

I have read your report on the Board of Governors and I think you have covered it very well indeed. I incline strongly to the view that as far as possible the members of the

Board of Governors should be multimillionaires. While this should not be completely the deciding factor, there is no doubt that men who have amassed a considerable fortune are able men, make good governors, and would in addition be able to donate substantially.[10]

Against this background, events proceeded apace. A meeting with the province's Committee on University Affairs in July 1962 was more encouraging to the Brock advocates than any previous such encounter, although no official sanction was yet given by the committee or the government to the proposed institution. On 31 October 1962, Brock University became incorporated; in November, a fund-raising dinner was held with representatives of the major industries of Lincoln and Welland counties. The $80,000 needed for organizational purposes over the next year was raised easily in the few weeks following the dinner. In 1963, through the activities of the board, a site was chosen for the building of the campus, funds were finally secured from the provincial government to purchase land that was made available to the university by Ontario Hydro, and, after much initial scepticism, Brock obtained from the Committee on University Affairs and the government of Ontario official sanction and independent status.[11]

From the small regional universities founded in the early 1960s to the established, well-endowed, 'national' institutions, the participation of the private sector was instrumental in the expansion and development process. At the University of Toronto, for example, the Board of Governors outlined a plan for doubling the university's enrolment between 1957 and 1969. The key elements in the program was a $51,000,000 national campaign begun in 1958. According to a brochure published in that year, the project was intended to be a 'triple alliance of government, business and the people.'[12] The co-chairmen of the campaign were Toronto board members – Wallace McCutcheon, of Argus Corporation, and Neil J. McKinnon, the president of the Canadian Imperial Bank of Commerce. The management committee included an equally impressive list of corporate personnel. Indeed, William Dunlop, the minister of education, suggested that any new appointees to the Toronto board should have similar roots in the business community in light of the campaign ahead. 'I realized the desirability, even the necessity, of a reasonably wide distribution [of Toronto board members], but the argument used this time was that, since a financial campaign is coming up, men should be appointed who know how to push a campaign and are on the ground when needed.'[13]

For the University of Toronto, this approach proved wise. By November 1959, the university reported that the Board of Governors itself has 'set the pace' by donating gifts totalling $462,000. The campaign received a major boost from the City of Toronto when the mayor, Nathan Phillips, declared November 'the University of Toronto Campaign Month.'[14] Bolstered by the private donations raised through the national fund, the university received from the government the necessary capital and operating support to expand its campus downtown and to build satellite campuses in Mississauga and Scarborough.

At the University of Waterloo, the crucial role played by the business community was evident not only in the events leading to the founding of the institution but in the organization of the academic program as well. In the Kitchener-Waterloo area, Waterloo College, a Lutheran-controlled university, had been for three decades the major institute of higher learning. But in the mid 1950s as pressures for expansion were felt throughout the province, the institution's board discussed the possibility of expanding its facilities in order to meet the growing need. To their dismay, however, the board members discovered that the government of Ontario had no intention of changing its long-standing policy of financing only non-denominational universities.

In response, the college decided to follow the path taken in the past by other denominational universities in order to receive at least partial government funding. The process involved establishing a non-sectarian affiliate with its own governing body which would offer arts, science, and professional training not available at the college itself. In order to gain increasing respectability from both the government and the community as a whole, the college also took the bold step of appointing its first lay president – J.G. Hagey, a member of the Waterloo College Board of Governors and the public relations manager of B.F. Goodrich, one of the region's largest employers.[15]

In co-operation with Ira C. Needles, the president of B.F. Goodrich, Hagey began the process of raising support for extended educational facilities in the Kitchener-Waterloo area. In September 1955, Hagey called a meeting of several of the region's most prominent community leaders: C.M. Dare, president of Dare Biscuit Company; A.M. Snider, of Sunshine Limited; C.A. Pollock, president of Dominion Electrohome Industries; E.J. Shoemaker, president of McBrine Luggate and Company; and Dr S.F. Leavine, a prominent Kitchener physician. A tentative list of possible members for a board of governors of the new college was drawn up in which 29 of 32 prospects were prominent businessmen. It was decided that the six individuals mentioned above would form the nucleus of the Founding Board. The decision was also taken in December to establish a non-denominational faculty which would be affiliated with Waterloo College. In April 1956, Waterloo College Associate Faculties became a legal entity with a board of governors drawn largely from the list compiled in the previous year.[16]

Unlike other universities that evolved from denominational origins, the Associate Faculties was unable to reach agreement with its mentor, Waterloo College. The Lutheran Synod of America was distressed by the sudden erosion of its own authority. Thus, even though the Associate Faculties operated as an affiliate of Waterloo College for three years, it developed in an increasingly independent fashion. The success it had in rousing popular and government support was related largely to the innovative nature of the academic programs it proceeded to introduce. When the Board of Governors discussed the types of subjects the university would teach, it arrived at the following conclusion:

It was fairly evident that the answer was to be found somewhere in the area of science or applied science. During this period Canada's booming economy had brought sharply into focus a national shortage of both engineers and trained technicians. The launching of Russia's sputnik had dramatized the need for accelerated scientific activity in the western world. And right at home the board of the Associate Faculties, predominantly made up of area industrialists, was thoroughly familiar with the need.[17]

The foundation upon which the reputation of Waterloo would be built was a co-operative engineering program in which students would spend two-thirds of each year in the classroom and one-third working directly in industry. The essence of the program was favourably received by the Canadian Engineering Institute, the National Conference of Canadian Universities, and the education committee of the Canadian Manufacturers Association, all of whom were consulted by the board. The board met as well with representatives of thirty-five industrialists in Toronto in 1956 who were also highly impressed.

By 1959, when the Associate Faculties received its own university charter, 250 companies were participating in the co-operative engineering program. Furthermore, 'more than 600 companies have expressed an interest in accepting Waterloo's engineering students as soon as they can organize their operating programs to do so.' The institution boasted as well that financial support totalling more than $1,300,000 had been donated or pledged by industry and individuals. 'Waterloo's working relationship with industry augurs well for future financial support from industry. In the recent fund-raising drive campaign, cooperating companies subscribed generously. This source of potential revenues increases as the cooperative engineering program expands.'[18]

The success of the new venture was attributed largely to the activities of the Board under the aegis of Hagey and Needles. The former became the University of Waterloo's first president; the latter its first board chairman.

The Board of Governors was made up of professionals, businessmen and journalists, all by the nature of their work very much aware of the immediate demands of the society in which they lived. The President had spent his life, both his business and leisure hours, closely related to community concerns ... [as well as in] advertising and public relations. The Chairman of the Board of Governors, Ira Needles, has been a leader in Canadian industry and active in the affairs of the Canadian Manufacturers Association for many years ... Needles wrote literally hundreds of letters to Canadian companies and it was largely these letters which brought the first students in from industry.[19]

Throughout the province there were other examples of how crucial the role of the business community was in raising political and financial support for the expansion of facilities in both old and new universities. In Peterborough, for instance, the first step leading to the opening of Trent University in 1964 was taken by Reginald R. Faryon, the president of Quaker Oats Company, who sent a letter to business and civic leaders urging that funds received by the city from the sale of a natural gas distribution system be used to build a university. The Canadian General Electric Company played a pivotal role in the project by donating 100 acres of land just north of Peterborough for the site of the new university. And by November 1963, the organizing committee had raised $2,000,000 in the private sector for the founding of the new institution. This series of events was particularly impressive in light of the refusal of the government to support the venture in 1960. In that year Premier Robarts had said, 'If a university is set up in Peterborough, we will wait and see what support they get from their own community'.[20] That university organizers were fully aware of the mutual benefits flowing from their association with the community – especially the corporate community – was revealed in this statement by Thomas Symons, the founding president of Trent University:

On the most basic but nonetheless important level, the University will be an enormous economic boon to the whole region. It will be one of the largest employers and largest consumers of goods and services in the region. Not only will it pour money into the local economy in the form of wages and therefore, increased buying power, but it will demand merchandising and maintenance in large quantities; not only new buildings and new equipment, but food, fuel and supplies of every sort, as well as increased services such as buses, telephones and electricity.[21]

In northwestern Ontario, where agitation for extended post-secondary facilities had been carried on since the end of the Second World War,[22] Minister of Education Dunlop told the Fort William community in the early 1950s that, unless they could mobilize their own resources, the government would not approve a new institution. Consequently, in 1955, $175,000 was raised from public and private resources in the community and in 1956 the Lakehead

Technical Institute received permission to offer university courses, a step which led to official chartering of the institute in 1962.[23]

Indeed, the tendency for prominent businessmen to play leading roles in the governing of Ontario universities increased from the 1950s to the early 1970s. In 1951, for example, eighty individuals identified by John Porter as members of the economic élite in Canada held positions on boards of governors of the fifteen major Canadian universities. 'That the university governorship stands out as a symbol of honour and worth is perhaps illustrated by the fact that 30 of the 80 persons in the economic elite who held these positions were among the top 100 rankers of the corporate world.' He confirmed the existence of a procedure discussed in the cases of Brock and Waterloo in which 'when new universities appear, the chairman and chancellors are selected from the board room of the nearest dominant corporation.'[24]

In 1972, Wallace Clement found that '240 elite members held a governing position in one of the private schools, universities or other institutions of higher learning.'[25] And a case study of eight Ontario universities in 1974 found that 500 different corporations and financial institutions were represented on the boards of governors. The survey concluded that 41 per cent of the total membership of such boards was held by members of the economic élite.[26] It is important to note that the survey did not include individuals with kinship ties to the economic élite and those who had close ties to corporations without themselves holding directorships. The effect, of course, of including such individuals would be to raise the percentages of those linked closely with the business community far above the 41 per cent level.

Thus the involvement of businessmen in the development of the university system was considered essential if the system was to grow. The prestige they brought to the various projects, the money they raised, the money they contributed, the influence they held in political and corporate circles, were vital in a political culture that continued to pay great deference to the doyens of corporate capitalism. As we have seen, this deference was not eroded even during a period when the universities had become publicly funded enterprises. One university comptroller candidly outlined the reasons for appointing wealthy businessmen to the boards of contemporary universities:

First of all, because they have money themselves or manage it for someone else, they have the required experience. Secondly, they might be persuaded to part with some of it once they get a first hand knowledge of the need [for expanded educational facilities]. And they know other people of means and can talk them into giving a few thousand or a few hundred thousand, whatever it takes. Thirdly, it's the thing to do – don't you see? – to appoint businessmen. Society expects it. People look up to them, especially government people. If the business community feels there's a need for a university and shows its interest by putting up a good chunk of money, this is a pretty persuasive argument for a provincial grant.[27]

The genesis of York University was not unlike that of other new institutions discussed in the previous section. The paths of individuals from two distinct interest groups – one from the upper echelons of the business community and the other with deep roots in the cultural life of Toronto – converged in a common quest for expanded educational facilities in the Toronto area. In the summer of 1955, a committee from the North Toronto YMCA initiated discussions about the role the Y might play in advancing the cause of adult education in Canada. Across the continent, the YMCA had a long history of involvement in the development of colleges and universities. Various branches of the organization had operated or been affiliated with a number of post-secondary institutions in cities such as Boston, Chicago, and Montreal.[28]

At the same time, under the aegis of Air Marshal W.A. Curtis, vice-chairman of A.V. Roe & Company, a group of individuals associated with the aircraft and transportation industry was considering the need for universities to respond more quickly to the changing dimensions of Canadian industrial development. Against the background of startling statistical evidence, projecting the rapid rise of university-aged youth in the Toronto area over the next decade, Air Marshal Curtis had posed the possibility of starting a new university during informal discussions at the 1956 conference on scientific and technical manpower at St Andrew's, New Brunswick.[29]

In that same year, the Y arranged for the two groups to pool their intellectual resources and, after establishing a formal committee on 'the university project,' invited Curtis and several of his associates to join it. Because of his high profile in influential circles, Curtis was appointed chairman of the group. The committee included: three representatives from the North Toronto Y, A.A. Clarke, A.R. Jordan, and A.R. Hackett; Arthur Margison, a consulting engineer; T. Loudon, a former head of the Department of Aeronautical and Civil Engineering at the University of Toronto and later associated with De Havilland Aircraft Company; E.T. Alberts, a Toronto insurance executive; and Stanley Deeks, the executive director of the Industrial Foundation on Education (and formerly an engineer with A.V. Roe and Company).

In November 1957 a delegation from the committee headed by Curtis met with W.J. Dunlop, the Ontario minister of education, who expressed interest in, but offered no official sanction of, the proposed university project. In fact, the plans of the York University Organizing Committee (as it was now called) were still in a highly embryonic stage. The committee had yet to decide if its interest lay in establishing an adult evening college on the one hand, a full-time day school on the other hand, or some combination of the two.

As discussions proceeded, however, it was increasingly evident that, for the majority of committee members, a full-fledged university lay on the horizon. They believed that by maintaining direct affiliation with the YMCA, the project would be constrained by an organization with limited resources and limited educational aspirations. According to the minutes of an organizing committee meeting in September 1958: 'For reasons of long-term financing, staff appointments and normal growth, a stage of development would undoubtedly be reached when it would be necessary to separate the operation of the York University committee from the YMCA and continue as a separate entity, although retaining an affinity with its former parent group.'

In the meantime, the committee membership had been enlarged in order to draw further upon the technical and business expertise of individuals both within and outside the academic world. In January 1958, J.R. Kidd, a professor with long involvement in the development of adult education, joined the group. In May of that year, G. Arthur Lascelles, commissioner of finance for Metropolitan Toronto, A. Douglas McKee, president of Perina Limited, Douglas F. Kent, president and general manager of Kendall (Canada) Limited; and Walter R. McLachlan, president of Orenda Engines Limited, also became members.[30]

In December 1958, following the official severing of relations with the YMCA, and after the decision had been made by the committee to seek a university charter from the province, a delegation met with Premier Frost. The meeting had been arranged by Oakley Dalgleish, the publisher and editor of the *Globe and Mail* and a close associate of the premier.

Frost encouraged the committee to pursue a charter, but he cautioned that this implied no promise of financial support from the government. He reiterated his inclination to finance the development of higher education in Ontario by expanding the facilities of existing universities. He was particularly worried about the York committee's request for capital aid to purchase 400 acres of land for a proposed site of the new campus. The premier suggested that if, in fact, a new institution were built, it would be more economical for the organizers to buy land outside Metropolitan Toronto – where the cost would be less prohibitive. Frost also let it be known that, whatever the future held, the committee would have to gain the support of the University of Toronto and of the community as a whole (in order for the project to gain credibility).[31]

By March 1959, the committee had obtained an official charter from the provincial Legislative Assembly authorizing it to offer university courses. Financial support, however, had not yet been secured. In order to establish the type of credibility spoken of by Frost, the new Provisional Board of Governors, whose members were drawn from the organizing committee, discussed the need to obtain the support of prominent and influential individuals in the business community. According to J.R. Kidd: 'As far as businessmen are concerned, I think it will be wise to find those who already have positions of influence but who are obviously moving ahead in their own field ... I think we should keep our eyes open for able men who move to Toronto and who have not yet taken on many commitments in this city.'[32] He suggested as well that other interest groups, including new Canadians and labourers should also be represented on the permanent board of the university. With these considerations in mind, each member of the provisional board was asked to submit a list of possible candidates for the new Board of Governors.

Events on other fronts proceeded apace. Following extensive and heated negotiations, the York board worked out an arrangement with the University of Toronto, in which the former would remain an affiliate of the latter for not less than four and not more than eight years.[33] While in its formative stages York might well benefit from the revered reputation of Toronto through this association, some board members worried about the institution's subsequent ability to establish its own identity. Furthermore, the board's limited experience in academic planning, the rather stringent affiliation terms, and the weighty financial problems left the project – and the university's long-term future – still foundering on the shoals of uncertainty.

But in May of 1959, Curtis had begun to seek the makings of a solution. He received a letter from Dr Murray Ross, vice-president of the University of Toronto, who had been authorized by its president, Claude Bissell, to work closely with the York board in drawing up the affiliation agreement. Ross wrote that York could become a vital, novel, and exceptional institution by embarking on bold educational directions. Over the years he had grown impatient with Toronto's failure to broaden its curricular offerings and to modernize its teaching methods. For York, he saw new opportunities. He noted that while York would have to remain quite small for several years, it could establish its distinctive character by focusing on a 'few well integrated courses' that had yet to make their presence felt in Canadian universities. 'Emphasis,' he suggested,

should be given to the social sciences ... One must consider the fact that there has been tremendous interest in and development of the Social Sciences in the United States universities and that in Canada, the Social Sciences have not received comparable attention nor have they been developed in the universities to the same extent as in the physical sciences. Here is an area in which an enterprising university could readily capture the field.[34]

Furthermore, York should stress the value of small classes and make the tutorial system (as opposed to the large, impersonal lecture system) its basis for classroom instruction.

According to Curtis, not only did Ross's letter provide a new direction for creative action, but it convinced him and his committee that the author should become the first president of York University. 'There was so much new look to this thinking that when I read the letter to our committee, they agreed unanimously that he was the man we should have as president, and authorized me to explore the possibility.'[35]

Ross, however, did not accept the subsequent offer immediately. He noted that he was postponing any decision 'until there is some indication that a strong Board [of Governors] for York can be organized.' He told Eric Phillips, the chairman of the University of Toronto board:

Potentially there is a good group of men interested in York: Bob Winters, Bill McLean, Allen Lambert, Ted Walker, John Proctor. Air Marshal Curtis is hopeful that Mrs. John David Eaton and Peter Scott will join the above group to form the nucleus of the new Board ... I think the group requires someone like yourself to tell them the job is important and that they should get on with it.[36]

Efforts to attract these, and other, prominent individuals were successful, and the permanent board (replacing the provisional board) was constituted in 1959. Ross officially accepted the presidency in December that year.[37]

The new board brought an impressive list of corporate associations to the fledgling institution: Robert Winters, chairman of Rio Tinto Mines, became the first chairman of the York board. Also appointed to the board in 1959 were: Allen Lambert, president of the Toronto-Dominion Bank; W.C. Harris, of Harris Partners; John D. Leitch, chairman of Maple Leaf Mills; William Pearson Scott, president of Wood Gundy (Securities); John S. Proctor, executive vice-president of the Bank of Nova Scotia; and Edwin H. Walker, president of General Motors of Canada. Other appointees included David B. Mansur, a financial consultant; Edgar Burton, chairman of the Robert Simpson Company; Mrs John David Eaton, wife of the president of the T. Eaton Company; F.G. Gardiner, a lawyer and former chairman of the Metropolitan Toronto council; Bertrand Gerstein, president of People's Credit Jewellers; John M. Gray, chairman of Macmillan Company of Canada; J. William Horsey, chairman emeritus of Salada Foods; W.F. McLean, president of Canada Packers; L.G. Lumbers, president of Canada Wire & Cable Company; and A.J. Little, a partner in Clarkson Gordon, all of whom were appointed between 1960 and 1963.[38] W.A.

Curtis, the only member retained from the provisional board, was appointed the first chancellor of York University.

Members of the board with links other than in the business community were: William Mahoney, vice-president of the Canadian Labour Congress and national director of the United Steel Workers of America; Senator (and banker) D'Arcy Leonard; Dr R.F. Farquarson, chairman of the Medical Research Council; and Dr W.F. James, a consulting geologist.

Why did these individuals agree to serve on York's board? Individually, their motives were undoubtedly mixed. Wilfrid Curtis, as mentioned, had special concerns about the future of the transportation industry in Canada and believed that universities had a crucial role to play in building expertise in this area. On the other hand, Mrs Eaton became quickly involved in the university's cultural affairs and strongly supported the establishment of a fine arts program. Bertrand Gerstein, a retail jeweller, with 'no previous involvement in community affairs,' was anxious to find a non-business outlet for his energies and interests. David Mansur, a veteran in the construction and real estate business, was attracted by the newness of the institution and was excited by the prospect of helping build this vital enterprise 'from the ground up.'[39]

If their private motivations varied, in general the board members (the majority of whom were university graduates) were swept up in the raging enthusiasm for the expansion of university facilities in Ontario. This was an area of increasingly high priority and those involved at the board level were individuals whose stars in the business world were also rising. The prestige value of a board appointment was evident to most. To be selected 'by one's peers,' according to David Mansur, was a badge of honour in the heady days of university development.

To some, the benefits of board membership may have proven even more concrete over the years. Minutes from a meeting of the Board of Governors revealed that in 1969 York had short- and long-term investments in private companies totalling $2,275,633. The companies listed were the Toronto Dominion Bank, Simpson's, British American Oil, Ford Motor Credit Company, and General Motors Acceptance Corporation. The membership of the board at that time included the president of the Toronto Dominion Bank, the vice-president of Simpson's, the vice-president of General Motors, and a former director of the Ford Motor Company.[40]

Despite these direct links to some of the companies they headed, financial rewards could hardly have been a major lure to the original board members. As we shall see, the price these individuals paid for joining outstripped any direct profits they might accrue from university investments in their own companies. Yet the contacts made and the club-like atmosphere that evolved in this élite community might well have contributed in a small way to the general health of Canadian business. Furthermore, in light of the massive expansion occuring in the entire field of higher education, Ontario's universities made no small contribution to economic growth in the province during the 1960s. The university was big business and the corporate executives overseeing this expansion were well aware of the problems and opportunities this presented. They believed that they were needed and this too inspired many of them to join.

By 1960, York's business-dominated Board of Governors was firmly in place. But the question persists: once appointed, precisely what functions did board members fill? It is evident that while some were more active than others in the daily affairs of the university, all of the governors were intended to be much more than mere figureheads. Far and away their main responsibilities were to contribute personally to the financial coffers of the university; to seek large donations from their own companies; to use their influence in raising funds from among other major corporations; to secure large loans from Canadian financial institutions; to establish the institutional infrastructure of the university; and to lobby for political and financial support at the government level.

In its first academic year, 1960–61, York operated on a small scale out of Falconer Hall at the University of Toronto. In 1961 the university moved to Glendon College, the site of an old family estate, then owned by the University of Toronto and located in a fashionable part of Toronto. For its first three years, York offered a limited number of courses in the arts, but engaged simultaneously in the process of planning its curriculum development for the post-affiliation period. The university also undertook the search for a permanent site which would permit it to increase its enrolment, build residences, and move into the fields of graduate and professional education.[41]

These were lofty, expensive plans, and the financial future remained uncertain. Like all new universities, York was seriously handicapped by an absence of endowment funds which older institutions had gathered over previous decades. Furthermore, York was incapable of getting a head start in collecting private funds, since its arrangement with the University of Toronto forbade it to campaign in the corporate sector until the latter had completed its own fund-raising drive in 1964.[42] This restriction indicated the enormous difficulty that universities faced in carrying out long-range subscription campaigns in the Canadian business community. Clearly, Toronto sought to avoid direct competition in this area from a daughter institution. According to Henry Borden, the vice-chairman of the Toronto board, the $51 million fund-raising campaign had been a hard, up-hill struggle. In December of 1963, he told Leslie Frost, 'We do not believe that a general appeal to the public for funds to the University for any appreciable amount in the reasonably near future would have any hope of success and we certainly could not at this time recommend or endorse such an appeal.'[43] Overcoming such evident obstacles to private fund-raising would be one important measure of the success and value of York's business-led board.

The first step involved securing large donations from York board members themselves. In 1962 the university was able to inform the provincial government (from whom it sought capital and operating support) that 'the University will provide private moneys [from board members] in an amount comparable to that of any university in the province.[44] According to a fund-raising specialist whom York retained in 1964, such contributions comprised seed money essential to any successful appeal among other Canadian businesses. The image then presented would not be of a struggling university, scrounging for funds in a desperate fashion, but of a confident, well-endowed institution, already well on its way to success on the strength of large donations from its own members.

It must be remembered that the Governors of the University and corporations and foundations which they control or can successfully influence are also 'key prospects.' Corporate executives and individual philanthropists will expect to be informed of the level at which these corporations and the Board as a group are prepared to lend support. The process of pace-setting is a double-barrelled one – as to the amount of gifts and as to promptness with which the decision is made and commitment given. All must be at the highest level to ensure success.[45]

A memo to several board members from A.T. Lambert, the president of the Toronto-Dominion Bank and the chairman of the board's finance committee, explained the process through which donations were to be solicited:

I have spoken to Mr. Walker with regard to General Motors, and to Mr. McLean with regard to Canada Packers, and while confirmation of amounts has not been received, these are actively being considered. Mr. Harris and Mr. Proctor will approach the Bank of Nova Scotia. Mr. Winters and Mr. Burton will be speaking to the Canadian Imperial Bank of Commerce. I have given an indication of my thinking with respect to the Toronto-Dominion Bank.[46]

In December 1964, at a meeting of the Board of Governors, a list was presented of 224 companies in Canada with an accompanying account of their pre-tax profits for 1958 and 1959. According to the minutes of the meeting: 'Members were asked to say who they think should make contact [including themselves] and how much target could be, based on any previous knowledge of corporate giving.'[47] That the wealthiest board members had indeed made substantial contributions to the university, and that this fact was advertised in the wider campaign to other potential donors, was revealed in a letter to Mrs Thomas Bata, of Bata Shoe Company, dated 11 March 1965, which read in part:

As an assurance to all who may contribute to the York University Founders Fund that the Board of Governors has accepted the challenge to provide a University of the highest calibre, they have personally pledged in the aggregate the sum of one million dollars to the Founders Fund which is in addition to the subscription from the various corporations with which they are connected.[48]

Board members associated with large financial institutions proved their value in other ways. Since government grants for capital and operating expenses were distributed only on an annual basis, and since they often fell short of the university's immediate and perceived future needs, it was essential for the institution to have access – as any private corporation would – to substantial bank loans. In 1965, the Board of Governors authorized debenture borrowing of $2 million (at 5½ per cent per annum) from the Toronto-Dominion Bank, whose president, Allen Lambert, was a member of the University financial committee.[49] On at least four other occasions throughout 1966, correspondence was exchanged with the Toronto-Dominion Bank regarding loans to the university.

To expedite the collection process and to consolidate possible links with other financial institutions, it was reported that a York account had been opened not only at the Toronto-Dominion Bank but also at the Canadian Imperial Bank of Commerce. Further, 'Mr. Lambert has suggested that it might be appropriate to open a third account in the Bank of Nova Scotia to process cheques for contributions drawn on that bank.'[50]

The connections between the Board of Governors and the business community were exploited not simply for the purpose of raising private funds, but the prominent corporate positions of board members also helped the university secure a working relationship with the provincial government. As noted earlier, when the organizing committee was ready to submit its initial plans to the government in 1958, it called upon Oakley Dalgleish, the publisher of the *Globe and Mail*, to arrange a meeting with the premier of the province. Later, in 1962, when the university's public grant fell $700,000 short of its request, the chairman of the Board of Governors, 'Bob' Winters, wrote a personal letter to 'Les' Frost, the former premier and currently a member of the Committee on University Affairs, in order to seek redress.[51] (This obvious personal relationship between the two was particularly interesting in light of the fact that they were prominent members of opposing political parties.)

It should be noted, however, that there was nothing 'automatic' about the government's response to the university on such matters. Indeed, in a firm reply to the university written six days before Winters wrote to Frost, Premier John Robarts explained that the government faced many requests from a variety of institutions, and simply could not afford to meet all of their demands: 'It may be that some effort will have to be made to revise your operating budget ... We cannot accept the position that we will automatically pick up the deficits of every university in the province.[52] Clearly, Ontario universities operated within a competitive economic environment. But the fact that they were represented by prominent corporate personnel was considered a prerequisite for securing financial viability and provided them, as well, with the type of access to the highest levels of government which, in their view, they would otherwise have had difficulty obtaining.

The Founders Fund Campaign, as the university fund-raising drive was titled, was the product of a highly sophisticated process, orchestrated in minute detail from beginning to end. As early as 1958, the university organizers had been approached by G.A. Brakeley and Company on the possibility of its running York's fund-raising drive. Brakeley's credentials seemed impressive. It had already been involved in similar campaigns on behalf of the universities of Toronto, British Columbia, Western Ontario, McMaster, McGill, Queen's, and Assumption (Windsor). A lengthy brochure, replete with a healthy combination of self-glorification and independent compliments on its past success, underlined its qualifications for the task. It claimed that universities could not achieve success in the critical area of private fund-raising unless they engaged in a nearly scientific plan, conducted by experts experienced in the art of tapping the private sector's resources.[53] The days in which philanthropy could be obtained through the efforts of a few generous individuals had long since passed.

Since York was as yet incapable of undertaking such a campaign (because of its affiliation agreement with the University of Toronto), the company was not hired immediately. But in 1964, its services were engaged for a fee of $85,000.[54] Through a tried and proven technique called 'The Survey, the Analysis and the Plan,' Brakeley's outlined the process that would be followed in this impending community project. In a detailed questionnaire submitted to the administration, the president and his advisers were asked to respond to a series of questions about the university's goals, objectives, and building plans. From this information a campaign theme would be elicited that would facilitate the ability of potential donors to relate quickly to the needs of the university.

Once the formal process was completed, the consultants would interview the president and each of the board members to gain a further insight into the dynamics and current problems of the university. This latter process was considered preferable to soliciting written briefs from all the board members since they might hesitate to reveal confidentialities in writing. Such information would enable the campaign organizers to anticipate and guard against any embarrassing publicity that might arise in the course of the fund drive. By the autumn of 1964, the preliminary process had been completed. It was time to outline, in detail, through the 'analysis,' the direction to be followed in the months ahead.

Of first priority was a carefully contrived prediction of how much money the university could expect to raise. After considering the personal resources of the board members, the number of potential large donors in the corporate community, the state of the Canadian economy, and the possible competition from corporate fund drives at other universities, Brakeley's arrived at the figure of $15,000,000. Once again, as we noted earlier, the 'pace-setting' contributions of key individuals and corporations were considered crucial in ensuring the success of the campaign. Furthermore, the heavy dependence on a small number of large donors was to be as necessary an ingredient of the York campaign as it was for universities across the country. Brakeley's explained:

Our survey and those subsequent discussions revealed the possibility of raising a sum in the neighbourhood of eight million dollars through the pursuit of what might be termed normal methods of campaigning directed by the outstanding leadership known to be available and paced by exemplary gifts at the top level. The balance of seven million dollars can only be raised in special gifts at the seven figure level ... These special and unusually large gifts *must* be secured and available as pace setters if even the modest amount of eight million dollars in the lower levels is to be secured.[55]

One further difficulty, inherent in the problems of a new university, placed York at a disadvantage to wealthier institutions. 'The University of Toronto fund-raising result included alumni at over $250,000 and a substantial sum from small businesses, which latter lacking Toronto's alumni contacts, are not likely to be as susceptible to the appeal of York.'

Five basic committees, presided over by York board members, were established in order to concentrate on specific areas of the campaign. A Toronto corporate gifts division would appeal to companies in that city; a Toronto personal gifts division would seek out individual contributions; a national gifts division would campaign outside of Toronto; a public information division would be in charge of the media campaign; and an administrative division would handle the daily business of the fund drive. All of this was carefully mapped on an extensive chart outlining responsibilities and jurisdictions. The entire campaign was presided over by a management committee.

All of the participants were expected to follow a very strict schedule in meeting their goals. For example, from 31 August to 26 September 1964, the solicitation of 'key prospects' was to be conducted and completed. This included obtaining advance pledges from especially large corporations and from the members of the Board of Governors, all of which was to be done before any public announcements. During this period, in which the long-term potential of the campaign would be determined, the management committee was expected to 'meet fortnightly' to discuss the course of the drive.

On 19 October the solicitation of advance 'national gifts' was scheduled to begin and the governors were to be approached personally for even greater contributions. In February 1965, after the large corporate donors had been solicited, the public campaign was to begin in earnest.

The latter was launched by an elaborate 'media dinner' on 19 December 1964, to which the owners, managers, and / or editors of Toronto's major media outlets were invited. The guest list included John Bassett of the *Toronto Telegram*, Beland Honderich of the *Toronto Star*, J.L. Cooper of the *Globe and Mail*. Prominent officials, as well, represented radio stations CFRB, CHFI, CHUM, CKFH, CKEY, and television networks CFTO and CBC (radio and TV); Maclean-Hunter publishing company and *Saturday Night* representatives were also invited. The menu was planned meticulously: a seafood cocktail, filet mignon or roast beef, and ample liquor before, during, and after dinner.

A very careful tabulation of subsequent media coverage of the university was kept on file. A memo to H.D. Barbour (the Brakeley official heading the campaign) noted that coverage in the written media had increased from 154 stories in November of 1964 to 251 stories in March of 1965.[56]

The key months of the campaign, following the media dinner, were February and March 1965. In this period, great emphasis was placed on canvassing individual donors and those corporate contributors that could be further influenced by public (as opposed to private) appeals. Throughout March, 'cultivation literature' was mailed out, canvassers were assigned to specific areas, and the canvassing itself, which began on 9 March, was to be completed on 30 April.[57] The 'clean-up' period was to occur during May, and the final report was to be issued by Brakeley's on 31 May. In rapid-fire succession, outlined with military-like precision, the public was assaulted by the York campaigners.

The main brochure used in the campaign was an attractively packaged, easily read pamphlet entitled *Plant Now That the Seeds May Grow*, issued in March 1965. It described the national needs and local pressures for a new university in Toronto, and it outlined the expansion plans of the university – an approach consistent with the view that, for the public to be responsive, it needed to know exactly what it was paying for.

York, noted the brochure, would be 'especially well placed to address the problems of urban life' and it detailed the immediate and long-range building plans that covered development in the sciences, the social sciences, the humanities, and the professions. The booklet also discussed the 'unique philosophy of York,' in which, through a college system, the perils of a factory-like, mass production university would be avoided. Each college would serve no more than one thousand students at a time.

Finally, in an effort to demonstrate the university's impressive credentials, the pamphlet listed all the department heads with their academic degrees, and all the board members with their corporate affiliations.

The campaign was planned to the ultimate degree, even to the point of sending out different form letters to contributors of varying amounts. There were three such categories: those who donated over $50,000; those between $1,000 and $50,000; and those who gave less than $1,000.[58] That gratitude itself was intended to serve as an incentive for potential donors was demonstrated in the 'personalized' form letter that was sent to prospective large donors: 'Those who make substantial contributions to the Founders Fund may have their names permanently recorded on the original Founders College by a bronze plaque at the entrance to certain rooms, a list of which is attached to the brochure.'[59]

The campaign ended in the spring of 1965, and before evaluating its success, some specific aspects of corporate giving to York University should be noted. The performance of individual Board members was indeed impressive. While initial projections called for them to contribute collectively one million dollars, by January 1965, they had actually pledged $1,167,500. The records show, furthermore, that the companies of which they were the top executives donated at least an additional $1,325,000.

The pattern of a relatively small number of large companies contributing major donations was as typical of the York campaign as the Industrial Foundation on Education had shown it had been for Canada as a whole. If the Board of Governors is included as a single corporate entity, the records reveal that nine companies or foundations contributed over $250,000 each, accounting for a grand total of $4,699,500 – which was 45 per cent of the total donations raised as of 31 March 1965. Fifteen more corporations gave at least $100,000 each, totalling $1,820,000 – comprising 17 per cent of the total; 31 corporations contributed over $50,000 – constituting 18 per cent of the total; 29 companies contributed over $25,000 – accounting for just over 8 per cent of all funds raised to that date. Altogether, 231 corporations, individuals, or foundations gave grants of over $1,000. Donations of under $1,000 yielded $127,694 – a fraction more than 1 per cent of the total funds pledged as of 31 March 1965.

In terms of sectoral donations, the banks and insurance companies, the resources-related industries, and the food and beverage industries (especially the breweries) were among the most prominent contributors, a pattern consistent with the over-all trends discussed earlier.

In summary, the York Founders Fund campaign, like the wider university appeals in the Canadian corporate community, must be considered a qualified success. The campaign featured some impressive donations by a relatively small number of contributors (although apart from the Board of Governors, there was only one seven-figure donation). But it faced some palpable disappointments as well. By mid 1966, the fund had achieved just under 70 per cent of its fifteen million dollar goal ($10,411,840).[60] Even though the Founders Fund office was closed in October, 1965, contributions continued to trickle in until 1970 when the $15 million dollar figure (less expenses and including interest from investments) was finally obtained.[61]

Throughout the campaign, the organizers reported that in a number of areas and industries the 'key' prospects had not come through. At the end of 1964, in the electrical and allied industries, only half of the 91 prospects had contributed. In the food and beverage sector, despite some large individual contributions, only seven of 24 prospects had pledged donations. Thirty of 65 companies which were solicited in the paper, publishing, and printing sector donated to the fund. Similarly, appeals through the National Gifts division in Vancouver and Montreal had fallen short as well.[62]

What the campaign underlined was that corporate aid to higher education in Canada had been pushed to the limit. The fact that the Founders Fund goal was not achieved until 1970 suggested that if York had been interested in campaigning after 1966 for more private support (beyond the Founders Fund), it would have found the task next to impossible. Indeed, a campaign undertaken by the university in 1971 and 1972 fell flat.[63] Corporate aid to York, as for the province as a whole, did not keep pace with government support over this period. In 1965, 68.1 per cent of York's operating income came from government sources. By 1969 that figure had climbed to 73.2 per cent, and in the latter year, only .6 per cent of the operating budget was covered by private corporate funds. Between 1964 and 1970 government funds accounted for 87 per cent of York's capital income, despite the Founders Fund project. For the entire province these trends were even more evident. While government aid increased from 72.5 per cent to 79.7 per cent over the period 1965–69, company support declined from 3 per cent to less than 2 per cent of total university income.[64]

None the less, the 'margin of freedom' that York had gained from private corporate support enabled it to move ahead quickly with a building program that would not have been wholly sustained by public grants alone. The role of board members in using their influence to seek out these sources was crucial, and it explains the stern defence of a business-dominated board of governors delivered by Murray Ross in the late 1960s when this type of structure was increasingly criticized as unrepresentative of the community at large. According to Ross:

At York we usually have to present bills to the government before we can secure funds for payment, but seldom are architects, contractors, union workers, and others willing to wait for such payments. We therefore have to have a line-of-credit with the bank to permit us to keep many construction jobs moving ahead and on schedule. At present our line-of-credit is $6,000,000. I doubt if any council of faculty and students could secure such a credit rating ...

The Board of Governors controls expenditures in line with budget estimates. This is not an extraordinarily difficult task and yet there are times when it requires a degree of judgement, experience and toughness that few faculty possess. And thirdly the Board raises private funds. In the past three years the York Board has raised over $15,000,000 in private moneys.[65]

Apart from its central role in the fund-raising campaign, as Ross implied, the board played a pivotal part in establishing the university's infrastructure. Of utmost importance was its decision to expand York's facilities by building a new campus (to open in 1965) on a site at the northern fringes of metropolitan Toronto. Board members participated directly in the long, arduous process of securing the property and negotiating (with three levels of government) the transfer of land to the university.[66]

While day-to-day activities were carried out by full-time administrators, who served on a variety of board committees, the board itself held ultimate authority for the hiring of architects, for the approval of the university's 'master plan,' and for determining York's future enrolment.[67] Once basic decisions had been taken, academics and administrators assumed responsibility for determining the scope and content of York's academic offerings, though the board still held the power to approve the funding of all programs. Over the years the board largely left curriculum decisions in the hands of the academics since this was an area in which the governors had little expertise.[68] Murray Ross claimed, in 1970, 'at no time has the Board rejected or vetoed academic plans proposed by the Senate.'[69]

In the end, the prominent corporate status of York's governors had made their appointment to the board (or that of similar individuals) inevitable. Their activity, in the eyes of the president, had made their continued participation invaluable. But their experience in fund-raising indicated that, while higher education was a popular philanthropic cause for the private sector, in light of heavy government funding the sky was by no means the limit.

FOUR

Provincial Planning 1945–67

As we have already noted, the major financial responsibility for ensuring the extension of post-secondary educational facilities was assigned by business, academics, and the public at large to the government and to government agencies. Keynesian ideology – the state practice of engaging in significant public spending within the context of a free-enterprise economy – had swept the country in dramatic form after the Second World War.

Yet within the higher educational sector, the bureaucratic structures through which these developments would occur were, in the late 1940s, barely visible, let alone sophisticated. The number of government officials in Ontario who dealt with university matters could literally be counted on the fingers of one hand.[1] Higher education was a mere and minor adjunct of the Department of Education. Contact between universities and government was minimal, informal, and irregular. Furthermore, the process of interaction was highly subjective: decisions favourable to the university community were frequently influenced by the degree of private sympathy held by the premier for the institutions themselves.

By the late 1960s, however, the size of the government bureaucracy dealing with higher education was growing by leaps and bounds. By 1971, there were some nine hundred government employees involved exclusively with higher education through the new, separate Ministry of [community] Colleges and Universities.[2] Formula financing, systems analysis, and entrenched committee structures had all replaced the more primitive planning techniques of an earlier day.

And yet, as this chapter will demonstrate, despite the mammoth increase in government activity, the state eschewed the approach of seizing direct control over the university system. No master plan was framed within which specific decisions were made. The universities demanded the right, and were encouraged by the government, to make their own plans, individually and then collectively.

The government's role remained largely responsive, and its responses were *ad hoc* in nature. As specific problems arose, it responded in a piecemeal fashion. The private sector – in this case the 'autonomous' universities and their supporting agencies – was assigned primary responsibility for ensuring its own development. Heavy public spending did not lead to extensive public control.

Before the Second World War, higher education had enjoyed a secure (though not exalted) place in the social life of Ontario. With the notable exception of Mitchell Hepburn (premier from 1934 to 1943), politicians periodically paid tribute to the worthy contributions of Ontario universities.[3] The University of Toronto, officially known as the 'provincial university,' was especially well placed, both physically and hierarchically, to earn the respectful scrutiny of provincial politicians. Queen's and Western, on the other hand, while perceived as important parts of the higher educational community, often languished in the shadow of their senior sister. Regularly they bemoaned their financial deprivation, since their solvency was tied to the goodwill of the premier and to whatever surplus funds they could secure from the public treasury in any given year.[4] But if they were generally underfinanced, only infrequently were the province's three provincially assisted universities forced to involve themselves directly in the trials and tribulations of daily political life. Before the war, they served a small, though probably respected, élite. If they appeared far removed in their ivory towers, they were at least free to pursue traditional intellectual goals and were largely untouched by interfering politicians.

Indeed, as E.E. Stewart has noted, if, by 1950, the universities had secured institutional autonomy, it was more for the reason of benign government neglect than active government respect for the principle of academic freedom. While mostly ignoring the activities of the universities, on at least two occasions provincial premiers publicly rebuked University of Toronto professors who were considered either subversive or disloyal.[5] Such incidents, however, were the exception, not the rule.

That there were very few debates on higher education between 1917 and 1950 in the provincial legislature, that not one recorded vote on a university matter took place in that period, and that universities (apart from the war period) received precious little attention from politicians, newspaper editors, or the public at large, could be explained in part by the simple, informal, and unsensational manner through which university-government relations were carried on. In the eyes of succeeding provincial governments, the great questions of university governance and administration had been resolved once and for all in 1906 when provincial legislation brought the University of Toronto into the modern world. Against the background of a public investigation, coupled with wide demands for greater efficiency and academic autonomy, a two-tiered governing structure (later emulated by every other non-denominational university in Ontario) was created at Toronto. The Board of Governors, consisting of prominent community leaders, oversaw the financial side of university affairs, while senior professors, through the Senate, controlled the academic sector.[6] The provincial government, then, eschewed any responsibility for directly governing Ontario's universities.

The manner in which public funds were sought and obtained was simple and direct. Each year, the premier would receive from the universities statements of their projected needs and / or deficits. Sometimes the institution would send a delegate – either the president or the chairman of its board of governors (or both) – to meet with the premier (or his designate) and present its case. Often, contact was only through the mail. If the province had a healthy surplus of funds after other provincial needs were serviced, then university costs might be covered. If not, their deficits would be carried forward. The fact that the premier was frequently the minister of education as well, allowed such discussion to be conducted through quiet consultations with a minimum of bureaucratic delay.[7]

The degree to which this process could be affected by the personality and posture of the premier was revealed by the contrast between the approaches of the Hepburn and the Drew administrations towards higher education in Ontario. Hepburn's cavalier attitude towards the universities was demonstrated not only by his public condemnation of Professors George Grube and Frank Underhill for their alleged anti-war statements in 1939, but by his refusal to accept an honorary doctorate from the University of Toronto.[8] Furthermore, during the Depression, he regularly underfunded the universities. While this neglect could be explained in part by the difficult economic environment of the time, in 1939, even as conditions improved, Hepburn actually reduced grants to the three non-denominational institutions.[9]

The approach of George Drew (premier from 1943 to 1948) reflected through the statements and actions of his treasurer, Leslie Frost, was far more positive. Under the Drew administration, not only were grants to universities restored to, and then increased over, previous levels, but the important role played by the universities in the prosecution of the war effort was acknowledged and duly praised by his government:

The Government has recognized the importance of our universities in our national structure. Research is of tremendous importance during war time. After the war ... we shall be faced with greater competition in the world markets and in our domestic market. Our skills and knowledge, therefore, must take the place of tariff barriers which will be lowered or removed. The Government has determined that to the extent of its power it will make available to our workers and our industries the advantage of scientific research. In this great Province, it was felt particularly that science should be called to the assistance of our primary producers on the farms, in the forests, and in the mines. It was accordingly felt that our universities should be freed from the burden of debt that is hampering their efforts and that, additionally, grants should be made to them which permit them now in time of war to organize for peace. Accordingly, grants of $816,000 to Toronto University and $250,000 each to Queen's and Western were made – a total in all of $1,316,000.[10]

From 1944 to 1948, the provincial government met a variety of other financial needs in the post-secondary educational community, including special grants to Ontario medical schools, and support for an Institute of Child Study at the University of Toronto. McMaster University, which partially freed itself from Baptist control in 1947, obtained provincial grants for the first time in that year, and Carleton College, an institute of adult learning with wider ambitions, secured public funding as well. In 1952, Carleton achieved official university status. Symptomatic of the government's growing preoccupation with the relationship between educational development and economic growth, grants were also given by the Drew administration to institutes of trade and vocational training in Haileybury, Port Arthur, Hamilton, Kirkland Lake, Ottawa, Windsor, and Sault Ste Marie. The Ryerson Institute of Technology was established with provincial support in Toronto in 1948.[11]

Despite these important post-war developments, the relationship between the universities and government remained unsophisticated and highly informal. Until 1964, higher education continued to fall under the jurisdiction of the Department of Education which, itself, was often included in the responsibilities of the premier or, as in the case of Dana Porter (minister of education, 1948–51), was only part of the minister's wider cabinet duties (Porter being also attorney general during this period). Despite their higher public profile and increased responsibilities during the war, the universities continued to submit their requests for funds in the traditional manner. Apart from merely asking them their opinions, the government had no systematic way of determining the real needs of the universities.

How inconsistently this was done was revealed by the fact that in 1945 the University of Toronto submitted a very detailed statement of its activities and projected financial needs.[12] But in 1949 the statements of Western and Queen's were very sketchy indeed, lacking the depth and comprehensiveness of the former.[13] In fact, the president of the University of Western Ontario, G.E. Hall, was criticized by the minister for presenting budget projections that were both overly ambitious and insufficiently documented. Furthermore, the minister claimed that the request was submitted after the provincial budget was drawn up, and that it contained statements different from those made in a personal discussion between himself and Hall. 'It is clear from the whole record that the President has been too late and too vague in presenting his recommendations to the treasury.' Hall had publicly criticized the government for inadequately supporting his university and this too aroused the ire of the minister. 'Quite frankly when I saw Dr. Hall's statement in the *Globe and Mail* this morning, I was disturbed and disappointed. I think there was absolutely no justification for [such] statements from a man in his position.'[14]

By the early 1950s, it was becoming increasingly clear that higher education demanded the careful attention of officials within the Department of Education. The entrance of the federal government into the financing area through its direct support for universities (following the recommendations of the Massey Report in 1951), the growing number of chartered and publicly funded institutions in Ontario, and the wider ambitions of the sector as a whole, required closer scrutiny by the government. From the universities' perspective, the relationship was also unsatisfactory. In 1949, President Hall had been unrestrained in his criticisms in the *Globe and Mail*. Complaining about both insufficient funding and the *ad hoc* process through which universities sought government support, Hall concluded: 'The presidents, deans and other officials in our universities have had to foresake education to become executive supersalesmen, leaders of delegations and beggars, so that universities may even remain in existence. In doing so they are neglecting the responsible leadership which is their duty.' He called for a system similar to that which existed in Britain, where university needs were evaluated regularly by a politically independent university grants commission. He felt as well that university needs should be re-examined on the basis of five-year projections.[15]

His concerns had been expressed earlier by others in the university community, including W.E. Phillips, the chairman of the Board of Governors at the University of Toronto. Phillips, whose advice was frequently offered to and solicited by the minister or the premier throughout his tenure at Toronto, argued that the informal method for evaluating university needs was in dire need of improvement. In a letter to the premier, Phillips claimed that the process was haphazard, piecemeal, and arbitrary. Instead of merely totalling its deficit on an annual basis and seeking support on that basis from the government, each university, he felt, required a long-range view of its plans and potential resources.[16] Clearly, however, he hoped the government would initiate such a process, since long-term budgeting was a 'practical possibility only when fundamental decisions relating to the role of the university are clearly established.' He proposed a primitive formula-financing system (which emerged in a more sophisticated form in the late 1960s) based on a five-year projection in which a 'maximum amount [of provincial funds] could be developed on the basis of a Unit cost per student in attendance and would obviously vary with the actual number of students in attendance in each succeeding year.'

His comments were written against the background of a dramatically increasing enrolment due to the influx of postwar veterans. Probably because enrolment declined in 1949 as veterans graduated, his recommendations did not appear to gain wide popularity in the university community, nor were they taken up by the Department of Education.

None the less, in light of the kinds of problems described above, one important change was made by the government. In 1951, R.C. Wallace, a highly respected professor who had recently retired from his position as principal of Queen's University, was hired as a part-time adviser to the Minister of Education.[17] He was assigned the responsibility of evaluating university funding requests and reporting his findings to the minister; he also had direct access to the premier when circumstances required it. In 1952, Wallace reported to the minister (Dunlop) on a meeting he had had with Premier Frost in which Frost had asked him 'to have a conference with you [Dunlop] to see what can be done to obviate any unnecessary duplication in university work in the Universities in Ontario. He [Frost] is concerned that there not be an expansion which would necessitate new support from the Government if that expansion does not seem to be necessary and if the work is already taken care of in a sister institution'.[18] Renowned (or notorious) for his frugal spending habits,[19] Frost was becoming increasingly worried about the growing aspirations of the province's universities and about the potential drain this would create on provincial resources. It was intended that Wallace would oversee and limit these ambitions in his recommendations to the minister.

In mid 1952, Wallace met with all the universities individually, heard their requests, and submitted a report to the minister. Its purpose was to evaluate the status and project the requirements of individual departments and professions in the province. After noting that 'there has been only limited contact and exchange of ideas between university authorities in Ontario,' he continued:

Legal training, library training, aeronautic engineering, physiotherapy, are not given and probably will not be offered in the future outside of Toronto. Applied Science except in the first year (or, in the case of Carleton College, the first two years) will be confined to Toronto and Queen's. Medicine is adequately looked after at Toronto, Western, Queen's, and Ottawa. It seems improbable that McMaster will embark on the whole course of medical training. Dentistry is offered only in Toronto. It will be less expensive to expand facilities there than to establish a new faculty at Western. Journalism is adequately provided for at Western and Carleton College (at least as far as English-speaking needs are concerned). There would not be justification for new ventures in this field. Geography has become so integral a part of the Social Sciences that all the Universities either offer it now or will do so in the future. It is the responsibility of all universities to offer a well rounded course in the humanities, the pure sciences, and the social sciences, and there can be little consolidation, except that visits from experts in specialized fields, from university to university, are helpful and stimulating.

For the population of Ontario there are adequate university facilities at the present time. There may not be adequate funds to meet their needs in the future.[20]

These statements are significant for two reasons. First, they reveal that, in 1952, despite the recent creation and public funding of two new universities (McMaster and Carleton), the province's perceptions about the need for future university facilities were cautious and conservative. Neither Wallace nor the government foresaw the unprecedented increase in the university-aged population, or the explosive demand for capital resources that would confront the province in the years ahead.

Second, Wallace's evaluation confirms the fact that the universities were responsible for initiating expansion plans in specific courses and faculties, an approach consistent with their long-standing autonomy. The government's response to such plans was (and would be) determined by its perceptions of the public need for such facilities. If provincial support for a new school of engineering, for example, would, in the opinion of the government, lead to redundancy, then the proposal would not be favourably received. The converse was also true. Yet there is no evidence that Wallace or the government had anything more than a very general idea of how these needs could be determined. His report offered no evaluation of changing demographic trends, nor had he consulted specific professionals in order to widen his perspective. Furthermore, the information in his report was presented in such a way as to be consistent with the political goal of frugal public spending.

A year later, Wallace prepared another report which traced the history of public spending on higher education in Ontario since 1921.[21] He noted that, from 1921 to 1951, Ontario had increased grants to colleges and universities only 3.2 times. Furthermore, in 1921, while public funding covered 70 per cent of each institution's costs, in 1951, only 50 per cent of university expenses were financed by the government. Frugality had, indeed, typified government spending patterns.

Wallace explained as well that, although a 1921 report on university financing had recommended that no new buildings be erected by the universities without first consulting the government, 'this procedure has not been followed to the letter.' Over the years, the universities had certainly informed the government of their expansion plans, but because the practice of university autonomy was so deeply entrenched in the province, 'when a decision has been reached as to the final assistance that can be given, the use of the funds voted is left entirely to the discretion of the university authorities.' In this way, the province's planning capacity was further circumscribed by the independent authority of the universities. At best, the government could exert pressure on the universities to restrict their expansion or avoid duplication in an indirect (though certainly influential) way. Although potentially inefficient, this process was believed to be essential by Wallace in order to guarantee the independence of the universities.

The Wallace period (1952–55) was thus one of consolidation. Given the fact that university enrolment had actually fallen in the early 1950s with the departure of the veterans, there was no perceived need in government for any great extension of university facilities. According to Dunlop, Wallace had done precisely what was expected of him. He had brought such order and co-ordination to the whole area of university-government relations that the process of interaction was as smooth as it had ever been. In a note to Wallace in 1954, Dunlop wrote:

As the university presidents and principals have set out their requests for maintenance and capital costs (in detail and with reason), and as you have made your recommendations, I should like to suggest it is not necessary that you should see the Heads of the Universities this year as you have done in other years. You have done this so thoroughly and so efficiently that each University knows what is expected and how the system operates.[22]

Dunlop's high opinion, however, was apparently not shared by the premier himself. For while Frost had great respect for the integrity and intelligence of Wallace (which is why he had been appointed), he recalled in later years that Wallace had not been tough enough with universities, a view that only confirmed the high degree of conservative thinking in the Conservative government.[23] None the less, Frost must have felt it politically unwise to veto any of Wallace's financial recommendations.

When Wallace died in 1955, his responsibilities were assumed by J.G. Althouse, the chief director of education in the province. While Wallace's process of consultation with the universities remained unchanged under Althouse, the department's view about the future of higher education did not. This, in turn, would dramatically affect the planning process in a few brief years.

In October 1955, Althouse submitted a report to the minister of education which brought sharply into focus a number of important, changing features in Ontario's higher education.[24] Echoing the Sheffield projections, he estimated that, by 1965, the university population of 21,000 students would probably double. Whereas the universities had been criticized in the past for being too ambitious, they were now taken to task for being unprepared to cope with these significant changes.

The universities have declared that they do not intend to double their enrolment but rather to raise standards of admission very sharply. The figure of 10 per cent increase has been used in such statements. This means that the existing universities are planning to accommodate only about 23,000 in 1965 instead of the 42,000 who will desire to be accommodated.

Recognizing the shifting public attitudes already identified in chapter one, Althouse posed this question: 'Can the universities and Provincial Government defy public opinion and deny to 10,000 or 20,000 young persons who could pass today's tests, the right to attempt higher education?'

Althouse was equally pessimistic about a solution to this dilemma proposed by the universities. 'The device suggested by the Universities themselves is that of junior colleges. To be effective in providing an outlet for even 10,000 young people by 1965, such a plan would have to include 20 such institutions with an enrolment of 500 each.' He concluded that it 'will be difficult to find staff for twenty such institutions for they will have to compete both with the universities and with the secondary schools for instructors, and there will be an overall shortage of such instructors.'

Furthermore, he felt that junior colleges would be incapable of providing the 'training for leadership required in the industries, in business and in the professions.' he concluded:

A junior college cannot attempt specialized or professional training; the best it can offer is a sort of second rate general education. The professional schools must remain in the Universities; if these do not increase their accommodations substantially, Canadian industry, business and professions will be short of leaders, despite a heavy expenditure on junior colleges.

In such forthright and insistent language, Althouse proposed the following solutions. He suggested that educational resources in northern Ontario be strengthened significantly. At the Lakehead, where a technical institute already existed, he recommended that it be turned into a junior college and ultimately offer full university courses as resources permitted. In Sudbury, a school of engineering should be created in affiliation with Queen's or Toronto. He called for the establishment of four more polytechnical institutes like Ryerson. More scholarship, bursary, and student aid funds should also be offered. And, finally, the government should:

Indicate to the Universities that they will be expected to accommodate from 50 to 75 per cent more students by 1965 than they do today ... The present situation with respect to medical practitioners, dentists, business administrators, engineers, pharmacists and secondary school teachers and many others must be improved, not aggravated.

It is significant that Althouse did not advocate the creation of any new universities. He preferred, instead, to see the existing universities expand their own facilities, a view that was basically consistent with that of Premier Frost.[25] Implicitly, he was recommending that the government take greater initiatives than it had in the past to ensure that the universities meet these various objectives.

The degree to which Althouse's views were accepted by the government was revealed by the publication in 1956 of the province's submission to the Royal Commission on Canada's Economic Prospects. This document contained the most extensive statement of government policy on higher education that had existed in years. Citing the startling enrolment projections, the report re-emphasized how ill prepared Ontario might be to face the future. Developing the utilitarian theme, the report argued that 'the advance of higher education is essential to Canada's development as a modern industrial power. Without large numbers of university graduates, neither industry nor the government, nor the educational system, nor the medical services can be expanded as the growing stature of the nation requires.'[26] The report also cast a heavy shadow over the proposed solution of junior colleges for the reasons outlined by Althouse.

The document's main effect was to raise awareness among academics and politicians about the educational needs of the future. In one case, the president of the University of Toronto, Sidney Smith, upon reading the report, paid a personal visit to George Gathercole, head of the province's Department of Economics and one of the report's chief authors. Smith told Gathercole that he had been heavily influenced by the statistics and arguments of the brief. He admitted that, while in the past he had held to the view that raising admission standards was necessary in order to preserve the quality of education, he now understood that the universities themselves, and in particular the University of Toronto, had the responsibility to open their doors more widely in the future.[27]

Yet there was no detailed solution on the horizon. As the brief to the Royal Commission had noted (p. 135), 'a discussion of future capital outlays can only be put into proper perspective by reference to the methods that may be adopted to meet the anticipated heavy increase in university and college enrolment. As yet university authorities have given no indication as to how they are likely to proceed.' Nor, for that matter, it should be noted, had the government.

Despite the growing consciousness about the need for universities to widen their responsibilities, increase their enrolments, and serve specific economic functions, the system suffered from a curious kind of paralysis. On the one hand, despite the admonitions of Althouse, the government neither had the administrative tools nor the political will to provide new facilities or to compel the universities to expand quickly. The added pressure of a premier committed to frugal public spending also prevented the system from growing rapidly. On the other hand, while the universities themselves understood that the future was to be far different from the past in terms of the numbers of students to be served, there was a continuing feeling among certain 'traditionalists' that to expand quickly would be to sacrifice their commitment to quality education.[28] Yet to the extent that the universities *were* interested in expanding their facilities, they felt that the government was still too unwilling to increase adequately financial support.

Change, however, was certainly in the air. In the midst of these neutralizing and sometimes contradictory pressures, the government recognized, at least at an elementary level, the need for rational economic planning. In other areas of the economy, the province had already taken one significant step. In 1951, it had created the Office of the Provincial Economist under the direction of veteran civil servant, George Gathercole. Around him he soon gathered an impressive coterie of economic 'experts' known popularly as the 'brains' trust.'[29] Their responsibilities involved not merely studying changing economic trends, demographic patterns, rural-urban migration, and so on but also determining the ways in which such changes would affect wider areas of social policy. Conscious of the growing demands on government by the private sector, welfare agencies, and educators, this group submitted numerous studies to the premier in the mid 1950s. In 1956, these activities were formalized. Gathercole was appointed the deputy minister of the new Department of Economics.

The department compiled such studies as the province's brief to the Royal Commission on Canada's Economic Prospects and worked closely with Althouse in the Department of Education in drawing up enrolment projections.

This latter task was facilitated by the open-mindedness of Althouse who, in the view of Gathercole, did not object to the frequent presence of economists within the educational sector.[30]

In early 1956, the province's universities were all asked to submit statements on their expansion plans for the next five years. These projections were then evaluated by Althouse who used them as a basis for recommending grants in the immediate year and for forecasting funding trends in the years ahead. Almost all of the capital and operating grant requests were scaled down by Althouse, but usually on the basis that he did not foresee how a particular university could complete its projected building program over a single year. For example, with reference to the University of Toronto, he wrote:

the amount required for capital expenditures in 1958 / 59 set at $11,500,000 by Mr. Stone [the vice-president of the university] is far in excess of the amount of construction likely to be completed for that year. Consequently, I have set down only $7,500,000 for that year ... For operating costs I have not put in the full amount for two reasons: 1) additional funds ought to be forthcoming from other sources and 2) with a reduced building programme in 1958 / 59, the operating costs for the five year period should not be as high as indicated in the President's letter.'[31]

There was no attempt, however, to force the universities to redirect their funds from one project or faculty to another. They were still responsible for determining their own academic and professional priorities.

After the death of Althouse in 1956, the Department of Education set the planning process on a road still travelled by the Ministry of Colleges and Universities. The educational needs of the province were growing so quickly and in such a complex fashion that the work of one became the work of several. In late 1956, the minister announced that the premier had appointed a committee consisting of the provincial treasurer, the minister of education, and senior officials from these latter two departments to evaluate the needs and recommend funding policy for the province's universities.[32] To facilitate its evaluation process, the committee sought information from the universities that was more detailed, systematic, and long-term than in the past.

The role of the Department of Economics was becoming increasingly important in the data-gathering process. In 1958, it conducted the most extensive survey of university-related developments in the modern history of the province.[33] The report noted that, although current university expansion plans would ensure that anticipated enrolment pressures could be accommodated to 1960, they would not do so by 1965. It documented, as well, how poorly served was the population of northern Ontario. While containing 11 per cent of the provincial population, the region accounted for only 5 per cent of university students, and the gap was widening.

The report then outlined in brief terms the expansion plans of every university. Herein lay a partial insight into the characteristics of each university that would emerge in the next decade. While most schools were planning to extend such facilities as student residences, physical plants, and administrative buildings, their other projections reveal that they were independently creating their own priorities, and that they were attempting to create for themselves independent identities. Virtually every institution was planning to move heavily into the important and extensive fields of science and engineering. McMaster, notably, sought funds for a nuclear reactor. Ottawa, always strong in the civil professions, anticipated extending facilities in its law and social science faculties. Queen's sought support for a political science and economics building, reflecting its strong applied liberal arts tradition. Carleton, a new university, was planning a faculty of architecture. Both Western and Toronto intended to extend their offerings in professional fields of education. All of these plans, however, were purely tentative, and were subject to closer scrutiny by the provincial government in the years ahead.

Against the background of such impressive plans, the committee advisory system was formalized further in 1958 when a new group – the Advisory Committee on University Affairs (CUA) – was appointed by the premier to carry on the responsibility of evaluating university demands and providing funding recommendations to the minister of education.[34] The nature of the committee membership was significant. C.F. Canon, the chief director of education (Althouse's successor), was its chairman. But his colleagues were all men with backgrounds in economics and finance. George Gathercole, the deputy minister of economics, H.H. Walker, the chief accountant in the Department of Education, and H.H. Cotnam, from the Treasury Department, were appointed as well. Political pressure in later years would widen the representation of the committee considerably, but in this initial phase, since its chief concern was the scope of provincial support for university facilities and since the dominant issue was the role of higher education in the burgeoning economy, it only seemed sensible to the premier that the committee should consist predominantly of civil servants with a competent grasp of economic and accounting problems. Yet the committee was to operate only on a part-time basis. All of its members continued to hold heavy responsibilities in other areas of government.[35]

There was one further appointment to the committee which was significant in another way. Samuel Beatty, the chancellor of the University of Toronto and a highly respected mathematician, was hired as a part-time adviser to the committee.[36] The appointment sparked considerable controversy. Eric Phillips, the chairman of the Board of Governors at Toronto, wrote an angry letter to Premier Frost claiming that the Beatty appointment was 'extraordinary' and 'improper.' Further, he was incensed that he was not consulted about this step. Finally, he described as 'fantastic' that 'Dr. Beatty may wish to visit our university' to discuss financial affairs. In Phillips' mind, the conflict of interest problem was insurmountable.[37] According to observers at the time, Phillips very much resented the possible erosion of his own private relationship with Premier Frost through which he frequently discussed university problems, particularly as they related to the University of Toronto.[38] Indeed, in the above letter, he expressed the hope that the new committee (which he claimed to have had a part in creating through discussions with Frost) would not change the traditional approach of having the chairmen of university boards directly involved in negotiations with the government. 'I can see no good reason to depart from this pattern,' he asserted.

Yet Frost's appointment of Beatty was, itself, based on his desire to reward the accomplishments of a personal friend and respected scholar. Beatty did not play a large role on the committee nor, according to one former member, was he really expected to.[39] His appointment had been in the form of a sinecure during a time when the politics of higher education in Ontario were still informal enough to allow the new Committee on University Affairs to be used in this fashion. A more structured and official advisory committee was slowly evolving, but it was not yet entrenched.

The establishment of the new body marked a major step forward in the co-ordination of activities in the area of higher education. But while the committee made some important strides in terms of information-gathering and analysis, its scope of activity was severely limited. This can be demonstrated through an analysis of the committee's minutes, through interviews with former members, and through an examination of internal department documents.

Between October 1958, and December 1960, when it was restructured once again, the committee met twenty times. The meetings were generally held on a monthly basis, although there were frequently large gaps between sessions. For example, from 2 June until 3 September 1959, and from 4 August until 5 December 1960, there were no meetings.[40] The committee's time was spent largely preparing for the annual provincial budget debates which usually began in February or March. Between the autumn and new year, then, the committee would receive briefs from the universities, evaluate funding requests, and submit its recommendations. Each meeting lasted approximately two to three hours.

Unlike its later practice, however, the committee never visited any of the province's universities. According to J.R. McCarthy, the committee's secretary and the province's superintendent of curriculum, the committee members were so busy with other responsibilities, that some were unable to attend monthly meetings, let alone 'become familiar with the operation and requirements of the province's universities.'[41] While university representatives sometimes met the committee at Queen's Park, frequently communication was carried on exclusively through the mail. But some universities were so uncertain about the committee's function and status that they sent their briefs directly to the minister or to the premier. According to McCarthy, this resulted in 'overlapping and confusion' among the three offices.[42]

In retrospect, more than one committee member confirmed McCarthy's view that the meetings and discussions were not exhaustive. 'The information provided varied from one institution to another and was so incomplete that it was difficult to make any estimate of need.' One participant did not recall receiving any of the material before the meeting at which it was to be discussed. So the time for reading, absorbing, and deliberating was certainly brief. On one occasion, the financial decisions concerning all of the province's universities for the coming year were taken in one two-hour meeting.[43]

One example of this patchwork process in action reveals how deficient the system could be. Father E.C. Lebel, from Essex College in Windsor, appeared before the committee to support his funding requests and claimed that the minister of education had approved his institution's development plans. When told that the Department of Education did not approve individual expansion programs, Father Lebel corrected himself and said that the minister had 'not opposed' his university's plans.[44] The lines of authority were obviously unclear.

In another case, Queen's University noted in a long brief how unfairly it had been treated in financial terms relative to other institutions. Principal Mackintosh contended that, since there was no specific formula followed in the allocation of funds, his institution had received far less funding per student than all of the established universities and less than some of the new universities as well. He pointed out that Ottawa, a denominational institution, which received partial aid from the province, appeared to be getting more for its 'secular' courses than Queen's. All of this was particularly distressing in light of the fact that Queen's enrolment was increasing faster than all but two universities in the province.[45]

The role of the committee, then, was seriously limited. It saw itself not as an instigator of policy but as a respondent, on behalf of the province, to initiatives taken by the universities themselves. With no 'objective' formula for the distribution of grants, it functioned on a piecemeal basis. Yet despite its obvious weaknesses, it was still the best forum at the government's disposal for evaluating university needs, and its financial recommendations were followed closely during its tenure.

Against the background of the type of criticism levelled at the committee on university affairs by one of its own staff and echoed by others within the university community, the CUA was restructured in December 1960. Two key changes were made. The committee's membership was widened to include for the first time individuals from outside government. Joining Dana Porter, George Gathercole, and John R. McCarthy were Floyd Chalmers, a well-known publisher and philanthropist, Robert W. Mitchell, the president of Supertest Petroleum Company, and T. D'Arcy Leonard, a senator. When he retired as premier, Leslie Frost also joined the committee, replacing John Robarts who became premier in 1961.[46]

The committee also had wider terms of reference so that, technically, all matters related to higher education, budgetary or otherwise, would require committee comment or involvement. The earlier committee had focused mainly on financial matters. Now the CUA was to 'coordinate the development of higher educational facilities' and 'to provide a clearing house for university problems.'[47] The implication was that provincial policy on higher education would flow from the deliberations of the CUA. It was to be an adviser, a scrutineer, and a planner.

This was a tall order for a committee which had no full-time members, which lacked its own research staff, and whose data base had not increased proportionately with its responsibilities. The committee lacked reliable enrolment projections for the next decade; it was not aware of how many students were currently registered or expected to register in specific faculties; and it was compelled to make major decisions in areas such as the authorization and chartering of new universities where no elaborate government policy yet existed. Saddled with the extraordinary task of mapping the future of higher education in Ontario, it was forced to function within a kind of policy vacuum where no master plan had been conceived or outlined by the Department of Education.

Furthermore, it faced the suspicions of individuals and groups within the academic community who believed that the organizational changes made in 1961 had not gone far enough. Not only had J.R. McCarthy recommended the creation of a further education branch within the Department of Education to handle higher educational matters, as well as a strengthened CUA with its own staff, but many academics had advocated a system for the distribution of grants similar to that in England. There, an impartial university grants commission, with wide authority in the university community, allocated funds largely free of government involvement or interference. The Department of Education believed, however, that because fewer students attended university in Britain than Ontario and because the British government paid more of the universities' costs than the Ontario government, the former's administrative solutions were not applicable to the province's unique problems.[48]

Generally, the universities supported the revised CUA with its wider representation, but they continued to carry on a persistent campaign for academic
participation on the committee, fearing that aging politicians, civil servants, and
businessmen were not the best exponents of university interests.[49] Not until 1964
did their efforts finally bear fruit.

In the meantime, the committee confronted its task in an environment where
university services were required at an unprecedented rate. In the absence of a
master plan, and mindful of the jealous manner through which the universities
guarded their traditional autonomy, the CUA, under the urging of Leslie Frost,
embarked on a portentous path. In March 1962, the committee called a meeting
of all the presidents of the universities of Ontario to impress upon them the scope
of the problems ahead. Two important events resulted from this meeting. The
presidents agreed to form an official association called the Committee of Presidents of the Provincially Assisted Universities of Ontario (CPUO). Second, they
agreed to undertake an immediate study of the future of higher education in the
province.

What Frost and the committee had succeeded in doing was to turn the
responsibility of planning back to the universities themselves. If the CUA and the
CPUO could co-operate on major projects, the government would avoid the
charge of interfering unjustly in university affairs. The implications of this new
arrangement will be discussed more fully later, but in the short run at least it
appeared that an acceptable compromise had been struck.

To assist the presidents' committee, the CUA authorized the most comprehensive study of enrolment trends every done in the province. Robert W. Jackson, of
the Ontario College of Education, was asked to draw up a series of projections
which were then passed by the CUA to the CPUO. The latter chose, as the most
realistic estimate, a projection which called for an enrolment of 74,000 undergraduates by 1970, a recommendation that was included in the report of the
presidents' special committee.[50]

Thus, for the first time, through the perspective of the Deutsch report (as the
presidents' study was called), a province-wide perspective was gained on the
future of higher education in Ontario. Each university was expected to adjust its
expansion plans in order to fulfil its share of the enrolment projections to 1970.[51]
Here, then, were the rudiments of a provincial plan, but it was planning of a
particularly limited sort. The chief variable in determining the size of the system
was the number of students who could be expected to enrol. In this way, the
universities perceived themselves to be responding to the market demand for
places in the post-secondary system. Apart from a brief discussion of medical
training facilities, no comprehensive effort had been made either by the CUA or
the presidents' committee to determine the needs of specific professions or

industries, nor was there yet any study on the future of qualified manpower in Ontario. Despite the faith of government and business in the economic value of investment in higher education, there was no developed or reliable method for relating the specific economic needs of the province to the type of facilities (existing or planned) in the burgeoning university system. In this unpredictable environment, the universities, acting autonomously and freely, were still expected to create their own priorities, though now under the watchful eyes of the committee of presidents (their own collective instrument) and the CUA. There was, then, more government involvement and better methods of evaluation than in the past, but this reliance on the model of *social demand* could hardly be viewed as sophisticated planning within the higher educational sector.[52]

The Deutsch report made a series of other important suggestions which formed the basis of CUA recommendations and government actions in 1964 and 1965. Since one of the universities' major problems was a shortage of teaching personnel, a new scholarship program was created to encourage students to pursue teaching careers. Special grants were given to those universities involved in graduate work to expand their programs. On the recommendation of the presidents, the CUA arranged for a substantial extension of library resources directed especially to the new and 'emerging' universities. A most telling indication of how influential the universities were in programming their own future in the province was the fact that the Deutsch report's recommendation to create two new liberal arts colleges in Metropolitan Toronto and two more in the Niagara region and Peterborough, was ultimately followed by the government on the endorsement of the CUA. The University of Toronto expanded its campus to Scarborough and Mississauga, and Brock and Trent universities were chartered in St Catharines and Peterborough respectively.[53] Finally, the presidents' recommendation to build a system of community colleges for the purpose of training students in the skilled and semi-skilled trades and vocations was adopted by the government (with some revisions).[54]

But because the Deutsch report had been undertaken and completed so quickly, even in the minds of the presidents, it was no more than a skeleton for future planning in the province. By the end of 1963, new and troubling questions were being raised about the decision-making processes and particularly about the CUA's relationship with the government on the one hand and the universities on the other. Because the CUA's funding recommendations were being followed to the letter by the government, the universities began to see the committee as the 'executive arm' of the government itself, rather than as a spokesman for university interests or even as an objective scrutineer of university needs in the province. Thus, when the CUA made unpopular decisions – such as the scaling down of university requests for capital or operating grants – it inspired their individual and collective wrath through the committee of presidents.[55] These encounters angered members of the CUA, but they none the less raised questions, even among the members themselves, about the committee's proper function.

In November 1963, a lengthy discussion of this problem took place in the presence of the minister and the premier during a CUA meeting. In a rather exasperated tone, Leslie Frost denied that the CUA was the 'executive arm' of the government.[56] In spite of this, he defended such actions as the presence of the provincial treasurer at certain CUA meetings, a presence that the presidents felt violated the independence of the committee, since they feared that the treasurer would exert undue influence over the CUA. Frost claimed that the presidents would always be dissatisfied with any unfavourable decisions. What they demanded from the CUA, he claimed, was 'absolute perfection.' They failed to admit that their sometimes extravagant demands needed to be curbed.

If the universities' complaints were predictable and sometimes irritating to the CUA, it was still evident that the combined demands for increased public funding and institutional autonomy would grow more insistent in the years ahead. According to E.E. Stewart, a former deputy minister of university affairs and secretary of the CUA, this posed a difficult dilemma. Canadian universities, he claimed, were:

literally filled with this notion of university autonomy and the right to make their own decisions. So it wasn't possible nor do I think that anyone around the government that I recall ever contemplated a sort of moving in and taking over and drawing up the plans and making all of the key decisions, but you can see we had a vacuum in the Ontario educational system. We had an elementary and high school system that were publicly run in the combination between the local school boards and the Department of Education, and we had this small group of universities that were supposedly independent.[57]

As we shall see, this conflict was never completely resolved, but in the short term a number of steps were taken.

In 1964, the government created a new Department of University Affairs and expanded considerably the supporting bureaucratic agencies. Several new branches of the ministry were struck, including an architectural services Board, a financial requests office, a research office, a student awards office, an accounts branch, and a strengthened office of the deputy minister.[58] Furthermore, the government widened the representation of the Committee on University Affairs to include academic representatives nominated by the committee of presidents and the Ontario Confederation of University Faculty Associations (OCUFA).[59] While the system still departed significantly from the British approach favoured by most academic spokesmen, the presidents, at least, were appeased by the move. Premier Robarts, they claimed, 'spoke of the advisory committee's function in terms that practically approximated the kinds of grants commission that the universities had been asking for.'[60]

If the universities were preoccupied with the question of the decision-making process, the government was beginning to see the problem of higher education more in terms of dollars and cents. In a speech on university-government relations in 1966, the minister of both the Department of Education and of the new Department of University Affairs, William Davis, raised this question in a carefully worded but resolute fashion. The government, he asserted, had no desire or intention to engage in activities that might threaten university autonomy or academic freedom or to deny the necessary funds for university expansion. But he added, 'I think there is justification in asking whether the universities have shown sufficient imagination and innovation in meeting the challenge of offering quality education to ever increasing number of students within the bounds of reasonable costs.'[61] He wondered whether in their haste to expand, the universities had given sufficient attention to some of the 'new techniques and devices as a means of obtaining improved educational results.'

The key notion in Davis's speech was 'accountability.' While convinced of the need to extend post-secondary educational facilities, society, he concluded, was beginning to ask some serious questions about the allocation of its enormous expenditures. If it detected wasteful, redundant, or unwise spending, then it would demand that the government undertake the kind of co-ordination needed. He challenged the universities to face the task ahead, justify themselves, and ensure that the freedoms they had earned in the past would be vigilantly preserved in the future.

A more precise and controversial stimulus to university co-ordination ended the year of 1966. In one of their many joint ventures, the CPUO and the CUA cosponsored a commission under J.W.T. Spinks to study the future of graduate education in Ontario. Spinks, the president of the University of Saskatchewan, was joined on the commission by G.O. Arlt, president of the Council of Graduate Schools in the United States, and by F.K. Hare, master of Birkbeck College, University of London.[62]

The work of the Spinks commission was steeped in enormous controversy even before the report was officially released. According to a leaked version of the study, it appeared to take the most extreme approach possible in encouraging co-ordination in graduate studies among Ontario universities. It called for a province-wide University of Ontario, a superstructure modelled on the University of California which would be presided over by a board of regents with both government and lay membership, and an academic senate on which each of Ontario's universities would be represented.

Such a proposal appeared to strike at the very heart of a system founded on the principle of institutional uniqueness. Furthermore, the fact that Clark Kerr had been fired recently as president of the University of California by the governor of that state was seen as feeble testimony to the guarantee of independence that this type of system could offer the universities.[63]

The response to the recommendation was immediate and unflattering. One by one, presidents polled by the media condemned the concept as 'unfeasible,' 'unnecessary,' or 'unworkable,' and threatening to the identity of the smaller universities.[64] An editorial in the *Orillia Packet and Times* reflected the degree of opposition aroused even in a community with no university:

The sort of super university envisaged by the recent Spinks' report in which all the universities would be reduced to so many campuses of one giant province-wide university is indicative of the Orwellian trend of the times in which individual standards of freedom of choice are being removed in the name of administrative convenience.[65]

Even the minister himself, who had already insisted that the universities rationalize their activities, made it clear that he did not have this type of proposal in mind: 'I feel ... the recommendation overlooked the very heterogeneous family of highly individualistic universities we have developed in Ontario'.[66] Thus, while the universities and the government may not have resolved to each others' satisfaction the degree of independence to which the former were entitled, the Spinks' commission reinforced one fact: Ontario had no intention of establishing the kind of direct political or administrative control over its universities that other jurisdictions had experienced, no matter how practical or economically attractive the prospect.

The remainder of the Spinks' commission's recommendations were much less offensive to the universities than the call for a University of Ontario, but in one key passage the report identified a central weakness of a university system built on the basis of educational 'entrepreneurialism':

The most striking characteristic of higher – not only graduate – education in Ontario is the complete absence of a master plan of an educational policy and of a coordinating authority for the provincially supported institutions. Here are fourteen fully chartered, nominally autonomous universities with the freedom of action of independent private institutions. They are free to declare their own objectives and to develop their own programs without regard or reference to their neighbours or to the needs of the Province. They compete with each other for their share of annual appropriations and the direction and rate of their development is determined not by rational and unified planning but by their individual ingenuity in securing funds.[67]

This indictment had at least a catalytic effect. The commission's proposals for a formula-financing system for the distribution of capital and operating grants, a process of appraising graduate programs to avoid duplication and proliferation, and an inter-library loan system, were already under study at the time of the report's publication, or were instituted as a result of its recommendations.[68]

Perhaps the most important of these, the formula-financing system for the distribution of operating grants, resolved in part the planning difficulties of the entreprenurial university system. The formula was tied to the number of students each university enrolled annually. The basic income unit (BIU) was the monetary value assigned to students for the purpose of funding the universities. In the first year of the formula (1967), a general arts student in a three-year program was assigned a BIU value of $1,320, while a PhD student was worth approximately six times that figure. The monetary value of other students varied according to the program and year in which they were enrolled, and fell somewhere between the BA and PhD student levels. A university's income for operating purposes, then, would be a multiple of the number of students registered in various faculties and the value of the BIU for that year.[69]

The rationale for this type of formula, which was conceived by Douglas Wright of the CUA and refined with the assistance of delegates from the committee of presidents, was explained by Wright in a detailed brief.

Through their long history, universities have generally enjoyed autonomy: independent control over their own internal actions. The preservation of this autonomy is defended on every hand. Yet the increasing dependence of the university on the state (and the state on the university with its expertise) necessarily jeopardizes university autonomy. Universities cannot escape accountability for the public money they spend, but detailed scrutiny leading to line-by-line budgeting control would erode autonomy until universities would become only extensions of the state in a process which is identifiable in some other social institutions.[70]

The task at hand was to devise a system of financing which achieved public accountability and simultaneously preserved institutional autonomy. Wright eschewed the approach which placed in government hands the responsibility of determining faculty / student ratios, faculty salaries, teaching loads, class sizes, etc., as an unacceptable violation of university freedom. He favoured instead a process through which university income would be determined by an average costing of different programs (applied to all universities) and multiplied by the number of students (consumers) in each program. The university's grant, then, would be applied to the institution's 'general purposes and budgeting' free of government direction.

The new system reinforced the private nature of planning post-secondary education even in a period of extensive government involvement in the post-secondary system. According to the CUA itself, it accomplished the goal of ensuring efficiency in the allotment of funds, but it also removed from the CUA the need to seek more and more information from the universities even as their demands increased. Under the old line-by-line evaluation process, it had been necessary to review every planned expenditure of each university before funding decisions were made. Under the formula system, each institution would be interviewed but questioned only generally about its over-all request. On the basis of such interviews, the CUA would arrive at a formula for the coming year. Furthermore, the universities no longer risked having private donations counted against them in the funding process. No account of individual or private contributions would be taken by the committee in setting the formula level. Thus, there would be an added incentive for the universities to seek non-governmental support. In short, 'the formula system gives freedom to the individual institution to order priorities and take necessary decisions.'[71]

This, then, was a refinement and extension of the earlier planning decision to tie university funding to projected enrolment. The market principle embodied in the model of social demand continued to reign supreme. It should be noted, as well, that the operating formula described above and the capital formula which was currently being devised were conceived in the absence of a master plan or even a thorough investigation of the future of higher education in the province. Both the CPUO and OCUFA had been clamouring for such a study, but the report of the Commission on Post-Secondary Education was not authorized by the government until 1969, and was not completed until 1972 – *after* the unprecedented period of expansion had reached its peak.[72] The autonomy and independence of publicly supported, but privately run, universities of Ontario *had* been vigilantly preserved throughout the 1960s. By the early 1970s, in a very different political and economic environment, the most persistent question facing the universities was 'at what price?'

FIVE

The Curriculum, Professionalism, and the Market Economy

From the preceding account, it is evident that the university system which evolved in Ontario during the postwar period was shaped by the values, the culture, and the political forces of a mixed capitalist economy. For all intents and purposes, the universities were publicly funded, privately operated, and primarily designed to fulfil economic functions. Yet one major question remains. How, precisely, did the universities set out to satisfy their *raison d'être*? If the main purpose of higher education was to contribute to economic prosperity, then how did the universities engage in this task?

This chapter focuses on what must be considered the most important aspect of higher education, the development of its academic programs. The general question explored here is the relationship of the curriculum to the economic requirements of society as a whole. The discussion begins with an examination of the link (if any) between undergraduate education and economic development. We are faced at the outset with an apparent anomaly. If, in the minds of politicians, businessmen, and the public, the chief aim of higher education was to contribute to economic growth, then how can one account for the development during the 1960s of undergraduate curricula that were diverse, experimental, and 'impractical' in their conception and orientation? Would the interests of the academic and business communities not be in conflict over the nature of undergraduate education?

The remainder of the chapter examines the development of graduate and professional education where fewer philosophical conflicts between those inside and outside the university might have been anticipated. Professionally trained students, after all, were expected by both teachers and employers to make immediate and direct contributions to Canadian society. The entire thrust of this type of training was unmistakably utilitarian as the universities undertook to train teachers, lawyers, doctors, engineers, and architects. On the performance of these graduates, external impressions about the value of Canadian universities could be formed. Employers could discern how well university professors had prepared their students to handle responsibilities in the working world. Economists could evaluate how productive the new graduates were on the job and how much of this productivity could be attributed to their educational training. And, based on the numbers graduated, governments could measure the universities' ability to respond to the shortages of professionals in the market place. Around the success of professional education, in fact, revolved the ultimate justification for the utilitarian university. This chapter explores the assumptions behind, the methods used for, and the success achieved in fulfilling these economic functions.

For a period of at least forty years before 1960, the undergraduate curriculum requirements of non-denominational Canadian universities were, with some exceptions, uniform and unchanging. Higher education was distinctly and unapologetically élitist, serving no more than 6 per cent of university-aged youth.[1] There were few professors in each discipline, and most were burdened with heavy teaching loads. For students, BA programs were heavily prescribed, and the number of course options and academic specialties strictly limited. The academic atmosphere was intense, paternalistic, and hierarchical – and, for many students, intimidating. But there were apparently few dissenters. One of the most famous degree-holders from the University of Toronto recalls his classroom experience in this way:

The University of Toronto that I knew as a student from 1932 to 1937, and as a teacher during a brief period in the war, derived its quality and flavour from individuals – strong minded, unorthodox, concerned with morals without being moralistic, living and working in an environment that they themselves had created. In the classrooms students expected and welcomed the grand manner and authoritative stance; and if they mimicked or ridiculed their instructors, it was a form of flattery.[2]

For arts students, course content drew heavily from the works of the towering scholars of the western world. English courses were steeped in the writings of Milton, Johnson, Shaw, and Shakespeare. History, philosophy, and political science classes traced the roots and development of European civilization, of which Canada was but a minor part. If the limits of essential knowledge were not specifically defined, there appeared at least to be a consensus about the need to instil in the minds of students a 'consciousness of Western values' and an appreciation of their 'cultural inheritance.'

Throughout the 1950s, a typical three-year undergraduate arts program consisted of four or five prescribed subjects (plus one or two options) in first year, including English, a foreign language, mathematics or science, and history, and a course in the social sciences. Several Ontario universities demanded philosophy and Latin as well, and naturally, in the denominational universities, the study of religion was a vital and compulsory ingredient of the curriculum.

In the upper years, some flexibility was allowed as general or pass course students chose one or two subjects of 'concentration' in third year, and honours students pursued their specific interests in fourth year with heavier research requirements, often including the preparation of an undergraduate thesis. Through 'concentration,' it was intended that students would master the essential elements of a specific subject.

The honours program at the University of Toronto was unusual in that most students chose the four-year course of study upon entering first year, while in other institutions this selection was delayed until second or third year. Toronto's honours program was renowned for being especially rigorous, although students were rewarded with the privileges of working in smaller groups than pass-course students, of being able to take higher quality courses not offered to the latter, and of associating more closely with university professors than did students in three-year programs.[3]

With the exception of the University of Toronto, however, where special emphasis was placed on the great intellectual value of the demanding honours program, the vast majority of Ontario students registered in three-year courses where the academic demands were believed to be rigorous enough. Furthermore, the incentive to pursue honours studies over general studies for vocational reasons was not as prevalent in the late 1950s as it would be a decade later when changing economic conditions began to restrict job prospects for general BA students. According to Sidney Smith, the president of the University of Toronto, despite the deep public concern about the need for science and engineering graduates:

the demand for arts graduates ... is already very great and will increase. Many of the leaders of Canadian industry who conferred recently at St. Andrew's, New Brunswick, mentioned the need for good BA's and their hope that the crucial shortage of engineers and scientists would not cause an imbalance in the universities that would endanger their integrity and effectiveness.[4]

Employment (placement) centres at many universities during this period confirmed the view that there were abundant career opportunities for all undergraduates, whatever their degrees, especially in primary and secondary school teaching.[5] Here, then, was an important insight into the general relationship between the undergraduate curriculum and the economic needs of Canadian society. Universities could offer compulsory, demanding, and traditional courses of study with little direct concern about the vocational requirements of Canadian society, on the confident assumption that all graduates – in the arts and elsewhere – would be absorbed into, and productively occupied by, a growing economy.

Once the future enrolment crisis in higher education was recognized in 1956, the universities took initial steps to increase the quantity while maintaining the quality and form of their traditional curricula. At Queen's, for example, where administrators and faculty were intent on preserving the school's relatively small size (even as admission pressures increased), the principal admitted that some changes were necessary:

A clear view of the matter requires an understanding of certain facts. The first is that there is a very urgent need in the country for a much larger number of university graduates in almost all fields, and at the moment especially, particularly in engineering, scientific research, teaching and in business.[6]

In 1959 an Honours Bachelor of Science program was created, and by 1963–4, following other additions to the Arts and Science curricula, approval was received from the Ministry of Education to build a second college of education in Ontario on the Queen's campus. But while choices for areas of concentration were widened, the basic curriculum requirements of the past several decades remained intact.

The same was true on other Ontario campuses where concern focused less on curriculum reform than on exploiting the current system and resources to the fullest.[7] Throughout this period, university senates and arts and sciences councils were masters of their own institutions' academic destinies, free from the direct control of provincial authorities, generally in accord about what constituted the basic elements of a proper higher education, and confident that their graduates would be gainfully employed. As F.E.L. Priestley noted in 1964: 'the universities are still dedicated, particularly in the humanities, to a belief in the value of a rigorous intellectual discipline, of the cultivation of a careful and penetrating scholarship by acquiring a degree of mastery of a subject.'[8]

During the 1960s, however, new pressures pushed the universities down the road of academic reform, as the previous consensus yielded to experimentation, liberalization, and pluralism within the academic community. The general pattern of curriculum development during the first half of the 1960s involved the dual process of increasing the number of programs and courses offered in the faculties of arts and science, and of decreasing (though not eliminating) the number of compulsory courses required for the BA degree. The availability of more options was undoubtedly a response to the broader range of subjects in which new and younger faculty were competent to teach. A common tendency for universities, as well, was to stress the value for students of majoring in more than one subject in their pursuit of general or honours degree. In 1963, Windsor offered for the first time programs in sociology and economics, sociology and anthropology, and sociology and political science. Queen's, too, created a degree program in sociology, reflecting the increasing attention being paid to the behavioural sciences during this period.[9]

The types of courses created by faculty and chosen by students revealed something of the cultural preoccupation with the power of Russia and with the cold war. At Toronto, for example, it was observed that many students were substituting Russian for German as their chosen foreign language. (In western Canada, Slavic languages became increasingly popular in the early 1960s.) A considerable interest in East Asian (and later Latin American) studies was evident at several universities, as the emergence of developing countries captured the attention of scholars and students in the social sciences.

As the pressures for pluralism and greater freedom of choice increased, several universities abandoned some long-standing compulsory courses, which had traditionally been defended on the grounds that such prescribed courses provided academic programs with an intellectual coherence otherwise unobtainable. Both Western and Windsor reduced the number of required courses for the BA from 17 to 16 in 1963 and 1966, respectively. In 1962, McMaster created a new program which represented the first major curriculum change in twenty-five years. Students were offered more elective courses and greater freedom of choice, though they were still required to take courses in divisions other than their own majors so as to avoid excessive specialization. Most notably, the requirement that religion be taken was dropped from the degree qualifications of this former Baptist college.

Institutions like Carleton, which had traditionally compelled students to select a philosophy course in first or second year, now allowed students to take philosophy or history or another humanities course of their own choosing. But a proposal that the general course be radically altered as a whole was rejected since that institution sought to maintain what it felt was a solid three-year course which, in difficulty, 'lies somewhere between most three year courses and [four year] honours courses.'

Symptomatic of the increasing concern about overspecialization in a period when career training attracted more and more students, was the revision made at Western in 1964, where the traditional practice of offering separate courses for science and arts students was replaced by a new 'common first year program.' In essence, explained the president of Western: 'programmes I and II are replaced by an offering of subjects from four divisions of Humanities, Social Sciences, Mathematics, and Natural Science, and Miscellaneous, within certain specified limits. It is believed that the additional flexibility provided by the new program may be of great benefit in determining programs for second and subsequent years.'

The academic philosophy of 'general education,' – which had made a notable, if uneven, impact in the United States between 1920 and 1950 – was becoming increasingly prominent in Ontario a decade later. Achieving distinction at Columbia after the First World War and once again, after 1945, at Harvard, general education was seen in both periods as a necessary component through which higher education could be prevented from becoming too professionally and vocationally oriented. The goal of general education, as stated in 1945, was to sustain 'the liberal tradition within a curriculum that recognized the legitimacy of individual interests and talents while at the same time it established a common bond of general learning.' While general education involved 'that part of a student's whole education which looks first to all of his life as a responsible human being and citizen,' specialized education 'indicates that part which looks to the student's competence in some occupation.' According to Frederick Rudolph, most American academics after the Second World War professed a desire to keep their courses of study from infusing students with a narrowly focused 'irresponsible competence.'[10]

As we have seen, the general education approach had a considerable impact on Ontario higher education, and one university – York – attempted to implement general education theories in a comprehensive and holistic fashion. In order to prevent 'narrow specialization,' all first-year students at York were compelled to take interdisciplinary courses in social science, humanities, and natural science. The program at York was drawn up by academics who had been heavily influenced by the developments in the United States described in the last paragraph.

Throughout the decade, then, academic choices were broadened, compulsory courses in the traditional and 'classical' subjects were all but eliminated and, under the added pressure of the student movement, individual students were given far more freedom and responsibility to structure their own academic programs. Toronto abolished its traditional honours program and devoted far more of its academic resources to the traditionally 'under-privileged' pass and general courses. Similarly, radical changes were implemented at Queen's, McMaster, and Carleton as universities attempted to 'more truly answer the mood of young people today.'

The question persists: how well did the universities respond, during this period of innovation and reform, to the needs of the professions and industries who favoured the expansion of higher education for utilitarian reasons? The general statements of the Industrial Foundation on Education, the Canadian Manufacturers Association, and the Ontario Chamber of Commerce, previously alluded to, confirm this highly practical bias in their view of the university's role. The observer could be forgiven for concluding that, in the minds of Canadian businessmen, the training of professionals was the only function of higher education. Since the majority of Canadian students were still enrolled in general arts courses, and since arts programs themselves became increasingly experimental during the 1960s, were businessmen completely blind or indifferent to this 'non-practical' aspect of higher education? How were the two reconciled?

The answer is found in a perusal of the business trade journals where the specific interests of particular industries were more clearly defined.[11] From this source emerges a theme that was both broader in scope and more subtle in flavour than the researcher might have been led to expect.

For what becomes increasingly apparent is that business saw no contradiction between the potential value of practical and non-practical training. In virtually every major industry and commercial enterprise, businessmen were firm in their conviction that intensive student exposure to the liberal arts was as vital to the well-being of the economy as was specific professional training. This perception was born of the very complexity of the economy itself which rendered inadequate any narrow or specialized learning, even in the major professions.[12] There was, then, a surprising congruence of views among business spokesmen and proponents of general education in the academic community. This appraisal of the oil industry, for example, explained the problem from the corporate perspective:

The oil industry is one of the most technical and automated industries. Its operations require the service of many professionals, technicians and specialists. But a closer look at the industry – or any major industry for that matter – shows its actions and growth depend on decisions of a social and economic nature that involve much more than the routine use of a slide rule, the seismograph or electronic computer ... We want people who can think, people who can understand the philosophy as well as the mechanics of their particular operation.[13]

The requirements of all industries were subject to such rapid transformation, particularly in light of the wider use of the computer, that virtually all employees required retraining once they began working in a major industry. No employer believed that a four-year business degree or even a master's degree, in and of themselves, prepared students adequately for the unpredictable problems they would face in their new jobs.

The changed business environment affects senior executives too. It used to be that the ability to design a better mouse trap virtually assured business success. Today, however, the emphasis is on hiring, retraining and motivating good mouse trap designers; marketing the device rather than selling it; providing an adequate organization and control system; and planning ahead, using market research for the day when mouse traps become a thing of the past.[14]

What employers sought from the universities was the imaginative student who would become the adaptable employee, capable of meeting new challenges and solving complicated problems. In the words of the president of Imperial Oil, 'industry has found that it can train an educated man, but it cannot necessarily educate the trained man.'[15]

These views were confirmed in other statements and surveys. According to the president of Bell Telephone in a speech to the Canadian Chamber of Commerce, 'Education [in schools and universities] should be primarily concerned with teaching how to learn.' The task of teaching specific skills for a specific job, he contended, would be best left to the companies themselves, most of which were already engaging in some form of on-the-job training at all levels.

The Economic Council of Canada agreed in its own survey, in 1964, that 'companies are anxious that new employees have basic education which will permit training and retraining to meet continuing job requirements.'[16] Arts courses that broadened the horizons and enriched the perspectives of future employees were an essential background to professional training and a professional career.

Indeed, in a frame of mind that might well have surprised those ambitious students hell-bent on the road to success through specialized training, many employers were sharply critical of the deficiencies these very students brought to the job. Because many business-oriented students had left their interest in liberal arts far behind, they were often lacking such basic skills as the ability to 'read, write and think clearly.' The editor of *Oil in Canada* cited University of Alberta president, Walter H. Johns, in a discussion of the problem. In the applied chemistry field, a company which hired many PhDs in 'a vast industrial empire,' informed Dr Johns that, 'there are hundreds of technically qualified employees who are handicapped by a lack of ability to formulate and communicate ideas beyond the merely technical.' Another business leader in the utilities field told Dr Johns that men graduating from engineering schools were technically competent enough but they 'were almost completely illiterate in the humanities and social sciences.' The magazine editors despaired of the problem and concluded firmly that professional training must include 'a blending of academic subjects with the essential technical subjects.'[17]

That humanities and social science courses were deemed absolutely essential by employers in a variety of professions was underlined in an article in the *Canadian Chartered Accountant*. The intellectual and academic scope of business managers of the future needed to be broadened if only for their very practical corporate interest in a changing, shrinking world. According to the author, business training must not only include learning the tools of the trade, but also such things as 'the nature of life in foreign countries, more than one language, and academic work that broadens [students'] bases of information and makes them generally analytical in their approach to the world in which the businesses they serve operate.'[18]

Other observers in the chartered accountancy profession predicted that the demands on the future accountant would reach beyond his current qualifications. In an era when major corporate decisions were increasingly the product of committee deliberations, the accountant, if he hoped to move into the 'senior management group,' would have to do more than merely audit books. He might be called in as a tax consultant, or he could be required to work closely with senior officials in solving high-level problems. Tomorrow's accountant, then, should be university-trained, and 'it therefore seems probable that in the future the profession will expect the chartered accountant to have acquired a broad liberal education through attendance at university.'[19]

In an effort to quantify the real value of an educated and imaginative employee, the director of training at a large pulp and paper firm posed the following economic model. According to him, most companies of similar size in the same industry had equivalent costs in such basic areas as raw materials, wages, taxes, and insurance. Thus the only key potential difference among such companies would be the quality of their personnel, especially at the highest levels, and the quality of these employees would be determined by the excellence of their educational training. Herein lay a company's competitive advantage: 'We will require employees who can think logically and keep abreast of technological improvements.'[20] Imaginative, flexible managers would be an undoubted asset to a far-sighted corporation.

As an editorial in *Cost and Management* pointed out, the very nature of a successful manager in a modern corporation demanded an integration of academic and technical skills. It reviewed an apparent confusion in management circles over the aims, objectives and methods of executive development programs:

This divergence of views has come about because the job of the top manager is so nebulous, complex and all embracing ... management education is not aimed at indoctrinating the trained with facts and theories; it's aimed at altering his basic attitudes and responses and fostering in him a state of mind that will react automatically on sound principles whatever the challenge may be. In this respect, the aims of management education are closely allied to the aims of the liberal arts programme and to say that a manager's view-point cannot be broadened and enlarged by a systematic program of studies is to invalidate the whole basis of academic education.[21]

In short, the 'manager can never afford to stop learning,' contended *Industrial Canada*,[22] and business writers and spokesmen appeared committed to the view that only a broadly based university education incorporating the liberal arts would provide adequate basic training.

Although they were preoccupied with different concerns, then, the views of businessmen reinforced those of academics on the issue of the liberal arts. The latter could not but be enthralled at the rapid expansion of their own professional opportunities in the humanities and social science fields during the 1960s.[23] While arts professors may not necessarily have prepared their students for careers in science and business, it is clear that the subjects they taught were viewed as essential by the business community itself. This symbiotic relationship explains a great deal about the depth of support for the extension of higher education in Canada. Because the demand for graduates was strong, whatever their academic degrees, all forms of post-secondary education – from engineering to fine arts – were seen as profitable forms of public investment.

Those academics who recoiled at the utilitarian imperative behind university growth prospered as much as those who cared little for the abstract or humanistic aims of higher education. If proponents of general education were committed to creating modern-day renaissance men, businessmen did not object, so long as these new renaissance men had among their array of talents the capability of managing a complex corporation. Indeed, the views of businessmen about the value of higher education seemed entirely consistent with those of Claude Bissell, who cited Peter Drucker's evaluation of recent trends:

Knowledge is the only real capital today. The development of educated people is the most important capital formation, and their number, quality and utilization the most meaningful index of the wealth-producing capacity of a country ... Support of education has changed from a contribution to an overhead cost to a capital investment by which the financial question has changed from 'Isn't it too much?' to 'Is it enough?'[24]

Beyond this general endorsement of the value of arts subjects and general education, businessmen said very little about the content of arts courses. At times, some strong statements were delivered on the need for schools and universities to teach the value and superiority of free-enterprise ideology.

In its brief to the 1955 Royal Commission on Canada's Economic Prospects, the Canadian Manufacturers Association implored schools to 'lay stress on the teaching of an economic system that is founded on private initiative and personal responsibility and freedom.' And the editors of the Royal Bank of Canada's *Monthly Letter* believed it inadequate for schools to teach only constitutional history and politics: 'It is a fatal mistake to believe that democratic education consists of teaching children some of the facts about our government and making them learn the provisions of the British North America Act. The survival of democracy depends on the ability of people to make realistic choices in light of adequate information.' But its over-all message was consistent with the more general views outlined earlier. 'Canada needs broadly educated men and women in all fields of endeavour so that sound judgement operates on sound knowledge.'[25]

For the most part, then, corporate spokesmen left the teaching of academic courses to the educational experts within the 'autonomous' universities.[26] Apart from some notable exceptions, businessmen were not intimately familiar with the process or methods of learning. They were more concerned about the results. So long as the demand for educated citizens was apparent, so long as their tangible experience proved that the educated were more productive on the job, then they were satisfied that the system was working. The task was to facilitate its ability to do more of the same.

If the concerns of the business community about the development of undergraduate education were expressed in broad and generally imprecise terms, their views about professional training were somewhat easier to decipher. For business, as for society as a whole, the prime function of higher education was to produce the manpower necessary to contribute to economic growth and prosperity. In order to understand in greater depth the relationship of higher education to the development of the Canadian economy, it is vital to gain a clear insight into the process through which universities developed their professional programs.

As Mark Blaug has noted, there have been three types of models used in planning the expansion of higher education in western capitalist countries: the 'social demand' model, the 'rate of return on investment' approach, and the process of 'manpower planning.'[27] As we noted in the last chapter, social demand – the technique of predicting the number of students who will enrol in universities over a given period – was used in Ontario during the 1960s by the committee of presidents and the Committee on University Affairs. This model involved studying past trends in the proportion of university-aged youth enrolled in post-secondary institutions and then estimating, in aggregate terms, | the number of students who would be registered in the future.

While the Jackson projections, drawn up in 1962 and revised in 1963, were used with considerable effect in estimating the number of undergraduates by 1970, clearly they were inadequate in dealing with the future of graduate and professional schools. Planning in the latter areas was based on a number of different political and philosophical assumptions. First, while Ontario was committed to the notion that students should have both equal opportunity and universal access to a university education, these egalitarian notions were not intended to apply to every level of the post-secondary system. That is, while education ministers continually espoused the view that all students who desired an undergraduate education should have the right to obtain one, the same was not true of all who desired a second or third degree in the graduate and professional fields.

Enrolment in some of these areas was more rigorously controlled by the professions and the universities on the assumption that a surplus of doctors or lawyers or engineers would be a wasted investment (as well as a possible threat to the incomes of existing professionals). Thus, in a number of cases, qualified applicants were refused entry into professional schools during the 1960s.[28] Conversely, the implied assumption about undergraduate education was that Ontario could never produce too many BA students, since a basic post-secondary education was considered a social and academic right for the intellectually competent.

Furthermore, the need to rationalize the expansion of professional and graduate programs meant that no single university could provide courses in any field it wanted, although every university attempted to provide a full complement of undergraduate arts and science programs. Thus, students living in northern Ontario, for example, who wanted to attend law school, would be at a considerable disadvantage to those living in southern Ontario where several law schools existed by 1960.[29] The former would be compelled to travel long distances, incur added expenses, and leave their homes and families.

Since the social demand approach was based on the universities responding to the pressure for entry by students themselves, and since professional educators needed to know exactly how many of their graduates would be absorbed in order to determine how many to admit to the classrooms, theoretically, a more sophisticated type of planning model was required for the latter.

The rate-of-return-on-investment method was one approach that attempted | to take into account in more specific terms the costs and benefits of public and | private spending on higher education. Through this process, economists |

attempted to determine how much investment higher education warranted by measuring the output in employee productivity or privately earned income, and / or the gross domestic product that could be accounted for by educational training itself.[30]

A typical analysis employing this model was a study undertaken by the Economic Council in 1965 which involved comparing the incomes of the educated with the less educated and then contrasting the situation in Canada with that in the United States. In a widely cited conclusion, the Economic Council found that economic growth in Canada was historically tied to increasing investments in educational training:

The benefits of increased education, according to certain calculations and assumptions, are estimated to have accounted for a share in the general order of one quarter of the *increase* both in the average standard of living and in the productivity of Canadians from 1911 to 1961. Although this is a large contribution, it is apparently substantially lower than that indicated in comparable estimates for the United States.[31]

As a general supporting document for those favouring increased investment in all areas of higher education, this report was highly useful. It suggested that if so much of Canada's economic development since the turn of the century had been accounted for by the gradual increase in educational achievement by its citizens, and since the higher standard of living in the United States appeared to depend so heavily on its better educational standards, then Canada could scarcely spend too much on educational development. Both the public and private returns were highly profitable. But as a guide for determining the allocation of public funds to specific professional faculties, this model had severe limitations.

A disconcertingly large portion of the economic studies of education during the 1960's made much over the evidence of high average returns to educational investments and the supposed importance of this to educational policy makers. The concern should have been on improving policy makers' insights regarding the points of probably rapidly diminishing returns to increased investments. The fact that well qualified economists treated high average returns to educational investment as reliable guides to investment decisions raises some interesting questions about the sociology of economic science.[32]

Relying so heavily on the average rate of return as a sufficient index for measuring the value of educational investments, these economists were merely translating the conventional political wisdom into economic terms. More specific data were deemed unnecessary since manpower shortages in all fields showed no signs of becoming manpower surpluses in the near or distant future. Perhaps the rate-of-return theorists assumed that the professions themselves were aware of how many doctors or lawyers would be needed in the years ahead. Perhaps, in fairness, they hoped only to provide a general context within which further studies might proceed.[33] In any event, the task of determining the specific manpower needs of the Canadian economy was left to other economists and other planners employing different models and methods of analysis.

While the social demand model was designed to respond to the number of students seeking higher education, and while the rate-of-return approach provided only the most general insight into the extent of educational investment required by universities, manpower planning had a more precise purpose. It was intended to 'gear the expansion of the educational system to quantitative forecasts of the demand for highly qualified manpower.'[34] In this way, it was hoped that, over a given period, both excessive shortages and surpluses in the production of skilled employees could be avoided. Furthermore, through manpower planning, ideally, the time lags between the recognition of a need and the training of a skilled employee could be reconciled. Finally, manpower planning should ensure that individuals would be employed in jobs that fully utilized their specific talents.

What is perhaps most significant about educational policy in the professional area is that neither the provincial government nor the universities undertook a comprehensive manpower survey (covering all fields) until close to the end of the 1960s.[35] There were, however, a number of partial or informal studies carried out by specific professions or government agencies and some of these will be referred to in the following discussion. This section, then, will discuss manpower planning within the context of its importance to the development of certain specific professions. The strengths and weaknesses of this model will be outlined as the discussion proceeds.

The most common difficulty in all manpower surveys was the basic, but overwhelming, problem of gathering accurate and dependable data. Since the training of required manpower demanded a precise understanding of the types of occupations that existed in the province, it was essential for manpower forecasters to prepare detailed lists and definitions of skilled services that were performed. But according to the authors of a study prepared for the Commission on Post-Secondary Education, 'occupational classification systems which have been devised are unsatisfactory for the purpose of manpower forecasting.'[36]

For example, the authors discovered enormous inconsistencies in merely attempting to define an engineer. If an engineer were defined as someone holding an engineering degree from a recognized university (which was the definition used by professional engineering associations), then how would the researcher take into account those technicians who performed many of the essential tasks of the engineer but who did not have a university degree? Conversely, many engineers might have performed the jobs of technicians, thereby complicating efforts to determine how many technicians exist or would be needed in the future. Indeed, the 1961 Canadian census was found to have been woefully inadequate on this crucial issue of occupational definition: 'There is reason to believe that a substantial number of technicians were counted as engineers in the 1961 census of Canada and that the extent of overstatement of the number of engineers relative to technicians varied between provinces. Over a quarter of the engineers in Canada in the census did not possess a university degree.'[37]

Such problems may have arisen from the vagueness of the questioning techniques used by census takers and manpower forecasters. While some technicians, for reasons of occupational status, might have knowingly falsified their job classification, others may well have perceived themselves as engineers by virtue of the tasks they performed. As the previous study pointed out, 'technicians [in Canada] sometimes supervise engineers or do their work ... Moreover, the best technology diploma courses may turn out more highly qualified graduates than weaker engineering schools.'

Even if the census takers had been more careful and had sought to prepare job definitions on the basis of the type of work performed, they would have run into equally awesome difficulties. One of the most widely used dictionaries of occupations was prepared by the International Labour Organization in 1958. While it described, for example, the job of engineering technicians, 'it provides no information on the different levels of work within the broad category from least sophisticated and demanding to the most.'[38] The definition, as well, was found to give little indication of the 'great variety of specific types of specialization.'

Pursuing this problem, the authors of the study for the Commission on Post-Secondary Education found the best and most detailed definitions in the *Dictionary of Occupational Titles*, but here the definitions were so specific and precise as to defy categorization. In fact, a study done for the Committee of Presidents of the Universities of Ontario in 1970 discovered that the three most important manpower studies done in Canada during the 1960s used different definitions of the term 'engineer,' making comparisons among them, and projections based on them, exceedingly difficult.[39] Indeed, concluded the most comprehensive study of engineering education ever done in Ontario:

Surprisingly little is known about our engineering manpower resources even though they are of growing importance in Canada. There is a dearth of data concerning the number of engineers, where they come from, and to what level or in what specialties they are educated. We cannot state with any certainty the fields in which they are employed, what functions they perform, how much they earn, or how they are distributed geographically across Canada or throughout the industry.[40]

This type of problem might have been at least partially alleviated during the 1960s if employers themselves had kept an adequate inventory of the type of work done by their employees. But a survey undertaken for the Economic Council of Canada in 1966 of seventeen of the largest companies in a variety of Canadian industries found that, while most employers believed in the value of manpower planning, they simply lacked the required data which would facilitate adequate long-term forecasting on the types of employees needed even within their own companies.[41]

In the health-care sector, where a plethora of statistical information was assembled throughout the 1960s, the problem of gathering reliable data was equally formidable. In the field of medicine, the measurement of the state of health of society – or the morbidity rate – was crucial to the process of determining how many doctors would be needed in the future. But according to the Royal Commission on Health Services in 1964:

scientific efforts to quantify the non-fatal characteristics of morbidity are relatively new, and little or no effort has so far been made in Canada to establish an integrated system of data collection to supplement the well established mortality statistics ... Because of inadequate data it will be necessary to refer to sources which are often limited in scope or outdated, and some judgement regarding their general validity will be made.[42]

Several years later, few improvements appeared to have been made in the data-gathering process. According to the authors of the report of the Ontario Committee on the Healing Arts in 1970:

Repeatedly we have been struck by the lack of firm statistical data relating to many aspects of health care. Frequently, we discovered that professional groups appearing before us made statements and allegations which could not be substantiated by factual evidence. Moreover, there are few, if any, scientific indices available for the precise measurement of the productivity or efficiency of the health system. Still less are there agreed means of measuring total costs and social benefits of particular programs, or means of controlling, let alone reducing, costs in the health industry. Professional practitioners and technical 'experts' usually fail to agree on the most appropriate means of studying, not to say solving, the problems with which we have grappled. Necessarily a certain rough and ready commonsense and a due regard for the present art of the possible have had to inform and limit the scope of our inquiry.[43]

Even after some enormous changes had occurred in the expansion of facilities for training health-care manpower during the 1960s and early 1970s, planners continued to conduct studies and make projections on the basis of incomplete and possibly inaccurate data. For example, in 1973, a study done by the Association of Universities and Colleges in Canada on the enrolment plans of Canadian medical schools, discovered that, even in this basic area, hard information was difficult to come by:

Directors of programs were asked whether they considered the need for more graduates to be urgent; if they thought an increase to be desirable, or if they were uncertain. Interestingly enough in only four of the 20 disciplines for which opinions were ventured were the respondents unanimously agreed that there was a need for more in the field. In all the others there were some who were uncertain or who thought that the output should not be increased ... It is doubtful that it will be possible to obtain this information until the present flurry in health education and health care has settled; when the roles of the various professionals and the patterns are more clearly established. So rapid are the changes and so confusing the effect of expansion and innovation, it is hard to determine precisely what is happening at any given moment let alone predict future needs ... The present picture is one of great activity and inevitable confusion.[44]

The factors which the authors admitted raised questions about the accuracy of the survey results were such problems as incomplete returns, confusion over nomenclature, misunderstanding of a survey, double counting, difficulty in discovering the existence of programs, in making projections, and in determining the maximum output of medical schools.

Universities encountered similar difficulties in other areas of professional planning throughout the 1960s. Those institutions planning to launch architectural programs discovered in 1963 that no information existed on 'the number of architects produced each year, the capacity of Canadian schools of architecture, the number of applications accepted or rejected by schools.' In fact, discovered one researcher, 'the whole question has not been given serious thinking.'[45]

Even within the profession itself, uncertainty prevailed about the need for more architectural schools in Ontario. A meeting of the Ontario Association of Architects in November of 1964 was unable to determine the local, regional, and national need for more architects. One member's opinion was that there were already enough professional architects in the province, but that the construction industry 'urgently needed trained architectural assistants and technicians.' Another member felt it essential that in any study of this problem, 'consideration should be given to the volume of construction which is now carried on in which architects are involved, in relation to the total volume of construction.'[46] Neither of these speakers presented statistical data to the meeting.

Similarly, in the area of social work, York University was told by the deputy minister of welfare in Ottawa in 1965 that 'no national manpower survey in the social welfare field has been carried out since 1960, and therefore we are unable to provide you with recent statistics on the number of social workers and the training of employed personnel.'[47]

What is striking, as well, is how inconsistent solid information was from faculty to faculty within universities. For example, in 1957, the University of Toronto published a report which attempted to project the enrolment of professional faculties to 1970. In the field of forestry, it was known that a hundred jobs had been offered to the twenty-three graduating students from the 1956 class, indicating both the scope and type of demand that existed for forestry graduates. But no such information existed on the fate or future of graduates from the Institute of Business Administration.[48] None the less, construction and enrolment changes occurred in unprecedented terms against the background of an *assumed* demand for graduates from virtually all professional faculties over the next decade.

The difficulty of determining both the types of professionals already working in business and industry and the numbers of specialists needed in the future was a problem common to most professions. As late as 1974, no adequate inventory existed on the distribution of lawyers working in corporate law, real estate law, family law, or criminal law, and the possibility of providing such information in the future was considered extraordinarily difficult.[49]

The specific types of business professionals required by industry could scarcely be tabulated by manpower planners throughout the 1960s since the distribution of such skilled professionals (university-trained or otherwise) was unknown. Instead, business leaders stressed the need for broadly trained, innovative graduates who could adapt themselves to any number of fields.[50] Finally, the data-gathering process was hindered by misunderstanding and controversy over the problems of skill substitution and para-professional work.[51] In most fields, practitioners and educators had not resolved satisfactorily such problems as whether technicians could perform the work of professionals, dental hygienists the work of dentists, bookkeepers the work of accountants, or landscape technologists the work of architects.

Despite the basic data-gathering inadequacies, decisions were made and statistical justifications offered for expanding professional education facilities in many areas. In the health-services sector where, unlike in many areas, a number of major manpower studies were carried out in the 1950s and 60s (in the *hope* of ensuring systematic planning), an insight can be gained into the manner in which forecasters rationalized their recommendations for expansion.

The most common index used to measure the adequacy of health care – whether in the fields of medicine, dentistry, or pharmacy – was the profession-al / population ratio. The Health Survey Committee Report (1951), the (Hall) Royal Commission on Health Services (1964), and the (Dowie) Ontario Commit-tee on the Healing Arts (1970) all put great emphasis on such ratios in the course of their studies. How Ontario compared to Canada as a whole, or how Canada measured up to the ratios in other western countries in this regard, formed an important part of these studies' analyses. For some observers, any decrease in such ratios over a certain period in the history of Canada indicated a serious decline in the quality and supply of medical facilities.

In 1961, R.F. Farquarson, the chairman of the Medical Research Council of Canada, compared the performance of Canada with that of the United States in the areas of physician and dentist versus populations ratios. He concluded that Canada was lagging too far behind. He called for an increase in the capacity of the existing schools and for the building of new ones in order to achieve a ratio of 1: 2,500 for dentists and 1: 879 for doctors by 1980. But this blithe use of ratios was challenged by L.Z.G. Stevenson of McGill University who said that Far-quarson had failed in his analysis to account for certain crucial facts. He argued that in some medical specialties there were too many doctors and in others too few, so that a general ratio was meaningless. He noted, as well, that comparing Canada to the US was an inadequate form of measurement since there was considerable controversy within the US over what the best physician / popula-tion ratio should be. Finally, he claimed that, whereas Sweden had a far lower physician / population ratio than Canada, the quality of medical care there was excellent. R.G. Ellis, dean of the Faculty of Dentistry at Toronto, also chal-lenged Dr Farquarson's argument on the grounds that what the profession required was not more dentists but more efficient use of dental auxiliaries such as dental hygienists and dental technicians.[52]

Even with the publication in 1964 of the most sophisticated study ever done in Canada on the quality and adequacy of health services – *Medical Education in Canada* by J.A. McFarlane *et al.* – the analytical problems seemed to increase as the questions became more complex. Despite the fact that several studies for the commission used physician / population ratios as their measurement of the adequacy of health services in the country, one of the authors seemed to cast some serious aspersions on the value of his own work. McFarlane noted (p. 186) that while

the physician / population ratio may be used as a crude descriptive index of the medical manpower of the country as a whole at a particular time ... one cannot conclude from changes in the ratio that needs are being met, or are not being met. Whether the supply of physicians is inadequate, sufficient, or overabundant cannot be judged in isolation from a consideration of such factors as the supply of hospital beds of various types, the financial resources of families, the degree of urban development and of regional organization of health facilities, and of special importance ... the geographical distribution of the physicians themselves.

Yet for most of these questions, the author admitted that statistical information was not available. Furthermore, it was noted that equally qualified manpower planners using the same data but slightly different assumptions could create projections that would vary so greatly as to be of suspect value. If, for example, the attrition rate of medical students at the end of the first year was estimated at 15 per cent (instead of 12 per cent) over the period 1963–64 to 1977–78, 'then the reduction in output would be nearly 900 graduates. This would be equivalent to the entire output of a medical school receiving a class of 68 annually for 15 years.'[53]

Other imponderables could drastically affect decisions to create new facilities over this period. If teaching methods became more efficient, if financial barriers for medical students were reduced or increased, if the immigration / emigration rate of medical school graduates changed as a result of some unforeseen political event, then the long-term projections might prove inadequate. Improved pension plans for doctors or dentists might change retirement patterns, just as changing technology, better drugs, or improved knowledge about health care in the community at large would alter medical practices.[54] Basing projected future needs on past trends, then, and formulating conclusions on the basis of incomplete data, raised serious doubts about the value of all such studies – doubts acknowledged by the authors themselves.

Despite these limitations, the Hall commission made a series of specific and influential recommendations. Combining its subjective judgements with 'objective' ratio indicators against the considered feasibility of a rapid building program, the commission selected from among the several ratios presented to it by its researchers and called for the building of five new medical schools in Canada by the mid 1970s. On the basis of these recommendations, which were endorsed by the Committee on University Affairs in September 1964, the Ontario government announced two months later that Ontario's medical schools would all receive increased funds to expand their facilities and that capital would be provided for the building of a new school at McMaster University in Hamilton.[55]

The commission recommended – and both the CUA and the government agreed – that a new dental school was justified in the province. Following representations by the Ontario Dental Association and the University of Western Ontario, the premier announced that funds would be provided for the construction of a new dental school at Western, although the background discussions were subject to the same kind of statistical and theoretical uncertainties as those which had characterized the debates about the need for new medical schools. Interestingly enough, the Hall commission rejected the recommendation of its own research study on the need for a new school of pharmacy in Canada, indicating how unpersuasive the 'factual' data was on that issue.[56]

That the Hall commission had failed to answer all questions regarding health needs in Ontario was indicated by the creation of the Ontario Committee on the Healing Arts, which reported in 1970. While the committee focused more heavily on the organization of the health-care system and on the role of professional organizations than had its predecessor, it too attempted to project manpower needs in the province through the next two decades. Yet the committee's work revealed that, if anything, the problems of accurately predicting manpower needs had become more, not less, difficult over the 1960s. For example, in the field of pharmacy, the authors discovered that the pharmacist / population ratio had decreased from 1: 2,740 to 1: 4,423 between 1955 and 1968.

This, by itself, did not necessarily mean that the public was served less adequately than in the past. 'Pharmacists may be devoting much more of their time to work as pharmacist rather than as store clerks, managers and owners,' and the average time taken to prepare prescriptions may have fallen as an increasing number of drugs came from pharmaceutical firms ready for dispensing to the patient. Furthermore, even though the number of pharmacists had decreased steadily in Ontario since 1955, as small outlets were taken over by large chains, 'the size of a pharmacy may well have increased enough to offset the decline in numbers [and] there might be fairly large economics of scale in the dispensing of present drug pharmaceutical products.' Yet for the majority of commissioners, future developments *did* appear to justify the creation of a new school of pharmacy in the province. The increasing use of chemotherapy would require a greater use of pharmacists' services; the very high demand for pharmacists in the hospitals of the province and the critical need for continuing education of practising pharmacists were reasons enough to build a new school outside of Toronto.

That this rationale was little better than educated guesswork was indicated by yet a further divergent opinion from the chairman of the committee himself, who submitted a minority report challenging the recommendation. He felt that there was simply not enough information in such areas as the occupational role of the pharmacists, the educational requirements for pharmacists, or the student recruitment process to justify the costs of building a new school. He cited, as well, a report of the Committee of Presidents of the Universities of Ontario which agreed that any further training of pharmacists should occur outside the university setting.

Nor did the chairman agree with the committee's recommendation to build a new dental school in Ontario. He believed that not enough was known about the different kinds of dental care needs, or about the effect of the possible development of public dental care on the profession. Furthermore, he contended that future needs could be filled by the more efficient and widespread use of dental auxiliary workers. The majority members of the committee, on the other hand, believed that the unfavourable geographical distribution of dentists and the effect of increasing public consciousness about the need for good dental care would increase the demand for dentists in the future and would justify another school.

The statistics and arguments, then, could be interpreted in a variety of ways, as the authors appeared to raise more questions about the future of health care than their manpower planning studies answered. Despite the great faith that lobbyists and professional groups put in statistics and ratios, the committee concluded:

In the present state of social and economic knowledge the criteria for 'adequacy' of a public service must be arbitrary; there are no precise means of measuring the optimal quality of the service which 'might be available'. Therefore in considering the adequacy of physicians or other health professionals 'manpower supply', we are thrown back upon judgements which are to a considerable extent subjective.[57]

There were other problems that contributed to the lack of precision and imperfections inherent in manpower studies. Manpower planners were forced to rely, in part, upon the type of information that employers could provide about their own future plans. Yet employers themselves were often incapable of projecting their future requirements within the vagaries of the market economy. One survey for the Economic Council of Canada found that:

most companies consider the biggest problems confronted in attempting to project future manpower requirements to be those of forecasting company sales or shares of market, and predicting the influence of technological change. The latter may on the one hand have caused certain jobs to disappear as in the case of some forms of mechanization and automation. On the other hand the rapidly developing use of the computer has created large numbers of new jobs in roles such as systems design and programming.[58]

In a market economy where students were free to choose those professions they wished to enter, it would appear to have been vital during the 1960s to understand not merely what employers' demands were for the future, but also how students made their choices about which professions to enter, so that adjustments in recruiting techniques and admission policies could be made over the long term. Yet as E.B. Harvey pointed out, no comprehensive study on student career patterns had been done in Ontario. His own investigation of this problem was not completed until 1972, only after the expansion phase of higher education had reached its peak.[59]

A similar study had been published in 1969 in the *Canadian Medical Association Journal* in which the career choices of the 1965 graduating class from the Toronto medical school were traced over several years, in order to determine the type of medical specialties these students entered. Yet the conclusions of this study were highly tentative and were presented with some serious qualifications.[60] Neither the Hall report nor the Committee on the Healing Arts had access to such information in projecting the future supply of doctors and dentists. Both, in fact, emphasized how little was known about the desired distribution of medical specialists in Canada and Ontario.[61] Yet the authors were compelled by governments to make long-term projections even in the absence of such data.

What was true of the planning process in the health services sector was characteristic of other professional fields as well. The perceptions of planners of the manner in which expansion should occur were derived from a wide variety of dissimilar statistical profiles of the industries or professions that the schools were intended to serve. The process was largely a general and often subjective one, in which the 'impressions' of a dean, the 'opinion' of a professional organization, or the 'evaluations' of a consultant were given great weight by the academic planners, no matter how unscientific the sources of information.

Occasionally buttressed by some very convincing statistics, the planning documents derived their conclusions from the very *general* belief that the economy was improving, that professional education was increasingly required, and that the demands for trained graduates were far greater than the supply. In some cases, where precise information on the need for trained manpower was unavailable, enrolment pressure – that is, social demand – was used as the basic rationale for increasing facilities. Decisions about the number and location of schools were then made on the basis of subjective and *political* factors, though all were rationalized within the context of utilitarian and economic arguments.[62] Imprecise and potentially error-ridden as it was, this was the main approach through which the development plans of Canadian universities were tied to the perceived needs of the provincial and national economies. The theory and practice of the manpower approach were simply too deficient to allow for the development and application of dependable methods of economic planning. As the president of the University of Toronto noted in 1956:

Faculties of engineering are found in the greatest number, then commerce, medicine, law, nursing, pedagogy, music, home economics, pharmacy, physical education, agriculture, dentistry, architecture, social work, forestry, journalism. We all know of the national shortages of personnel in most of these programs ... The firmest prediction we can make about the unpredictable future is that the facilities for professional training will expand.[63]

Some further examples in the non-medical fields should bear out the validity of these conclusions. In the late 1950s, as we have seen, business and government leaders stressed with great vigour the need for newly trained engineers in Canada.[64] As a result, new schools of engineering were established at universities with well-developed science programs. Western, McMaster, Carleton, Ottawa, and Waterloo all had new programs in place by 1958. (Queen's and Toronto already had long-established schools of engineering.) And yet, almost immediately, the vagaries of the economy resulted in a 'temporary saturation of engineers' in the market place.[65] In September 1959, enrolment in engineering faculties dropped as 'graduates were finding it not so easy to secure employment.' This rather shocking situation was due, in all probability, to the fact that the federal government cancelled a contract it had undertaken in 1956 with the AVRO corporation to build a supersonic interceptor, the Arrow. Consequently, engineering staff in the affected industries decreased by some 42 per cent: 501 engineers and 675 scientists in Canada lost their jobs, a large number of whom emigrated to the United States.

As the economy gradually recovered in the early 1960s, university engineering faculties increased their capacities once again in light of the increasing demand for engineers' services. In 1965, the Committee on University Affairs again pondered the future of engineering education in Canada. The committee's first full-time chairman, and the founding dean of the engineering faculty at the University of Waterloo, Douglas Wright, prepared a report attempting to project future needs. He discovered that past trends since the Second World War provided precious little guidance to the future on this issue:

It is very difficult to project future engineering enrolments. On the one hand, there may be a further reduction in the proportion of high school graduates entering engineering, tending in the long run to a figure as low as six per cent. However with the very rapid rate of increase in the proportion of students entering the Institutes of Technology in the province, the distribution may have reached stability already. There is, further, a well publicized present shortage of new graduates – reflecting freshmen enrolments of some years ago when 8% of the Grade 13 class chose to enter engineering, which may indicate that the economy needs this many graduates at least.

... About all that can be said in conclusion is that there is bound to be continuing fluctuation over cycles of five and ten years' duration, and that enrolments might tend to vary between such wide limits as six and ten per cent of the Grade 13 population.[66]

Thus, even in terms of measuring the social demand for engineering places in Canadian universities, the future was highly uncertain. How, then, should decisions about the required expansion of the engineering profession be determined? According to Wright:

In considering the means through which further expansion may be undertaken several important questions arise. Where should the further expansion take place? Should other new facilities of engineering be created? To what extent should universities be 'persuaded' to provide for further expansion in a faculty? Such questions would seem to require careful study by the universities and the Advisory Committee on University Affairs. The only relevant observation that may be appropriate here is that Ontario now has a substantially larger number of engineering schools, relatively, than any other Province in Canada, than any American state, or any European country.

The fact was that professional planning in such areas as engineering, accounting, law, and business, depended heavily upon the growth of the economy as a whole. But if the economic development of Canada were itself unpredictable, how accurate could manpower projections be? In 1970, a study on the need for engineers to 1981 assumed that the 'real Gross National Product [would grow] at a compound annual rate of 4% per annum.' By the late 1970s, however, that rate of growth was being surpassed, although unemployment in the economy as a whole continued to rise.[67]

In 1957, the Law Society of Upper Canada had made its momentous decision which resulted in the establishment of new common law schools at Queen's, Western, and the University of Ottawa. Prior to that, Osgoode Hall and the University of Toronto were the only training grounds for lawyers in Ontario. In the absence of specific information on how many lawyers would be needed in the years ahead, the Law Society realized that it could not afford to train the number of lawyers clamouring for admission. It ruled that any university with adequate facilities could offer legal training programs. The key element here appeared to be social demand.

The Law Society had expected that after the last of the post-war veterans had passed through the system in the mid 1950s, enrolment at Toronto and Osgoode Hall would decline and Osgoode Hall would return to its position as the only law school in the province. But in 1955, 'the figure [at Toronto] climbed to 670 students in actual attendance at the school, and it appeared that a new level, approximately double the old, had been established.'[68] Osgoode's own facilities were heavily strained, since as a private institution it received no government grants. After meeting with executives from all Ontario colleges and universities, the Law Society announced, in 1957, the decision described above.

It was projected in that year that by 1969, there would be approximately 1,500 to 1,700 law students in Ontario. Yet it was obvious in 1964 that, by 1970, first-year enrolment alone would surpass the projections made in 1957 for all three years of legal training combined. These pressures led to the creation of a new law school at the University of Windsor in 1969 and to the transfer of Osgoode Hall Law School to the new campus of York University, where training facilities were substantially increased. In the midst of such expansion, while the need for lawyers was assumed and apparently borne out by the ease with which lawyers obtained employment, there was little reliable information on the proper distribution of lawyers within the various legal specialties.

Until 1967, there was only one school of architecture in Ontario, located at the University of Toronto. Over the years, the school had expressed a desire to limit its enrolment despite increasing pressure for admission, on the argument that to grow too quickly would be to threaten the faculty's educational standards. As the annual report of the president of the university noted in 1957, 'The school of architecture indicates that it would be wise to control enrolment, and it recommends that there be not more than 270 students at any one time.'[69] It was indicated, as well, that two 'outstanding' schools – Liverpool and the Massachusetts Institute of Technology – had fewer than two hundred students.

By the mid 1960s however, for a variety of reasons, several universities sought to establish architectural schools on their respective campuses. For York, its location in the fastest growing metropolitan area in Ontario justified, both economically and demographically, the creation of an architectural faculty which, furthermore, would be consistent with the university's plans to create a School of Environmental Design. Planners at the University of Waterloo, on the other hand, believed that 'there was no correlation between a successful School of Architecture and the size of the urban area in which it was located.' Moreover, they argued that a large urban area tended to tempt professional faculty to establish lucrative consulting practices. The fact that Waterloo already had a successful engineering program provided, according to university spokesmen, a solid base upon which to build an equally successful school of architecture.

Queen's University, too, emphasized the value of its own engineering faculty in seeking support for an architectural training program. And Carleton drew upon the theme of regional disparity within Ontario in defending its claim for a new faculty. Noting that there were no architectural training facilities in eastern Ontario, the university stressed that Ottawa had the second largest group of practising architects in the province, both in private practice and public service with the federal government.[70]

The Committee on University Affairs, which was burdened with the task of selecting from among these presentations, consulted the University of Toronto, the Ontario Association of Architects, and the Royal Architectural Institute of Canada before making its decision. Because the manpower needs of the future were uncertain, neither the OAA nor the RAIC could offer precise recommendations as to whether there should be one or two new schools created in Ontario, though the director of the University of Toronto school felt that there should not be another school established in Toronto.[71] However inexact and contradictory the specific recommendations, all were agreed that, in light of the continually heavy immigration of architects into Canada, new training facilities within the province *were* justified. The CUA was left the task of determining how many new schools should be publicly funded and where they should be located. Statistical evidence could not resolve this essentially political problem for the committee or the government.

The CUA ultimately decided that both Carleton and Waterloo should be permitted to move ahead. Since York had no school of engineering and since training facilities already existed in Toronto, it was considered inappropriate to construct a new facility on that campus. York, furthermore, had just received support for a new faculty of fine arts, and the CUA feared an embarrassment of riches at that institution (which in the view of some members had been expanding too rapidly in the professional field anyway).[72]

Even in the field of secondary school teaching, where fewer planning problems should have existed, the Department of Education was forced to make 'emergency' arrangements in order to meet student demand. In 1977, demographer Robert Jackson noted that in light of 'compulsory attendance and general acceptance of some form of secondary education for all ... if we have satisfactory population projections it is a relatively simple task to project total school enrolment.' Twenty-one years earlier, W.G. Fleming, of the Ontario College of Education's Department of Educational Research, had set out to fulfil this 'relatively simple task.' He predicted that by 1968 / 69 there would be 362,800 students in the high schools of Ontario. In fact there were 500,000. The 1,300 teachers whom he thought it would be necessary to hire in the same year became 5,619. And while he predicted that there would be 11,000 teachers in total by the end of the 1960s, there were, in reality, over 30,000.[73]

How was this unexpected demand for teachers met throughout the 1960s? Until 1963, the Ontario College of Education in Toronto was the only high school teacher-training institute in the province. Normally, students would study there for one year after completing the requirements for a BA at a recognized university. But as early as 1955, in an attempt to cope with the secondary student bulge, special steps were taken to circumscribe this traditional training route. Upon receipt of a 'letter of permission' from an Ontario school board, would-be teachers were excused from the full year at OCE if they enrolled instead in a fifteen-week course (over two summers) at the college. As late as 1969 (when the program was finally phased out), fully 20 per cent of newly hired teachers were still working under the auspices of letters of permission. After years of criticism from teachers and ministry officials about the questionable quality of the program, it was finally abolished.

Part of the teacher-training slack was picked up during the 1960s by two new colleges – Althouse in London (1963) and McArthur in Kingston (1965). In both cases, facilities were immediately overloaded. Althouse did not obtain its own building until 1966. And at McArthur, which enrolled 900 students annually instead of a planned 600, the pressure for accommodation on the residents of Kingston was so great that 'the college was forced to arrange for the use of space in hotels and motels and faced difficulties in providing transportation.'[74] Emergency planning remained the order of the day.

According to Robert Jackson and W.G. Fleming, the strain put on the system merely in attempting to cope with numbers long delayed efforts that should have gone towards evaluating and improving the teacher training process. That Ontario succeeded in meeting high school demands through these *ad hoc* responses was indeed surprising. But for aspiring school teachers in the mid 1970s, the negative consequences of such short-term planning would become devastatingly evident.

If consistency and inadequate data were endemic to the process of planning in the professional fields as a whole, this was even truer of graduate planning in the arts and sciences. Whereas the justification for expanding facilities in the former area was almost always tied to a consideration (however inexact) of the need for qualified manpower, in the latter field other more 'academic' motives influenced the planning process.

For reasons of prestige, status, and institutional reputation, most universities favoured the healthy development of their graduate programs. As A.N. Bourns, a former member of the Committee on University Affairs and later president of McMaster University, recalled:

Every university, small and large, wished to develop and expand at the graduate level ... and it could be argued that the prestige consideration played a role at the time.

The main argument was that the only way in which we could attract first rate faculty and hence provide first rate undergraduate education was to allow faculty an involvement with students at the graduate level.[75]

In its examination of the status of graduate studies in Ontario, the Spinks commission found in 1966 'a very general wish to proceed as rapidly as possible at the master's level in most of the younger universities.'[76] And as a Senate Committee on Graduate Studies at McMaster University concluded in 1968: 'within the academic world the university's short term reputation is coming more and more to reflect the quality of its graduate schools.'[77]

The academic community, then, required little beyond academic rationalizations to justify its desire to expand graduate offerings. For the Committee on University Affairs, however, economic considerations played an equally vital role. Following the publication of the undergraduate enrolment projections by Robert Jackson in 1963, the committee realized that there would be a drastic shortage of qualified faculty to teach in Ontario universities unless graduate training facilities were quickly extended.[78] Given the demand for qualified teachers in the United States and Britain, the prospect of attracting sufficient numbers of teachers from abroad appeared equally dismal. But exactly how many faculty would be needed in the years ahead, and in what academic areas were the requirements the greatest?

In 1964, the Humanities Research Council addressed this problem in a survey of 162 departments in 34 universities across Canada.[79] While an earlier study by the Canadian Universities Foundation had released 'terrifying statistics' on the future need for university teachers in all departments, the results had been expressed in aggregate, not divisional or disciplinary, terms. A second study by the CUF on the supply of trained graduates had concluded, pessimistically, that at 35 institutions across Canada only 242 students would qualify for a doctorate in 1964. But neither of these studies had addressed the issue of the specific demand for the services of those with higher degrees.

At first glance, the results of the HRC survey indicated that the crisis was not so great since a majority of departments reported that the PhD was not required for permanent employment. In History, for example, this meant that of the responding departments, only 52 PhD graduates across Canada would be required by 1965–67, while 85 would actually be graduating with the doctorate. The supply, based on current enrolment patterns, seemed more than ample in this and a number of other areas.

But the authors of the questionnaire advised its readers to be cautious in interpreting the results. First, a number of departments did not respond to the questionnaire so their needs were unknown; second, the PhD graduates who are 'fresh from the graduate schools have had little or no university teaching experience and cannot be expected to assume full responsibility as university instructors at once.' Third, new universities were planned for the future and their demands were unclear. Furthermore, universities were increasingly demanding scholars with impressive publication records, and this would create pressures on universities to hire academics of proven research ability as well as with impressive degrees.

On closer examination, the responses to the questionnaires revealed that the departmental chairmen themselves were anything but clear about their own faculty plans. The rate of growth of undergraduate departments was, in many instances, unknown, so that graduate projections were tentative and understated further by the fact that many chairmen did not take seriously 'the warning that in six years the number of full-time university students in Canada will double.' The HRC report noted as well: 'If in 1970 there are twice as many students in Canadian universities as there are now, does it follow that there will be twice as many undergraduates studying classics in X university as there are now?' The possibility of year-round university operation might also affect staffing needs in a positive manner, while the potential use of closed-circuit television would have the reverse effect. Consideration would also have to be given to the possibility that graduates in the humanities might want to work outside the university. Finally, the impact of professors hired from abroad, and of those returning from other professions to the teaching field, was also unknown.

The statistics, then, only added to the uncertainty of planning in the graduate area, and the HRC study concluded: 'it must be said quite frankly that no one has yet made a realistic and dependable estimate of the total number of instructors required in each of the Humanities disciplines in Canadian universities for the period ending in 1970.' The over-all conclusion, however, brought the study full circle and reinforced the general view that expansion of graduate schools was, in fact, necessary, and that careful steps should be taken to nourish and sustain quality graduate education.

In its own investigation of the Ontario situation, the Spinks commission discovered similar problems in projecting future needs in the sciences as well as in the social sciences and humanities. According to the commission, even the Ontario Economic Council was dubious about the viability of the manpower planning process. The commission observed that:

Existing estimates are of two main kinds – those which predict the need for university teachers as a function of predicted enrolment and output, and those put forward by the various specialized professions with respect to their own fields. Neither sort is satisfactory for the purpose of wise planning for graduate education. The demographically-based predictions of the first sort yield only very broad answers, and do not get down to cases, especially as regards specialization. Internal professional estimates usually reflect the optimism of the present practitioners. It is difficult, for example, for a chemist not to feel that Ontario is going to need a lot more chemists in the near future.

Yet, despite these doubts, the authors arrived at a conclusion that would appear extraordinary within a very few years.

We recognize that there is an almost inexhaustible market for higher degree graduates in Ontario, and since Ontario has traditionally also helped to staff the universities and professions of all Canada, the problem of demand is an acute one. The economic situation of Canada and the explosive growth of the universities requires the maximum possible production of doctors of philosophy.[80]

Within the context of this general belief in the need for more Canadian-trained university teachers, but limited by a lack of reliable data on how and where these skilled professionals should be distributed within the university system, the CUA was forced to rely upon a very subjective decision-making process in allotting grants for graduate programs. Reva Gerstein, a former member of the CUA, described as '*ad hoc*' the approach in which decisions about the potential problem of duplication or over-extension of graduate and professional programs in the early 1960s were taken amid a great deal of uncertainty.[81] The committee relied, as well, on financial incentives to determine priorities within the system. In 1964, it created a graduate fellowship program for students in the humanities and social sciences through which it was hoped that graduates would be lured into university teaching careers. According to Douglas Wright, the first full-time chairman of the CUA, the general philosophy of the committee with regard to undergraduate planning applied to the graduate sector as well. Apart from certain professional fields, such as law and medicine (where enrolment was rigidly controlled), a key variable which determined the size and priority of specific university programs was student preference.

The pattern we have followed is one that is really demand planning, social demand as some call it, in which the demand of qualified people for places of study is the principal determinant. This puts the burden of responsibility on the individual and since the responsibility for the outcome is largely his, that seems to me to be ethically and philosophically quite proper. And in my experience, it has on the whole worked very well. People are able to make responsible decisions and I would say much better than the so-called planners.[82]

So long as graduate students continued to find jobs, so long as the universities were provided with funds to enhance their reputations by extending graduate offerings, then the institutions could continue to develop on the strength of demonstrable public support. But in this area, as well as in the professional sector, there was simply no proven way of relating the perceived requirement for master's and doctoral students to the development of graduate programs, since perceptions themselves were often in conflict. By the end of the decade, the context within which the universities functioned was beginning to change. As will be shown in Chapter Six, graduate programs would pay a heavy price for shifting public views about the value of higher education.

If a key purpose of professional education was to meet the growing demands of a utilitarian society, how successfully did the curricula of professional programs themselves respond to this requirement? Whereas the thrust of undergraduate education was largely preparatory, the programs of the professional schools were designed to train students directly to take their positions in the working world. This final section examines the success of the universities in adjusting their training programs to the demands of industry, the professions, and the economy.

The importance assigned the development of professional education in Ontario in the post-war period was not a typical response to this issue throughout the history of the province. Nineteenth-century educators tended to view professional education with considerable suspicion and the university's role in this process with little enthusiasm.[83] The overwhelming emphasis of university teaching was on the training of undergraduates in the classical and liberal arts. With the possible exception of medicine, practical and vocational training were treated as something of a travesty and a violation of the university's time-honoured academic tradition. As Principal Dawson of McGill University noted in 1863: 'If we have any provision for educational qualifications in the civil and military services of this country, it is a dead letter.' Dentists and pharmacists, for example, were sometimes seen as untrustworthy merchants peddling their wares under the guise of medical respectability. Although this was undoubtedly an unfair characterization of all such practitioners, the absence of regulation in these professions and the minimal qualifications required for practice did little to alter such negative images.

In order to eliminate the most blatant instances of malpractice, the Ontario government recognized several professional groups as official spokesmen for their respective trades and granted them the power to license aspiring professionals. In 1868, for example, the Royal College of Dental Surgeons of Ontario had been officially sanctioned and given the power to license, certify, and train dentists. A provincial act in 1871 gave similar recognition to pharmacists, and in 1872, the Law Society of Upper Canada officially gained the right to oversee the training of solicitors and law clerks.

Significantly, the government made no effort to dominate or even regulate the professions; they demanded, and were assumed, to be basically self-governing. Thus they determined both the method and process of training future colleagues. The educational approach generally involved several years of apprenticeship training outside the framework of traditional educational institutions. The Law Society of Upper Canada, for example, demanded that all students work in law offices for a period of five years, after which time they could be certified to practice.

But because of the need to standardize teaching methods, most professional groups began establishing their own colleges where lectures and examinations were offered as a complement to the apprenticeship process. These colleges, however, had a rocky history in the late nineteenth century. The Royal College of Dental Surgeons, originally opened in 1869, closed one year later and reopened in 1875. The Law Society's Osgoode Hall began in 1862, closed in 1868 for economic reasons, reopened in 1873 for five years, and did not receive permanent status until 1889. Throughout the 1870s and 80s, the Ontario College of Pharmacy also had an on-again, off-again history.

Because of the economic pressures faced by such colleges, because of the desire of students to supplement their own apprenticeship training with a broader educational base, and because of the growing belief in the minds of university officials that professional training as a form of higher education necessitated a wider academic foundation, a new tendency emerged in the last part of the nineteenth century. The medical, pharmacy, and dental professions all affiliated their own colleges with non-denominational universities. In this way the professions gained for their students the prestige of a university degree (such as a bachelor of pharmacy), and the universities were able to expand their own science offerings (thereby increasing their public grants as a result of their association with the professions). Furthermore, the increasing urbanization and industrialization of Canadian society required the training of more professionals, and with the teaching facilities that the universities offered enrolments could be considerably increased.

The professions, none the less, retained considerable control over the training of their respective students. They were generally heavily involved in drawing up appropriate curriculum programs, though university senates did have ultimate authority in this regard. In the case of dentistry, the Royal College of Dental Surgeons held membership on the faculty council of the School of Dentistry at the University of Toronto. Most significantly, the professions generally set the final licensing exams for students and held total control over the apprenticeship portion of the training program. Throughout this period, as a number of observers have noted, the professions were accorded the right to resolve their problems free from extensive government regulation and to co-operate with the universities without government interference.

While suspicions often characterized the relationship between the universities and their professional affiliates, for the most part they coexisted peacefully – strengthening their bonds in the years ahead and providing each other with economic and academic benefits. All of this reflected the increasing status accorded professional education throughout the first half of the twentieth century, though in the eyes of some academics this reputation was secured at the expense of the traditional university function.

By the mid 1950s and 60s, certain common features were typical of the relations between the professions and the universities with which they were affiliated. The bulk of the academic function rested in the hands of the universities themselves, although the professional associations retained powers that could prove very influential if applied. In the field of pharmacy, for example, the Ontario College of Pharmacy had the authority to grant degrees but had held this power in abeyance since 1953, turning this function over to the University of Toronto. In the field of medical training, 'the professional associations, that is the Canadian Medical Association and the Ontario Medical Association, have no role in specifying curricular content. However, the Medical Council of Canada indirectly, and the College of Physicians and Surgeons in Ontario, have the legal right to define curriculum within the Ontario medical schools. In recent years, however, the latter agency has delegated this responsibility to the Universities.'[84]

While professional organizations argued that their powers to license, accredit, and certify trainees were necessary to protect society from the abuse of unqualified practitioners and to ensure that economic and social needs were adequately met, there was no unanimity on this question among observers in the field. Two background studies for the Commission on Post-Secondary Education, the final report of the commission itself, and the report of the Committee on the Healing Arts, all recommended that the responsibility for licensing be removed from the professions and that educational training in the professional areas be, without qualification, under the control of the universities:

At present many self-governing professional organizations guard entry into their professions, deciding and enforcing conditions of admission. For post-secondary education, the principal issue in this area is the increasingly close and rigid link which professional bodies have tended to forge between formal education and admission to professional practice. In recent years broadened access to post-secondary learning has increased the number of qualified applicants seeking admission to professional careers. But many professional associations – often in the name of preservation of standards – have responded, not by increasing their membership, but by stiffening the educational requirements needed for admission to the profession. They have frequently stipulated the need for additional diplomas, degrees, or years of schooling, often in any field of university study. Similarly as the range of professional services needed by society has expanded, certain professions have replied not by diversifying their structure through the development of appropriate para-professionals, but by having all tasks performed within the profession.[85]

According to a number of critics, differences of opinion between professional practitioners and academics raised serious questions about how well the universities were serving the social and economic needs of the community. Such conflicts surfaced in discussions about the content of the curriculum itself. On the one side were those who believed that the major goal of the universities was to prepare students for specific vocational functions. On the other side were the academically oriented who believed that theory and research deserved greater attention. For example, in business courses, especially at the graduate level, an exhaustive study for the Council of Ontario Universities found a dichotomy between those stressing management training and those emphasizing more academic forms of business education. Courses in public administration, arts administration, and health administration gained considerable popularity in the 1960s, but because they stressed the need for a strong backing in political science and other social sciences, they downplayed the management side as opposed to the public policy side of business training. The public administration program at Queen's University and the business administration course at the University of Toronto were singled out for this deficiency. Both were criticized for responding inadequately to the current needs of the Canadian corporate community.[86]

Similarly, the Professional Engineers of Ontario, in their brief for the Lapp report, argued that the engineering schools were paying too little attention to the needs of the profession itself. They felt that aside from the basic science and specialized engineering courses, the universities should offer courses on such professional matters as the organization of the engineering profession, the ethics of practice, employment practices, and independent practice. Furthermore, the engineers felt that the educational program should be complemented by two years of 'acceptable engineering experience as a prerequisite for certification.' They praised the co-operative engineering program at the University of Waterloo where students spent one-third of every academic year working in industry.[87] That there were indeed differences even among the universities about the proper way to best meet the needs of society in this field was indicated by the fact that Waterloo offered the only such program in the province.

Even among the professional groups themselves, views were not unanimous. Both the Institute of Chartered Accountants and the Institute of Canadian Bankers argued, somewhat heretically, that for the professions to control curriculum would be disadvantageous to the notion of quality teaching since the universities were more aware of changes in theory, technique, and science than were professionals in the field. They feared an educational system controlled by professionals would be both resistant to change and possibly self-serving.[88]

Curiously, there were those in the academic community who disagreed with this testimony to their sensitivity. The CPUO contended that without professional input into the determination of course content, 'academics might be resistant to change because of their failure to recognize the problems of a changing society and their stubborn insistence on scholastic achievement at the expense of professional relevance.'[89]

Whether because academics were too conservative or because the professions too accreditation-conscious, there was considerable criticism of the universities for their failure to relate educational training to the real needs of the outside community. As the Committee on the Healing Arts observed about the health services professions, 'the existing pattern of education for workers in the health services has evolved without benefit of an overall plan of administration.' Both medicine and dentistry were criticized for emphasizing training and curing at the expense of the preventive and social aspects of health care:

The rewards, in income and professional status, are relatively low for [the latter] type of work than for other aspects of medical practice. Furthermore, and perhaps more importantly, the system is ill organized for the provision of 'comprehensive health care': including preventive medicine. The necessary technology is now divided among poorly coordinated groupings of practitioners, hospitals, community services and public health agencies.

The committee did commend recent changes in the nature of dental education which stressed more clinical work than in the past, since 'such changes are overdue in what has been a relatively rigid and unchanging program of studies.' Dentists were advised as well to pay greater attention to the value of working with auxiliary personnel in whom they had expressed too little interest traditionally for what the committee concluded were reasons of status and self-interest.[90]

In other areas as well, discrepancies were found between the perceived or actual needs of society and the thrust of curriculum development. In engineering, the Lapp report discovered that the current curricula reflected the conviction that Canada's industrial sophistication would develop more quickly than it actually had. With a high proportion of mathematics and science, as opposed to technology and business administration, courses, engineering programs were developed 'apparently on the premise that a significant fraction of engineering graduates would be making their careers in the innovative activities of research, development and design. The lack of any reliable predictors for technology, coupled with the current air of uncertainty in the economy and policies relating to national resources, makes it difficult to match curricula to the future demand for skilled personnel.'[91]

Similar dislocations were found in the field of social work by a critical observer of educational trends in Canada. After discussing the uncertainty about directions social work should take in universities in the late 1960s, the author discussed similar weaknesses of programs in community colleges:

The lack of clarity and confusion around purpose ... is even more apparent if one considers the social service worker programmes as well. These programmes, growing up very quickly and in a short space of time, have had to develop without the benefit of research or much curricular expertise. In most instances faculty recruited have not had prior experiences in social work education or in curriculum development. The model which one might expect these faculty to choose would likely be their own Master of Social Work (MSW) experience. In fact a perusal of several calendars for social service worker programmes in Ontario would appear to support this. This has resulted in curricula for community colleges, in Ontario at least, which resemble watered down MSW programmes of the late 1950's and early 1960's. They are caught up in teaching the familiar methodologies of Case work, Group work, and Community organization. Ironically this has occurred at the same time as schools of social work, particularly in Canada, have been moving away from a methodological approach. This means that community college graduates will have training that is compatible with current practice in agencies which are still staffed primarily by graduates of an earlier period, but may be increasingly incompatible with the social work philosophy and practice of newer graduates of Canadian schools of social work. While the university graduate is being given a theoretical base which will hopefully equip him to understand and adapt to a variety of practice situations, the community college graduate with a shallow theoretical base may be more vulnerable to obsolescence.[92]

In commenting upon recent developments at the university level, another respected social worker and professor suggested that the approach of tying social work education to the graduate level of the university was having negative effects. Besides leading to the creation of a relatively small élite of social work 'professionals,' such programs and their graduates were becoming 'severed from the mainstream of social activities and from the great mass of social knowledge and skill.' He contended that what the profession needed were different levels of training with the possibility of movement from one level to another and that the universities should therefore be an 'organic element' in the educational process.[93]

The case of law is particularly interesting as an example of how intense conflict could be between the professions and the academics over what constituted adequate training for professional practice. While the Law Society of Upper Canada yielded control over its training program to the universities in 1957, its Legal Education Committee prescribed certain basic courses that each law school would be required to offer if the law degree were to be ultimately recognized. Furthermore, part of the compromise reached between the Law Society and the law schools involved a process in which the former agreed to surrender control over the three-year pre-articling program to the universities, and preserved for itself authority over the articling year and the bar admission program (the licensing examination for entry to the profession in the province).

With the law schools controlling three-fifths of the training program and the Law Society two-fifths, the compromise stood. The result was the longest legal training process in Canada, and according to one author the longest in the world.[94] Since that date, critics have argued that the practice of law could be better served by a condensed training period involving either the shortening of the class-room period, and / or the elimination of the articling or bar admission programs. For historical and political – not academic – reasons, law students in Ontario were subjected to this questionable training process.

This conflict between the profession and the schools found expression as late as 1970, following a study done on the future of legal training in Ontario. The McKinnon commission observed that because the functions of the law had expanded dramatically in recent years as lawyers moved increasingly into the fields of family law, taxation, debtor and creditor law, estate and corporate law, 'the practising lawyers have found it difficult to keep up with these changes.'[95]

Despite the growth of these various specialties, the commission found a general consensus (with which it concurred) that the number of years required to become a lawyer should be shortened. Where disagreement arose, however, was on the commission's recommendation to eliminate the articling year. Students had complained to the commission about the quality of this year of apprenticeship during which time they were inadequately supervised and often compelled to perform trivial tasks. Furthermore, the increasing difficulty that students were having in even obtaining articling employment in light of heavy competition convinced the commission of the need for radical change.

While Osgoode Hall Law School (now at York University) supported this recommendation with some qualifications, as did the Committee of Ontario Law Deans, the Law Society itself, and many lawyers individually, were emphatically opposed to the proposed change. They were convinced that the practical training obtained during the articling year was absolutely essential for future lawyers. A typical comment from one lawyer captured the mood of the profession as a whole: 'To turn lawyers loose on the public when they may have never met a client, never attended in a real courtroom, never been in the Registry office and never observed or participated in a functioning law office can only promote ineptness and bring discredit to the profession.'[96]

The commission was also criticized by this lawyer for not considering the possibility of 'introducing more practice-oriented aspects into the law school curriculum.' The rift within the legal community over this issue was so great that no action was taken on shortening the legal training program. Presumably, both the academic and professional sectors remained dissatisfied with this failure to reconcile the training process with the perceived needs of the profession itself.

Finally, there were differences among the universities, the professions, and independent observers (and sometimes differences within these groups themselves) about proper procedures for the admission of students to professional and graduate schools, over teaching techniques and examination methods, and over the issue of the retraining of professionals. Both the Hall commission in 1964 and the Committee on the Healing Arts in 1970, for example, found universities using different methods to determine who qualified for admission to Ontario medical schools. In the early 1960s, apart from the use of high school grades (where standards varied from region to region), most medical schools interviewed prospective medical students before admitting them. Yet the Hall commission found that 'most chairmen of selection committees doubt the value [of these interviews] for predicting academic performance.' Towards the end of the decade, as medical schools became larger, some institutions ended this practice and relied exclusively on the student's previous academic performance.[97]

The new McMaster medical school, however, moved in precisely the opposite direction, not only interviewing prospective students but de-emphasizing grades as a primary admission criterion.[98] McMaster engaged in the heretical procedure of admitting a large portion of its applicants who had no background in science on the assumption that students with varied experiences in public service would prove to be at least as competent in medicine as those whose preparation had been based exclusively on academic training in a limited field.

Some schools also continued to have a two-year pre-medical training program for aspiring doctors, whereas others (such as Toronto) dropped this requirement. And while the medical profession placed heavy emphasis on the importance of the licensing exam that all students were required to take after their university training and before their admission to the profession, at least one renowned professor of medicine concluded that 'the exam is a crude testing instrument for this purpose'.[99] This type of diversity, of course, had its advantages, but it underlined as well the fundamental differences among doctors and educators about how best to meet the health needs of the community.

On the issue of continuing education, there was considerable controversy in most fields about the best method for ensuring that professionals maintain their competence in a period of rapid technological and scientific change. In pharmacy, for example, it was discovered in 1971 that courses offered to practising pharmacists were highly unsatisfactory: 'These programs have tended to project their information as if all pharmacists were clustered around a norm irrespective of time of graduation. This has tended to make the programs too sophisticated for some, useful to others, and not at a high enough level for recent graduates.'[100]

In engineering, the Lapp report found an urgent need to create regular programs for the continuing education and requalification of professionals. It recommended that 'periodic requalification [perhaps every five years] be initiated so as to require successful completion of a course of study in either control or management, or a combination of these two, together with a structured program in applied humanities.' Yet both academic and professional organizations felt that this recommendation was too specific and that more study was needed. While accepting in principle the need for retraining, they argued that the profession should play a greater role in determining the structure and content of the program than the Lapp commission had allowed.[101]

In amplifying the difference over this issue, the Commission on Post-Secondary Education recommended that professionals be compelled to requalify every ten years, only to have this suggestion denounced by the Ontario Region of the Canadian Society for Mechanical Engineering who felt that peer scrutiny was protection enough against the emergence of incompetent engineers. Yet in a different survey, professional engineers were found to favour requalification every five years, but they lamented the shortage of educational facilities and funds available for such a program.[102]

And in dentistry, the Committee on the Healing Arts found that although formal lectures and informal clinics were available for dentists to upgrade their skills, 'the committee is not satisfied that these existing arrangements for continuing education in dentistry go far enough towards ensuring that dental practitioners will keep abreast of improvements in dental knowledge through their professional lives.'[103] A program of retesting dentists every five years was recommended by the committee, though it was never implemented.

Thus, despite the unprecedented expansion of higher education in all areas, the province's ability to relate the needs of the economy to educational investment had not been refined by the end of the 1960s. Indeed, as late as 1977, two authors with much experience in the field concluded:

Although manpower planning has been widely discussed during the past decade, in fact very little manpower planning goes on in Canada. Aside from *ad hoc* efforts to look at supply and demand in particular sectors, such as the Royal Commission on Health Services, there has been little on-going manpower planning. The Department of Manpower and Immigration has prepared several forecasts of likely demand but it has not yet included a reconciliation of supply estimates with demand.[104]

The planning process was piecemeal and inconsistent, with decisions taken on the basis of subjective, political, and sometimes arbitrary considerations. What propelled the system on was the general belief that heavy investment in higher education produced profitable returns. But below the surface of that article of faith, specific questions and obvious anomalies went unaddressed.

Could it be otherwise, however, in a political economy and political culture in which the private decisions of competing universities determined academic priorities, where professions were their own regulators and certifiers (often for reasons of self-interest), and where the government, as a mere spectator at worst and a co-ordinator of these private decisions at best, functioned within an unpredictable and uncontrolled economic setting? For some, this process of private planning was the system's very strength. Yet as the dislocations of the economy and the disappointments of students in the early 70s indicated, it was also the system's fundamental weakness.

SIX

More Scholar for the Dollar 1968-73

Propelled by buoyant economic conditions, favoured by free-spending politicians, and buttressed by widespread public support, higher education during the
1960s became one of Ontario's major growth industries. Between 1962 and 1968,
full-time enrolment in the province's universities increased from 39,000 to over
92,000. Public funding of higher education rose from $76,000,000 in 1965 to
$360,000,000 in 1969. Over the same period, the proportion of the total provin-
cial budget absorbed by higher education rose from under 1 per cent to 11 per
cent.[1] The spin-off effects of educational investment into other areas of the
provincial economy, if uncalculated, were unmistakably evident.[2] By 1968,
popular faith in the economic value of higher education reached unprecedented
heights.

By the beginning of the new decade, however, in a shift as dramatic as that
which had inspired the rapid expansion of the system, the public attitude
towards higher education became suddenly critical. Shrinking employment
opportunities for university graduates and a growing concern about the extent
of public spending as a whole combined to transform the pervasive conventional
wisdom. The new disfavour in which universities were held had a serious impact
upon the planning and decision-making processes. The rapid adjustment that
the universities were forced to make merely highlighted and exposed the *ad hoc*
planning methods under which the system had long laboured. This chapter
explores the reasons for the erosion of public faith in the economic importance
of university education and how this affected the planning process in the early
1970s. The major themes of this study are reinforced in the analysis that follows.
The vulnerability of the post-secondary system to shifting perceptions of its
economic importance and the continuing difficulty the system had in achieving
specific economic goals were as evident in a period of economic downturn as
they had been during an era of unprecedented prosperity.

'There is no groundswell for increased support to universities. In fact the opposite is true,'[3] declared the deputy minister of university affairs in 1969. 'There is the feeling,' echoed the minister himself, 'that we have reached the end of the line; that we cannot afford to increase to any significant degree the amounts being directed to universities in future years.'[4]

Such an abrupt shift in attitude about the investment value of higher education seemed to occur literally overnight. In 1967, a Department of Manpower survey had found that there were unfilled jobs in almost all fields across the country. Industry was crying out for qualified employees. Opportunities were abundant; incomes were increasing; the optimistic projections of the Economic Council of Canada in 1965 seemed entirely justified. As late as 1968, the treasurer of Ontario could still declare: 'Education is our principal tool for increasing the productive capacity of the economy, for creating a better society, and for providing the opportunity for every citizen to develop his fullest potential.'[5]

On what basis, then, could a series of studies conclude that such faith in the social and economic value of higher education had been misplaced, that universities absorbed far too much public funding, and that the trend of reducing the student's share of educational costs should be abruptly reversed?

The scale of Canada's recent investment in higher education was documented by Stephen Peitchinis in a report prepared for the Council of Ministers of Education in Canada. He found that between 1961 and 1969, capital and operating expenditures on post-secondary education had increased from $315,000,000 to almost two billion dollars.[6] Furthermore, it was costing more every year to educate each student. Although tuition fees had been raised in most parts of the country in 1965 (evoking considerable student protest[7]), the proportion that Ontario students contributed towards institutional costs had fallen from 28.8 per cent in 1963 to 17.3 per cent in 1969.[8] In dollar terms, that did not make university cheaper for the student, but it did make it far more expensive for the tax-payer. If the costs of institutional support and student aid were to continue rising, as Peitchinis claimed they would, then in the face of 'competing social priorities'[9] Canadians would have to decide how much further to extend their commitment to post-secondary education. Apparently the Ontario government had detected a shift in public sentiment on this issue. What rationale was there for such disenchantment?

We noted in Chapter Five how strongly various economists supported the view that both public and private investment in higher education would produce measurable 'profits' both for the individual and for society as a whole. But by the early 1970s, in the face of changing economic conditions, the rate-of-return theorists began to examine previous assumptions more critically and in more precise terms.

In a paper entitled 'The University Degree as a Union Card,' and later in a full-length study, David Dodge, an economist at Queen's University, disputed the popular thesis that enormous investments in higher education produced profitable social returns.[10] The traditional method for calculating rate of return entailed measuring the public investment in classroom hours, libraries, faculty salaries, etc., against the incomes of university graduates. The latter were then compared with the salaries of 'similar individuals' who did not attend college, and the differences represented society's profit on its educational investment. A further assumption was that an individual's salary was a close reflection of his productive worth to his employer and to society as a whole.

The technique of comparing the earnings of the educated with the less educated was considered reliable only if the subjects resembled each other in all respects other than their level of education. But according to Dodge, economists (such as those discussed in the last chapter) had paid too little attention to the influence of non-educational factors in their discussion of income differentials and employee productivity. Native ability, family background, class origins, the ability to learn quickly on the job, all played a more important role in determining an employee's productivity than recent economists had assumed, and none of these related directly to the employee's educational experience.[11]

Furthermore, in such lucrative professions as accounting and engineering, the level of incomes earned was found to be greatly influenced by the barrier-to-entry techniques imposed by the professions themselves. Such artificial controls forced incomes up irrespective of the contribution of an employee's educational training to his qualifications or productivity on the job.[12] And in the less specialized occupations, the university degree was being used less as a measurement of the quality of, or potential of, employees than as an artificial means of discriminating among them before hiring.

These conditions, then, raised questions about the profitability or social rate of return on government investment in higher education. Indeed, in the professions of engineering, science, and accountancy, Dodge came to the surprising conclusion that such returns were 'negative at a discount rate of five per cent or greater.'[13]

By simply including more variables in his analysis than had other economists in previous rate-of-return studies, Dodge challenged conventional views about the value of extensive investment in higher education. The radical departure in the thinking of some economists seemed to be contagious. Other studies, both within and outside Canada, came to similar conclusions. In an investigation of the economic returns to graduate study in science, business, and engineering, Dodge and David Stager found that only in the case of Masters of Business Administration programs 'did the rate of return exceed five per cent.' In both engineering and science, there were 'large negative returns [or losses]... We conclude that there appears to have been an over-allocation of public and private resource to investment in graduate education in science and engineering in the mid 1960's.'[14]

Even the relatively high rate of return in graduate business programs discovered by the above authors was questioned by a sceptical observer of developments in the business community. In 1971, *Industrial Canada*, the publication of the Canadian Manufacturers Association, published a two-part article by a professor of business administration at the Harvard Business School, J. Sterling Livingston, which criticized the widely held assumption that management training programs adequately prepared students to perform competently in the business world.[15] Citing a variety of studies on the performance of 'well educated' managers, the author reached a number of surprising conclusions. One evaluation of nearly a thousand graduates of the Harvard Business School contended that 'academic success and business achievement have relatively little association with each other.' This investigation had sought 'without success to find a correlation between grades and such measures of achievement as title, salary, and a person's own satisfaction with his career progress.' Another study found that scholarly success in undergraduate training was an equally inaccurate guide to an individual's management potential. 'The routes to the top [in the business world] are apt to hold just as many or more men who graduated below the highest one-third of their college class than above on a per capita basis.'

Further investigations reported by Livingston revealed that the rate of turnover in highly responsible managerial jobs was greater among the highly trained than the less trained. Over half of the graduates of MIT's master's program in management changed jobs in their first three years out of school, and by the fifth year 73 per cent had generally switched jobs at least once and some were 'on their third and fourth jobs.' While the reasons for such mobility among the highly trained might at first glance be attributed to their search for more responsible and better paid employment, it was found, in fact, that 'most of the men who leave their jobs have mediocre to poor records of performance.' In analysing the career progress of young management-level employees working for a branch of the American Telephone and Telegraph Company, two researchers found that those 'who consistently fail to meet company expectations are more likely to leave the organization than are those who turn in stronger performances.'

How could these trends be explained? Deficient management training within universities was found to be the main culprit.

One reason why highly educated men fail to build successful careers in management is that they do not learn from their formal education what they need to know to perform their jobs effectively. In fact, the tasks that are important in getting results usually are left to be learned on the job, where few managers ever master them simply because no one teaches them how.

In emphasizing problem-solving and decision-making skills in their curricula, management education programs were found to neglect the development of skills required to 'find the problems that need to be solved, to plan for the attainment of desired results and to carry out operating plans once they are made.'

In a widely cited study published in 1970, Ivar Berg found that virtually no systematic studies had been carried out to investigate the relationship between levels of education and subsequent job performance. In one area where this, in fact, had been done – the American armed forces – Berg found that years of education are: '*a*) only moderately related to objective measures of aptitude, *b*) a poor predictor of success in training, and *c*) almost unrelated to objective measures of proficiency on the job'.[16] And in Canada, David Sewell came to similar conclusions. 'The data we examined tend to support the hypothesis that persons with varying levels of formal education are capable of performing equally effectively in many occupations.' The 'common sense' explanation of this situation was that on-the-job training 'may be a good substitute for formal education in the formation of many skills ... If there indeed is considerable substitutionality among these means of forming skills, the search for the formal education "requirements" of occupations becomes a futile exercise.'[17]

Rethinking the relationship of educational investment to economic growth in such critical terms led the Economic Council of Canada to reverse its own position on this issue. In 1971, the council argued that the costs of higher education had been so great throughout the 1960s that the actual rate of return on investment in the entire country had been higher in 1961 than in 1967. Thus, while the student's private investment was paying off in relatively higher wages (although not necessarily because his degree had increased his productive capacities), society's investment in him apparently was not. The council suggested that, in light of this, universities might consider charging students more for their education.[18]

In a series of convocation addresses in 1968 and 1969, William Davis, the minister of university affairs in Ontario, made his own contribution to this mood of growing scepticism. While he refused to minimize both the enormous achievements and the unmistakable potential of post-secondary education, he detected an increasing concern about the extent of the taxpayer's commitment to the province's universities. 'No longer is it possible to assume that public support will continue to be forthcoming at the level of need anticipated by the universities solely on the strenth of the role which they have performed traditionally for so many years.'[19] He advised the universities to define their priorities more carefully, to establish their relevance to the community, and to take their case to the public.

If anyone had introduced the topic of cost-benefit analysis into a discussion of university operation a few years ago he would have been drummed out of the academic community with righteous indignation. Today, however, we hear many references to terms such as cost-benefit analysis, operations research and systems management in conjunction with planning for university development. I would suggest that the danger lies, not in the adoption by the academic community of modern management methods, but rather from the possibility that universities may fail to identify accurately and effectively, both for themselves and society at large, the aims, goals and objectives of higher education.[20]

While the tone of such addresses was invariably conciliatory and polite, the sentiments they embodied were expressed in more shrill terms by other spokesmen in the weeks and months ahead. Given the scope of public investment in higher education, the universities were believed increasingly to be both inefficient and bathed in luxury. An investigation by the Department of University Affairs in 1969 found, for example, that university residences were 'unnecessarily costly,' and cited this observation in the magazine, *Canadian University*:

The day is past when large square buildings with multiple bedrooms straddling along hallways were considered substantial housing. Now 'the new thinking' dictates buildings of architectural magnificence outside and inside, clusters of rooms around stair landings instead of hallways, one-student-to-one room accommodation and a new luxury in furnishings that in some cases provides the student with a better physical environment than he enjoyed at home.[21]

This view was further reinforced by a Gallup poll in March 1971 in which 49 per cent of Canadians agreed that the costs of education were simply too high, with the largest number of those sampled identifying such items as 'buildings, equipment, too many frills and too much waste and inefficiency' as the major components of such expense. Only 3 per cent thought costs were too low and 32 per cent felt that they were about right. By contrast, in April 1965, 89 per cent of Canadians had believed that more money would be needed for education in the next few years, while only 7 per cent felt that the reverse was true.[22]

In May 1970, the minister was less oblique on this issue than he had been in the past. 'I somehow sense,' he claimed, 'that we haven't really used our dollars [in higher educational spending] in the most effective ways.' Ministry statements emphasized 'efficiency' in educational spending as the order of the day. 'The public is willing to have large amounts of public money granted to educational institutions only if these resources are expended efficiently and effectively,' warned one press release.[23] And in 1971, when the new minister of colleges and universities, John White, announced spending increases that were considered inadequate by the universities, he aroused even more consternation when he defended this allocation with the crudely utilitarian (but memorable) phrase that the government was now seeking 'more scholar for the dollar.'[24] One year earlier, Davis both captured and helped create the prevailing public attitude of the early 1970s when he noted that 'there was a time in the not too distant past when the majority of our citizens believed that almost any amount invested in education, particularly at the higher levels, constituted a wise investment on the part of the public. That feeling no longer seems to be so general or unquestionable.[25]

Such statements were not mere fickleness on the part of a vacillating government. They evolved out of a downward shift in the fortunes of the national economy. Whereas higher education had once been extolled as the key to continued economic prosperity, it was apparent by the early 1970s that the province's universities had become part of the economic problem.

The post-secondary educational system was directly affected by the two most severe economic difficulties facing Canada in the late 1960s and throughout the 1970s: rising unemployment and spiralling inflation. In the post-war world, economic growth in Canada was stimulated by a combined development of the primary manufacturing industries, especially in natural resources, and of secondary manufacturing, particularly in Ontario. As we have seen, the demands generated by these sectors provided a solid foundation upon which the educational system was expanded and defended by optimistic politicians. The heavy involvement of government in such economic endeavours was, as already suggested, a common trend in developing capitalist economies in which the state increasingly 'socialized' many of the overhead costs of industrial production and economic development. Railways, highways, oil pipelines on the one hand and unemployment and welfare payments on the other were among those costs which private industry was both unprepared and unable to absorb.

Within the industrial process, changes in the mode of production severely affected the type of trained manpower required. In the late 1950s and early 60s, it was evident that skilled workers and professionals were vital to develop, modernize, and operate the complex technology needed to run major industries. The division of labour demanded within such industries inspired the expansion both of the community college system in the province (with its heavy vocational bias) and the university system (which emphasized the training of managers, teachers, professionals, and scientists).

But, as observers like O'Connor and Galbraith have noted, the type of industrial technology developed increasingly required investment in non-human, as opposed to human, capital.[26] Heavy industry, especially, was becoming capital, as opposed to labour, intensive. Perhaps, ironically, the skilled and semi-skilled helped create much of the technology which began (and continues) to render many of their services redundant. Even as this process evolved, enrolment increased tremendously in Canadian universities and colleges. Confident that they would obtain lucrative jobs with higher education, students also realized that they could not hope to obtain satisfactory employment without some form of post-secondary training. But by the late 1960s and early 70s, the effect of these structural changes within industry was beginning to be felt. The gradual decline in the need for human capital investment served 'to expand total production and accelerated the growth of relative surplus population.'[27]

While this problem was evident in many western societies, it was exacerbated in Canada by a steady decline in the manufacturing sector where the vast majority of productive and specialized jobs still existed. Between 1965 and 1971, the proportion of the work force employed in manufacturing industries declined from 24.5 per cent to 21.3 per cent: in the western world, only Greece and Ireland had smaller percentages. In Ontario, similar trends were evident: between 1966 and 1972, while the province's total work force grew by 27 per cent, the number employed in manufacturing declined slightly from 776,831 to 772,000.[28]

This situation was explained, in large measure, by the close integration of the Canadian and American economies. Chapter Two of this study noted the extent of foreign ownership in primary and secondary industries in Canada by the late 1960s.[29] As one frequent commentator on this issue observed:

since World War II Canada's manufacturing industries can increasingly be characterized as warehouse assembly operations which rely on imports of technology, machinery and parts, and components. Moreover, as U.S. investment has more and more derived from the reinvestment of profits made in Canada from loans on the Canadian money market, the net flow of interest and dividends out of Canada has surpassed the inflow of new investment.[30]

As American companies devoted more of their resources to producing jobs and technological innovation in their own country, the opportunities for those trained in Canada diminished. The Science Council of Canada noted that between 1969 and 1971, of 25,000 scientists and engineers who graduated in Canada, only 2,000 obtained work in the manufacturing industries. By contrast, in the early 1960s, half the graduates in these fields had been hired by manufacturing companies.[31]

What prevented unemployment levels from climbing higher than they already were in Canada was the rapid expansion of the service sector of the economy, especially that segment operated and financed by the government. Those auxiliary agencies, institutions, and corporations established to buttress the private sector, themselves absorbed an increasingly large portion of the work force in the three decades following the war. Between 1961 and 1971, the percentage of those directly employed in the public sector rose from 10.8 to 12.2 per cent. Another 6 per cent were supported indirectly by government funds. The traditional response of governments in capitalist countries to rising unemployment since the Second World War has been to stimulate the private sector through tax concessions and direct grants and to expand further the number of workers employed in the service sectors. Through a combination of rising taxes, private borrowing, and the issuing of currency, Canadian governments financed their own massive expansion during this period.[32] And, as the demands on government by its own employees and creditors increased, public expenditures were quickly outstripping public revenues.

Herein lay the second source of economic difficulty for universities across the country. The public sector drained resources but produced little in the way of immediate, tangible, and obvious economic return. While civil servants, the unemployed, and universities demanded heavy financial support, their *direct* contribution to economic productivity was minimal. Thus, government spending became one important ingredient of rising inflation in the late 1960s and early 70s.[33]

Since the private sector remained the main engine of economic growth in Canada, conventional wisdom dictated that taxing corporations too heavily would discourage private investment. On the other hand, higher taxation of individuals, whose contributions to government revenues were already far outstripping those of corporations, might inspire political discontent and further fuel inflation by pushing up wage demands to compensate for these rising taxes. By the early 1970s, the solution attempted by most governments in Canada to this dilemma was to encourage private expansion and limit public spending.[34] In this way, it was hoped that the economy would be stimulated, inflation would be curbed, and government deficits would fall.

It was in this complex and contradictory economic context that the statements of Premier Davis, his ministers, and the 'new' economists should be understood. Universities were encouraged to limit their aspirations and operate 'efficiently' because they were perceived increasingly as a public burden instead of a 'shrewd investment.'[35] Had they still been viewed positively, then perhaps their growing economic problems might have been treated with greater sympathy. But the times had changed. If the growing deficit in the province's budget raised questions about the validity of the rate-of-return-on-investment theories, persistent increases in unemployment and underemployment among university graduates raised serious questions about the value of manpower planning projections as well.

As noted in chapter five, while many specific questions about the need for qualified manpower were left unanswered, the general assumption upon which universities prepared for expansion was that shortages existed in most fields. But after 1969, the unemployment rate surpassed 5 per cent and reached 7 per cent by 1975. For those under the age of 25, the rate was consistently higher than for the population as a whole. 'Softness' in the economy resulted in 10 per cent fewer companies sending recruiting teams to universities across the country in 1971. The problem was particularly acute for graduates in the liberal arts who were most likely 'to get the cold shoulder in favour of more specifically trained diploma graduates from community colleges.' In 1972, a Manpower and Immigration Department survey of 735 companies in Canada discovered that they had hired 38 per cent fewer arts graduates than in the previous year which, itself, had been 37 per cent below the 1970 figure.[36]

Even those in highly specialized graduate fields were beginning to suffer the effects of an undulating economy. A study done by the Graduate Student's Union at the University of Toronto found that of 190 PhD graduates seeking employment, only 150 had found jobs and less than half the 158 PhDs seeking employment as university teachers had obtained such posts. Opportunities for professionals including engineers, accountants, and scientists, were found to have decreased by 30 per cent in 1971, according to a survey of 1,400 companies conducted by the Technical Services Council of Toronto, an industry-run placement service. Only 19 per cent of graduates in chemistry from 34 universities at all degree levels found jobs in their field in 1971.[37] A national study involving 1,268 university departments discovered that the majority 'saw both a present and future oversupply of doctoral graduates in their fields.'[38]

A study on the 'market situation' for university graduates in Canada in 1971, conducted by the Department of Manpower and Immigration, found supply exceeding demand in virtually every discipline, every faculty, and at every degree level.[39] In a representative survey in Ontario E.B. Harvey discovered that only half of the undergraduates receiving their degrees in 1972 had found employment for which they had been trained.[40] And when the federal government's pamphlet, *Career Outlook* – once an incontestable tribute to the economic value of a university degree – reported that students in all areas were experiencing difficulty in finding both full- and part-time work, it became clear that university graduates were neither shielded from, nor capable of solving, the country's employment problems. A typical experience was described to E.B. Harvey by one Ontario student:

In May 1970, I graduated from Queen's University with a B.A. and an excellent and wide range of work experience. I then spent the next 10 months in utter and complete frustration job-hunting. Finally, I got a fairly good job, totally unrelated to my training and wishes but this was a short-term position. In the summer of '71 I began summer school and have returned to university to make up necessary courses in psychology, hoping there is some sort of job market in the discipline. However, it does not prove as stimulating as my work in English and I plan to return to work for an additional year to pay off student debts ... Most of my friends graduating in my year were similarly jobless.[41]

All of this was not to suggest that higher education had failed to fill gaps in the labour market in the past, only that now the emergence of large numbers of graduates, combined with a slow-down in the economy, had 'reduced the demand for a once scarce commodity.'[42] Thus, the economists were suggesting that, in a period of low unemployment, it cost too much to train a skilled worker, and in periods of high unemployment, the university was becoming a costly holding ground for unproductive citizens.

While the general assumptions about the investment value of higher education appeared to be changing, some economists and educators seemed both appalled and bemused by this unpredicted situation. Their comments, once again, pointed to deficiencies in the planning process. Frank Kelly, of the Science Council of Canada, noted bluntly that the over-abundance of PhDs resulted from a 'massive goof in manpower forecasting.'[43] He claimed that when asked to predict their requirements throughout the 1960s, companies kept 'mindlessly forecasting five per cent to ten per cent annual increases in research and manpower.' Universities and governments, he contended, were even more sanguine about the employment possibilities of university graduates. Max von Zur-Muehlen, an economist for Statistics Canada, pointed out how paradoxical it was that while up to two-thirds of PhD graduates might not find jobs for which they were trained, only 56 per cent of all new professors hired in Canada in 1971 were Canadians.[44]

One indication of how volatile the employment situation was from year to year was contained in a statement by George Kerr, the minister of colleges and universities in Ontario. He wondered how effectively students in high schools were being advised about future employment prospects. 'One minute we hear of a need for more lawyers in a certain area and the next minute we hear that the opportunities are no longer there; these fluctuate on an annual basis. So it is hard to be accurate in this type of information.'[45] Indeed, conditions were so changeable that, in 1973, after two years of negative reports, the *Financial Post* reported that job prospects were improving for professional students, though they were still poor for arts graduates.[46] Indeed, in that year, conditions across the country showed a marked variation from industry to industry, profession to profession, and region to region.[47] Caught in the web of these fluctuating circumstances, students in the early 1970s found their own educational plans subject to unpredicted and *ad hoc* revisions. According to E.B. Harvey:

It is evident that our 1972 sample is strongly aware of the upgrading and professionalization trends in the labour force. However, they seem to be confronting a double bind. Despite their attempts to upgrade their qualifications by specializing in fields that are relatively open for employment, they are still confronted by rapidly deteriorating labour market conditions. These graduates as a group represent those caught in the middle; they started their educational training during an expansive period when higher education led to higher status jobs and graduated in time to experience serious difficulties in obtaining an adequate position in the labour force. In short, their increasing awareness of unfavourable economic conditions has not helped this group in securing satisfactory employment.[48]

Against this type of uncertain background, Harvey and Lennards concluded that 'economic analyses alone are not a sufficient basis for educational policy formation.'[49] Like others in the university community, these authors met public criticism of the university's role by stressing more intensely than ever that higher education had incalculable non-monetary benefits that would not show up on the return side of an accountant's ledger. In response to David Dodge's work, for example, John Deutsch, the principal of Queen's University, claimed that 'the economic value of education is only one aspect, and in my mind not the most important one.'[50] Even the Economic Council of Canada qualified its own conclusions by arguing that, whatever the university's economic function, it undoubtedly produced a 'well informed, more tolerant and understanding citizenry,' a society more culturally enriched, and the opportunity for all people to develop their intellectual capacities to the fullest. In short, affirmed the council, 'education must serve the goals of cultural development and equality of opportunity as well as the objective goal of economic growth.'[51]

In the mid 1960s, as has been noted, it was assumed that greater social equality was one cultural and economic benefit that would flow from heavy public investment in higher education. But what if it were shown that in spite of such massive spending, the benefits of post-secondary education were still unevenly distributed in favour of students from privileged families? Furthermore, what if existing programs of student assistance were found to be ineffective in confronting this problem? Under these conditions, the entire approach to achieving the elusive goal of equality of opportunity might be open to question, with enormous implications for the financing of post-secondary education.

In the midst of the concern over increasing educational costs, this was the debate in which Ontario became embroiled. It was a tortuously complex controversy, evoking a multitude of viewpoints, each presented as the 'right' solution for tying a program of student assistance to the principle of social justice.[52] The following is an attempt to expose the essence, and explain the political significance, of two antithetical views (rather than to explore the minute details and subtle differences among all proposals).

The first view, and the easiest to comprehend, had been offered by the Canadian Union of Students in 1966. In March of that year, CUS published a study on accessibility to higher education that had received wide financial backing from public and private institutions in Canada. The report statistically validated the widely believed view that higher education remained the preserve of the middle and upper classes. Twenty-three per cent of the Canadian population – those in the higher income classes – accounted for nearly 50 per cent of students enrolled in Canadian universities. Another two-thirds of the Canadian people – those of working class status – comprised only 35 per cent of the university population.[53]

For CUS, this inequitable situation merely confirmed the argument that financial factors such as high tuition fees provided extraordinary barriers for the poor in their efforts to obtain a university education. The existence of high costs imposed psychological barriers as well. A university education had to be treated by society, and seen by its citizens, as a right, readily available to all, not as a luxury, accessible traditionally to a privileged elite. Thus, argued CUS, in the interests of widening accessibility, tuition fees must be abolished and living stipends provided for all students. The organization also dismissed extensive loan schemes as further disincentives for the poor, since lower-income families were the least likely to undertake large debts in order to finance a university education.[54]

But in 1969, the Cook-Stager report, *Student Financial Assistance Programs*, took issue with these claims on several counts. First, it was asserted that the public was concerned about the growing costs of higher education and student aid (an issue CUS had not addressed), and cited this editorial in the *Globe and Mail* as one indication of such sentiment:

Full time students in Ontario have increased from 71,000 in 1964/65 to a projected 162,000 in 1969/70. Student loans, grants, fellowships, and scholarships have gone from $17 million to $71 million and are extended to approximately 40 per cent of students ... How long will the majority of Canadians who benefit only indirectly accept this existing system of financing?

Thus, in light of the expense, *total* subsidization of the university system, including student living costs, would not likely be tolerated by the taxpayers.

Second, the authors argued, while the goal of universal access to higher education for all income classes was a worthy one, and one to which they were committed, it was no longer certain that this end could be achieved by merely reducing fees and providing living stipends for all. A survey of high school students convinced them that most students had decided upon their educational futures in grades nine and ten, in *ignorance* of the costs of university education. Their perceptions, therefore, were moulded by cultural and environmental factors, as opposed to economic considerations exclusively. Thus, lowering fees and providing grants would be an 'inefficient' *and* ineffective method for achieving wider accessibility.

On the other hand, the authors agreed with the Canadian Union of Students that, for those students who did attend university, the funds allotted through the present awards scheme in Ontario were insufficient. The awards neither covered the students' living costs nor took into account their foregone earnings – that is, the income they would have earned had they worked instead of attending university. Thus any future aid scheme should reflect these expenses more adequately.[55]

Third, and most important, Cook and Stager argued that eliminating fees and providing stipends would *violate* the principle of social justice. Since it was evident that the university was still an academic haven for the upper-income classes, any further subsidization directed at the entire student population would merely extend the privileges of the rich without, as mentioned, increasing the participation rate of the poor. This point was supported by a study on the income redistribution effects of expenditure on universities, which demonstrated that the taxes of the poor were already being used to boost the incomes of wealthier university graduates. 'Students whose families earn between $3,000 and $7,000 receive less benefits than their total contribution to the costs of education while students whose families earn more than $7,000 receive a proportionately greater amount.'[56] Therefore, while CUS had always argued that abolishing fees would be a progressive step, Cook and Stager (among others) now contended that such a change would be economically and socially regressive.

Here, then, was more 'evidence' that the private rewards of higher education were outstripping those of the public. If equality of opportunity could not be served by lowering fees, then public expenditures could be checked by raising them. In a proposal that was adopted by two other major studies on financing higher education, Cook and Stager recommended that students pay a higher proportion of their 'instructional' costs, while the government should devote its resources to subsidizing university research.[57]

Yet the principle of equality of opportunity was not intended to be sacrificed in this proposal. Under a 'contingency repayment student assistance plan,' Cook and Stager recommended that all students be entitled to borrow sufficient funds to cover their total tuition and living costs. To shield themselves from the criticism that under such a plan students would accumulate debts they might never be able to repay, the authors suggested that the amount of repayment be contingent on the income a student earned after graduation. If he had no income, his debt would be forgiven.

The Cook-Stager proposal was not hailed by all as the best solution to the problems it addressed. But taken together with the Peitchinis report and the draft report of the Commission on Post-Secondary Education, whose proposals for student aid were similar in principle (if different in detail), a resolution to a once contradictory set of goals was introduced into the public forum. Now fees could be raised, public expenditures could be curbed *in the interests of social justice*. If Cook and Stager were right, then a much greater burden of educational costs could be borne by the individual student without violating the principle of equality of opportunity.

When the government raised tuition fees by an average of $100 and lifted the loan ceiling in the student awards program from $600 to $800 in 1972, it appeared to have embarked in the general direction outlined by recent researchers. The budget speech of the minister reflected these changing perceptions:

There have been strong cost pressures in the area of post-secondary education in the past several years. At the same time fees have remained substantially unchanged ... The government believes it inequitable for taxpayers to bear all the cost increases; rather, the student who benefits directly should bear a larger part of the costs of post-secondary education.[58]

The piecemeal changes which followed could hardly be viewed as radical. The modifications in the fee and loan levels scarcely even approached the scale recommended by Cook and Stager, Wright, or Peitchinis. None the less, they raised the spectre of such changes and fuelled the rhetorical fires of those who were not so sure that the contradictions had been resolved.

Among the sceptics were university students themselves who, for very different reasons, provoked questions in the mind of business leaders, politicians, and the public at large about the investment value of higher education. The 'student movement' which swept across North America in the mid 1960s and early 70s subjected universities to the type of political unrest that tested the mettle of campus administrators and added to the growing uncertainty about the legitimacy of public support for higher education.

Since universities thrive on the creation and conflict of ideas, they have always been forums for the expression of dissenting and heretical views.[59] At one level, then, campus activism of the 1960s might be viewed as little more than a demographic phenomenon: the mere presence of an unprecedented number of university students produced an unprecedented number of political dissenters. Yet the events of that era were, in part at least, the product of unique sociological and historical conditions.[60]

For student critics, universities became symbols of the paradoxes and limitations of liberal-capitalist democracy. It is significant that the first, and perhaps most sensational, student eruption at the University of California (Berkeley) in 1964 occurred when a 'liberal' university was attacked for denying a group of activists 'freedom of speech.' In subsequent years, the concerns central to student politics became deeper and more fundamental. Blessed on the one hand with the rewards of the most prosperous economy in history, many students were, at the same time, appalled at the failure of society to eliminate the persistent problems of widespread poverty and deprivation.

The poor, as the previous discussion pointed out, had yet to make significant inroads into the universities themselves. As vehicles for the affluent into lucrative and prestigious careers, universities were condemned by student activists as institutions which perpetuated social and economic disparity. The university, furthermore, was not simply a neutral institution engaged in the timeless pursuit of free and disinterested inquiry. In performing research for corporations, government, and the military, and in training skilled manpower, it was involved in creating 'a new working class for the capitalist economy.'[61] Business-dominated boards of governors became targets of political dissidents because they symbolized the ability of capital to wield power throughout society. Consequently, the 'democratization' of university governments became, for many students, a vital priority.[62]

In the United States, the immediate problems of the Vietnam war (into which students were drafted after 1967), the violence of racial tension, and the location

of many universities near deprived areas of large cities, heightened the contradictions between society's lofty aspirations and its evident brutal realities, producing hundreds of confrontations on the campuses of the nation. While the
political activities of Canadian students were generally more subdued, the media
invariably sensationalized some of the more newsworthy campus conflicts.[63]

The majority of students, in fact (much to the dismay of political organizers),
eschewed direct political action, and among students themselves there were
many conflicts between radicals, moderates, and conservatives.[64] But sufficient
evidence was emerging that, in general, students were more questioning of the
status quo than at any time in the recent past.[65] Opinion polls revealed how
bemused and, at times, revolted were corporate leaders, tax-payers, and parents
by this growing polarization between the generations. In a 1969 poll, for example, Canadians listed a litany of complaints against the nation's youth. Seventy
per cent of those interviewed believed young people to be slovenly, undisciplined, lazy, defiant, demanding, and indulged. In September 1971, while 16 per
cent of those interviewed considered the current generation of young people to
be 'better' than previous generations, 38 per cent felt that it was 'worse'.[66]

There was considerable comment in business journals about the apparent
antipathy of students towards 'free enterprise.'[67] One article warned corporate
executives that 'someday radicals might be picketing your plant.'[68] W.O. Twaits,
president of Imperial Oil Limited, blamed the schools and universities themselves for failing to teach students about the realities of the business world.
'Corporate profits are not understood. People don't understand competitive
pricing,' he complained. He charged that universities were increasingly occupied
by 'talkers' instead of 'doers,' and 'the public is getting the idea that the
universities are filled with radicals.'[69]

None of this, of course, helped the image of the universities. Politicians, such
as Liberal MPP Eddie Sargent, demanded that something decisive be done about
campus unrest 'in view of the moral revulsion of the Canadian public to
demonstrations, sit-ins and property damage in universities.'[70] University affairs
minister Davis attempted to minimize the problem of student activism, but he
conceded that the universities, increasingly perceived as public burdens, could
scarcely benefit from this type of internal dissension. 'More than ever before,
higher education has become a focal point of public attention ... the greatest
amount of attention [is] usually related to the *problem* areas, of which student
activism, in its various forms, and the *costs of education* have tended, of late, to
be the most prominent.[71]

The environment in which problems in higher education were being discussed
was radically different in the early 1970s from what had been in 1960.

Complaints over the spending of too little money had turned into protests over the disbursement of too much. Traditional methods, which had been believed to guarantee equality of opportunity, were now being questioned by both liberal academics and radical students. Despite the obvious (and admitted) limitations of their own research, economists were now hailing a new economic orthodoxy. Students, they claimed, benefited more from higher education than society as a whole; consequently, they should bear a larger share of the financial burden.

The degree to which political sentiment had changed could be measured by comparing the content of opposition speeches in the Legislature in 1968 to those of 1970. In the former year, both NDP and Liberal spokesmen had sided with the university presidents in their clamour over inadequate government funding.[72] But two years later, Walter Pitman, NDP education critic, warned: 'We can no longer look at education to solve all the problems of government and the provinces and this society,'[73] and Tim Reid of the Liberals demanded that the universities be brought to account for their wastage of public funds. In rebuttal, Davis correctly charged that the approach taken by the opposition was 'not totally consistent with some of their previous observations, particularly their concern with the validity of investment in education.'[74]

The political effects of these changing perceptions were immediate, widespread and serious. They highlighted the *ad hoc* methods through which university and government officials responded to new and unexpected problems, and they exposed the presence of a policy vacuum in the field of higher education at a time when the consensus over the value of the 'educational investment' was breaking down. A number of incidents portended difficulties ahead for the university community. First, in 1968, the government allowed for an increase in the basic income unit that fell far short of the request made by the committee of presidents on behalf of the universities. While the latter had sought an 11.1 per cent increase, the government provided only 5.5 per cent more than in the previous year. This scaling down of the universities' request was not unusual. What was unique was that for the first time in recent years, the government had rejected the advice of the Committee on University Affairs on this issue: the CUA had sought an increase in the BIU of 6.2 per cent.[75]

In 1969, the presidents filed a formal complaint to the Committee on University Affairs concerning a recent decision by the Department of University Affairs to accept no financial responsibility for any new program that had not been approved by the CUA. The presidents saw this as a violation of the universities' traditional autonomy in planning. It seemed, as well, to entail the type of detailed scrutiny of university programs never intended by the formula financing system.[76] The prevailing fear within the department was that the universities were expanding too quickly and spending too freely. The CUA was called upon, although originally without specific policy directives, to seek out and impede the growth of 'redundant' programs.

Discussion over these issues was carried out openly, but conflict between the CUA, the Department of University Affairs, and the government, simmered at a less public level as well after 1970, and indicated how damaging university authorities believed the new economic environment was on the decision-making process. The premier's response to the rapidly increasing public debt (at all levels of government) had been to strengthen the role of the Treasury Board in overseeing public expenditures.

In accordance with the recommendations of the Committee on Government Productivity, the provincial government implemented in 1969 a procedure called program budgeting, which was designed 'to achieve long term planning by each department, integrated through the Treasury Board Secretariat.'[77] The government's goal was to limit expenditures and reduce the deficit without increasing taxes in the years ahead. To this end, each government department was asked, in 1970, to prepare a five-year forecast 'within constraint levels determined by the Treasury Board Secretariat.'[78]

On 8 January, 1970, the Committee on University Affairs recommended (among other things) that the basic income unit for 1970–71 be increased by 6 per cent to $1,650.[79] But on 14 January, C.E. Brannan of the Treasury Board informed E.E. Stewart, the deputy minister of university affairs and the secretary of the Committee on University Affairs, of constraint levels for the coming year. He said that the BIU should not exceed $1,640. He suggested, as well, that the CUA revise downward its request that government support for capital projects be increased from 95 to 100 per cent of cost, 'in light of the need for general constraint.' His memo also advised that the loan ceiling on the Student Awards Program be raised (thereby reducing aid distributed in the form of grants); that the committee should consider the elimination of the Ontario graduate fellowship, the Ontario scholarship program for grade 13 students, and teacher education awards; and that fees be introduced in colleges of education equivalent to those in university arts and science programs.

Three lengthy letters – from Douglas Wright (CUA chairman) to Stewart, from Stewart to Brannan (Treasury Board), and from Davis to Charles McNaughton (provincial treasurer) – objected strenuously to the specific recommendations of the Treasury Board and to the 'style of approach' used by the board to impose constraint levels. For example, Davis argued to McNaughton that the recommendation to hold the BIU level at $1,640 'is contrary both to the principles of program budgeting which we are attempting to introduce and to the well-established advisory system which has worked effectively for so many years in Ontario, through the Committee on University Affairs.' He continued:

'One might go so far as to say that the integrity of the Committee is called into question. For if the Treasury Board is going to make the kinds of decisions that Mr. Brannan has set out on its behalf, then there is reason to ask why we need an advisory body at all.' Davis did not question the right of the board to establish the total amount of money available to each department, but 'the means by which that money should most effectively be distributed and used, is surely a matter that should be left to those organizations who are devoting full time and energy to the study of such matters.' He noted that this was the third occasion in the past two years in which the Treasury Board had attempted to direct the department's allotment of money instead of restricting itself merely to establishing a global figure.

His letter provided an example of how counter-productive he believed the Treasury Board's actions were. He recalled that, while the Treasury Board had committed itself to spending $70,000,000 for health sciences development in 1970–71, he had personally objected that this amount was 'excessive,' but approval was apparently given nevertheless: 'There are going to be many people who will find it difficult to understand how a government can provide so much in the way of funds to one relatively small segment of higher education, for which plans are most indefinite to say the least, whereas it finds it difficult to provide the $114 million required for all the remaining capital needs of the universities combined.'

The argument of the CUA and the minister was based on the view that, if Ontario were committed to providing open access to all qualified students, then the financial recommendations of the CUA were the basis for ensuring that this policy was carried out in the future. But internal departmental documents revealed how much uncertainty existed within the government about the political and economic feasibility of this very goal. In a memorandum prepared by the staff of the Department of University Affairs in April, 1971, the policies of the Treasury Board and the department itself were critically evaluated.[80] The authors noted that the recent Treasury Board guidelines were founded on the premise that a 'constant proportion of students' should be served by the universities. That meant that 13.9 per cent of the 18–24 age group would be admitted in the years ahead. But according to the report:

this produces vast differences from *current government policy* which is essentially open ended and is based on ... the expressed policy of the Ontario government to provide a place in the university for every qualified person who applies for entrance. Although what constitutes a 'qualified' application is somewhat loosely defined, the policy is nevertheless open-ended ... the number of people who attend is growing faster than the general population from which they are drawn.

The report then confronted the crucial difficulty in the planning process outlined in this study. So long as students were finding jobs in the market place, then the open-ended enrolment policy (based on social demand) posed no immediate problem. The tasks of producing skilled manpower and of ensuring wide accessibility to higher education could be pursued simultaneously.

When this policy [of open-ended enrolment] was first spelled out in the early 1960's there seemed to be an underlying assumption that there were great economic benefits which would be automatically reaped from all investment in education, especially at the post-secondary level. As it now appears, increased educational expenditure will not automatically result in a better economy, and in fact many people who graduate from university may be under-employed despite consistent Government investment in their education.

The report noted that in the current situation, the lack of policy was potentially debilitating.

This is perhaps the place to reiterate the necessity for spelling out objectives as an integral part of the development of government policy. Under-employment of university graduates, while always unfortunate, is not necessarily a concern of educational policy if the objective is simply to increase the general educational level of the population. If the objective, however, is more directly related to the economy of the Province, unemployed or under-employed graduates are very much related to educational policy. It appears that the latter consideration was an important implicit policy objective of the large Government expenditures on the university in Ontario during the 1960's. In any case the necessity to outline objectives against which system performance can be monitored is demonstrated by the present situation.

Apart from the government's intention of saving money, then, the constraint program of the Treasury Board was conceived and carried out in the absence of a fully considered philosophy on the purposes of post-secondary education in a period of declining employment opportunities for university graduates.

Despite its fears about the arbitrary nature of Treasury Board decisions, about the effect of the latter's guidelines on the autonomy of the universities, and about the uncertain impact of recommended fee increases, the CUA was compelled to implement cost-cutting measures that brought it into increasing conflict with the universities themselves.

Despite some solid co-operative achievements (in the area of the operating grants formula, a capital grants formula, and the appraisal of graduate programs – see page 173), there were signs that the spirit of partnership between the

CUA and the university presidents' committee was subject to increasing strain. The presidents were distraught by what they perceived to be a serious distortion in the role that the Committee on University Affairs was intended to play. What they had expected to be an independent 'buffer' (whose major function was to oversee the requests of the universities while protecting them from the government) was becoming, in their view, 'much more an instrument of government that it was a buffer.'[81]

In 1971, the CUA was particularly concerned about the rapid growth of graduate studies in the province. To check this trend, it recommended that a quota be placed on the entry of foreign graduate students studying in Ontario. It called for a substantial increase in graduate tuition fees, as well as a limit of $1,800 on remuneration that graduate teaching assistants and researchers could receive from provincial formula funds. Following protests and representations by the presidents, all of these proposals were either withdrawn or substantially modified. The two organizations also succeeded in blunting the effects of a ministry embargo on the extension of all new graduate programs by drawing up criteria allowing for exceptions to this restriction.[82]

But in the crucial area of operating grants, the presidents remained dissatisfied with the funding levels recommended by the CUA and with those actually approved by the ministry. Between 1968 and 1973, BIU levels approved by the government consistently fell short of those increases recommended by the universities and the CUA.[83] Furthermore, John White, the new ('more scholar for the dollar') minister, augmented his constraint program in 1971 by reducing the funds allotted to Ontario graduate fellowships by $1.5 million; $4.5 million were shaved off the Ontario student awards budget; another $12.5 million fell from the previous year's capital expenditures.[84]

The presidents had looked to the CUA to shield the universities from such harsh financial decisions, but according to the former the spirit of co-operation between the two bodies was 'broken with a vengeance' in early 1972. Followed by a flurry of publicity, Phyllis Grosskurth, an English professor from the University of Toronto, resigned from the Committee on University Affairs, charging that the Treasury Board had interfered in the activities of the committee. Several days before the CUA was to make its annual recommendations to the government, a Treasury Board document was circulated to the committee, once again posing a number of alternatives for limiting expenditures in postsecondary education. It concluded: 'in order to guide the department in preparing the 1972/73 estimates, decisions as to which constraint alternatives should be following in meeting limitations are required.'[85]

Grosskurth argued that the document limited the committee's freedom of action by suggesting that it select from among a restricted set of alternatives that had already been drafted at the cabinet level. Thus, 'while the CUA would appear to be free to challenge its assumptions, it could do so only in the knowledge that the Cabinet was already considering measures discussed in advance with neither the CUA nor the universities concerned.'[86]

The presidents' worst fears were confirmed when the minister announced several significant changes in policy which had been outlined in the Treasury Board document itself. Among the most controversial were the increase of undergraduate fees by $100; the raising of the loan ceiling in the Ontario Student Awards Program from $600 to $800; and the imposition of a third-term tuition fee for graduate students.[87] On the first two issues, the CUA had given its 'reluctant' approval, much to the chagrin of the presidents and student spokesmen. On the last, the committee had not even been consulted and strongly disapproved of the minister's action. The measure sparked a discussion within the CUA itself which brought into question its entire function.

Dr. Rossiter [a CUA member] stated that the most serious implication of a third term fee was that the committee had not been consulted about the desirability [of taking such a step]. He stated that this lack of consultation produced a situation where there is a serious question as to what in fact the function of the committee should be ... Mr. [Leslie] Frost stated that there was a serious question as to the independence of the committee at this point.[88]

Although no longer chairman of the CUA when the above comments were made, Douglas Wright expressed a different point of view. He stated, in retrospect, that neither the presidents nor Phyllis Grosskurth had understood the role of the CUA. 'They had never read its terms of reference.' The CUA was not intended to be a buffer, he contended. Its role was merely to proffer advice which the government, the ultimate decision-maker, could deal with as it pleased. According to Wright, the Treasury Board document was an unexceptional paper, drawn up by the government to measure the cost of various programs. The CUA examined it and made 'its own independent recommendations as it always had done.'[89] And in this case the government had exercised its legal authority to reject the committee's counsel.

The process, in fact, was no different from that carried out by Treasury Board in 1970, although, as stated, both Wright and the minister, William Davis (now the premier) had been as critical of the Treasury Board in private correspondence as Grosskurth was in her public statement in 1972. And if the CUA's role had been misunderstood, the final report of the Commission on Post-Secondary Education suggested that there had been good reason for this confusion. While the CUA's terms of reference in 1964 had 'unambiguously' restricted it to an advisory role, in times of rapid growth, when the investment value of higher education was unquestioned, the committee had served mainly as an advocate of the universities, joining with them to expand the system on an unparalleled basis. 'The Committee on University Affairs found that it could scarcely recommend an expansion that was rapid enough. Its typical recommendations for larger increases in capital and operating grants were carried to the Treasury Board and apparently accepted without much argument.' In practice, then, the government seldom found it necessary to exercise its authority over the universities through its legal control of the CUA. But in a period of increasing financial restraint, when disagreements over funding levels were far more frequent, the presidents looked to the CUA to serve as a powerful spokesman, protecting university interests as it had done in the past:

It was assumed that the CUA, of mixed academic and lay representation, was either an advocate of universities speaking to government or a neutral body with real powers of its own, standing between institutions and government. That it was neither became clear only later, under the impact of greater financial stringencies, the government demonstrated that the CUA was not an advocate, or an intermediary, but an advisory appendage whose counsel it could accept, modify or reject.[90]

Times had changed the way in which the CUA was used, and it appeared that there was no longer an effective intermediary shielding the universities from government control. Yet government policy appeared, to the presidents, to be shaped on an *ad hoc* basis, since the only underlying philosophy sustaining it was 'fiscal restraint.' The arbitrary freeze on all capital construction in Ontario universities, announced by the ministry in November 1972, merely reinforced this impression. To the presidents, the events of that year had proved the CUA to be either a meek follower or an impotent protestor of government actions.

The presidents' brief to the CUA in December of 1972 was a shrill condemnation of actions taken in the past year: 'The universities have been faced with uncertainties, sudden changes in policy, unexpected constraints and very frequently a crisis atmosphere which have combined to make it nearly impossible to fill their role in an effective way to achieve the purposes which we all share.'[91] In their individual appearances before the CUA, institutions catalogued particular problems in functioning within restrained budgets.[92] While they could hardly be expected to understate their difficulties, actions spoke louder than words. Trent faced a $200,000 operating deficit, including a $50,000 reduction in its library book purchasing budget. Brock University provoked a sit-in among two hundred students when budget cuts caused the release of eleven part-time faculty members. The province-wide freeze on capital expenditures forced Western to withdraw tenders that had already been offered to prospective builders, and plans to renovate existing buildings were also shelved. Queen's documented the problems faced in what it described as the 'steady state situation or the difficulty of maintaining an institution's vitality when new programs are not evolving.' The universities' freedom to manoeuvre, which had been entrenched in a period of expansion, seemed now, to the presidents, to be in great danger, subject to the vagaries of the financial climate.

The planning process was complicated further by the serious problem of inaccurate enrolment projections between 1969 and 1972. As noted earlier, the model used to determine funding levels was based on social demand, that is, the demand for places in the university system by students applying for admission. So long as applicants were academically qualified, the province was committed to ensuring their access to the universities. In a period of increasing fiscal restraint, it was especially important for universities to provide the government with some idea of how high funding needs would climb in the years ahead. This could only be done on the basis of reliable enrolment projections. But from 1968 to 1970, enrolment estimates fell significantly short of the numbers of students actually registering in Ontario universities.

A series of inter-departmental memoranda revealed how much confusion and disruption this situation caused within the university system. In 1969, Wright noted that,

when individual universities have enrolment that exceeds expectations, it is not always easy to recruit the necessary additional staff immediately, and classes are temporarily enlarged, leading to some real loss in quality in the short run, and, significantly, operating budget surpluses are established. It has also become evident that in fiscal 1969–70 there will again be a total enrolment over-run in the province which, while not nearly as large as last year will obviously be of concern to Treasury.[93]

According to H.H. Walker, the new deputy minister, these difficulties had arisen, in part, from the fact that the universities' enrolment projections were based on figures considered unreliable by the Department of University Affairs.[94] The universities, on the other hand, believed that the department was unprepared to cope with the possibility that enrolment would exceed expectations in 1971, as it had in the previous two years. 'I do not wish to be an alarmist,' wrote J.B. Macdonald, the executive director of the presidents' committee, 'but unless something is done quickly I can see the very real prospects of a situation early next fall [1971] in which some thousands of applicants to university cannot find places.'[95] The response of the government was twofold: to create a formula stabilization fund in which universities would be allowed a margin of error of 1 per cent in their projections; second, the government insisted that the universities establish an application data centre to co-ordinate the admission procedures and annual enrolment estimates of universities throughout the province.[96]

But as university officials grappled with the problem of meeting possible enrolment over-runs in the years ahead, the system suddenly faced the opposite problem in the fall of 1971. In that term, students *under-enrolled* in the province's universities. Expected to rise by over 9 per cent, undergraduate registration rose by only 5 per cent.[97]

In order to assess the reasons for this unusual situation, the Department of Colleges and Universities sponsored a survey of those students who had not returned to university or community college in the fall of 1971. The study included both new applicants and upper-year students who had been accepted and were expected to enrol, but who had failed to register. Two thousand, seven hundred and two questionnaires were prepared and yielded a response of 499 cases.

While the survey was limited by the fact that no previous studies had been done on the same problem through which meaningful comparisons could be made, the results were revealing none the less:

When we asked respondents specifically why they did not attend college or university this year, we found that more than one half of the expressed comments related to financial reasons or to the limited job market. To be more exact nearly one third of the group indicated that they simply could not afford to get the money [sic] to attend this year, while another 25 per cent of the respondents stated that they had found a good full time job and had decided to earn some money. In addition to this, 7 per cent of the respondents complained about the perceived difficulty in getting jobs after graduation. [Approximately 4 out of 10 "drop outs" also] cited that disillusionment or lack of motivation led them to discontinue.[98]

Those students no longer motivated to pursue their studies cited general disillusionment with particular courses, facilities, environment, or staff of the institutions as the reasons for not returning.

This situation recurred, with an even greater impact, in 1972. In that year, enrolment fell 6 per cent short of anticipated registration. Ironically, the formula system which had originally been designed to respond to the prospect of rapidly increasing enrolment now threatened to add to the universities' problem of inadequate funding. Unless some immediate action were taken, the universities would not be able to meet their accounts.

Once again, *ad hoc* actions were required. To the relief of the universities, the ministry responded by introducing a 'slip year' formula system in January 1973, in which a university's formula entitlement would be based on its previous year's enrolment if it had been higher than in the current year.[99] The planning process, then, had been disrupted at the most basic level of enrolment projections, since no university could be certain of its size – even in the short term – in the midst of such an unpredictable economic environment.

In 1974, in an effort to secure greater stability in the funding process, a new procedure was adopted by the government. Under a 'global budgeting' system, the total operating grant for the provincial university system would be established by the government (on the recommendation of the CUA) without direct reference to university enrolment.[100] Each university's annual grant would be determined by the level and program distribution of its own student population. Enrolment, then, would continue to decide the distribution of grants among the universities, but the total provincial operating grant would be decided on the basis of less 'objective' criteria, much as it had been before the formula system was introduced in 1967. In this way, university funding could more easily be integrated into the provincial restraint program.

The prevailing uncertainty among education planners was exacerbated by disagreements between the universities and the government over the basic task of information-gathering. Efforts to rationalize the development of higher education in a period of economic restraint led the ministry to broaden its data base concerning the operations of the province's universities. While the Council of Ontario Universities (the renamed presidents' committee) was prepared to meet the ministry's demands to a point, there was considerable concern among the universities about the extent of information sought and the uses to which it would be put. The COU adopted a plan to establish a data bank that would provide a central clearing-house for all information needed by the universities, the CUA, and the ministry to plan for the future.

The COU was prepared to forward specific requests from the data bank to the government. It was intended, however, that the information would be provided mainly on a system-wide basis. Requests for information about individual universities posed, for the COU, a more 'complicated' problem. The presidents decided that the ministry should limit requests for information to 'numbers' – whether of students, faculty, staff, or dollars.

This policy would tend to reserve to the universities consideration of the quality aspects in dealing with the questions of who shall be taught, what shall be taught, who shall teach and how shall resources be allocated. The universities need for their part to develop a collective capacity to examine questions of province-wide need and prevention of undesirable duplication. Competent exercise of such a capacity will satisfy the Government and make intrusions into university decision making by CUA or DUA unnecessary.[101]

The COU, however, was overly sanguine if it felt that this statement of policy would resolve all future problems surrounding the data gathering issue. In 1971, when the ministry notified the CUA that it required data on a variety of issues hitherto unrequested, even Douglas Wright, chairman of the CUA, challenged the suitability of such a questionnaire. 'We should avoid collecting information in more detail or more frequently than is reasonable or necessary.' Specifically, he wondered why the universities should be asked for added information about the 'intake of students by program' when the Department of University Affairs already collected that material in a slightly different form. In the area of graduate enrolment, he noted that 'universities may, quite legitimately, claim that they cannot provide much valid information on long term prospects without another year's experience in the light of uncertainties associated with the policies. The credibility of the CUA/DUA information gathering program would be reinforced if such factors were anticipated and acknowledged.'[102]

The universities, in fact, were so disturbed at the extent of the information sought that they refused to provide the relevant material until they had met with the CUA to discuss the parameters of such requests. In citing several examples of how badly conceived were some of the questions, J.B. Macdonald noted that it was impossible to enumerate course registration of students in the Humanities and Social Sciences since many took courses in both. He wondered why 'diploma, non-degree and make-up students were included on some forms regarding enrolment and not others.'[103] And he claimed that there was 'very strong objection to collecting information for continuing staff, particularly "citizenship at birth." '

This last issue, particularly, produced enormous tension and debate within the university community and highlighted the fundamental conflict between the government's desire to rationalize its investment in higher education and the universities' insistence on autonomy in planning during a period of fiscal restraint. The request for information on the citizenship of faculty arose out of the growing debate in the province about the percentage of foreign faculty and graduate students occupying places within the Ontario post-secondary system.

The issue had received most sensational prominence in 1969 with the publication of *The Struggle for Canadian Universities*, by Carleton University professors Robin Mathews and James Steele. Over the next several years, scores of articles, speeches, debates, and books raised the discussion to feverish proportions across the country. Critics pointed to instances of discrimination against Canadians in the hiring policies of Canadian universities; to the fact that the proportion of Canadian professors had actually decreased during the 1960s; to the surprisingly low level of Canadian content, particularly in humanities and social science courses; and to the inability of foreign-trained faculty to supervise Canadian research topics.[104]

The general response among university faculty and administrators to this problem was critical and defensive. The presidents, for example, stressed the necessity for Canadian universities to maintain an 'international outlook' and the obligation of universities to keep their doors open to scholars and students from other countries.[105] As the University of Toronto had told the Committee on University Affairs in 1967: 'We have to be able to recruit in the United States since it would damage the entire Canadian academic community if we acquired all our needed staff from the other Canadian universities. In this we have had some success. Sixty per cent of the 106 new members of staff appointed in the first six months of 1966 came from the United States.'

The committee of presidents, while agreeing in 1969 to examine the issue, rejected suggestions that quotas be placed on the number of foreign graduate students in Ontario or on the number of non-Canadian faculty hired on the grounds that 'scholarship is universal and that citizenship is not a meaningful [hiring] criteria.'[106]

While professing no desire to interfere with the hiring practices of Canadian universities, officials within the Department of University Affairs were increasingly concerned about the apparent unwillingness of the universities to take any action on this problem. They were especially distressed at the universities' use of public funds to train and hire non-Canadians at the expense of Canadian citizens, particularly in a period of fiscal restraint. In the fall of 1970, E.E. Stewart, the deputy minister of university affairs, received a brief from Robin Mathews stating that in twenty of the largest faculties of English in Canada, Canadian professors constituted only 48.5 per cent of the staff, and one Ontario department had only 37 per cent Canadian professors. The University of Toronto department of English was singled out for its presistent refusal to address itself to this problem. Stewart was shocked at the contents of the brief. In a letter to Douglas Wright, he explained:

My first reaction was that this is just another missive on the issue of Canadianism from Professor Mathews ... But if he is even close to the mark about the attitudes of the Department of English at the University of Toronto towards courses in Canadian literature, and/or the admission of Canadian students to graduate programs, there would seem to be some case for concern. Even more damaging, however, is the refusal of the University of Toronto to produce the figures on the citizenship of graduate students so that there might be a general reaction as to the validity of the Mathews' complaint.[107]

In 1970, the Committee on University Affairs responded to the issue by seeking information from the universities on the citizenship of faculty and graduate students from each university. No individual names were requested. The committee sought, instead, a departmental breakdown of the data.

Reaction within the university community was extremely hostile. York University refused to submit the material on the ground that requests for such information violated the human rights code in Ontario.[108] After consulting with the director of the Ontario Human Rights Commission, however, the CUA found that, while it would be contrary to the code to ask an applicant for a faculty position about his citizenship status, 'it is not contrary to the code to ask for such information after an employee is hired.'[109] In 1971, the committee again sought such information, and again the universities were hesitant to provide it until meeting with the CUA. In July of that year, a meeting was held between the executives of the COU and Wright, and, for the moment, agreement was reached on this and other issues discussed earlier.[110]

The debate appeared to have climaxed in 1973 with the publication of the report of the parliamentary Committee on Cultural and Economic Nationalism in Ontario, an all-party document which took a very strong stand on the need to strengthen the Canadian presence in Canadian universities. The report noted that the number of new faculty hired from outside Canada was still unacceptably high, but lamented the fact that economic restraints would prevent the situation from being reversed for many years. A brief from McMaster University highlighted the dilemma:

We have now reached the stage in many but not all disciplines where our universities are graduating a substantial number of young scholars who would be qualified for junior faculty appointments. As well, some of our universities have attained a reputation for excellence sufficient to attract the return of some mature and highly respected Canadian scholars who established themselves abroad. It is both a paradox and a dilemma that having reached the point of developing the human resources that could significantly increase the proportion of Canadian faculty in our universities, we find ourselves in a situation of slowdown if not actual contraction, both in relation to student population and to the commitment of public funds.[111]

The debate, then, had brought into focus the conflict over the type and extent of information required to plan the university system rationally, the disagreements about the role of higher education around the issue of cultural nationalism, the justification for public investment in institutions hiring so many non-Canadians, and the difficulty of addressing this issue in a period of severe fiscal stringency.

The uncertainty and disagreement over adequate levels of spending reinforced the need for a long-term view of higher education in Ontario. The 'master plan' whose absence had been conspicuous for a decade had taken concrete shape with the minister's announcement in June 1967 that a Commission on Post-Secondary Education was being created in order to project the pattern of development of higher education within the province.[112] But it was not until May 1969, that a chairman for the commission was actually chosen. The government had sought a number of individuals of 'national stature' to preside over the commission, but no acceptable candidates could be secured. The ultimate choice of Dr Douglas Wright did little to cool the relations between the universities and the government.

According to the executive director of the Council of Ontario Universities, the presidents had not been consulted before his selection.[113] They viewed Wright's appointment as a conflict of interest since he was already the chairman of the Committee on University Affairs and, because the presidents were becoming increasingly critical of the activities of the committee itself, they were not optimistic about the future of the new commission. Fears were also expressed within the university community that Wright was too much of a 'technocrat' to deal sensitively with the 'human' aspects of higher education, and that he was too willing to impose the type of constraint levels demanded by the government.[114] The presidents decided to proceed with an extensive study of their own which they would submit to the commission as a brief.[115]

Fears over the 'erosion' of university autonomy were heightened by publication of the Wright report, or the draft report of the Commission on Post-Secondary Education, in early 1972. In accordance with the principle of ensuring accountability to the public in the expenditure of funds for higher education, the commission recommended the creation of a new provincial structure for decision making in which a 'co-ordinating board,' consisting of equal numbers of representatives from the lay and university communities, would oversee the activities of the universities on a province-wide basis. Its powers would be paramount: to establish new faculties, determine admission policies, and distribute funds among the institutions. The commission was convinced that such a structure would eliminate the tensions of the present system in which the role of the CUA had grown uncertain and confused. The new body would hold specifically defined powers, thereby shielding the universities from the government, on the one hand, but co-ordinating the system in the public interest on the other.[116]

But the COU was appalled at this proposed 'radical' change in the decision-making process. What the draft report recommended, it declared, 'was to remove from the universities all the freedoms essential to the very idea of a university. Autonomy in the decisions about who shall teach, what shall be taught, and who shall do the teaching is not a self-serving rallying cry of universities: it is an essential condition for universities to meet their true obligations to society.'[117] Thus, if co-ordination in these areas was necessary, it should be done by a body within the university community, so that the traditional freedoms of Ontario's universities could be preserved. In deference to the notion of public accountability, the presidents proposed an alternative model which recognized the need for further co-operation but allowed their own organization a greater role in the process.[118]

The final report of the Commission on Post-Secondary Education seriously modified the earlier proposal – at which the presidents expressed great relief.[119] But in the heated atmosphere of the early 1970s, the draft report had been viewed as yet another assault on the freedom of the universities in a period of fiscal constraint in higher education.

One further series of events revealed how sensitive the universities were to perceived threats to their autonomy. In 1969, proposals had been made in the committee of presidents to expand the organization's research capacity to facilitate and extend the process of planning and analysis, and to provide an effective collective voice for the entire university community. In its initial form, the new structure called upon each university to surrender some degree of autonomy to the new 'Congress of Universities' by delegating to it 'sufficient powers of initiative and decision making to carry forward at an accelerated pace the process of collective action so well begun under the auspices of the Committee of Presidents.'[120] Thus, the new body could demonstrate to the province how serious the universities were about co-ordinating their activities, while preserving for the institutions freedom of action within their own organization.

Significantly, the proposal for granting the proposed congress legislative powers was rejected by the individual universities themselves as a possible infringement on their autonomy. The Council of Ontario Universities, which ultimately came into being in 1971, lacked the 'powers of coercion' outlined in the earlier proposal, and was to function solely on the basis of voluntary action. The approach that the COU intended to follow in its dealings with the CUA and the government was defined as the principle of 'collective autonomy.'[121]

Against a background of shifting spending priorities and increasing financial restraints, then, the Council of Ontario Universities broadened its scope of activity tremendously. By 1972, it functioned with an expanded secretariat, a strengthened research division, and a budget of some one million dollars. It sponsored the activities of twelve standing committees, seventeen affiliate organizations, and ten special subcommittees, which worked on specific projects with other agencies such as the Ontario Confederation of University Faculty Associations and the Committee on University Affairs.

In an effort to deepen its own political impact, the COU no longer presented itself as a 'presidents'' organization exclusively.[122] By allowing each Ontario university president to attend meetings, accompanied by one academic representative from his own university, the COU hoped to reflect the interests of the entire university community (an approach that never fully satisfied university faculty organizations).[123] It presented briefs regularly to the CUA, it issued numerous press statements; and it initiated its own studies on various aspects of higher education in Ontario.

The COU had thus evolved from a rather informal spokesman for university interests to a massive lobby whose major energies in the early 1970s revolved around defending the cause of higher education to a government and a public that no longer held universities in such high esteem. One publication, for example, challenged the prevailing view that professors were underworked.[124] Considering their teaching, research, counselling, and administrative activities, they were found to work longer than the average labourer. The COU's brief to the Commission on Post-Secondary Education – later published as *Towards 2000* – was a sustained defence of the utilitarian value of higher education in 'post-industrial society.'

In the past, this type of rationalization and organized pressure on the past of the universities had been unnecessary, since there was little conflict between government and post-secondary institutions about the aspirations and functions of higher education. In the new era, however, the Council of Ontario Universities, together with a revitalized Ontario Confederation of University Faculty Associations and the Ontario Federation of Students, were forced to take their places alongside other lobbyists in relentless appeals for government sympathy and public funds.[125] Ironically, as the COU's resources increased, its special influence diminished – yet another sign of the political impact of economic restraint.

The most noticeable area in which the COU practised the principle of 'collective autonomy' was the field of graduate studies. As noted earlier, pressures for the co-ordination and rationalization of graduate and professional programs had been stimulated in 1966 with the publication of the report of the Spinks commission. Fearing the arbitrary limitation of graduate programs by the CUA or the government, the committee of presidents had established, in 1967, an 'appraisals' committee which undertook an on-going evaluation of new graduate programs proposed by Ontario universities. Significantly, however, the powers of the appraisals committee were strictly limited. It was

> explicitly forbidden to engage itself with questions concerning the 'need' for any specific programmes; not commissioned to assess the relative quality of the offerings of our different universities, but [burdened instead] with the sufficiently difficult and responsible task of determining that each programme which it approved would provide students with an educational opportunity fully consistent with the acceptable standards generally established for relevant disciplines in universities inside and outside Canada.

Questions of manpower requirements, program cost, or comparative program quality were outside the prerogative of the appraisals committee. Between 1967 and 1969, the vast majority of programs appraised at both the master's and doctoral levels were approved immediately or authorized to proceed within a year. Of 52 programs proposed in the first three years, only five were refused authorization.[126]

The government and the Committee on University Affairs remained dissatisfied with this limited type of rationalization. In 1971, against the background of the policy of fiscal restraint, the ministry imposed an arbitrary embargo on the extension of all graduate programs. The presidents were spurred to action once again. For the short term, following discussions between the universities and the Committee on University Affairs, numerous modifications were made to this policy. In turn, the presidents agreed that a broader, deeper, and more systematic type of analysis would be undertaken of the graduate programs of Ontario universities.

Special consultants, including some from outside Ontario, would be called in to evaluate the quality of each discipline in every university where graduate studies were offered. While these assessments were designed to make specific recommendations covering the period to 1978, it was hoped that they would provide projections beyond that year if such forecasts were possible. While the quality of graduate programs remained of major concern, the consultants were instructed, as well, to comment on the need for graduate places both in terms of social demand (enrolment pressure) and manpower requirements (employment prospects) of graduate students.

Between 1972 and 1974, the Advisory Committee on Academic Planning (ACAP) published nineteen studies on various graduate disciplines in the province. Although the studies addressed the social demand and manpower issues in varying degrees of detail, common to most of the reports was the considerable difficulty of predicting with any degree of precision, the nature and impact of these market demands. Indeed, in light of recent experience, the COU warned from the outset of forecasting difficulties that lay ahead.

How can one decide the number to recommend for total provincial enrolment of graduate students in economics? in chemistry? in religion? in planning and environmental studies? in education? Is the problem made easier or harder by asking specifically about Ph.D. enrolment? Even if one could feel confidence in employment forecasts for highly qualified manpower, one would not have solved the problem, for there are motives other than vocational which drive young people to advanced study. Since there are these cultural and societal factors and since employment forecasting is subject to the uncertainties of the economic and industrial future, and because of the high vocational and geographical mobility of the holders of graduate degrees, some persons have said we should not ask our consultants for such figures. But, of course, one must have future enrolment figures in mind to do any planning of universities. If there is an over-expansion problem now, it is at least in part due to unstated assumptions of the planners of ten or so years ago. It is thought that the best approach is to consider employment forecasts, enrolment trends, undergraduate interest and other relevant data, to make the best recommendation one can and, most importantly, to state its margins of error.[127]

These fears were borne out in virtually every discipline assessment undertaken by ACAP. Consultants faced a variety of difficulties as they tackled the manpower problem. Thus, for example, the methodological deficiencies of manpower studies done only two or three years earlier in the field of engineering, the unpredictable dimensions of technological change in fields affecting the need for environmental planners, and the uncertain future of the gross national product, all rendered precise projections on the need for skilled manpower virtually impossible.[128] Indeed, the problems inherent in manpower planning were as serious in the early 1970s as they had been in the mid 1960s. What had changed was the readiness of educational planners to admit, in an uncertain economic environment, the potential limitations of their assumptions and analyses.

In the field of education, for example, the consultants found it impossible to predict the need for masters and doctors in statistical terms.

In nearly every country, there is an absence of information concerning, for example, how individuals with counselling qualifications are actually used in the system, and what kind of skills directly contribute to the performance of particular roles. This links with a second problem: that of substitutionality. It is possible to argue that few of the highly developed skills of the education profession are of a kind that are solely and exclusively relevant to performance of narrowly defined tasks. The skill and knowledge obtained by a person who has a high level of training in educational administration do not remain unemployed and unexploited until he is promoted to a principalship. The administrative functions of the school, in common with other specialist functions, are not embodied in a single role, but form part of the responsibility of a large number of staff. Manpower forecasts tend to assume a clarity and fixity of role definition and near zero levels of skill substitutionality that cannot be justified in the present context.[129]

Because of these difficulties, the consultants attempted to predict future enrolments exclusively on the basis of social demand, although here too unknown changes in the demand for trained graduate students in education could affect the educational plans of individual students in uncertain ways.

In the field of environmental studies, the consultants plainly rejected the predictions of a recent study done for the Central Mortgage and Housing Corporation that estimated a surplus of 1,200 to 1,300 graduates by 1981. The author was accused by the ACAP planning consultants of using an extremely narrow definition of 'professional planner.' In their view, he did not account sufficiently for the employment possibilities of environmental planners in such fields as advocacy planning for citizen groups concerned with environmental issues, or of the increasing needs of local and regional governments, as well as other public agencies concerned 'with special functions or services.' While the consultants saw no need to increase enrolments beyond those currently planned by the universities, 'we see no grounds for recommending a cut-back in the Ontario planning school enrolments on the basis of manpower needs alone.'[130] They did, however, recommend that developments in this field be appraised on a regular basis in light of prevailing uncertainties.

Finally, in engineering, consultants refuted the 1970 claim of the Lapp report (see chapter five) that, because of possible overproduction, a number of doctoral programs be dropped from Ontario universities. Lapp was criticized for failing to examine adequately the various branches of engineering: chemical, electrical, mechanical, and civil. For this reason, assessments were carried out in each of these areas. None of the reports was as pessimistic as Lapp had been about the employment prospects of graduate engineers. Indeed, in 1974, when the report on chemical engineering was published, consultants found that the situation had already changed from the previous few years. This led them to the following conclusion about the value and effects of manpower planning:

Examples of inaccurate and misleading forecasts are numerous, and it is difficult to assess the damage to national needs and economies created by such erroneous forecasts. Probably the most damaging results from erroneous surveys are on the careers of young people who believe implicitly in the accuracy of the forecasts and proceed to make career decisions which may not be their preferred choice. Even at this period in time, students are witnessing a complete reversal of the predictions of the past three years that there will be a scarcity of jobs for engineers in the next decade. Thus as we observe, as a result of these forecasts, dramatic reductions in engineering, at the same time we also observe that, in fact, a serious shortage of engineers can occur during the next five years.[131]

Because of the possible development of job prospects for engineers in such new fields as environmental control and regulation, air safety, and medicine, the consultants in chemical engineering 'were only mildly concerned with the question of the job market for Ph.D.s.' In a spirit somewhat reminiscent of that a decade earlier, their recommendations reflected a rather unexpected optimism.

By 1973, decision-makers in Ontario's system of higher education faced difficult and portentous choices. The final report of the Commission on Post-Secondary Education, completed the year before and not released till 1973, highlighted the unresolved controversies over how post-secondary education should be utilized, governed, and financed in a period when society no longer had simple and certain answers to these questions. Initiated in an atmosphere where public support for universities was still strong, the report was completed in an era when such enthusiasm had been considerably undermined. Perhaps in response to thses shifting winds, the report attempted to speak to a variety of interests in its pursuit of a broad consensus.

On the one hand, it acknowledged the failure of the universities to respond consistently and accurately to the economic needs of business and industry, dismissing manpower planning as 'unsatisfactory' and cost-benefit approaches as 'partial and distorting.' On the other hand, it defended the universities by pointing to their many diverse educational and social functions in a complex technological age. Adult education should be extended; opportunities in the arts should be more widely available to the community, as should the chance for members of the working force to learn new skills. The problems of quality of life and the use of leisure time all demanded the creative utilization of higher education as well.

On the one hand, the report recognized the need for universities to be accountable to the public; on the other, it insisted on preserving academic freedom and institutional autonomy. It therefore recommended a new provincial structure allowing for the extensive participation of representatives of the lay community (not dominated by business) to accomplish the first end and facilitated the participation of members of the university community (including faculty and students) to accomplish the second.

It accepted as a 'categorical necessity' the achievement of universal accessibility to post-secondary education and made recommendations encouraging the wider participation of disadvantaged groups. But at the same time, it recognized the prevailing concern over the costs of pursuing this end and devised a financing system which would, as Peitchinis and Cook and Stager recommended, turn a higher portion of the costs over to the individual student.[132]

As noted by Dr Wright (the original chairman of the commission), it had, however, 'drawn most of its people from the existing system of universities and colleges and government advisory councils ... I think it has to be acknowledged that they were insiders and not outsiders.'[133] Thus, the very positive value attributed to higher education in the future of the province (which in many ways paralleled the views of the presidents themselves) may have been a case of educators serving as their own best advocates. If higher education were no longer viewed by the government as a viable instrument for 'improving society,'[134] then grand plans for the further expansion of the system would be unlikely to see the light of day. And by the mid 1970s there was precious little evidence of any such ebullient sentiment.

SEVEN

Students, Staff, and the State: The Politics of Scarcity 1974–80

The process of financial retrenchment ushered in at the beginning of the 1970s continued largely unabated throughout the rest of the decade. At best, the universities endured what John Deutsch had described as the era of the 'steady state' or 'the problem of maintaining viability when new programs are not evolving.'[1] At worst, they suffered through a depressing period of permanent underfunding. While they managed to avoid both massive lay-offs of full-time faculty and the closure of 'uneconomical' institutions, the impact of continuing restraint was none the less considerable. Higher education absorbed a diminishing proportion of public funds; corporate support of Canadian universities was further eroded; and an entire generation of highly trained doctoral graduates faced the dismal prospect of permanent underemployment. Perhaps the most significant development involved the emergence of collective bargaining, including the unionization of large sections of university faculty – a prospect considered ludicrous (if pondered at all) only a few years earlier.

By 1980, government policy, shaped primarily by economic imperatives, had produced an opposite, if still unequal, reaction within the university community. Presidents, students, and faculty (unionized or not) could protest inadequate grants but could do little to alter them. The full historical significance of these strains was, of course, unclear by the end of the 1970s, and this chapter only cautiously engages the discussion. But the events themselves were compelling enough to justify examination; for while the myriad tensions found new forms of expression, the problems that created them were already well known. Unfortunately, workable solutions remained as elusive as ever.

University lobbyists in the last half of the 1970s complained accurately, and with tedious regularity, about the inadequacy of government support for higher education. Annual grants failed to keep pace with inflation, failed to match consistently the recommended increases of the government's own advisory body, and failed to meet fully the cost of the government's declared 'objectives' for post-secondary education. Equipment and facilities were deteriorating, library budgets were evaporating, and new hirings reached a virtual standstill.[2]

Within the public sector, however, none of these problems was unique to the universities, and none departed significantly from the patterns established in the first part of the decade. Indeed, in December 1977, following its re-election (once again on a minority basis), the Conservative government inaugurated a new restraint program designed to balance the provincial budget by 1981.[3] This, of course, had a debilitating effect on most publicly funded programs and institutions. But more significant was the compilation of new statistics demonstrating that within the public sector as a whole, and in the education field specifically, the standing of the universities had slipped considerably. While grants per student in elementary and secondary schools had increased 33.2 per cent (in real terms) between 1970/71 and 1979/80, during the same period grants per university student *fell* by 13.1 per cent. Despite their own severe budgetary problems, hospitals too, fared better than the universities in the last part of the decade. Between 1972/73 and 1979/80, the universities' share of total provincial expenditures declined between 12 and 15 per cent (depending on the inclusion or exclusion of debt servicing).

Community colleges by no means prospered during this period either, but they also bore less of the financial brunt than the universities. Between 1973/74 and 1977/78, per student grants to the former *exceeded* those of the latter by 8 per cent. Perceived as more pragmatic educational institutions, colleges maintained a more favourable public image. While university enrolments slipped and as their graduates entered the market place with fewer options and lower expectations, the colleges were forced to refuse admission to thousands of qualified applicants who were undoubtedly responding to the CAATs' more enviable placement records. At Ryerson, an institution long praised by the media for its service to industry, seven of 26 departments in 1977 turned away one-third of the qualified applicants.[4]

The government's own preoccupation with vocationally oriented training was indicated by its creation in 1976 of an Ontario Industrial Training Council. In response to the high unemployment levels among young people between 18 and 24 years of age, in reaction to the failure of universities and colleges to serve adequately the needs of youth lacking academic inclination or ability, and in recognition of the unwillingness of business to pay the high costs of skilled training, the ministry authorized this new body to evaluate, recommend, and co-ordinate efforts to reconcile manpower surpluses with industrial requirements. In no other post-secondary area did the government embark on comparable initiatives during this period.[5]

Furthermore, the support Ontario provided its universities compared unfavourably with the situation in other provinces. From 1974/75 and 1980/81, Ontario's position declined from seventh to tenth in terms of grants per full-time student, and over the same period the other nine provinces increased their operating grants at a rate 'about 65 per cent greater than in Ontario.' On the other hand, in 1978/79, the province supported its hospitals and elementary and secondary schools at the third highest level across the country.[6]

The financial difficulties of Ontario universities worsened in 1977 as a result of a new federal-provincial funding arrangement in the fields of higher education, medical insurance, and hospital support. For the latter two areas, conditional terms were attached to the funds provided by Ottawa through the Established Programs Financing Act. In the former, the provinces were freed from specific guidelines. Ontario used this new found flexibility to redirect funds once spent on higher education to alternative priorities. According to Liberal MPP, John Sweeney, in 1979 Ontario diverted to other purposes $37 million of the $88 million intended for higher education. The provincial government did not dispute that it had disbursed Ottawa's money in this way. It claimed only, and correctly, that Ontario was not *legally* obliged to allot these resources to postsecondary education. Partly in response to provincial spending restraints, which effectively increased the federal share of university operating costs above the 50 per cent level it was intended to cover, Ottawa announced in the fall of 1981 plans to reduce its commitments and direct remaining grants to prescribed 'national purposes – in this case, job-oriented educational programs.'[7]

The declining priority of post-secondary education can be demonstrated, at least indirectly, in another way. In 1978 both the Liberals and New Democratic party were prepared to withdraw their support for the minority Conservative government unless it modified plans to increase drastically provincial health insurance premiums. At no time, however, did the economic fate of the universities inspire from the opposition parties such militant political threats.[8]

The litany of financial woes seemed endless, evoking this depressing conclusion from the Council of Ontario Universities: 'By direction or indirection, a shift in priorities has occurred in provincial government spending patterns in Ontario despite the government's assertion that higher education in Ontario continues to be a matter of high priority ... Where once the province did more than most to support its universities, it now does less than most.'[9] In the words of the Ontario Council on University Affairs, the government's advisory body, by 1979 Ontario housed a university 'system on the brink'.

Institutions seeking economic respite from benefactors beyond the provincial government failed to find it. Research support from the federal government, always a source of concern among university officials, experienced further erosion in the 1970s. In 1974 Ottawa actually reduced its support of university-based research activities, and from 1975 to 1979, real dollar contributions to this area remained constant. From 1967 to 1979, for the country as a whole, the ratio of research and development to the gross national product steadily declined. Compared to other industrialized countries, Canada was especially parsimonious in this area. Germany and Japan, for example, increased their contributions to research and development throughout the 1970s, and while the United States' and the United Kingdom's funding of R&D suffered some erosion, by the end of the decade their proportional spending in this field was still more than double that of Canada's.[10]

Private sector support for higher education, never substantial in Canada at the best of times, was even less impressive as times grew worse. In fact, most 'charitable' organizations faced increasing difficulty raising funds in the 1970s, but Canadian universities suffered more than the average. Annual surveys of approximately three hundred major companies between 1971 and 1978 revealed that the percentage of the corporate donation dollar going to higher education fell from 37 to 25 per cent. The studies also confirmed the continuation of patterns outlined in chapter three: American-controlled subsidiaries of companies operating in Canada gave less of their charitable contributions to universities than did Canadian-controlled companies.

One corporate executive from the 'food group' explained declining company interest in universities in this way. 'We have a growing feeling that the universities have been extravagant in both over-building and in operations and in keeping excess staff. We are switching our giving from universities to community projects in areas where we operate.' Some companies, too, expressed concern about the 'productivity' of professors who 'spend too little time teaching ... and too much time researching books and articles for a fee.' The alleged fostering of 'anti-business' attitudes among undergraduates concerned other corporate leaders as did the inadequate level of literacy among recent graduates working in industry.[11]

Since capital building projects had slowed to a virtual halt, and since this had traditionally consumed the highest proportion of corporate support for universities, yet another reason could be found for diminishing company interest in higher education. Significantly, the priority for business did not shift to operating areas – still considered the responsibility of government – but increasingly to student aid and scholarship programs designed to seek out and reward the country's most promising and productive citizens.

Despite these changes, it was unlikely that corporate aid to universities would ultimately disappear, anymore than would the value companies derived from the existence of publicly funded higher education. As Richard Hopkinson, president of the Institute of Donations and Public Affairs Research, concluded, 'universities are not charities in the sense that health and welfare, culture or other causes are ... Industry draws many of its executives from universities [and] works with them in the research area.' There was some feeling, in fact, that as government support for universities declined, the private sector might usefully occupy the vacuum, further reducing government control of higher education and giving the universities an opportunity 'to develop courses for the student body which would give some understanding of the meaning, importance and rationale for the private sector in Canada.'[12]

With some exceptions, then, corporate leaders appeared to believe that the financial squeeze on Canadian universities was no particular evil.[13] If it forced them to streamline their operations, eliminate redundant faculty, and drop programs that produced surplus graduates, then so much the better. With fewer dollars, universities might well produce more value for each scholar – a development that would make both public and private support of higher education, from the corporate perspective, easier to justify.

If the supply of operating funds squeezed the universities at one end, the uneven demand for graduates continued to impose strains at the other. The employment conditions for degree-holders did not prove as catastrophic in the late 1970s as some had feared earlier, but throughout the decade the situation proved far from enviable for large numbers of new graduates.

An Ontario survey of 1974 graduates conducted by Statistics Canada revealed the following conditions: the unemployment rate three months after graduation for those with bachelor's degrees was 11.9 per cent; for community college graduates, 9 per cent. For graduates from the humanities, social and behavioral sciences 20 per cent were unemployed. And after more than a year on the labour market, 'the graduates' unemployment rate was still high by traditional standards': 7.2 per cent for bachelor degree-holders and 6 per cent for college grads.[14] A nation-wide survey covering 45 per cent of the 97,000 students who graduated from colleges and universities in 1976 confirmed the earlier patterns: two years after graduation, 8.2 per cent of university degree-holders were unemployed, as were 6.7 per cent of former community college students.[15]

These findings were somewhat moderated by an Ontario Ministry of Education study of 1979 university graduates: eighteen months after graduation, 4.9 per cent were unemployed. And initial results of a 1980 Statistics Canada survey of university and college graduates across the country (year of graduation unspecified), showed a 2.8 per cent unemployment rate for university graduates and a 4.3 per cent rate for college graduates. This finding produced ecstatic exclamations from a spokesman for the Council of Ontario Universities. 'The myth about the unemployed graduate,' he claimed, 'has been exploded.'[16]

His glee was probably unwarranted. Like any statistical research project, unemployment surveys produced results that were influenced very much by the type of questions asked and variables used. The last survey cited, for example, which combined those graduating in the 1970s with their counterparts in the 1960s (when conditions were generally better) unsurprisingly found lower levels of unemployment for university graduates than those studies (also cited above) which looked only at 1970s degree-holders. Survey results which distinguished graduates on a regional basis would differ from those which looked only at national samples. Those which confined themselves to the graduates of a single year were bound to depart in their findings from those that did not. Finally, a full profile of employment conditions for university graduates was bound to elude those who failed to distinguish among types of jobs that the educated held. One searches, at times in vain, for consistent approaches used in employment surveys during the 1970s. Newspaper headlines bemoaning the plight of university graduates were followed within months by those which hailed the marketability of a university degree.[17] Still, from amid the mire it is possible to emerge with a clear if imperfect picture of the fate of university graduates in the last part of the decade.

On the basis of survey results already noted, it appears that the employment situation for university students was uncertain and variable. Consistently, however, the unemployment rate of students graduating with bachelor's degrees (in the 1970s) was higher than that for community college graduates. Graduates in the humanities fared worst of all. On the other hand, engineering, science, and the health disciplines continued to offer promising employment opportunities. In terms of salary, university graduates earned at the end of the 1970s considerably more than working Canadians without degrees and almost $3,000 more than college graduates.

While the proportion of women graduating from universities and colleges climbed considerably in the 1970s, the rewards they reaped compared poorly with those of men. According to the survey of 1976 graduates, the average university and college male was found to earn $2,000 more per year than the average female. 'This income gap was greater at the college level than among university graduates,'[18] and widest among employees of the federal government. While the expansion of post-secondary education had opened career doors for women, market vagaries combined with traditional prejudice to reinforce their traditionally inferior status in the working world.

The most serious problem confronting university graduates, and the real story of employment patterns in the 1970s, was the dilemma of underemployment. According to a 1973 national survey, 21 per cent of persons with general degrees held jobs that required no post-secondary education. The survey covered the entire population. 'Had only the young being included, it is likely that the percentage would have been higher.'[19]

A 1976 survey also found that over one-third of university degree holders were underemployed (i.e., over-qualified) and only 42 per cent of university graduates believed that their jobs were directly related to their education (compared to 65 per cent of college graduates). Evidently university graduates were increasingly displacing their less educated counterparts in jobs traditionally held by the latter. And post-secondary students of the 1970s, in numbers far greater than in the past, were taking up jobs unrelated to their educational training. While many resigned themselves to their fate, and while some even found new life in these unexpected career placements, Statistics Canada concluded that 'the hard reality of today's labour market is a rude jolt to many graduates fresh out of college or university. Disappointments may run high during the first few years after graduation.'[20]

Disappointment would appear to have been especially the fate of graduates from Ontario colleges of education. So unprepared was the province to deal with the (predicted) drop in school enrolments in the 1970s, that in the midst of the crisis (1977) the government sponsored a commission to investigate the problem, headed by Robert Jackson, a demographer and former director of OISE. Precise statistics on the number of unemployed education graduates were hard to come by since the colleges did not keep track of the employment histories of their graduating students. What was known, however, was shocking enough. In 1971, of the total number of graduates (qualified to teach both elementary and secondary school), 63.3 per cent had teaching jobs in Ontario. By 1976/77 that figure had fallen to 43.28 per cent. Clearly, a significant proportion of the remaining graduates were working elsewhere. But according to Jackson, there was little room for complacency about the fate of many. In an effort to determine the career patterns of college graduates who had left teaching, four studies were conducted. While the results were far from comprehensive, they produced this conclusion:

The findings ... do not support the claim that teacher education can be considered a form of general education and a useful preparation for occupations unrelated to teaching. The reactions of the respondents were largely negative, some even in regard to the usefulness of their training for teaching in schools, although the experience gained in practice teaching was often viewed more positively. Admittedly, the respondents may have felt bitter and cynical about their experiences, and indeed some classified their undergraduate university education as also being of little value to them in their non-teaching positions. Possibly the value of both the undergraduate program and teacher training will become evident as time goes on, but certainly the responses I received raise grave doubts in this regard.

Undoubtedly, university and college graduates continued to fare better both in terms of employment opportunities and salaries throughout the 1970s than Canadians with no post-secondary education. Still, for aspiring degree-holders, the future was not what it used to be. 'Graduates of some programs may have to accept low paying jobs which provide little responsibility, little opportunity for individual initiative or advancement and hence minimal satisfaction. In a word these graduates may consider themselves underemployed.'[21]

Underemployment after three or four years of post-secondary education was one thing: after ten or eleven years, it was quite another. Doctoral graduates of the later 1970s were among the hardest hit by deteriorating employment opportunities. While statistical surveys of postgraduate students were often as confusingly contradictory as those for undergraduates, the fate of the former group is somewhat easier to decipher. The reason is simple. Most doctoral students aspired to full-time, tenure-stream teaching jobs within Canadian universities. But by the end of the decade most universities had stopped providing such opportunities.

Involuntary unemployment of doctoral graduates was relatively low throughout the decade. A survey by Brian Wolfe of 1976 Ontario PhD graduates revealed that, two years after graduation, only 3.1 per cent were actively looking for work.[22] However, the proportion of PhDs who considered themselves to be underemployed was far higher. According to the same study, one-third of all the employed graduates believed their jobs to be less than suitable for individuals with their education. In the humanities and physical sciences only 50 per cent felt their qualifications matched their employment.

In most respects, humanities graduates fared far worse than their counterparts from other disciplines. Less than 75 per cent of this group held full-time jobs, 17 per cent worked part-time, and 8 per cent were involuntarily unemployed. On the other hand, only 4.2 per cent of graduates from other areas were employed part-time.

A national survey conducted by Statistics Canada revealed that 47 per cent of all working PhDs were dissatisfied with their promotion and career prospects. Those working in universities had good reason for displeasure. According to a report by Linda Moffat, 'It appears that Ontario is moving rapidly to an academic job market which is almost entirely a short term, non-tenure stream market composed of young Ph.Ds who have not given up on the dream of a permanent academic position and of clinicians who expect to have only an intermittent association with the university.[23] Similarly, in a study cosponsored with the Ontario Confederation of University Faculty Associations, the Council of Ontario Universities, in a rare moment of critical self-evaluation, described the consequences of hiring policies practised by some of its own members. Intent on cutting costs, Ontario universities were 'turning increasingly toward term appointments ... One university – to take the extreme case – is reported to have announced its intention of having forty per cent of its faculty in non-tenurable positions. Others are pursuing similar, if less draconian objectives.' Such practices, according to COU and OCUFA, would 'create second-class citizens of the university community unable to participate fully in various aspects of its life and work or to plan their lives and careers with reasonable hope.'[24]

Aspiring university teachers faced a demographic problem as well. The vast majority of tenured faculty were still relatively young (on average 41 years in Ontario by 1976), and even those who retired were frequently not being replaced. If attrition rates failed to reduce staff complements sufficiently, then the fate of young, recently tenured faculty was also uncertain. At best, most new PhDs were being offered 'a series of one or two year teaching appointments at a variety of different universities each with a heavy teaching load and often a rather low salary.'[25]

At this level too, women, who had entered graduate programs in greater numbers during the late 1960s and early 70s than they had previously, found themselves at the lowest end of the professional scale. 'Women are more frequently in the highly mobile low rank appointments than men and are subject to more family related job mobility than are men.' In addition, 'the probability of a female earning less than $15,000 was almost twice that of males.'[26]

Had the slack been taken up by institutions beyond the university world, then the prospects for secure, lucrative employment might have been enhanced. The survey of 1976 Ontario doctoral graduates found 17 per cent working for government and only 10.7 per cent working for industry. The implications of this situation were serious. It suggested 'that most of Canada's research and development is being done at Canadian universities. If this is the case, the impending decline in faculty appointments may affect Canada's research potential because young scientists with new ideas may not have access to the resources they need.' Industry's poor showing in this area was undoubtedly complicated by the dependent branch-plant nature of the Canadian economy. As we noted earlier, corporations preferred to sponsor research in the residence of the parent company as opposed to the countries of their foreign subsidiaries.[27]

Thus the effect of funding restraints on the personal lives of graduates and the intellectual resources of the nation, particularly in the areas of the humanities, were profound, and by 1980 showed no signs of improvement. According to Brian Wolfe:

One must be concerned about the effects of possible reductions in enrolment in humanities at all levels (i.e. undergraduate and graduate levels). Although from an individual point of view, the decision not to enrol in a humanities program may be correct, the costs to society of large numbers of potential students making this decision may be very high.[28]

As it had in the past, economic exigency shaped the politics of higher education in the last half of the 1970s. New players starred in old roles in the final act of this spectacle. With choreography far from crisp, performers from the Ministry of Colleges and Universities, the Council of Ontario Universities, and the Ontario Council of University Affairs (which in 1974 replaced the Committee on University affairs) once again pirouetted their way through a three-cornered dance, each catering to its own section of a bemused provincial audience. At stake was the future of higher education in Ontario.

The most reliable indicator of the low priority accorded Ontario's universities can be found in the province's successive budgetary allotments. But other developments are almost as telling. Between 1971 and 1975, the Ministry of Colleges and Universities was presided over by no less than five different cabinet members. Within that period no one held the post for longer than twenty months. Two occupied it for less than a year. Only with the appointment of Harry Parrott (1975–78) and Dr Bette Stephenson (1978–) was a modicum of stability re-established in the portfolio. By contrast, between 1959 and 1971, the ministry (which remained part of the Department of Education until 1964), had been headed by only two men – John Robarts and William Davis – both of whom ascended to the premiership. In the earlier period, the high-profile and popular education posts served as useful stepping stones for upwardly mobile politicians. Though the political future of Dr Stephenson was unclear by the end of 1981, her predecessors endured – if briefly – the fortunes of a politically diminished and politically less rewarding office. As minister, Davis had had the enviable task of sponsoring a system in rapid growth. When universities appealed for funds, he was able to earn plaudits and avoid recriminations by largely acceding to their requests. The ministers of the 70s, however (including Stephenson), were bogged down in a far more adversarial relationship with the institutions they oversaw, and the experience took its toll in personal and political terms.

Though well enough liked by university officials, Jack McNie (1972–74) apparently aggravated his poor health in the demanding job and resigned within a year and a half.[29] On the other hand, John White (1971–72) and James Auld (1974–75) were perceived far less favourably by university spokesmen; they faced biting and sometimes rude criticisms across the conference table, and unkinder cuts still out of ear-shot. While both were considered influential in the cabinet, neither was seen as accessible or sympathetic to the non-utilitarian functions of the modern university. Auld, a master politician, regularly frustrated his inquisitors with cleverly elusive responses. Harry Parrott, the Woodstock dentist, meanwhile, was both accessible and sympathetic, but considered by the universities a weak link in cabinet circles. But his unpretentious style and dogged working schedule eased, in part, the personal tensions between university and ministry officials.

Though only in their positions for short periods, most ministers had special educational interests that were in part reflected in the policies they produced. George Kerr (February to September 1972) helped resolve the long-standing question of funding for church-related colleges and universities. Jack McNie's concern for adult education helped focus greater attention on this problem, and led to added financial assistance for part-time students. James Auld was especially interested in questions of university finance, and Parrott devoted more attention to the student aid question than all of his predecessors. In the words of one ministry official, 'it coloured everything he did.'

But the frequent turnover of ministers in many ways severely limited their ability to mould their department in their own images. University matters were left largely in the hands of deputy ministers, their assistants, and the advisory institutions already well entrenched. James Gordon Parr held the post of deputy minister of colleges and universities from 1973 to 1978. A former dean of engineering at the University of Windsor, he served as chairman of the Committee on University Affairs for a brief period before assuming the deputy's post. Parr brought to the ministry an unorthodox appearance (flashy bow ties and bold checked suits) and a conservative, if eclectic, set of academic values. His speeches and various convocation addresses, written with immense eloquence and literary style, exposed a probing mind and widely read background.[30] Almost passionate in his idealism about the purposes and potential of higher education, he was none the less fervently committed to the policy of fiscal restraint, and he grew impatient with the universities' continual carping about underfunding. For Parr, the end of expansion offered the universities a unique opportunity to exploit their autonomy and potential creativity by channelling admittedly diminished resources into imaginative academic endeavours. Why, for example, had the universities not used more effectively the abundant new technology to develop original teaching techniques (which could, in the long run, save public money)? Why had they opted for the expensive and inflationary promotion model of automatic progress through the ranks, with minimal emphasis on the criteria of merit? And why did university professors not endure the lean years with the confidence that they *were* in fact privileged – employed, unlike most working people, in jobs they loved?

While Parr devoted more of his working hours to the problems of the less mature and far less autonomous community colleges, when he did meet with university representatives, he would put these challenges to them, expecting to stimulate a high level intellectual exchange in response. Instead, he heard all too frequently the simple demand for more money. While he may well have seen himself as a devil's advocate in this role, more often than not the universities perceived him as the devil instead, with little sympathy for their cause. Yet his relatively long tenure in the position provided the ministry (and its changing round of ministers) with some stability in an otherwise turbulent period.

Since 1974, much of the ministry's day-to-day activity has been overseen by the assistant deputy minister, Ben Wilson, outwardly a more traditional civil servant, less philosophical and more uncomfortable defending unpopular decisions than his immediate superior. Few significant policy matters, from student aid to the formula system, failed to pass through his office for advice and comment. He regularly mediated between the ministry and university spokesmen, and though he was often the first to bear bad news, he was respected in most quarters for his brave pose and usual frankness.

What united these individuals, with their different talents, interests, and personalities, was, however, far more important than what distinguished them. In an era of fiscal restraint, their freedom of action was heavily constrained. While some coated with sugar the bitter pills they served, they were none the less compelled to feed their patients distasteful medicine.

As we have already seen, relations between the ministry and the Committee on University Affairs on the one hand and the CUA and the universities on the other were far from smooth in the early 1970s. Considered impotent by the COU and too soft on the universities by the government, the CUA was unenviably caught between the devil and the deep blue sea. Its image problems continued to be damaged by the absurd, anachronistic arrangement in which the deputy minister served also as the secretary of the CUA itself. When J.G. Parr moved directly from the chairmanship of the CUA to the deputy minister's post, the committee's claims to independence appeared even more tentative.

Reva Gerstein, a psychologist (and well-known Conservative), became chairman of the CUA in 1973 and attempted to reassert the committee's autonomy from government. The CUA no longer employed the deputy minister as its secretary and in fact permitted ministry officials to attend its meetings only upon invitation. It did, however, continue to depend upon ministry staff almost exclusively for research assistance. While Gerstein's brief term failed to prevent the drift to the policy of restraint, it did produce one other important innovation. The CUA's annual report now contained a full list of all recommendations made to the government and included as well the government's response to each.

Following the publication of the report of the Commission on Post-Secondary Education, the organizational structure of the CUA was revised. While the scope of the new Ontario Council on University Affairs (OCUA) was more limited than the role prescribed for it in the COPSE report, and while it remained unabashedly an advisory committee, its new title, new chairman, and substantially revised membership appeared to offer the possibility of a clean slate. By 1974, the universities, though regularly outraged by insufficient funding, had slowly adjusted to the new economic realities by privately lowering their expectations. Still, they harboured the hope that the new OCUA might flex its muscles on their behalf in a more effective way than the recent advisory body.

The new chairman was Stefan Dupré, a political science professor at Toronto, who had in recent years split his time between teaching and carrying out government studies in the field of educational policy. A reasonably popular choice, Dupré brought his deceptively clever talents to bear on the committee in a number of interesting and innovative ways. Upon taking the job, he insisted on direct access to the premier whenever he deemed it necessary. On the basis of a handshake, Davis accepted Dupré's terms.[31] In general, Dupré communicated with the ministry from an arm's length distance more effectively than had his predecessors. (A symbolic but significant step was the removal of the OCUA's quarters from the Mowat Block at Queen's Park, which housed the MCU, to a downtown office). Dupré always forewarned ministry officials of forthcoming council statements and generally received the same courtesy in return.

Among a wide variety of policy concerns, three important matters stand out in the work of Dupré and the OCUA. Continuing Gerstein's approach of publishing council recommendations and government responses, Dupré went one step further. In order to expose the *reasoning* behind council deliberations, the OCUA published its full set of memoranda to the minister which included its recommendations. The annual reports also contained the minister's letters in response, though these were generally far less fully argued. The result was a more extensive body of documents involving deliberation over university matters than had ever been produced publicly by such an advisory body.[32]

In the area of formulating advice on operating grants, the OCUA employed an exquisitely clever technocratic tactic which temporarily served the universities well. Fully aware that most financial decisions at the ministry level had been made in a policy vacuum, the council had obtained from the government in 1974 the most precise statement of 'objectives' for the funding of higher education in recent years. These were threefold: '1) to offset inflationary trends, 2) to maintain or improve existing levels of service, and 3) to accommodate predicted enrolment increases.' The council then proceeded to analyse closely and *cost* each of these goals. The first of these (offsetting inflationary trends) was a clear, even hopeful, sign for the universities. The second, however, was ambiguous; essentially, the council dismissed as rhetorical the government's alleged desire to *improve* service, since its recent funding provisions had made this impossible. Instead the OCUA reformulated this proposal to read only 'to maintain existing levels of service.' The third objective was equally equivocal. "Accommodating predicted enrolment increases' failed to address the historical distinction made in practice, if not in theory, between the treatment of undergraduate and graduate (including professional) enrolments. While the former was more or less open-ended, the latter area had employed over the years both direct and indirect enrolment controls. Thus the OCUA interpreted the government's third objective to mean the 'accommodation of predicted enrolment increases at the undergraduate level [only].' Finally, the OCUA added a fourth objective of its own: 'to maintain the financial viability of the university system.'

Having critically evaluated and revised government statements for semantic clarity and economic realism (which in the case of the second and third objectives might well impose greater financial restraints on the universities), the council then set out to assist the universities by stretching to the limits the amended objectives. It concluded, after comparing the latest budgetary allotments with official goals, that 'there is evidence that Government funding of the university system failed in [1975/76] to meet the costs of the Government's own objectives.' According to this formula, operating funds were $16.2 million less than they should have been.[33]

Partially in response to these arguments, which essentially placed a price tag on the government's own rhetoric, and determined as well by the extremely lean financial period from 1974 to 1976, the government, in accordance with OCUA's recommendations, increased the operating grants for 1976/77 by an almost unprecedented (in recent years) 14.4 per cent. For 1977/78, the OCUA's financial recommendations were also met, though a tuition fee increase in that year brought in part of the additional income from the system's users. Still, the latter increase failed to satisfy the universities and did little to rescue the system from the general impact of constraint.[34] The universities, however, had been partially protected by the government's decision (also on the advice of the OCUA) to revise the enrolment-based operating formula. Because annual registrations were fluctuating so unpredictably each institution's operating grant was now allotted on the basis of a three-year average of its (weighted) undergraduate student enrolment.

In subsequent years the government returned to its recent pattern of rejecting OCUA's advice on operating grants and, significantly, it no longer articulated its objectives as clearly as it had in 1974, rendering ineffective the 'costing' approach.[35] Reinforced by the commitment in late 1977 to balance the provincial budget, government spending in higher education quickly slipped back into the more controlled pattern.[36] Unfortunately for the universities, the same could not be said for inflation, especially after the ending of federal wage and price controls. Indeed, in 1978, when the OCUA, now headed by William Winegard, attempted in a meeting to impress the universities' resource requirements upon the ministry, Bette Stephenson did not dispute the arguments. She simply replied that there was no money.[37]

The other innovation introduced by Dupré involved the ever-controversial area of graduate studies. Dupré had concluded and the universities knew that the recent appraisal and discipline assessment programs (described earlier), while not without value, had done little to facilitate the process of long-term planning. By skirting around the manpower question, and by avoiding the issue of program cost, the whole approach had failed to serve the cause of rationalization. The OCUA's response was short-term but decisive. In 1975 it recommended a sustained freeze on the formula funding of all graduate programs in favour of institutional grants that would take no account of enrolment shifts. Now universities would no longer be financially rewarded for increasing the sizes of their graduate components and at the same time they would not be penalized for maintaining small faculties. In addition, support for any new graduate programs would be given only after a careful consideration of their need and desirability, and on 'information about their impact on the financial position of the entire university system.' The freeze was imposed in 1976 for a three-year period.[38]

Surprisingly, this heavy-handed action provoked little negative reaction from the Council of Ontario Universities. Privately, many institutions were relieved. The COU knew only too well how limited had been its success at practising the principle of 'collective autonomy' in the field of graduate studies. Representing diverse, and frankly self-interested institutions, it had yet to produce a formula equitable enough to avoid jealousy and resentment but pragmatic enough to rationalize the system. Eschewing responsibility (if not effort), it realized that the OCUA had temporarily lifted the burden from its shoulders. But the message was clear. If the COU did not produce a workable plan, it risked the imposition of direct and perhaps arbitrary restraining measures by the government itself.

By 1979, only marginal progress had been made. The COU adopted a 'quinquennial approach to graduate planning' in that year. The OCUA approved this model, though the two organizations still differed in their interpretation of some of the criteria to be used in accepting or rejecting proposed graduate programs. Furthermore, the entire approach was to continue to function on a voluntary basis, so that its effectiveness and impact, both on small institutions fighting for survival and established universities clinging to their reputations, was unclear. As the COU noted, 'no activity has occupied so much attention or employed so many resources as the planning of graduate studies. And no area has drawn more criticism.'[39] The realist would foresee little change on either count in the 1980s.

The inability of the universities to reconcile their collective responsibilities with their individual interests tended in some ways to reinforce the entrepreneurial spirit in the scramble for students and resources. In response to the pervasive utilitarian perceptions regarding the value of higher education, a number of universities attempted to 'market' their offerings to the public. On the one hand, some adopted a relatively moderate approach which involved the striking of community liaison committees and the advertising of special campus events to which the public was invited. On the other hand, more extreme and questionable tactics were used by institutions such as Guelph in order to recruit students. In 'lifestyle' advertisements that could easily have been mistaken for those promoting summer camp, designer jeans, or Canadian beer, Guelph at one stage took to the radio air-waves ten times a day for six weeks with a musical jingle that in a small, offensive way reflected as well the 'narcissist' fashions of the 1970s.

High school's behind me / I'm headin' on out
Wanna keep on learnin' / Gonna find myself
Find myself a place / Gonna check out Guelph
Myself and Guelph.[40]

Other universities used a combination of media and telephone soliciting which also tended to approach the limits if not overstep the 'recruitment guidelines' laid down by the Council of Ontario Universities. Responding to complaints of these solicitation methods, the COU sought (without complete success) to prohibit 'extravagant advertising campaigns and recruiting tours.' In this area, too, its authority lacked legal sanction.

Perhaps more serious was the emerging trend within universities to redirect funds to the most 'profitable' forms of academic activity. Arts courses thereby considered socially or economically 'irrelevant' thus risked financial impoverishment in favour of the more 'pragmatic' and 'popular' academic programs. One example of this can be gleaned from a memorandum distributed to the faculty by the dean of arts and science at Queen's University in late 1980.[41] His forecast of the university's economic future was gloomy indeed:

I regret to say that it now appears quite certain that the period of financial constraint will continue for yet some time and that is unrealistic to expect 'things' to get better in the foreseeable future. Inflation continues, the effects on the industrial-based economy are particularly marked, energy costs affect this Province more than most – the reasons are many but they all support the conclusion that we must expect the rates of increase in our fee and grant revenues to continue to fall well short of inflation rates well into and perhaps through the 1980's.

How should the university respond to this dilemma? The dean suggested that a programming strategy be developed based on the following assumptions.

i) Students, undergraduates and graduate, will increasingly be influenced in their choices of university programmes and courses by their perceptions of 'relevance' to employment opportunities after graduation. The challenge will be to develop new courses and programmes which reflect this trend but which incorporate those academic values and traditions which must continue as central elements in degree programmes offered by the Faculty of Arts and Science ...
iii) Our ability to devote time to research and scholarly work and our ability to influence those making decisions vital to our future will depend increasingly on the enrolment of graduate students, competitiveness for grant supported and contract research, and participation in 'visible' activities related to the development of public policy, applied research and the like.
iv) In instructional programmes and in research and scholarship there will be increasing competition among universities for reputation and public recognition

The enrolment shifts which the dean described were already in evidence by the late 1970s. Whereas the proportion of Canadian undergraduates registered in arts and science programs was 58.1 per cent in 1967/68, by 1976/77 it had fallen to 47.3 per cent. By contrast, business administration departments doubled their enrolments over the same period from 5.8 to 10 per cent.[42] Responding to such shifts in the manner recommended in the above memorandum might well prove to be 'sound' financial management on the part of Ontario universities. It might improve their image in the eyes of the Ontario government, re-establish their reputations in the business community, or stave off impoverishment. It might also turn the universities, alas, into little more than high-minded trade schools, a process scarcely impeded by the economic environment of the last decade.

One final effort to promote efficiency in this period of fiscal restraint involved an important administrative change within the Ministry of Colleges and Universities in 1978. For the first time since 1964, the MCU and Ministry of Education were reunited and assigned to a single cabinet member (Bette Stephenson). According to E.E. Stewart, the deputy minister in the Premier's Office (and a former deputy minister in the MCU), the reunification evolved in part from Premier Davis's own experience in the 1960s when he handled the two portfolios simultaneously. Furthermore, 'the combination was perceived as a mechanism for creating greater internal efficiency, since it was hoped, that among other things, some reduction in administrative staff was possible with the merger.'[43] According to a senior official in the ministry, Davis also justified the move on the belief that overseeing the growth of higher education was more complicated administratively than handling educational problems during the period of restraint. Thus while two separate educational portfolios were required in the past, this was no longer the case.

The reorganization was greeted both within the Ministry of Colleges and Universities and outside with universal disdain. To some, Davis's perception that governing growth was easier than governing restraint merely demonstrated how out of touch he was with the problems the universities faced. Rationalization demanded more not less planning. Now, however, the universities would have to share computer facilities, ministry personnel, and the minister's time with administrators and organizations from the primary and secondary level. And in the eyes of a number of officials within the ministry, Dr Stephenson was so overworked with her additional responsibilities that she was unable to give sufficient attention to university problems. Communication was considered by university spokesmen worse after the merger than before. And while efficiency had perhaps never been the ministry's and the universities' strong suit, contrary to Davis's expectations, things were now working more slowly than ever.

As we have seen, the environment of economic restraint affected a wide variety of policy areas during the 1970s. This was true as well of the ever-controversial programs designed to enhance the accessibility of the less privileged to Ontario universities.

Traditionally, the student assistance program had been based on an uneasy alliance between the federal and provincial governments, the former providing aid (since 1964) exclusively in the form of guaranteed loans (with interest payments subsidized until students graduated), and the latter supplementing these loans with a program of non-repayable grants. Both types of assistance were means-tested, and the entire scheme was administered provincially.

As discussed earlier, the Ontario Student Assistance Program (OSAP) compelled all students qualifying for grants (whatever their personal or family incomes) to first borrow $1,000. This central feature of the scheme had always aroused the ire of critics who claimed that it violated the very principle of equity that the program was intended to serve. They viewed the loan 'threshold' as a deterrent to students from low-income families who would be less inclined to accumulate education-related debts than their middle-class counterparts.

OSAP identified two categories of students: a) those considered to be financially 'dependent' on their parents and whose incomes were therefore tabulated in determining the size of the annual award: b) those deemed 'independent' and whose parental resources were thus excluded from the calculation of the award. The latter group generally included students beyond their fourth year of undergraduate study, married students, and students who had been in the workforce for at least two years before resuming their studies. The effect of these definitions was to concentrate grant aid to students in professional and graduate programs, and to provide loans only for all but the poorest undergraduates. Of course, married students at all levels were among the chief recipients of grant assistance.

In the fall of 1978, the student assistance program underwent significant revision. The amendments were based in part upon the recommendations of the Interim Committee on Financial Assistance for Students which issued its report in January of 1977. Appointed in 1975, the committee was co-chaired by Stefan Dupré, the chairman of the OCUA, and Norman Sisco, the chairman of the Ontario Council of Regents (which presided over the province's community colleges).

Instructed to formulate long-term recommendations on the financial arrangements and administrative requirements of student assistance in the province, the committee laboured under a variety of limitations. It failed either to analyse or have at its disposal information regarding the recent impact (if any) of OSAP on the accessibility of lower-income students to the province's universities. It felt pressured as well by the combined impact of the Ontario government's fiscal restraint policies and the federal government's anti-inflation program, both of which were designed, in part, to control spending in the public sector. Much to the committee's embarrassment, the Ontario government issued the *Report of the Special Program Review* in late 1975 in the midst of the committee's public hearings. This Henderson Report, among other things, called for fee increases up to 65 per cent, and for the elimination of the grant component of the student assistance in favour of loans only. The timing and content of the report damaged the credibility of the interim committee, at least in the eyes of the Ontario Federation of Students, which called (unsuccessfully) for the committee members to resign.

The interim committee also suffered from the failure of the Ministry of Colleges and Universities to provide adequate technical assistance, which forced last-minute adjustments, including the hiring of an outside consultant to help complete the study. Thus while the final 36-page report served the interests of brevity, it lacked the advantage of depth.[44]

The committee introduced its report with a cutting critique of the OSAP scheme. It found a 'complex of programs' that had evolved during the past decade on an *ad hoc* basis. 'While the amount of aid available to the individual student under the program had grown, the terms of eligibility and specific provisions had varied confusingly over the years.' Its suggested revisions were designed to serve two basic goals: first, to direct a larger portion of grant assistance to the 'genuinely' needy, and second, to provide financially strapped 'middle-income' students with access to cash in some form. To accomplish the first end, it recommended both eliminating the mandatory borrowing requirement and continuing the distribution of grants on the basis of a means test. Thus a lower-income student who had previously received the maximum award (approximately $1,000 in loan and $1,800 in grant) would receive the total award in grant only. For others, the amount of the grant would then vary according to personal resources and, instead of being forced to borrow the remainder of their asessed need, students would have the option of refusing the loans.

To accomplish the second goal, the committee recommended making available to all students (with no means test) interest-bearing loans which would be guaranteed by the government but arranged privately between the student and a financial institution. This proposal derived from the committee's recognition that many students from middle-income families, whom the government would be unlikely to subsidize heavily, had also felt the recent ravages of inflation and deserved some protection. Evidence of this was an impressive statistic revealing that in 1977 some 40 per cent of all Ontario students had been deemed needy enough to require assistance in either loan or grant form, despite OSAP's relatively restrictive entry qualifications. Since it was also assumed that lower-income students still constituted a proportionately small percentage of the total student population, economic pressures could be seen to have forced their way up the class ladder in Ontario. On the other hand, whether interest-bearing loans (which most students would be unable to start repaying until after graduation) constituted a realistic solution to this problem was questionable. For students relying heavily on such assistance, the compounded debt over several years could be extraordinary.[45]

Despite its open-ended mandate, the interim committee was fully aware of how pragmatic pressures narrowed its options. If it recommended a costly program, its proposals would be ignored by the government. But an overly frugal plan would render useless its efforts to improve student assistance in the province. The solution it produced, then, involved the redirecting of existing grant funds to the poorest, and the liberalization of some cost allowances to meet inflationary pressures.

But there was a price to be paid for this approach, and it was to be borne by unmarried graduate and professional students who had, because of their independent status, been the chief beneficiaries of grant assistance in the past. Now they would no longer qualify as 'independent': if they sought grant assistance, their family incomes would be taken into account, even if they lived away from or had left home years ago. Thus a single 24-year-old law student would be considered 'dependent' on his or her parents, while a married 21-year-old student, at whatever academic level, would be entitled to grant assistance with no reference to parental income. Because of the cost implications, neither the interim committee nor OSAP had reconciled their approaches with provincial laws governing the age of majority. While in most respects 18-year-olds were considered independent of their families, for the purposes of student assistance, this law, in effect, was not applied.

The government, unsurprisingly, adopted only some of the committee's recommendations. The elimination of the loan threshold was secured, and single professional and graduate students were no longer treated as independents. In addition, in accordance with the interim report, part-time students would, for the first time, be eligible for grants as well as loans. And the conditions governing the financial contributions that students were expected to make through summer savings and part-time earnings were liberalized.[46]

The government added one severe restriction to the new program. No student could receive grant assistance for more than four years of post-secondary education, a cost-saving regulation designed, according to the minister, to encourage students to complete their studies quickly. Beyond that, students would be entitled to loans only and all loans would continue to be means-tested. Thus the unconditional interest-bearing loan proposal for middle-income students was rejected.

With the elimination of compulsory borrowing, the potential for equity in the new program was obviously greater than in the past. But its true effectiveness could only be measured by analysing the application of the myriad regulations. And initial evidence pointed to several limitations. First, the definition of a 'low-income' student remained unrealistic. For 1980/81, only families with net incomes under $7,700 received full grant assistance for their children. The expected contribution of all parents rose in accordance with their earnings. On the other hand, the federal government loan program expected no contributions from parents whose incomes were below $8,900 (net). As William Winegard, the chairman of the Ontario Council on University Affairs wondered, how was it possible for any family with two or three children and a gross income of $12,000 (net circa $7,700) to contribute anything to the costs of their children's education?[47]

Other criticisms were directed towards the 'improved' summer savings requirements (still considered too restrictive), the inadequate living allowances of $25.00 per week first offered to those on the new program,[48] and the part-time student regulations. Furthermore, when the new scheme was inaugurated, a major computer foul-up delayed the distribution of grants to thousands of Ontario students well beyond the beginning of the fall term.

These revisions in the student assistance scheme were augmented by upward revisions of tuition fee levels in the late 1970s. In May 1976, the minister announced that fees for foreign students would be more than doubled, rising from the two-term rate of $585 (the 'Canadian' price) to the new level of $1,500, and tripled to $750 for a full academic year in community colleges. Two predictable justifications were offered for these increases: the need for Ontario to 'restrain the growth of government expenditures,' and in response to the 'public concern regarding the cost to the Ontario taxpayer of educating foreign students in our post-secondary institutions.'[49]

In 1977, fees for all university students were raised a further $100, and $75 for college students. They rose another 5 per cent in 1979 and again by 7.5 per cent in 1980. The minister on this latter occasion introduced a new twist. Universities would be allowed for the first time a limited degree of autonomy in setting their own tuition levels. Each was entitled to raise its fees a further 10 per cent without losing the difference in formula income which would have been the case previously. While the universities were anxious to receive the 'extra' income that this new regulation would provide, they worried about the negative impact higher fees would have on student enrolments.[50] Ironically, those universities that needed the money the most (the small, underpopulated, regional institutions) were the least inclined to charge the additional 10 per cent for fear of deterring potential students.

Despite the tortured investigations, endless debates, and recent amendments, the province of Ontario, like other jurisdictions, had essentially failed to increase the participation rates of the poor in post-secondary educational institutions.[51] At best, the new student aid regulations, while more equitable in part, involved shifting around current funds that were distributed among a financially squeezed but unmistakably middle-cass constituency. Policy in this field as well was shaped by the debilitating impact of economic restraint.

The long-term redistributive effects of student assistance, then, had been and would likely remain minimal. But could it be otherwise? Just as the universities could hardly be expected to plan sensibly for an unplanned economy, so too they could scarcely hope to produce social equity through a limited student-aid scheme within a society so riddled with income and class divisions. For while 'equality of opportunity' by the mid 1970s had become a motherhood concept and one which politicians could openly oppose only at their political peril, in effect this was a static sociological formula. Student aid, like other forms of social assistance, was designed to equalize the race for unequal rewards. It was never intended to bring about genuine equality of condition.[52] Of course, it failed even to accomplish the first end. But cast in the rhetoric of 'equality' and 'accessibility,' student assistance served to mystify and legitimize society's deeply entrenched social divisions by offering the poor the false promise of upward mobility. As it trained the élite at one end and failed to attract the impoverished at the other, the university continued to perpetuate the class disparities so characteristic of twentieth-century Canadian society.

The student movement – that international phenomenon replete with its lofty idealism, militant tactics, and its unpopular public image – had largely perished in Canada by the early 1970s. The activists who formed the core of radical student organizations had dropped out, graduated, or assumed lower profiles within non-university establishments by the turn of the decade. Yet the movement was far from forgotten. A new generation of activists sought to rekindle the flame and keep alive the spirit of political consciousness. Attempting to learn from the past, they softened their image, curbed rhetorical excesses in favour of informed research, re-entered the mainstream of political life, and in the end failed as badly as their predecessors to touch the souls of the vast majority of their fellow students. The dismal economic climate of the 1970s, perhaps surprisingly, produced little in the way of campus activism. Instead students pursued more doggedly and with greater competitiveness than ever those elusive career opportunities once taken for granted in the 1960s. Undergraduates of the 1970s had little time for and little interest in student politics.

In Ontario, the torch was borne by the Ontario Federation of Students, an organization created in the spring of 1972 following the demise of the Canadian Union of Students and the Ontario Union of Students.[53] The rationale for the establishment of OFS seemed sensible enough. Students continued to have specific interests in the area of tuition fee levels, financial assistance, and campus housing that could well benefit from any influence that an organized pressure group could exert on university administrators and the provincial government. In addition, those activists who sought to widen the concerns of a revitalized student movement by focusing attention on social problems beyond the university hoped to wield influence within the new organization.[54]

But the shadows of the Canadian Union of Students and the Ontario Union of Students loomed heavily over the new association. Convinced that the radicalism of its predecessors had alienated most students, organizers sought to limit OFS's scope for independent action. As a creature of participating student councils, it was required to seek broad approval for all policy statements and activities. Logistical difficulties and political divisions prevented the faithful adherence to this rule, resulting in battles between the OFS executive and its constituent councils reminiscent of similar conflicts in the 1960s. OFS's first major enterprise – a campaign against tuition fee increases in the fall of 1971 – reflected these tensions. A moderately successful referendum on university campuses denouncing the fee increase was followed by a disastrous demonstration at Queen's Park in November of that year in which only four hundred students from across the province took part. There had been considerable debate within the organization over the advisability of this tactic and OFS almost crumbled under the impact.[55]

None the less, the organization survived. On the strength of a bold decision in 1973 to raise the levy on its members from 40 cents to $1.50 per capita, OFS reasserted its presence and improved its image among sufficient numbers of students in the province.[56] Most Ontario campuses held referenda favouring the increase and the additional income enabled the organization to hire several full-time organizers, lobbyists, and researchers to fulfil the promise of creating 'a strong provincial student voice.' By 1976, OFS had six full-time employees. It was turning out well-researched briefs on provincial funding and student aid. It re-established contact at Queen's Park with education critics from the opposition parties, and it appeared regularly before a respectful Ontario Council on University Affairs to make its case. The cutbacks in university spending had provided OFS with a new focus for research and organization.

It did not abandon the broader political concerns which had informed the activities of its predecessors. It sought instead to contain within them specific proposals that appeared more realistic in the conservative Ontario environment. For example, while officially favouring the abolition of tuition fees and the restructuring of the taxation system, OFS seldom pressed these demands. Instead it devoted its efforts to preventing current fees from rising and to improving the student asistance program. And while its reports on university funding were more global, forceful, and in many ways more informative than similar briefs presented by faculty and administrative organizations, they included short-term recommendations that might well have been considered good NDP policy.[57]

To the degree that the organization gained credibility, it did so on the basis of a lobbying group that took its place alongside those representing faculty and university presidents. It used the media more effectively and even, on occassion, received favourable editorial comment. In its own ways OFS became institutionalized in the 1970s in a manner that would likely have earned it the wrath of the student organizations which preceded it. Undoubtedly it would have been found feeble, 'liberal,' and co-opted.

Yet when OFS ventured beyond these respectable forms of activism, it had little to show for its efforts. As the financial plight of the universities worsened, several OFS-inspired demonstrations were held at Queen's Park towards the end of the decade.[58] And while they were better organized than the débâcle of 1972, there is little evidence that they had any impact on government policy or on the consciousnesses of most Ontario students. Student assistance programs scarcely improved throughout the decade, tuition fees continued their steady rise in the late 1970s, and OFS succeeded no better than the COU or OCUFA in reversing provincial spending policies on higher education.

A clue to the reason for such limited impact was provided by a senior ministry official who, on the occasion of a demonstration at Queen's Park in March 1978, attempted to determine first-hand the level of political consciousness among Ontario students. He ventured into the crowd, tape-recorder in hand, and interviewed a number of participants. He found the majority he talked to to be ill-informed about the issues and unable to express themselves clearly. Some were sincere, others were there to observe or have a good time. He was convinced that if this soft support for OFS policies was characteristic of students who took the trouble to attend the demonstration, those who stayed away (which included 99 per cent of college and university students) were likely even more uninformed, apathetic, too busy studying, or supportive of the government. Though scarcely a scientific sample, this official's perceptions undoubtedly reflected those of his minister who met the demonstrators, endured their heckling, and left, confident that government policy faced only ineffective challenges in the area of higher education.

The conditions that had given OFS new life as an organization were the same that limited its success as a movement. Escalating fees, growing underemployment, inadequate student assistance, and expensive student housing all provided it with solid issues around which to agitate. The OCUA, its own publications, and even the establishment media offered it a platform. All it lacked in the face of the quiescent, individualistic, and depressed atmosphere of Ontario universities was broadly based and active student support.

Aging professors might allude nostalgically to that era when traditional university, revered though ignored by society at large, engaged quietly in 'free and disinterested inquiry'.[59] On the other hand, as we have already seen, the universities were scarcely dragged kicking and screaming into the modern world. With few exceptions, university teachers enthusiastically supported the rapid expansion of the 1960s. New facilities, higher enrolments, and wider course options raised the profile, respectability, and the financial rewards of the profession. Whereas the average salary for a Canadian professor was $4,156 in 1947/48, by 1970/71 the comparable figure had climbed to $16,096.[60]

If the high priority and heavy funding of Canadian universities had enriched the opportunities and lifestyles of professors in the 1960s, the financial pressures of the next decade interrupted these favourable trends. By 1980, most professors scarcely faced a return to the prospect of genteel poverty (in fact, for many, life had never been better), but, short of this extreme result, the new academic environment embodied political and administrative tensions that affected the character of many universities in substantial ways. Foremost among these was the emergence of collective bargaining, including the unionization of university faculty associations.

Faculty unionization first appeared in Quebec at the beginning of the decade. L'Association des Ingénieurs Professeurs en Sciences Appliqués de l'Université du Sherbrooke was certified in November of 1970. In 1971, faculty associations at three branches of the University of Quebec (Montreal, Chicoutimi, and Trois Rivières) and L'Association des Professeurs de L'Ecole Polytechnique obtained union status. By 1975, over 60 per cent of all Quebec professors were unionized, far and away the largest provincial proportion across Canada.[61]

By 1974, faculty at three English-Canadian institutions – Notre Dame in Nelson, BC, St Mary's in Halifax, and the University of Manitoba – had all been through the certification process. Carleton at Ottawa was the first Ontario institution to display the union banner (June 1975), followed later that year by the University of Ottawa, and in 1976 by York University. This flurry of activity in the mid 1970s did not augur a stampede in the province (or in the country) as some had predicted. But the growth of collective bargaining proceeded at a steady, if unspectacular, pace. By 1980, the list of unionized campuses had expanded to include Windsor, Laurentian (and its satellite Algoma) Lakehead, and Trent. A total of 3,669 faculty members, constituting 30 per cent of the Ontario university teaching population, was represented by certified unions. Voluntary or special agreements, involving the use of collective bargaining (short of certification) existed at the University of Toronto (including its affiliates at OISE and Victoria University) and Ryerson, which had maintained such an arrangement since 1964. For Canada as a whole, over 50 per cent of all eligible full-time faculty and professional librarians were covered by collective bargaining in 1978.[62]

Support for unionization emerged as well from the ranks of teaching assistants and part-time faculty during the 1970s. For these employees, certification was obtained first at the University of Toronto in 1974, York in 1975, and later at Ryerson, Lakehead, McMaster, and Carleton. Each of these organizations was originally a local of the Graduate Assistants' Association, a title that inaccurately reflected the non-graduate component of the group, and reinforced the image of teaching assistants as students, not employees. In 1980 the organization was renamed the Canadian Union of Educational Workers.

How can this trend towards the unionization of faculty be explained? The question must be addressed in both its 'global' and 'local' dimensions. The economic environment of the 1970s, which featured diminishing financial support for universities, the failure of salaries to keep pace with inflation, and the growing threat of lay-offs, especially of untenured faculty, provided general conditions favourable to the *possible* adoption of collective bargaining methods by Canadian professors. The impact of these conditions was especially jarring in comparison to the almost unlimited opportunities and rewards of the 1960s. Material expectations had been raised, but they could no longer be so easily fulfilled.[63] The example of American colleges and universities where collective bargaining and unionization had made significant inroads prior to the 1970s further demonstrated the viability and increasing popularity of this approach.[64] In 1971 the Canadian Association of University Teachers created its first collective bargaining committee whose importance gradually increased throughout the 1970s. It too served as a catalyst in unionization drives around the country.[65]

In addition, the rapid pace of unionization among white-collar employees across Canada during the 1960s, including those traditionally considered professional, removed from the collective bargaining model its exclusively working-class flavour. Throughout the country, elementary, secondary, and community college teachers had taken advantage of federal and provincial legislation which permitted their organizations to become certified.[66] Subsequently, as teachers' salaries and working arrangements improved, many university professors looked on with envy and not a little anger at the apparent erosion of their own status. While opponents of faculty unionization argued that the professional status of professors would be diminished by collective bargaining, the proponents of this model argued that, *without* effective means of protecting their positions, such deterioration was even more likely. The example of doctors, lawyers, and engineers, who had managed to preserve their professional status *and* improve their incomes through the activities of effective bargaining agencies, further exposed the special vulnerability of university professors.[67]

One other development, perhaps less clearly recognized than those described above, assisted the cause of collective bargaining advocates. This involved the 'bureaucratization' of the university itself. The massive expansion of higher education in the 1960s witnessed organizational and administrative changes similar to those which had recently transformed management patterns in government and large industries. University administrations grew rapidly as presidents augmented their advisory staffs with planning directors, budget analysts, and a plethora of vice-presidents, whose responsibilities were broken down further into a multitude of jurisdictions. By the 1970s, the presidents' administrative credentials were likely to be as strong as (or stronger than) their academic qualifications, whereas in the past the reverse had been true.[68]

As the Duff-Berdahl report on university government observed in 1966, this transition had not always been smooth in Canadian universities. Poor communications among presidents, boards, university senates, and faculty associations had frequently produced tension and mistrust in the planning and decision-making processes. As one solution to this problem, Duff-Berdahl had recommended that junior faculty be more fully represented on university senates which had traditionally been dominated by senior professors, deans, and administrators. The commission called as well for the wider involvement of faculty, through the senate, in planning and budgeting procedures.[69]

While some changes occurred as a result of this report, most universities by the early 1970s had not done enough to satisfy their academic staffs. Indeed, the addition of students to university senates (also recommended by Duff-Berdahl) in the view of many faculty further diluted the influence of professors in the governing of the university. A number of investigations produced a litany of complaints about decision-making in the university. Information was still far from open, and deans and presidents were accused of making arbitrary decisions in hiring, firing, and promotion. Grievance procedures were unsatisfactory and tenure, the only real form of job security, was increasingly under attack. Senates had become larger and more unwieldy so that professors often approached these problems without a uniform voice.[70] All of this was painfully evident when funding was *plentiful*. When restraint was imposed, tensions increased.

In the past faculty associations might well have been the appropriate outlet for the expression of such concerns. But increasingly, this was no longer possible. Traditionally, faculty associations had functioned mainly as informal social organizations, heavily influenced by presidents and senior professors. Problems were addressed in a quiet, *ad hoc* manner. Salary matters were handled on an individual as opposed to collective basis. Controversial and adversarial postures were largely eschewed by these conservative, sometimes cliquish, and largely powerless associations. More often than not, they functioned as a minor adjunct of administrations themselves.[71]

By the early 1970s, younger and more vocal professors increasingly viewed such organizations as weak, meek, and easily co-opted by clever and more politically astute presidents and deans. Hence on many campuses, concerted efforts were made to turn faculty associations into articulate and persistent advocates of the collective staff interest. In fact, most campus unions resulted from the transformation of faculty associations into certified bargaining agents. The changed environment was described this way by a supporter of faculty unionization:

The university has changed significantly in size and former intimate relationships between the professors and the deans, vice rectors and presidents have been transformed into bureaucratic, centralized and insulated, strict divisions of labour. The attempt to set up senates and consultative bodies with substantial professorial representation have largely failed because in the crunch, on the issues that really count, the administration either fails to consult, or after consultation, neglects to integrate such advice into its decision making process.[72]

To a greater or lesser degree, all Ontario universities experienced the impact of these institutional pressures. Yet not every university took the unionization route. How can one account for this disparity? While it is perhaps too early to provide a full theoretical and historical account of the process, it is possible to outline in a preliminary way evident patterns in the unionization drive. Indeed, the characteristics of those universities which witnessed the certification of their faculty associations are distinguishable in a number of important ways from those where the trend was resisted.

Four of the seven unionized campuses in Ontario – Carleton, York, Lakehead and Trent – shared one common trait. They were among the youngest, least established, and most financially pressed institutions in the province. Carleton and York grew especially rapidly through the late 1960s, each absorbing a significant share of Ontario's massive enrolment increase.[73] For example, between 1965/66 and 1969/70 when full-time undergraduate and graduate enrolment increased by 191 per cent for Ontario as a whole, York's rose by 537 per cent and Carleton's by 218 per cent. From 1960/61 to 1969/70, Carleton's enrolment increased by 500 per cent, while Ontario's rose 355 per cent. Both institutions carried an especially large part-time student burden in the late 1960s. While the province increased undergraduate part-time enrolments by 163 per cent between 1965/66 and 1969/70, Carleton's part-time complement rose by 368 per cent and York's by 221 per cent over the same period.

In addition, because these institutions had fewer graduate and professional students than the established universities, they received less funding per student (due to the vagaries of the operating grants formula) than a number of their sister institutions. Their potential operating income was restricted further in 1971 by the provincial embargo on new graduate programs. Statistics reveal that between 1974 and 1976, among Ontario's fifteen universities, in terms of per capita grants, York stood ninth and Carleton tenth. (Windsor was eighth, Lakehead eleventh, Laurentian thirteenth, and Trent fourteenth).[74]

When restraint was imposed suddenly in the early 1970s, the building plans of both York and Carleton were interrupted. At the same time, inadequate increases in operating support hindered the maintenance of newly established programs. Of course, these difficulties were system-wide, but the 'senior' universities – Western, Queen's, Toronto – were better able to absorb the impact since they had increased their capacities at a more gradual, less frantic pace. The less established institutions suffered to a greater degree the disruptive consequences of both forced growth and sudden restraint.

The administrations of both York and Carleton handled the transition from expansion to restraint in ways that fed faculty discontent. At York, while certification itself occurred much later, the souring of faculty-administration relations was evident in 1972. Following a serious shortfall in enrolment which most Ontario universities encountered in that year, York president, David Slater, announced that the university faced a deficit of over four million dollars and the possibility of dismissing 130 to 160 faculty members. In response, the Senate established a committee to examine the budgetary problems of the university in greater detail. That the committee succeeded in reducing the original deficit projection to $705,000 raised serious questions about the administrative competence of the president and his advisers. In the meantime internal political clashes ensued. Two senior administrators had resigned and Slater demanded a vote of loyalty from a third. Following the evident collapse of support for the president from faculty and administrators, he was instructed by the board of governors to resign or face dismissal. He chose the former course.[75]

While the poisoned atmosphere of early 1973 was partially cleared by the appointment of a new president, Ian Macdonald, after-effects were in evidence. The university's enduring financial problems, continuing concern among faculty about potential lay-offs, and the obvious need to restore and preserve order in the structure of faculty-administration relations encouraged discussion about unionization. Indeed when the York University Faculty Association applied for certification in 1975 (after having signed up over 60 per cent of the faculty), the university administration did not oppose its efforts. Macdonald believed that more could be gained by accepting and working within the union model than by fighting YUFA at that late date. The university had already experienced enough political turmoil to last a president's life time.[76]

In a number of important ways, Carleton's experience in the mid 1970s parallelled that of York's. Inadequate funding levels, unfavourable enrolment projections, and a mounting university deficit forced the Senate, in the fall of 1974, to consider procedures for the possible lay-off of full-time faculty. But before the Senate's report was complete, a meeting of the General Faculty Board was held in which a member of the administration suggested that if the university deficit were to be reduced to 'nil,' 78 full-time faculty members would still have to be released. One week later, in response to faculty fears, Michael Oliver, the president, announced that no full-time contracts would be terminated in the

1975/76 academic year. However, at a further meeting of the General Faculty Board on 22 November, the president announced that budget cuts of $400,000 in the area of academic staffing were still considered vital in the coming year. Subsequent *closed* deliberations of two presidential advisory bodies, the Academic Planning Committee and the Budget Review Committee, were held to determine how these cuts could be implemented. The possibility of lay-offs still appeared imminent to many faculty members.[77]

Indeed the 22 November meeting was the 'trigger' which set off plans for faculty unionization. 'Exactly one week after the General Faculty Board meeting at which President Oliver announced the bleak financial picture for Carleton in 1975/76, a general meeting of the Carleton University Academic Staff Association, called on the petition of fifteen members, gathered to discuss the establishment of collective bargaining for academics at Carleton.'[78] Union organizers later reported that concern over job security was the 'overt reason' for unionization at Carleton.

In the meantime, the president, who had taken office in July 1974, announced the appointment of two new vice-presidents and an administrative assistant, the latter of whom had accompanied him from McGill. While there was some justification for this 'elaboration of the bureaucracy' – something which one faculty member believed should have occurred much earlier at Carleton – many professors immediately perceived this action as an undue usurpation of power in the president's office.[79] When Oliver announced in early 1975 that he and the Board of Governors would reserve the ultimate right to determine how lay-offs would occur – irrespective of the recommendations of the 'Senate Document of the Release of Teaching Staff in Time of Financial Stringency' – this unfavourable perception of his approach to office was reinforced. According to the former president of the faculty association, these administrative and economic problems combined to fuel unrest and widen the base of support for unionization among the teaching staff: 'It is this feeling of powerlessness, the perception that Senate was being reduced to symbolic and often manipulated legitimizers and the belief that professors must retain a real role in institutional decision making which has convinced many professors to accept collective bargaining.'[80] Certification was achieved in the spring of 1975.

Thus the adroitness (or maladroitness) with which administrators handled both the financial pressures and the transition from traditional to modern forms of governing the university affected the institution's ability to stave off faculty unionization. For reasons described above, the youngest universities in the province were especially vulnerable to unionization campaigns.

As an established elder among Ontario universities, the University of Ottawa would hardly appear to be a likely candidate for faculty unionization. But on closer examination, it is evident that certification there (in 1975), as at Windsor and Laurentian, *was* characteristic of patterns evident elsewhere in Canada. Until 1965, Ottawa was controlled by the Oblate Fathers and survived as one of the province's last 'denominational' universities. While the university had, since the Second World War, received partial funding from the provincial government for its scientific and medical programs, it remained for the most part dependent on private financial aid. But the expansion crisis of the 1960s forced the institution to consider changing its status or be rendered incapable of meeting the enrolment pressures and program requirements of the years ahead. Hence it was re-established as a non-denominational university, controlled, as other 'public' campuses, by a lay-dominated board of governors, thereby entitling it to full government support. Thus this century-old institution, at least in structural terms, was reborn in the boom period of the 1960s.[81]

According to John Cowan, a renowned physiologist and the first president of the faculty union, Ottawa's transition from a denominational to a non-sectarian university had not proceeded entirely smoothly. A number of Oblate Fathers remained in key positions on the board, and throughout the 1960s and early 70s the university continued to be governed in a 'paternalistic' and 'undemocratic' fashion. Faculty grievances were inadequately addressed, money was tight, morale was low; in short, the anachronistic methods which governed faculty-administration relations in the past survived the structural changes within the institution. In this strained atmosphere, according to Cowan, it proved far easier than many expected to convince most faculty members that collective bargaining and certification were the most effective ways of both ensuring material security and restoring working relations with the administration.[82]

Similar problems and responses were evident at Windsor and Laurentian where denominational control existed until the early 1960s. Indeed the first faculty union in all of English Canada, at St Mary's in Halifax, came about in large part as a result of the institution's disruptive transition from a private and denominational to a public and secular university.[83] In general, it would appear that, while all universities endured problems in modernizing their governing structures, those which bore the burden of recent secularization faced added pressures, and were therefore more susceptible to the prospect of faculty unionization than many of their fellow institutions.[84]

To what degree did the unionization of middle-class university professors augur the 'proletarianization' of academic employees? The evidence suggests that collective bargaining procedures emerged within a conservative not a radical framework. Successful certification campaigns invariably depended on how well union organizers could demonstrate their desire to uphold, not overturn, academic traditions and university conventions.

While the initiators of union drives may well have been politically to the left of the colleagues they set out to organize, every successful campaign addressed the issues in pragmatic as opposed to ideological terms. No organizer could hope to sign up a majority of professors by employing traditional working-class rhetoric. Terms like 'solidarity,' 'struggle,' and 'exploitation' were completely eschewed. The possibility of strikes was consistently down-played. Instead, union advocates painstakingly presented facts, figures, and academically garbed argument to make their case. Appealing to the professional consciousness of a highly educated professoriate, pro-unionists were able to demonstrate that less educated high school teachers had secured better increments, and in many cases were better paid than university teachers, a direct result of their collective bargaining clout. Instances of administrative bungling were effectively, though not stridently, documented in faculty association newsletters and briefs. Strong faculty organizations were offered as the only viable models for restoring working order to the university and protecting its academic integrity. And unions were posed not as ends in themselves but as means to achieving some specific, essential tasks. At Carleton, for example, a curiously argued case favouring unionization appeared in one newsletter. The writer contended that his colleagues need not support unionization in principle to back the particular unionization of Carleton's faculty.[85] And union organizers at York aroused the support of the business school faculty by appealing to its concern about the lack of institutional 'procedure' at the university.[86]

Nor were faculty unions the proponents of economic egalitarianism. One of the chief obstacles in the way of faculty co-operation was the historical disparity in salary between law professors (among others) and arts and science teachers. Accordingly, the support for unionization among the law faculty at York was secured by YUFA's promise to preserve the income disparity in subsequent contracts. And to meet the criticisms of those who feared that unionization would elminate merit as a significant promotion criteria (as opposed to automatic progress through the salary and teaching ranks), Ottawa, Carleton, and York all built merit clauses into their contracts.

Indeed, the ability of union proponents to sign up sufficient support depended to a very large degree on how 'responsible,' conservative, and academically credible were the organizers themselves. Right-left splits did exist on the executives of most faculty associations, but unity was preserved and support increased by the tendency of the latter to allow the image and program of the proposed union to be shaped by the former. At York, for example, historian Jack Granatstein, the first chairman of the unionized faculty association, admits to having been willingly 'used' by the 'left wing' of the union for the purpose of signing up the more conservative faculty elements in the campaign.

Astonishing to some outsiders was the situation at Ottawa where members of the medical and science faculties, traditionally among the most conservative departments of any university, initiated the entire collective bargaining and unionization drives. John Cowan claims to have personally signed up some 120 members, spending an average of two hours in discussion with each. That these 'respectable' elements of the university were among the earliest union supporters prevented the administration from dismissing the campaign as the work of young, left-wing, malcontented professors.

The Ottawa case is an interesting, even extreme, example of how every conceivable alternative to unionization was exhausted before certification was sought. This included calling a referendum on certification itself – a step considered unnecessary, redundant, and potentially destructive to the union cause by most trade unionists. (The actual certification vote is considered to be the only referendum required.) Against the advice of the Canadian Association of University Teachers, Ottawa carried through with the pre-referendum, won it easily, and then successfully conducted the certification campaign. Even before the Ontario Labour Relations Board authorized the certification vote and compelled the university to negotiate with the newly formed union, the organizers sought (unsuccessfully) to convince the university to negotiate voluntarily. According to Cowan, all of these steps were necessary in order fully to defuse opposition and elicit support for the union on a campus-wide basis.

The Carleton faculty association, too, bent over backwards to demonstrate its 'responsibility' by printing in one issue of its newsletter a full-page article on the advantages *and* disadvantages of unionization. Although some pro-unionists questioned the wisdom of the association providing anti-unionists with ammunition in this over-zealous effort to be fair, the latter failed to stem the unionization tide.[87]

Those unconverted to the union cause (at Carleton and elsewhere) feared the effect on the university of this 'inappropriate' industrial relations model. For them the university was a special institution, based on collegial decision-making, in which faculty members *already* held extensive powers. As Toronto economist, John Crispo, explained: 'Of great potential concern in several quarters is the possible shift from what has been believed to have been collegial, deliberative and participatory relations to what is perceived as being adversary, bargaining and contractual relations ... from a community of scholars to a community of protagonists.[88] According to Crispo and others, academics living with unionization could also expect the erosion of excellence 'through a rigid lock-step salary system depending on little more than years of education and years of service'; they could suffer the imposition of productivity clauses and work rules in exchange for better salaries; they might be compelled to endure third-party interference in academic affairs if bargaining were to break down; and, inevitably, they would face a strike situation which could damage the university (a 'non-essential' public service) beyond repair. In short, demanded unionization foes, could the university ever benefit from or even survive an 'adversary system based on confrontation and raw economic power'?[89]

The responses to these arguments were predictable. Collegiality and genuinely co-operative decision-making, if ever a reality, were dismissed as myths in this age of bureaucratized administrations and financial restraints. According to Winnipeg law professor, Roland Penner, most faculty had *little* decision-making power, and 'the fundamental legal relationship of the non-administrative academic to the institution was that of employer to employee'.[90] Like it or not, pro-unionists asserted, both the status of professors and the integrity of the university would depend on the willingness of the former to take collective action. And by acting reasonably, administrators and academics could avoid the extreme consequences forecast by anti-union spokesmen.

By 1980, unionization was still a new and uncertain phenomenon in Ontario higher education. The long-term impact on universities employing the model was unknown. Equally unclear was the ability of other institutions to escape the future without it. Perhaps this much can be said. The trend to collective bargaining among academics reflected what the university had become: a mammoth corporate entity in a recessionary state. The metaphor, of course, could be pushed too far. Universities did not exist for the purpose of producing profits. But possibly, they fell just one step short. Forced to justify themselves on the basis of productive, 'required,' and 'relevant' scholarly output (in terms of both trained manpower and research), yet compelled to do so with limited resources, they developed characteristics common to public and private corporations undergoing similar pressures.

This may not have been what idealistic supporters of higher education had envisioned two decades earlier but, if they believed that universities could escape the combined impact of shifting economic conditions and internal institutional tensions, they had been living an illusion. Ontario's universities were reaping what a materialistic province and business-oriented, culturally blinkered government had sown. The ivory was peeling off the tower. It had yet to be determined whether the edifice was crumbling.

Conclusion

Academics can always be counted upon to defend in righteous and eloquent terms the prime function of a university: 'to create, transmit and extend knowledge.'[1] But as we have seen, the degree to which knowledge is advanced and truth pursued depends on forces external to the university itself.

This study has explored the impact on higher education of some central components of a mixed capitalist economy in post-war Canada. Following a discussion of the important economic role universities played during the war, we described how the pervasive commitment to economic development forced higher education to the forefront of public concern in the late 1950s and mid 1960s. Universities were perceived, both by the individual and by society as a whole, as a critical element in the process of generating and accumulating wealth, and for this reason they were generously supported.

How vital it was for competing universities to legitimize themselves in the eyes of government, business, and apparently, the public at large, by gaining the political and financial support of important business interests, was also noted. A university's status during this period, from the perspective of its own spokesmen, appeared to vary directly with the prestige and prominence of its private corporate sponsors.

Furthermore, the traditions of academic freedom combined with the ideology of free enterprise to produce a governing arrangement in which universities were privately run but publicly funded. While private corporate funding was, of course, eagerly sought by individual universities, both the institutions and their corporate donors depended primarily on government revenue to finance the huge investment in higher education. As noted in chapter two, such funding was not in itself viewed by business or the universities as a threat to the autonomy of the latter; in fact, it was encouraged. What was resisted was any effort by the government to administer the institutions directly. Government agencies in Ontario performed the role of co-ordinators, scrutineers and consultants, but at no time during the expansion phase did they impose predetermined priorities upon the universities. As one participant observed at an international conference on higher education in 1971: 'Direct intervention by government particularly in anything that might be regarded as "higher education" is not usually regarded as good democratic form. Western governments have generally sought to act indirectly.[2]

The process through which universities attempted to fulfil the economic functions expected of them in planning their own curricular priorities was examined. In the area of undergraduate education, the direct links between the curriculum and the economy were, at best, tenuous. Still, businessmen and academics frequently stressed the importance of a well-rounded undergraduate education as a vital background for professional training and employment. Thus the rapid expansion of undergraduate education could be rationalized, both by academics who favoured broadening the curriculum for purely pedagogical reasons and by 'pragmatists' who believed that students in all educational fields would ultimately contribute to the productivity of the economy.

The dynamic which generally determined the size of universities and the distribution of resources was the market force of social demand or enrolment pressure. One fact, however, should not be overlooked. Had it not been for the widespread faith in the economic value of higher education as a whole, the money spent on humanities and social science programs would not have been so freely available. The university's ability to pursue on a large scale its academic goals depended upon the perceived economic value of the post-secondary system as a whole.

In the field of professional and graduate studies, where the obvious and accepted goal was to train society's required manpower, the planning techniques were highly uncertain. The ability of universities to respond adequately and accurately to such needs was as suspect as the capitalist economy itself was unpredictable. Even with the periodic use of such techniques as manpower forecasting, accurate long-term planning could seldom be reliably achieved. But as long as manpower shortages persisted on an annual basis in the early and mid 1960s, heavy investment in a variety of professional programs could be rationalized even if the ultimate effects of such investment were unknown. And so long as students were obtaining jobs, then the democratic justification for the generous funding of higher education could be proclaimed as well.

Student assistance programs could be defended as an economic investment as well as a visible form of support for the disadvantaged. Two economists summarized the situation in this way:

The most important point to note about the expansion of higher education during the 1960's was that the behaviour of students was roughly consistent with the stated needs of the economy for more educated manpower. There was a generally strong feeling that Canada needed a more highly educated labour force – particularly scientists and engineers. Students appeared to respond to these needs, and merely by building more universities and providing financial assistance the goal of a more highly educated and technically trained labour force was achieved.[3]

Whereas the above economic ingredients served the universities in a positive fashion during the 1960s, towards the end of the decade they began producing the opposite effect. With the economic value of higher education increasingly in question, economists adjusted their models, created new assumptions, and arrived at new conclusions. In an economic setting featuring high inflation and growing unemployment, universities were neither protected from, nor capable of rescuing society from, its new dilemma. Thus at every level of the university system, financial restraints had an impact. From hiring policies to academic programming, from student activism to faculty unionization, university life absorbed the pressures of the materialistic society which enveloped it.

Rapid adjustments and *ad hoc* responses were the order of the day. Despite greater lobbying resources, the Council of Ontario Universities' political influence diminished in a provincial environment increasingly unreceptive to higher educational concerns. No longer sustained by the driving 'philosophy' of rapid (or even moderate) growth, Ontario's universities cast about for some novel and popular utilitarian justification.[4]

Were there viable alternatives to this type of educational planning and organization? The structure, logic, and cultural values of free enterprise economies suggest that there were not. While the approaches to educational planning in other jurisdictions differed in form from those in Ontario, in substance they were quite similar.[5] Western capitalist governments tended to eschew direct control over individual universities (although some exercised more restraint than others); most relied on the dynamic of social demand and market forces to determine the distribution of student places within universities: all experienced (especially towards the end of the 1960s) considerable difficulty in their application of manpower planning; and, by the mid 1970s, economic problems and shifting perceptions about the economic utility of the contemporary university seriously affected the financial status of institutions in many provinces and countries.[6] The over-riding problem was the inability of universities in 'free enterprise' economies to respond to the vicissitudes of the market itself.

Even as the economic problems of the early 1970s intensified, many educators continued to defend the traditional approach to educational planning. According to an Ontario study on the future of graduate engineering, planning in education could be no better than economic planning outside the university:

Since we think of Canada as a free enterprise society we must have faith in it, and accept the disadvantages that come with its great values. Doctoral studies are long in duration and their populations cannot adjust themselves quickly to changes in the economy. It is a logical consequence that there may be periods of oversupply and of overdemand of doctorates. The former should not be so serious since the Ph.D. should be versatile enough to find a useful and challenging task to perform for society.[7]

Some economists, however, appeared less sanguine about the strengths of the free market system. Citing an article in *Time* magazine, Handa and Skolnik noted:

A plausible case can be made that the Government should try to predict the future man-power needs for every occupation, and then channel the intake into universities, discipline by discipline. This kind of massive educational planning is done to various extents in Communist countries, as well as in Sweden and France. To a nation as committed to freedom of choice as the U.S., the very idea seems repellant. Yet what the U.S. now has may be even worse: economic manipulation of the manpower market without adequate long range planning[8]

Whatever economic benefits might flow from this type of approach would probably be outweighed by its negative impact upon the immediate interests of the academic and corporate communities. The erosion of university autonomy, the elimination of free enterprise in business and industry in favour of centralized state planning, and government control of the now independent professional organizations, would all violate the traditional practices and values of both business and academe.[9]

The persistent refusal of the federal government throughout the 1970s to follow the advice of the Science Council of Canada and establish an industrial strategy that might stem the decline of the manufacturing sector and generate productive employment is only one example of the failure of economic planning to make significant headway in Canada.[10] And the failure of the Ontario government to assert direct authority over the plethora of agencies, board, and commissions that emerged in the province during the post-war period is another indication of the limitations of government planning in a free-enterprise society. As Fred Schindeler has noted:

Classical liberal-democratic theory and the liberal institutions it created were both based on the assumption that the functions of the state should be strictly curtailed ... In Ontario particularly, the politicians who have held office since the end of the war seem to have been unable to adjust their liberal philosophies to the demands for a welfare state that have been forced upon them. Wanting to maintain a facade of limited government and yet compelled to intervene in more areas of public concern in order to survive, they have resorted to extradepartmental agencies as a compromise solution to their dilemma. This expedient salves their own liberal consciences and also meets the demands of the organized pressure groups that want the kind of control over their operations that can be achieved only through public authority but nevertheless fear direct government supervision of their activities – no doubt because they too were nurtured on the principles of classical liberalism.[11]

By 1980, even the conservative *Globe and Mail* had recognized the impact of this approach on the province's universities. 'What the Government hasn't done, and shows no signs of doing, is to develop a policy – a policy which the universities, plagued by uncertainty and forced to curtail or kill valuable programs, need in order to plan for the future.'[12]

Thus, ironically, the utilitarian multiversity has been a far from perfect instrument of economic development. Proponents of the 'idealistic' purposes of higher education might well take pleasure in this conclusion. For if economic planning worked more efficiently, then the materialistic, technocratic, and anti-intellectual character of the institution might be dangerously reinforced. And the failure of the modern university to carry out adequately the economic duties assigned to it during the last two decades perhaps suggests that the classical goals of pursuing truth, providing equal opportunity, and stimulating critical thought have in fact survived in a significant, if diminished, manner. But in these lofty areas as well, there seems to be little reason for optimism, and herein lay the most serious indictment of the contemporary university. A class-divided society continues to perpetuate élitism in the university; an unstable economy removes any guarantee of productive employment for graduates; and a consumerist, essentially anti-intellectual culture, fed by the mass media and shaped by capitalist values, has sullied the quality of higher education itself.[13]

These are severe conclusions, especially the last. Yet the veracity of the last is what has so badly damaged the university. If all the other problems existed, but the university continued to promote and encourage genuine contemplative, critical thought, then the other evils might well be tolerable. And there are undoubtedly many students and professors who do stimulate each other to heights of intellectual ecstacy in the classroom. On the other hand, every teacher, student, and administrator could tell his or her own story about how the institution has been diseased by the epidemic around it.

Students, especially the best ones, are frighteningly competitive and career-conscious in this economically depressed era. Faculty are increasingly cynical and appear to devote as much time applying for research grants in order to get out of the classroom as they spend preparing for teaching. Ideas are discussed, but are they ever taken seriously? While the 1960s obviously produced many of the structural problems the universities faced in the years that followed, it is hard for a graduate of that era (who has since taught university) not to be slightly nostalgic about the quality of education in much of that period. For a fleeting moment, intellectual life was dynamic, ideas were explored with intensity and commitment, and sincere efforts were made by many to take what they had learned (or taught) in the classroom into the community for the purpose of improving social conditions. Quickly that phase passed, and as the economy receded, higher education exposed more clearly than ever its careerist, consumerist essence. Academic 'relevance' in the 1960s meant the linking of critical thought with meaningful action. In the 1970s and early 80s, relevance was still in vogue, but its definition had changed. It now meant that higher education was a simple (if inefficient) economic and technocratic commodity in the service of business and government. And as a 1980 survey of public opinion in Ontario revealed, the better the university filled this role, the more public support it could expect.[14] University officials deceived themselves if they believed that the purely academic functions of higher education had much deep-rooted support in the community as a whole.

Readers may decry the bleak picture painted in these concluding comments. They may deplore the lack of 'solutions' to the problems described. Yet that very demand is an indication of one of the university's main deficiencies so evidenced by the events of the last two decades. The intellectual work most appreciated these days is that which produces instant, marketable answers to complex social problems. Instead, let this be a provocation to reflect on the dilemma, to engage in critical self-evaluation, and to rethink radically the entire post-secondary enterprise. If we do not approach the issues in this spirit, then the solutions we produce will not only not work, but, worse yet, the soul of the university might be poisoned forever even if they did.

Notes

INTRODUCTION

1 *Financial Post*, 21 Nov. 1981; Government of Canada, *Fiscal Arrangements in the Eighties: Proposals of the Government of Canada*, Nov, 1981
2 See W.G. Fleming, *Post-Secondary and Adult Education*, vol. IV of *Ontario's Educative Society* (Toronto: University of Toronto Press, 1971); R.S. Harris, *A History of Higher Education in Canada: 1663–1960* (Toronto: University of Toronto Press, 1976). For extended discussions of the historiography of higher education in Canada, see P. Axelrod, 'Historical Writing and Canadian Universities: The State of the Art,' *Queen's Quarterly* (spring 1982), and 'Higher Education in Canada,' *History of Education Quarterly*, (summer 1979).
3 See, for example, Ralph Miliband, *The State in Capitalist Society* (London: Quartet Books, 1973); Wallace Clement, *The Canadian Corporate Elite* (Toronto: McClelland and Stewart, 1975); E.S. Greenberg, *Serving the Few: Corporate Capitalism and the Bias of Government Policy* (New York: John Wiley, 1974); D.N. Smith, *Who Rules the Universities?* (New York: Monthly Review Press, 1974); R.W. Nelsen and D.A. Nock, eds., *Reading, Writing and Riches: Education and the Socio-Economic Order in North America* (Kitchener: Between the Lines, 1978); Stephen Schecter, 'Capitalism, Class and Educational Reform in Canada,' in Leo Panitch, ed. *The Canadian State: Political Economy and Political Power* (Toronto: University of Toronto Press, 1977); Denis Forcese, *The Canadian Class Structure* (Toronto: McGraw Hill-Ryerson, 1975).

CHAPTER ONE

1 R.S. Harris, *Quiet Evolution: A Study of the Educational System of Ontario* (Toronto: University of Toronto Press, 1967), 148
2 'Class, Bureaucracy and the School,' in D. Myers, ed., *The Failure of Educational Reform in Canada* (Toronto: McClelland and Stewart, 1973), 16
3 See N. Sutherland, 'Introduction,' in M. Katz and P. Mattingly, eds., *Education and Social Change: Themes from Ontario's Past* (New York: New York University Press, 1975)
4 *The School Promoters: Education and Social Class in Mid-Nineteenth Century Upper Canada* (Toronto: McClelland and Stewart, 1977). See also, D. Wilson, R. Stamp, L.-P. Audet, eds., *Canadian Education: A History* (Scarborough: Prentice Hall, 1970), chaps. 11–13.

5 *Annual Report of the Normal, Model, High and Public Schools of Ontario for the Year 1873,* Part III, 10, cited in D. Lawr and R. Gidney, eds., *Educating Canadians: A Documentary History of Public Education* (Toronto: Van Nostrand Reinhold, 1973), 96

6 'Report of the Chief Superintendent of Education for the Year 1880,' *Journals of the Legislative Assembly of New Brunswick, 1881,* cited in Lawr and Gidney, *Educating Canadians,* 93

7 Cited in ibid., 96

8 R. Stamp, 'The Campaign for Technical Education in Ontario, 1876–1914,' (unpublished PhD thesis, University of Western Ontario, 1970), 14, 212, 68

9 J.M. Gilmour, *Spatial Evolution of Manufacturing: Southern Ontario 1851–1891,* (Toronto: University of Toronto Press, 1972), 154, 169. In 1871 there were 105 brewing establishments in southern Ontario, employing 536 workers; in 1891 there were 82 breweries with 1,047 workers. Similarly, in agricultural implements, there were 173 companies in 1871 with 2,143 employees, and in 1891 there were 136 establishments employing 4,029. In both cases, the 'value of output' tripled in the twenty-year period.

10 *Royal Commission on the Relations of Labor and Capital in Canada,* 1889, cited in Lawr and Gidney, *Educating Canadians,* 162; see also *Report of the Commissioners Appointed to Enquire into the Working Mills and Factories of the Dominion,* 1882, 2–3, cited in ibid., 65–7.

11 Ibid., 158–9

12 Cited in Stamp, 'The Campaign,' 257, 261

13 Castell Hopkins, *Canadian Annual Review, 1911,* 438

14 *Report of the Royal Commission on the University of Toronto,* 1906, liv

15 See R.S. Harris, *A History of Higher Education in Canada: 1663–1960* (Toronto: University of Toronto Press, 1976); D.C. Masters, *Protestant Church Colleges in Canada,* (Toronto: University of Toronto Press, 1966); L.K. Shook, *Catholic Post-Secondary Education in English-Speaking Canada: A History,* (Toronto: University of Toronto Press, 1971)

16 For a discussion of the impact of 'progressivism' on the role of government in economic and social affairs, see R.C. Brown and R. Cook, *Canada, 1896–1921: A Nation Transformed* (Toronto: McClelland and Stewart, 1974) and H.V. Nelles, *The Politics of Development: Forests, Mines and Hydro-Electric Power in Ontario, 1849–1941* (Toronto: Macmillan, 1974)

17 See *University Government in Canada,* the report of a commission sponsored by the Canadian Association of University Teachers and the Association of Universities and Colleges of Canada (Toronto: University of Toronto Press, 1967), 19–41. See also chaps 2 and 3 of this book.

18 Cited in Hopkins, *Canadian Annual Review, 1913,* 424

19 See 'Resolutions' of the Royal Society of Canada in *Proceedings and Transactions of the Royal Society of Canada, 1915,* cited in T.H. Levere and R.A. Jarrell, eds., *A Curious Field Book: Science and Society in Canadian History* (Toronto: Oxford University Press 1974), 178, 182–7

20 R. Stamp, 'Vocational Objectives in Canadian Education: An Historical Overview,' in S. Ostry, ed., *Canadian Higher Education in the Seventies* (Ottawa, 1972), 255

21 R. Stamp, 'Canadian High Schools in the 1920's and 1930's: the Social Challenge to the Academic Tradition' (paper presented to annual conference of the Canadian Historical Association, 1978), 9

22 R. Stamp, 'Evolving Patterns of Education: English-Canada from the 1870's to 1914,' in D. Wilson, Stamp, Audet, eds., *Canadian Education,* 325

23 P. Oliver, *G. Howard Ferguson: Ontario Tory* (Toronto: University of Toronto Press, 1977), 234; and Stamp, 'Canadian High Schools,' 2–4

24 Stamp, 'Canadian High Schools,' 3

25 See E.E. Stewart, 'The Role of the Provincial Government in the Development of the Universities of Ontario, 1791–1964' (unpublished DEd thesis, University of Toronto, 1970), 355–69. On the question of academics serving government during the Depression, see M. Horn, 'Academics and Canadian Social and Economic Policy in the Depression and War Years,' *Journal of Canadian Studies*, (winter 1978–79).

26 Dr W.E. McNeil to the 1939 conference of the National Conference of Canadian Universities, cited in G. Pilkington, 'A History of the National Conference of Canadian Universities, 1911–1961' (unpublished DEd thesis, University of Toronto, 1974), 271

27 In 1955 higher education absorbed only .13 of the gross provincial product in Ontario; in 1970 it consumed 1.61 per cent (*The Learning Society*, the Report of the Commission on Post-Secondary Education in Ontario, Government of Ontario, 1972, 222). In 1951 18 per cent of the provincial budget went to the entire educational sector; by 1964, that figure had climbed to 33 per cent. Stewart, 'The Role,' 405

28 'Education for Democracy,' *Saturday Night*, 7 Dec. 1940

29 'Do You Deserve Democracy? A Letter to a Young Canadian Citizen,' *Food For Thought* (Oct. 1940)

30 Ibid. (Dec. 1940)

31 See University of Toronto, *President's Report, 1941*, 1, and 1943, 3; Queen's University *Principal's Report, 1941*, 2–3, 7.

32 See J.L. Granatstein, *Canada's War: The Politics of the Mackenzie King Government, 1939–1945* (Toronto: Oxford University Press, 1975), chap. 5.

33 *Report of the President, 1943*, 4

34 Pilkington, 'History of the NCCU,' 304, 311

35 See 'Report of Committee,' a Proposed Defence Training Course, drawn up by the General Committee's Sub-Committee on Courses, Ontario Department of Education, 13 Nov. 1941; R.C. Wallace to G.F. Rogers, 19 Dec. 1941; W. Sherwood Fox to G.F. Rogers, 20 Dec. 1941; RG2–P3, Archives of Ontario

36 *Globe and Mail*, 24 Dec. 1942. The events are described in Pilkington, 'History of the NCCU,' 329–33.

37 See also A.G. Bedford, *The University of Winnipeg: A History of the Founding Colleges* (Toronto: University of Toronto Press, 1976), 239; and 'Correspondence with Prime Minister Concerning Liberal Arts Courses in Canadian Universities,' from the Canadian Social Science Research Council, 6 Jan. 1943, RG2–P3, Archives of Ontario.

38 Janet R. Keith, 'Will Canada's Universities Meet Needs of Post-War?' *Saturday Night*, 15 Jan. 1944

39 Charles E. Burke, 'Science, Technology and Research in the Canadian Democracy,' 1948, pamphlet in the McMaster University Archives

40 M. Thistle, ed., *The MacKenzie-McNaughton Wartime Letters* (Toronto: University of Toronto Press, 1975), MacKenzie to McNaughton, 27 Oct. 1941, and xix–xx

41 *Principal's Report, 1941*, 11

42 Vernon Hill, 'Canadian Universities Train Youth for War and Leadership in Critical Post-War Period,' *Saturday Night*, 20 Jan. 1945

43 'A Frank Statement of its Origins and Developments, Present Status and Future Needs' (1944), McMaster University Archives

44 Harris, *A History of Higher Education in Canada*, 456; E.F. Sheffield, 'The Post-War Surge in Post-Secondary Education, 1945–1969,' in Wilson, Stamp, Audet eds., *Canadian Education;* D. Stager, 'Federal Government Grants to Canadian Universities, 1951–1967,' *Canadian Historical Review* vol. LIV, no. 3 (Sept. 1973), 287–90

45 Budget speech, 16 March, 1944, 17
46 *Report of the Royal Commission on the National Development of the Arts, Letters and Sciences* (Ottawa, 1951), 132-7, 141
47 For example, University of Toronto, *Report of the President 1951*; University of Western Ontario, *Report of the President, 1951*
48 Queen's University, *Principal's Report 1941*, 2-3
49 J.L. Granatstein, *The Politics of Survival: The Conservative Party in Canada, 1939-1945* (Toronto: University of Toronto Press, 1967), chap. 6; Granatstein, *Canada's War*, chap. 10; G. Caplan, *The Dilemma of Canadian Socialism: The CCF in Ontario* (Toronto: McClelland and Stewart, 1973), chap. 5; J. Manthorpe, *The Power and the Tories: Ontario Politics, 1943 to the Present* (Toronto: Macmillan, 1974), 36
50 Granatstein, *Canada's War*, 277; Canadian Institute of Public Opinion, *Public Opinion News Service*, 8 March 1944; 10 Oct. 1945
51 See O.J. Firestone, *Industry and Education* (University of Ottawa, 1969); C.P. Stacey, 'The 1940's,' and W. Kilbourn, 'The 1950's,' in J.M.S. Careless and R.C. Brown, eds., *The Canadians: Part I, 1867-1967* (Toronto: Macmillan, 1968); R. Bothwell, I. Drummond, J. English, *Canadian since 1945: Power, Politics and Provincialism* (Toronto: University of Toronto Press, 1981).
52 *How Your Tax Dollar is Spent* (Ottawa, 1972); T. Hockin, *Government in Canada* (Toronto: McGraw Hill, 1976); A. Rose, 'Social Services,' in Careless and Brown, eds., *The Canadians: Part II; and L. Feldman, *The Municipal Dynamic* (Toronto: Ontario Economic Council 1974)
53 See, for example,*Financial Post*, 6 Feb. 1960, and *Globe and Mail*, 10-14 July 1956.
54 *Public Opinion News Service*, 4 June 1951; 6 Oct. 1951; 1 March 1952; 19 March 1956
55 See R.A. Easterlin, 'An Explanation of the American Baby Boom following World War II,' in D.M. Heer, ed., *Readings in Population* (Englewood Cliffs: Prentice-Hall, 1968); Alan Sweezy, 'The Economic Explanation of Fertility Changes in the United States,' *Population Studies*, vol. 25, no. 2 (1971); W.E. Kalbach and W.M. McVey, *The Demographic Bases of Canadian Society* (Toronto: McGraw-Hill, 1971); B. MacLeod, C. Ivison, and N. Bidani, *Patterns and Trends in Ontario Population* (Toronto: OISE, 1972); Bothwell et al., *Canada since 1945*, chap. 3.
56 *Public Opinion News Service*, 30 Aug. 1947; 29 Aug. 1950; 7 Aug. 1954; 4 Jan. 1956; 2 Jan. 1957
57 'Canadian University and College Enrolment Projected to 1965,' NCCU, *Proceedings, 1955*, 34-6
58 C.T. Bissell, ed., *Canada's Crisis in Higher Education* (Toronto: University of Toronto Press, 1957), and *Halfway Up Parnassus: A Personal Account of the University of Toronto, 1932-1971* (Toronto: University of Toronto Press, 1974), 44
59 Stanley Deeks (an organizer of the conference and an employee of the Industrial Foundation on Education), private scrapbook of newspaper clippings, and interview 12 May 1976
60 Industrial Foundation on Education, *The Case for Corporate Giving to Higher Education, 1957*. See also chap.2 below.
61 *Final Report of the Royal Commission on Canada's Economic Prospects* (Ottawa, 1957), 452
62 *Public Opinion News Service*, 6 Jan. 1951; 16 May 1953. See also speech by Stanley Deeks in which he portrayed the Soviet Union as a 'vicious and uncompromising enemy,' *Belleville Intelligencer*, 20 May 1957
63 Wilson Woodside, *The University Question* (Toronto: Ryerson, 1958), 30
64 Cited in IFE, *The Case for Corporate Giving, 1957*, 4, 5

65 *Final Report*, 19

66 Budget statement of Dana Porter, 1 March 1956

67 'Colloquium held in the Senate Chamber of the University of Toronto, January 17, 1958, with the Principals and Presidents of Ontario Universities and the heads of mathematics departments,' RG2–P3, Archives of Ontario

68 Submission of Canadian Universities to the Royal Commission on Canada's Economic Prospects, presented by representatives of NCCU, 6 March 1956, 5

69 'Education: the Key to Survival,' *Cost and Management*, July 1961

70 Submission of Canadian Universities, 5

71 Submission of Ontario to the Royal Commission on Canada's Economic Prospects, 1956, 57

72 *The Case for Corporate Giving, 1957*, 3, 10

73 J.D. Barrington, cited in *Financial Post*, 15 Sept. 1956

74 *The Case for Corporate Giving, 1957*, 18

75 H.J. Somers, President of St Francis Xavier University, prepared for the Ottawa Conference on Canada's Crisis in Higher Education, 1956, 'Private and Corporate Support of Canadian Universities,' in Bissell, ed., *Canada's Crisis in Higher Education*

76 G. Bertram, *The Contribution of Education to Economic Growth*, a study prepared for the Economic Council of Canada, (Ottawa, 1966), 61–2. See also Economic Council of Canada, *Second Annual Review* (Ottawa, 1965), 87

77 *Public Opinion News Service*, 29 June 1963; 10 Feb. 1965

78 *Canadian Annual Review, 1963*, 352

79 *Public Opinion News Service*, 7 April 1965; 29 June 1963

80 See the following correspondence: the case of F.C., 17 Sept. 1947; memo from E.J. Yonge, executive assistant to minister, to M.E. Anderson, Department of Education, 17 Sept. 1947; J.A. to Dunlop, 28 July 1955; Dunlop to J.A., 6 Aug. 1955; Dunlop to P.K., 31 Aug. 1956, RG2–P3, Archives of Ontario

81 Editorial, 'As We See it,' July 1959

82 Proceedings, Canadian Labour Congress, 1962, 19; see also its Proceedings, 1958, 1960, 1964

83 'Annual Brief to the Prime Minister, Leslie Frost, and Members of the Ontario Cabinet,' 25 Feb. 1959, RG2–P3, Archives of Ontario

84 *Canadian Annual Review, 1961*, 164

85 *Winnipeg Tribune*, 20 Dec. 1960

86 *Canadian Annual Review, 1960, 1961*; J.S. Dupré *et al*, *Federalism and Policy Development: The Case of Adult Occupational Training in Ontario* (Toronto: University of Toronto Press, 1973)

87 *Debates*, Ontario Legislative Assembly, 26 March 1963, 2,115

88 *The Learning Society*, 147

89 *Canadian School Journal* (1954), 28; McMaster University, *President's Report*, 1959/60

90 Robert Warner, *Imperial Oil Review* (Feb. 1961)

91 IFE, *The Case for Corporate Giving*, 6; Stanley Deeks cited in the *Port Arthur News Chronicle*, 14 Aug. 1961; *Financial Post*, 28 May 1960 (editorial); IFE, 'Academic Casualty Rates and Student Aid,' RG2–P3, Archives of Ontario; IFE, *The Case for Increasing Student Motivation* (1960)

92 Queen's University, *Principal's Report, 1950/51*, 13; University of Toronto, *President's Report, 1951*, 4; University of Western Ontario, *President's Report, 1951*, 53

93 *Canada's Crisis in Higher Education*, 219; Report of the National Federation of Canadian University Students, 'Campaign to Secure Increased Government Aid for Universities,'

presented to 15th Congress of NFCUS at the University of Western Ontario, 1955, McMaster University Archives.

94 National Federation of Canadian University Students, 'Brief on Education,' 1960, RG2–P3, Archives of Ontario; e.g., Proceedings of CLC, 1962, 23

95 Tuition fees were eliminated at Memorial University in Newfoundland in 1966. In 1968, tuition was subject to means tests and ultimately reintroduced for all students. See F. Rowe, *Education and Culture in Newfoundland* (Scarborough: McGraw-Hill Ryerson, 1976), 68.

96 See, for example, the remarks of E.E. Stewart, the deputy minister of university affairs, *Globe and Mail*, 14 March 1969.

97 *Globe and Mail*, c. 1958, cited in G. Cook and D. Stager, *Student Financial Assistance Programs* (Toronto Institute for Policy Analysis, 1969); W.J. McCordiac in the *Canadian Banker*, vol 69 (1962), 93; *Toronto Star*, 10 Oct. 1958; IFE, *The Case for Increasing Student Aid* (1958), 7: 'Making education free implies the possibility of state control. It is a cherished tradition that free enterprise in higher education is a corollary of free enterprise in other areas of our society.'

98 *The Case for Increasing Student Aid* 4

99 *Debates*, Ontario Legislative Assembly, 25 March 1963, 2134. See also *Debates*, 19 Feb. 1965, 641, where both Davis and Robarts are quoted as opposing free tuition on the grounds that such a policy would violate free enterprise.

100 Ibid., 10 Feb. 1958, 70. For an overview of the type of student assistance that existed in Ontario before 1958, aid which had once been distributed in the form of limited bursaries and scholarships, see W.G. Fleming, *Post-Secondary and Adult Education*, vol. IV, *Ontario's Educative Society*, (Toronto: University of Toronto Press, 1971), 407–22.

101 Speech given at the opening of the Chemistry and Chemical Engineering Building at Waterloo College, 3 Dec. 1958, RG2–P3, Archives of Ontario

102 Fleming, *Post-Secondary and Adult Education*, 410

103 E.g., Cook and Stager, *Student Financial Assistance Programs*, 65; *House of Commons Debates*, 14 July 1964, 4,442

104 T.C. Douglas, *House of Commons Debates*, 14 July 1964, 4,467

105 See Bissell, ed., *Canada's Crisis in Higher Education*; Submission of Canadian Universities to the Royal Commission on Canada's Economic Prospects; Submission of the Canadian Manufacturers' Association to the Royal Commission on Canada's Economic Prospects

106 *Debates*, Ontario Legislative Assembly, 23 Feb. 1965, on the announcement of the establishment of the community college system in Ontario (published in pamphlet form by government of Ontario)

CHAPTER TWO

1 Economists and economic historians, with varying degrees of cynicism and support, agree that 'non-interference' by government is the capitalist ideal. See Milton Friedman, *Capitalism and Freedom* (Chicago: University of Chicago Press, 1962); R.L. Heilbroner, *The Making of Economic Society* (London: Prentice Hall, 4th ed., 1972); Paul Baran and Paul Sweezy, *Monopoly Capital: An Essay on the American Economic and Social Order* (Penguin, 1968); Joan Robinson, *Economic Philosophy* (Penguin, 1964). Sources which document the active role of government in Canadian economic affairs include, W.T. Easterbrook and H. Aitken, *Canadian Economic History* (Toronto: Macmillan, 1956); 'Conclusion,' in Harold Innis, *The Fur Trade in Canada* (Toronto: University of Toronto Press, 1970); and H.V. Nelles, *The Politics of Development* (Toronto: Macmillan, 1974).

2 See T. Hockin, *Government in Canada* (Toronto: McGraw-Hill, 1976), 23; F. Schindeler, *Responsible Government in Ontario* (Toronto: University of Toronto Press, 1969), chap. 2. See also J.E. Hodgetts, *The Canadian Civil Service* (Toronto: University of Toronto Press, 1973), and R. Deaton, 'The Fiscal Crisis of the State in Canada,' in D. Roussopoulos, ed., *The Political Economy of the State* (Montreal: Black Rose, 1973).

3 See Heilbroner, *The Making of Economic Society*, chap. 8

4 The comments of C.D. Howe, former minister in the St Laurent government, are an interesting insight into the views of an unrepentant free enterpriser regarding the relationship of business and government. 'The government will take the initiative and do what it can to coordinate the efforts of government, business and other interested groups in achieving full and effective utilization of industrial expansion in the interest of all citizens of the country,' cited in O.J. Firestone, *Industry and Education* (University of Ottawa, 1969), 72. See also Ralph Miliband, *The State in Capitalist Society* (London: Quartet Books, 1973).

5 See R.T. Naylor, 'The Rise and Fall of the Third Commerical Empire of the St. Lawrence,' in G. Teeple, eg., *Capitalism and the National Question in Canada* (Toronto: University of Toronto Press, 1972); G. Horowitz, 'Conservatism, Liberalism and Socialism,' in his *Canadian Labour in Politics* (Toronto: University of Toronto Press, 1968); Hockin, *Government in Canada*, chaps. 2, 3; Muriel Armstrong, *The Canadian Economy and its Problems* (Scarborough: Prentice-Hall, 1972), 100–3.

6 E.F. Sheffield, 'The Post War Surge in Post Secondary Education: 1945–1969,' in D. Wilson, R. Stamp, and L.P. Audet, eds., *Canadian Education: A History* (Scarborough: Prentice-Hall, 1970); J.S. Brubacher and W. Rudy, *Higher Education in Transition* (New York: Harper and Rowe, 1976), chap. 9, and 409; Queen's University, *Report of the Principal to the Board of Trustees, 1952/53*, (which compares private contributions to Queen's with those of American universities), 92; 'Sources of Support for Higher Education,' in T.H. McLeod, ed., *Post-Secondary Education in a Technological Society*, (Montreal: McGill-Queen's University Press, 1973), 28

7 See IFE, *The Case for Corporate Giving to Higher Education, 1957*, 4–5.

8 'Canada's Expanding Universities,' 27 Nov. 1961

9 H.J. Fraser, 'The University and Business,' in *Canadian Universities Today* (Toronto: University of Toronto Press, 1961), papers presented to the Royal Society of Canada, 1960

10 *The Case for Corporate Giving, 1957*, part I, 17

11 'What Does Business Owe to Education?' Aug. 1960

12 'The Business Community's Responsibility to Higher Education,' at Kenneth R. Wilson memorial luncheon of the Business Newspapers Association of Canada, 18 June 1964, reprinted in the *Monetary Times*, Sept. 1964

13 Richard Edsall, 'Education: The Boom That Never Goes Bust,' *Canadian Business*, Oct. 1963

14 'Education for Industry,' brief presented by the Ontario Chamber of Commerce, 4 Aug. 1964, RG2–P3, Archives of Ontario

15 Fraser, 'The University and Business,' in *Canadian Universities Today*

16 *The Case for Corporate Giving, 1957, 2*

17 Cited in University of Toronto, *President's Report, 1956*, 5

18 *The Case for Corporate Giving, 1957*, part II, 22. See also A.A. Cumming, in the *Monetary Times*, Sept. 1964. The intellectual – and financial – opportunism expressed in this point of view should not be overlooked. Why universities would be sufficiently autonomous if they raised only 15 per cent of their funds privately as opposed to raising nothing, was never clearly explained. Obviously, the argument was being rationalized solely in terms of what

business community spokesmen believed the private sector could afford. Whatever business contributed, it was evident that the government was seen to hold the major responsibility for financing higher education in Canada.

19 'What Does Business Owe to Education?'
20 See John Galbraith, *The New Industrial State* (Boston: Houghton-Mifflin, 1967), in which he describes the various planning techniques used increasingly by private corporations during the twentieth century.
21 J. Watson and M. Douglas, *Company Contributions in Canada* (Conference Board Study, 1963), 47
22 Albert A. Shea, ed., *Corporate Giving in Canada* (published for the Committee on Corporate Giving in Canada, 1953), 50. In a survey of 878 companies, only 5 per cent were found to allocate charitable donations by committee; the rest relied on individual decisions, usually by the president of the company.
23 'Management of Corporate Aid to Education,' *Chemistry in Canada*, vol. 12, no. 12 (Dec. 1960), where Pollard's article is cited
24 G.R. Finch and J.G. O'Neill, 'Policies for Corporate Giving,' *Business Quarterly*, Nov. 1961
25 Quotations from Watson and Douglas, *Company Contributions*, 32, 36–7, 16, 14, 10, 15
26 Quoted in Aileen D. Ross, 'Organized Philanthropy in an Urban Community,' *Canadian Journal of Economics and Political Science*, Nov. 1952, 482
27 H. Byleveld, 'Business Aid to Universities: A Margin of Freedom,' *Canadian Business*, Jan. 1967
28 Ibid.
29 Watson and Douglas, *Company Contributions*, 23
30 Finch and O'Neill, 'Policies for Corporate Giving.' It is possible that some companies took advantage of tax exemption clauses in the Income Tax Act, which by 1960 allowed companies to contribute 10 per cent of their pre-tax profits to charities. But as Watson and Douglas argued, 'Its possible significance as a stimulus ... seems to have been overrated,' if only because charitable donations consumed, in 1965, only about 1.4 per cent of all pre-tax profits in Canada (Byleveld, 'Business Aid to Universities').
31 *The Case for Corporate Giving, 1957*; and interview with Stanley Deeks, former executive director of the IFE, 23 May 1976
32 Quoted in C.T. Bissell, *Halfway Up Parnassus* (Toronto: University of Toronto Press, 1974), 48
33 University of Toronto, *President's Report, 1957*, 8
34 Deeks said that, when he left the IFE in 1962, he cancelled 23 speaking engagements. Interview, 23 May 1976
35 *The Case for Corporate Giving, 1958*, 6
36 Deeks has in his personal collection a thick scrap book of newspaper accounts of the St Andrew's Conference. He noted as well that it received wide television and radio coverage.
37 *The Case for Corporate Giving, 1958*, 19
38 Ibid., *1959*, i–ii
39 Ibid., 1960, 14–15; *1961*, i; *1962*, i
40 E.F. Sheffield, *University Costs and Sources of Support* (Ottawa: CUF, 1962), 28, 29
41 H. Byleveld, *Company Contributions in Canada, 1965*
42 Robert Neesham, in *Executive*, Nov. 1966. See also *Toronto Star*, 6 Jan. 1961; *Financial Post*, 31 Dec. 1966.
43 See *The Case for Corporate Giving, 1957–1962*, and Byleveld, *Company Contributions*. In 1957, research grants were 11 per cent of the total contribution; in 1965, they were estimated by Byleveld to be 5.4 per cent

44 IFE, *Scholarships and Bursaries Provided by Business and Industry, 1961*
45 *The Case for Corporate Giving, 1957*, 2; *1960*, ii
46 Watson and Douglas, *Company Contributions*, 32
47 'Chairmen: Can You Spare a Dime?' *Executive*, Feb. 1967
48 Borden to Leslie Frost, 16 Dec. 1963, RG2–P3, Archives of Ontario
49 *The Case for Corporate Giving, 1958, 1960, 1962*
50 See *Canadian Oil and Gas Industries*, Feb. 1959
51 Byleveld, *Company Contributions*
52 IFE, *Programmes of Industry and Commerce for Financial Assistance to Higher Education, 1958*; *The Case for Corporate Giving, 1962*; Byleveld, *Company Contributions*
53 *The Case for Corporate Giving, 1962*
54 Ibid., *1959, 1960, 1962*
55 *Foreign Direct Investment in Canada* (Ottawa, 1972), 19–20
56 *The Case for Corporate Giving, 1958, 1959*
57 Watson and Douglas, *Company Contributions in Canada*, 10. The authors reported that corporate giving to communities in which companies were located was a prime feature of giving practices. This sense of community involvement may have been true in the United States as well. Stanley Deeks agreed with this interpretation.
58 Brubacher and Rudy, *Higher Education in Transition*, chap. 9; Byleveld noted in *Canadian Business*, Jan. 1967, that, unlike the US, 'there are virtually no truly private universities left in Canada.' Allan Arlett, *A Canadian Directory to Foundations and Granting Agencies* (AUCC, 1973), found at least 26,000 foundations in the United States and 1,400 in Canada, with 450 of those located in Ontario.
59 Watson and Douglas, *Company Contributions*, 41. Of 64 subsidiaries surveyed, only one was permitted to give over $2,000 without head office approval; only two could spend over $1,000, and 58 could spend no more than $1,000 without head office authorization.
60 Imperial Oil, for example, was a major contributor to the fund-raising campaign at York University in 1965. On the Carleton situation, see the *President's Report, 1956–57*, 7
61 IFE, *Public Fund Raising by Canadian Universities and Colleges*, 1960, appendices 6, 7. The disparity between the national total and the total for the Maritimes is explained by the fact that Quebec universities (especially McGill) raised $3.7 million more than they sought.
62 See chap. 3 of this book in which York fund raising campaign is discussed.
63 *The Case for Corporate Giving, 1958, 1962*
64 For a historical account of this process, see T.W. Acheson, 'The National Policy and the Industrialization of the Maritimes,' *Acadiensis* vol. I, no. 2 (1972)
65 *The Case for Corporate Giving, 1958–1962*; see also note 40.

CHAPTER THREE

1 For general accounts of the expansion of higher education in Ontario, see R.S. Harris, *A History of Higher Education in Canada, 1663–1960* (Toronto: University of Toronto Press, 1976); W.G. Fleming, *Post-Secondary and Adult Education*, vol. IV of *Ontario's Educative Society* (Toronto: University of Toronto Press, 1971); E.E. Stewart, 'The Role of the Provincial Government in the Development of the Universities of Ontario, 1791–1964,' unpublished DEd thesis, University of Toronto, 1970; L.K. Shook, *Catholic Post-Secondary Education in English-Speaking Canada* (Toronto: University of Toronto Press, 1971); D.C. Masters, *Protestant Church Colleges in Canada: A History* (Toronto: University of Toronto Press, 1966).

2 Interview with George Gathercole (former aide to Frost), Aug. 1976; and 'notes' on meeting with Premier Frost, 18 Dec. 1958 (with members of Organizing Committee, York University), J.R. Kidd Papers, York University Archives. See chap. 4 for a discussion of the government role.

3 *Globe and Mail*, 27 Feb. 1957. Rowntree was exaggerating because throughout the 1950s and 60s numerous groups from a variety of communities in Ontario lobbied persistently and usually unsuccessfully for university facilities. Archive correspondence and interview with E.E. Stewart, former deputy minister of university affairs, 2 May 1976, reveal that full university facilities were sought by groups in North Bay, Sault Ste Marie, Oshawa, Barrie, Orillia, and Chesley.

4 *Canadian Journal of Economics and Political Science*, Nov. 1952, 482

5 E.E. Mitchelson, 'The Story of Brock University to Date,' 1964 (Brock University Library). See also *Debates*, Ontario Legislative Assembly, 1 May 1964, 2,712, where the founding of Brock is discussed.

6 This appraisal of Dunlop is offered by W.G. Fleming, *The Administrative Structure*, vol. II of *Ontario's Educative Society*, 11. See also, 'The Story of Brock University.'

7 G.P. Gilmour to John P. Robarts, 7 April 1960, and D.M. Hadden (business administrator, McMaster University) to J.R. McCarthy (Department of Education), 17 July 1962; RG2–P3, Archives of Ontario

8 Stanley Deeks, 'Brock University: The Conquest That Failed' n.d. (circa 1967). This is a detailed, unpublished, and little known account of the early history of Brock University by a former organizer and vice-president of Brock who was relieved of his responsibilities in 1963. While his interpretation is open to question, this volume is extremely useful since it contains copies of correspondence, internal documents, and briefs prepared by Brock officials. For information included in the following two paragraphs see the following correspondence: Chown to Deeks, 16 Feb. 1962, 6 April 1962, 4 May 1962, Deeks to Chown, 11 June 1962

9 Schmon to Deeks and Mitchelson, 12 Oct. 1962, ibid.

10 W.A. Martin to Deeks, ibid., 5 July 1963; see also 'Board of Governors,' report prepared by Deeks, 12 March 1963, reproduced in ibid.

11 Ibid., 152, 89–90, 127–40; and minutes of meeting of Committee on University Affairs, 19 July 1962, CUA Files, RG–32, Archives of Ontario

12 'Graduates for a New Age: The Story of Growth at the University of Toronto,' National Fund File, University of Toronto Archives. See also *Varsity*, 25 Oct. 1957.

13 W.J. Dunlop to Mr Justice O.J. Cowan, 2 Dec. 1958, RG2–P3, Archives of Ontario

14 National Fund, 'News Bulletin,' no. 2, 20 Nov. 1959, University of Toronto Archives; *Varsity*, 9 Oct. 1959

15 James Scott, *Of Mud and Dreams: University of Waterloo, 1957–67* (Toronto: Ryerson Press, 1967), 22–4

16 J.G. Hagey to W.J. Dunlop, 12 Oct. 1955, RG2–P3, Archives of Ontario

17 *Of Mud and Dreams*, 30. The meeting with industrialists is described on 37.

18 Brief presented to W.J. Dunlop, minister of education, by the University of Waterloo, 26 Oct. 1959, RG2–P3, Archives of Ontario.

19 *Of Mud and Dreams*, 13, 59

20 *Globe and Mail*, 8 June 1960. See also T.B. Symons, 'Trent University,' in R. Borg, ed. *Peterborough: Land of Shining Waters* (Peterborough, 1966); 'Report of the Committee on Higher Education,' appointed by the mayor of Peterborough in 1958, RG2–P3, Archives of Ontario.

21 'Trent University,' 500
22 See, for example, resolution passed by Fort William District Progressive Conservative Association calling for a new university, 7 Jan. 1958; also brief from the Canadian Slovak Veterans Branch (Fort William) to George Drew, 5 May 1948, RG2–P3, Archives of Ontario.
23 *Debates*, Ontario Legislative Assembly, 16 March 1955, 810; 20 Feb. 1956, 351; Fleming, *Post-Secondary and Adult Education*, 109
24 *The Vertical Mosaic*, (Toronto: University of Toronto Press, 1965), 300
25 *The Canadian Corporate Elite: An Analysis of Economic Power* (Toronto: McClelland and Stewart, 1975), 251
26 John Barkans and Norene Pupo, 'The Board of Governors and the Power Elite: A Case Study of Eight Canadian Universities,' *Sociological Focus* (summer 1974), 86. See also their 'Canadian Universities and the Economic Order,' in R.W. Nelson and D.A. Nock, eds., *Reading, Writing and Riches: Education and the Socio-Economic Order in North America* (Kitchener: Between the Lines Press, 1978).
27 Gordon McCaffrey, 'Canada's Newest Universities Need Executives to Start,' *Executive*, Nov. 1962 (citing an unnamed university comptroller)
28 Papers on the work of the 'special committee on the University project' of the North Toronto YMCA, J.R. Kidd Papers, York University Archives
29 Interview, D.M. Smyth, 1 Nov. 1977; see also his 'How York University Came into Being,' *Atkinson Balloon*, Sept. 1977.
30 Minutes, meeting of York Organizing Committee, 8 Feb. 1958, 20 May 1958, 9, 17 Sept. 1958, J.R. Kidd Papers, York University Archives
31 Notes on meeting with Premier, 18 Dec. 1958, ibid.
32 Minutes of meeting of Provisional Board of Governors, 24 March 1959. (Examples cited are individuals such as David Mansur, Mitchell Sharp, Robert Winters.)
33 Minutes of meeting of University of Toronto Board of Governors, 16 June 1960, copy in York University Archives
34 Address by W.A. Curtis to the Board of Governors and Senate of York University, 12 June 1968, York University Archives, in which Curtis recounts the early history of York. Ross's letter is cited here. For an elaboration of Ross's views on higher education, see *The New University* (Toronto: University of Toronto Press, 1961).
35 Curtis, Address
36 Ross to Phillips, 20 Aug. 1959, President's Papers, York University Archives. Eric Phillips, as well as being chairman of the Board of Governors of the University of Toronto was chairman of Argus Corporation, Massey Ferguson, and an executive member of the boards of some twenty other major companies in Canada.
37 Ross to Phillips, 3 Dec. 1959; Interview with Murray Ross, 12 Jan. 1978
38 These individuals are all listed in a fund-raising pamphlet published in 1964, entitled 'Plant Now That the Seeds May Grow,' President's Papers, York University Archives.
39 Interviews, Gerstein, 10 Sept. 1981; Mansur, 21 Aug. 1981
40 Minutes of meeting of York University Board of Governors, 10 Feb. 1969. Though this material has never been officially released, the author chanced upon an unofficial copy in 1970. Also: 'McMaster University, which has a director from Harding Carpets, Ltd., is having Robinson Memorial Theatre carpeted with rugs from Harding Carpets,' in Barkans and Pupo, 'The Board of Governors and the Power Elite,' 87.
41 See 'Report of the Interim Curriculum Committee,' April 1961, John Seeley Papers, York University Archives; R. Winters to J.P. Robarts, 23 Nov. 1962, RG–32, Archives of Ontario

42 Minutes of Executive Committee meeting of York's Board of Governors, 19 Sept. 1966, President's Papers, York University Archives

43 19 Dec. 1966, RG2–P3, Archives of Ontario

44 'Brief to the Province of Ontario,' 23 Nov. 1962, President's Papers, York University Archives

45 'Report on Fund Raising Potential and Campaign Plans for York University,' Toronto, July/64, revised, Sept./65, G.A. Brakeley and Co. Ltd., Founders Fund File, ibid.

46 Memo from Lambert to Winters, Ross, Scott, Harris, Barbour, 20 Aug. 1964, ibid.

47 Minutes, Board of Governors meeting, Dec. 1964, President's Papers, ibid.

48 By F.G. Gardiner, 11 March 1965, Founders Fund File, ibid.

49 Minutes of Finance Committee meeting, Board of Governors, 29 June 1965, President's Papers, ibid.

50 W. Small (secretary of Board of Governors) to R.H. Winters, 15 Dec. 1964, Founders Fund File, ibid. See also 'Statement of Investments,' 31 March 1966, ibid. This shows that university funds were spread around to several large banks and financial institutions, including General Motors Acceptance Corporation, Royal Bank of Canada, Canada Permanent Mortgage Corporation, Toronto-Dominion Bank, Bank of Nova Scotia, Bank of Montreal, Canadian Imperial Bank of Commerce, and Ford Credit Company Note [sic]. All of these institutions held at least $150,000 worth of short-term notes. British American Oil Debentures and Simpson's were also the recipients of university investments of $50,000 and $150,000 respectively from the Founders Fund.

51 9 May 1962, RG–32, CUA Files, Archives of Ontario

52 Robarts to Ross, 3 May 1962, in response to a letter from Ross to Robarts, 30 April 1962, ibid.

53 D.M. Sunday to W.A. Curtis, 25 Sept. 1958; brochure included with letter. Founders Fund File, York University Archives

54 Memo from Lambert to Winters, Ross, Scott, Harris, 20 Aug. 1964, ibid.

55 'A Report on Fund Raising Potential and Campaign Plan for York University,' July 1964, revised Sept. 1965, ibid.

56 W. Sanders to Barbour, 13 April 1965, ibid.

57 'A Report on Fund Raising Potential,' ibid.

58 Ross to Mrs Zimmer (Brakeley's employee), 23 Feb. 1965, ibid.

59 Gardiner to Mrs Thomas Bata, 11 March 1965, ibid.

60 'Report of Subscriptions Received in Excess of $1000,' 14 April 1966, ibid.

61 B. Parkes to Lambert, 15 May 1970, ibid.

62 See memo from Barbour to Lambert, Harris, Scott, Winters, 27 Jan. 1965

63 The York Archives contains a 'fund raising package' that was apparently never accompanied by an actual campaign.

64 Statistics are derived from the following sources: Reports of Ontario Minister of University Affairs, 1967–70; Dominion Bureau of Statistics, *Canadian Universities: Income and Expenditures, 1965–66 and 1968–69* (Ottawa, 1969 and 1973); Statistics Canada, *Historical Compendium of Education Statistics from Confederation to 1975* (Ottawa, 1978); Statistics Canada, *Financial Statistics of Education, 1969 and 1970* (Ottawa, 1975); W.G. Fleming, *The Expansion of the Education System*, vol. 1 of *Ontario's Educative Society* (Toronto: University of Toronto Press 1971).

65 Murray G. Ross, 'Should University Board be Abolished?' (n.d., *c* 1969). Ross was particularly opposed to the unicameral system of government being proposed, and ultimately adopted, at the University of Toronto, in which the powers of the Board of Governors and

the Senate were subsumed in a new system presided over by a 'Governing Council.' See also Murray Ross, *Those Ten Years* (York University, 1970), 36: 'There would be no York University without its Board of Governors.'

66 See the following documents: minutes of Organizing Committee meeting, 2 Jan. 1959, A.D. Margison to John Diefenbaker, Prime Minister of Canada (n.d., *c* April, 1959), and 'Agreement between the Corporation of the Township of North York and York University,' 10 Sept. 1959, J.R. Kidd Papers, York University Archives; R.H. Winters to J.P. Robarts, 23 Nov. 1962, CUA Files, RG–32, Archives of Ontario

67 See 'Report of the Building Committee,' 21 June 1960; minutes of Campus Planning Committee, 20 June 1962; and 'President's Report to Faculty and Staff,' Sept. 1962, in which Ross describes the various activities of the Board of Governors to date, President's Papers, York University Archives

68 Interviews: Murray Ross, 12 Jan. 1978; David Mansur, 21 Aug. 1981; Bertrand Gerstein, 10 Sept. 1981

69 *Those Ten Years*, 38

CHAPTER FOUR

1 Within the Ontario Department of Education, there were apparently no officials working full-time on university matters. Not until 1951 was anyone hired to work exclusively on university problems. See below. Also, interview with H.H. Walker, 17 Aug. 1976

2 'Estimates,' press release from Ministry of Colleges and Universities, May 1972. The majority of this increase was accounted for by the absorption of the community college sector into the new ministry, which replaced the Ministry of University Affairs in 1971.

3 See Peter Oliver, *G. Howard Ferguson: Ontario Tory* (Toronto: University of Toronto Press, 1977), 240, and E.E. Stewart, 'The Role of the Provincial Government in the Development of the Universities of Ontario, 1791–1964' unpublished DEd thesis, University of Toronto, 1970, 385–7, which describe the views of George Henry, premier from 1930 to 1934.

4 Dr W.E. McNeil to the 1939 conference of the National Conference of Canadian Universities, cited in G. Pilkington, 'A History of the National Conference of Canadian Universities, 1911–1961,' unpublished DEd thesis, University of Toronto, 1974, 271; Stewart, 'The Role,' 341–3 and 350–5

5 Stewart, 'The Role,' 341–2, 390; Oliver, *Ferguson*, 242–3

6 *Report of the Royal Commission on the University of Toronto* (Toronto, 1906); C. Humphries, 'James P. Whitney and the University of Toronto,' in *Profiles of a Province* (Toronto: Ontario Historical Society, 1967); R.S. Harris, 'The Establishment of a Provincial University in Ontario,' in D.F. Dadson, *On Higher Education: Five Lectures* (Toronto: University of Toronto Press, 1966)

7 For example, see G.E. Hall (president, University of Western Ontario) to C.F. Canon (deputy minister of education), 9 Oct. 1952, RG2–P3, Archives of Ontario, in which grants are discussed for the coming year.

8 See N. McKenty, *Mitch Hepburn* (Toronto: McClelland and Stewart, 1967), 189–90. It might be noted that Howard Ferguson also refused an honorary degree from Toronto, though he reasoned that accepting it might be perceived as a conflict of interest. Hepburn's motives were less judicious.

9 Stewart, 'The Role,' 369

10 Budget speech by Leslie Frost, 16 March 1944

11 Budgets of Ontario, 1944–57; G.P. Gilmour (president, McMaster University) to George Drew, 28 March 1947; M.M. MacOdrum, (Carleton president) to Dana Porter, 16 Feb.

1949; and Porter to MacOdrum, 24 Feb. 1949, RG2–P3, Archives of Ontario. See also W.G. Fleming, *Post-Secondary and Adult Education,* vol. IV of *Ontario's Educative Society* (Toronto: University of Toronto Press, 1971), 452 and 470–90.
12 See C.E. Higginbottom to George Drew, 26 June 1945. The statement contains details of meetings of the university's Finance Committee, money spent in each faculty, and names and salaries of all faculty members. RG2–P3, Archives of Ontario
13 R.C. Wallace (Queen's) to Dana Porter, 7 Dec. 1949; G.W. Thompson (Western) to Porter, March 1949, ibid. The statement from Carleton (MacOdrum to Porter, 3 Nov. 1951) is also quite brief.
14 Porter to Thompson, 12 March 1949, ibid.
15 12 March 1949
16 Phillips to Drew, 10 Sept. 1948, RG2–P3, Archives of Ontario
17 Interview with H.H. Walker, 17 Aug. 1976; Frost to Porter, 11 July 1951, ibid.
18 Wallace to Dunlop, 28 May 1952, ibid.
19 Interviews with George Gathercole, Sept. 1976, and with McCormick Smyth, 1 Nov. 1977
20 Wallace to Dunlop, 11 June 1952, RG2–P3, Archives of Ontario
21 'Evaluation of Programs of Universities,' Sept. 1953, ibid.
22 25 Oct. 1954, ibid.
23 Fleming, *Post-Secondary and Adult Education,* 22. Wallace was seen by Frost as being 'too gentle to crack the whip with the universities.'
24 Memorandum to Minister on Higher Education in Ontario, 1955–56, 28 Oct. 1955, RG2–P3, Archives of Ontario
25 Interview with Gathercole, 1976
26 Submission of Ontario to the Royal Commission on Canada's Economic Prospects, 1956, 63–5
27 Interview with George Gathercole, 1976
28 See for example the statement by G.P. Gilmour, president of McMaster University, in his book, *The University and Its Neighbours* (Toronto: Gage, 1954). He warned of the entrance into universities of students from families 'which do not naturally and continually prepare their children for university, homes where books are scarce, where taste is not severely disciplined and where education is looked on chiefly as a means of upgrading in the economic sense' (p. 54). See also H.W. McReady, 'The University and the Community,' *Queen's Quarterly,* vol. 64 (1957/58), 20
29 The other members were H.F. Brown, P.C. Clarke, H.H. Walker, and Chester Walters. Interview with Gathercole, 1976. See also G. Gathercole, 'The Record and Role of Planning in Economic Development,' *Canadian Public Administration,* vol. V, 2, (June, 1962), 194–199
30 Interview with Gathercole, 1976
31 'Explanation of Five Year Forecasts to Provincial and other Universities, Vote 416,' 24 May 1956, RG2–P3, Archives of Ontario
32 Dunlop describes these developments to W.H. Swift from Alberta, 2 Nov. 1956, ibid.
33 'A Survey of University Expansion and Costs in Ontario,' ibid.
34 See *Report of the Advisory Committee on University Affairs,* 1 Feb. 1964, 10
35 *Interviews* with Gathercole and Walker
36 Dunlop to Cotnam, 21 Oct. 1958, RG2–P3, Archives of Ontario
37 The issue is discussed and Phillips is quoted in the following correspondence: Farrell to Dunlop, 17 Nov. 1958, and Canon to Farrell, 25 Nov. 1958, ibid.
38 Interview with Gathercole

235 Notes to pp. 90–7

39 The issue appears to have been resolved when Beatty resigned his position as chancellor in 1959. See University of Toronto, *President's Report, 1959*, 11; interview with Gathercole
40 Minutes of meetings of CUA, RG32, Archives of Ontario
41 Memorandum to the Chief Director for the Information of the Minister, Re: Committee on University Affairs, 22 Nov. 1960, RG2–P3, ibid.
42 See Dunlop to Bissell (president, University of Toronto), 6 Nov. 1958, asking for information which on other occasions was sought by the committee itself. Ibid.
43 Quotation from 'Memorandum to the Chief Director,' 22 Nov. 1960; interviews with Gathercole and Walker
44 CUA minutes, 2 Jan. 1959
45 Mackintosh to Canon, 26 Jan. 1959, RG2–P3, Archives of Ontario
46 *Report of the Advisory Committee on University Affairs*, 19
47 *Globe and Mail*, 23 Nov. 1960, and Department of Education press release, 18 Nov. 1960
48 J.R. McCarthy, Memorandum: re an Ontario Board of Higher Education, A Proposal for the Integrated Development of Higher Education in Ontario, prepared by D.M. Smyth, Sept. 1960. RG2–P3, Archives of Ontario
49 CPUO, *Post-Secondary Education in Ontario, 1962–1970* (Jan. 1963), 23–31
50 Ibid., appendix: minutes of CUA meeting, March 1962
51 For example, see discussion in the Senate of York University, 19 Oct. 1962, where the CPUO's preliminary forecasts about York were discussed. Its projections influenced York's decision to raise its enrolment estimates from 4,000 to 7,000 by 1970.
52 Interview Douglas Wright, 8 April 1975. Wright, a member of the CUA from 1965 to 1971, and appointed its first full-time chairman in 1967, used the term 'social demand' to describe the planning process. Its purpose was to place the responsibility for the development of university priorities in the hands of those using the system, the students. See discussion of this model in chap. 5 below.
53 *Report of the Advisory Committee on University Affairs*. See also CPUO, *From the Sixties to the Seventies: An Appraisal of Higher Education in Ontario* (1966)
54 See the CPUO report, *The City College* (1965)
55 CPUO, *From the Sixties to the Seventies*, 40
56 Minutes, CUA meeting, 14 Nov. 1963, RG32, Archives of Ontario
57 Interview with Stewart, 2 May 1976
58 McCarthy, 'The Department of University Affairs and How It Developed,' *Canadian University*, Sept./Oct., 1966
59 Statement by Premier Robarts in Legislature on Introducing Bill to Establish Department of University Affairs, 22 April 1964, RG2–P3, Archives of Ontario
60 CPUO, *From the Sixties to the Seventies*, 45. See also Claude Bissell, 'The Presidents strongly supported the establishment of a Department of University Affairs especially when set against the alternative of control through a branch of the Department of Education.' University of Toronto, *Report of the President*, 1964, 5
61 'The Government of Ontario and the Universities of the Province,' *Gerstein Lectures* (Toronto: York University, 1966)
62 *Report of the Commission to Study the Development of Graduate Programmes in Ontario Universities* submitted to the CUA and the CPUO (1966)
63 Interview with Spinks in the *Financial Post*, c Jan. 1967. Spinks said that when the recommendation was formulated by the committee, Clark Kerr was still president of the University of California.

64 For statements by the various presidents, see the *Kitchener Waterloo Record*, 29 Dec. 1966; *Ottawa Fulcrum*, 11 Jan. 1967; *St. Catharines Standard*, 30 Dec. 1966.

65 5 Jan. 1967

66 *Debates*, Ontario Legislative Assembly, 5 June 1967, 4,264

67 *Report of the Commission*, 77

68 *Report of the Committee on University Affairs*, 1967, 10, 31. CPUO, *Campus and Forum*, Third Annual Review (1968–9), 8, discusses appraisals program.

69 *Report of the Committee on University Affairs*, 1967, 11–12

70 Memorandum on Formula Operating Grants, Wright to members of the CUA, 4 July 1965 (obtained from author), 3, 5

71 'The formula obviates the need for detailed scrutiny of proposed expenditures in each university.' *Report of the Committee on University Affairs*, 1967, 12, 13. See also Wright to Rev. R. Guindon, rector of the University of Ottawa, 8 Sept. 1967, RG2–P3, Archives of Ontario

72 Both the presidents and provincial faculty association felt that there was simply not enough information that would allow for adequate long-term planning. A recommendation calling for a 'commission under the joint sponsorship of the Committee on University Affairs and the Committee of Presidents to study the existing patterns of higher education in Ontario and to make recommendations for its development, integration and governance,' was contained in *From the Sixties to the Seventies* (1966), 94.

CHAPTER FIVE

1 W.B.W. Martin and A.J. Macdonnell, *Canadian Education: A Sociological Analysis* (Scarborough: Prentice-Hall, 1978), 22

2 Claude Bissell (former president of the University of Toronto), *Halfway Up Parnassus* (Toronto: University of Toronto Press, 1974), 15

3 See the following: Undergraduate Calendars from Toronto, Western, Queen's, and Ottawa, 1950–1958; R.S. Harris, *A History of Higher Education in Canada, 1663–1960* (Toronto: University of Toronto Press, 1976), 496-520; F.E.L. Priestley, *The Humanities in Canada*, published for the Humanities Research Council (Toronto: University of Toronto Press, 1964), chaps. 1 and 2; C.B. Macpherson *et al.*, *Undergraduate Instruction in Arts and Science* (Toronto: University of Toronto Press, 1967). At Toronto about 50 per cent of undergraduates registered in the honours program throughout the 1950s, but at other Ontario universities the proportion ranged from 5 to 20 per cent. For overviews of curriculum trends, see F. Rudolph, *Curriculum: A History of the American Undergraduate Course of Study since 1636* (San Francisco: Jossey-Bass, 1977); W. Kilbourn, 'Canadian History and Social Sciences, 1920–1960,' in C.F. Klinck, ed., *Literary History of Canada*, vol. II, (Toronto: University of Toronto Press, 1965), 22

4 University of Toronto, *President's Report, 1956*, 18

5 'Placement Reports' in *Report(s) of the President(s)*, Carleton University, 1957–61: McMaster University, 1960/61; University of Toronto, 1957–61

6 Queen's University, *Principal's Report, 1955/56*, 13

7 Queen's University, *Principal's Report(s), 1959/60*, 27; 1963/64, 16; McMaster University, *President's Report(s), 1959/60*, 1962/63; Carleton University, *President's Report, 1959/60*

8 *The Humanities in Canada*, 1

9 See the following sources for discussion of Ontario curriculum trends in the 1960s: Presidential Reports from University of Windsor, 1963/64; Queen's University, 1963/64; Uni-

versity of Western Ontario, 1963/64, 1964/65; McMaster University, 1961/62; Carleton University, 1963/64, 1968/69; University of Toronto, 1969/70; Report of the Interim Curriculum Committee, April 1961 (John Seeley Papers, York University Archives); undergraduate calendars, Ontario universities, 1960–1970; Macpherson *et al. Undergraduate Instruction.* 10 *Curriculum: A History of the American Undergraduate Course of Study since 1636*

11 Much of the material for this section and others in the book on business attitudes is based on a reading of some twenty business and trade journals in Canada between 1958 and 1965. The *Business Periodical Index* (1958–61) was of great assistance here. *The Canadian Periodical Index* was used for subsequent years. The publications of the Industrial Foundation on Education were also valuable.

12 For an interesting discussion of these changing corporate trends, see D.G. Willmot, 'Planning for Growth and Diversification,' *Monetary Times*, March 1963.

13 *Imperial Oil Review*, Sept. 1959

14 C.B. Buetow, consultant with the Thorne Group (Toronto), 'What You Can Do About Training,' *Industrial Canada*, Feb. 1968

15 *Imperial Oil Review*, Sept. 1959

16 Cited in Marcel Vincent, 'Business and Education Should Team Up,' *Canadian Business*, Nov. 1966, from which the previous quotation was also taken.

17 *Oil in Canada*, 8, 15 Jan. 1959

18 D.L. Bibby, 'Education and Training Power,' *Canadian Chartered Accountant*, Oct. 1963

19 Ibid., April 1963. See also K. Byrd, in ibid., Jan. 1964; J.N. Allan, 'Continuing Education for the Industrial Accountant,' *Cost and Management*, Sept. 1961; and 'Manpower in Changing Society,' *Industrial Canada*, March 1968

20 F.M. Ladd (director of training, Consolidated Paper Corporation), 'Employee Training: Why and How?' *Pulp and Paper*, May 1959. See also A.G. Stapleton (personnel director, General Motors), 'How G.M. Uses Employee Education as a Major Competitive Tool,' *Office Equipment and Methods*, May 1960.

21 *Cost and Management*, Sept. 1961

22 March 1966

23 The evidence thus far marshalled points to the widespread support for the expansion of higher education among Canadian academics. There were some dissenting protesters who undoubtedly remained committed to a more limited, élitist form of post-secondary education. See, for example, G.P. Gilmour, *The University and Its Neighbours* (Toronto: Gage, 1954), 54. But their voices failed, by and large, to rise above the din of their more pragmatic colleagues.

24 In *School Progress*, May 1960

25 Cited in 'What Does Business Owe to Education?,' *Trade and Commerce*, Aug. 1960

26 See, for example, D.G.M. Draper (chairman of the Chemical Education Division, Chemical Industries of Canada), *Chemistry in Canada*, Dec. 1960.

27 'Approaches to Educational Planning,' *Economic Journal*, vol. 77 (1967), 262

28 See, for example, the comments of the Dean of Medicine at the University of Toronto: 'In order to retain its reputation for sound standards in teaching and training, the graduating class should not increase beyond approximately 150.' Report of the Statistical and Fact Finding Subcommittee to the Advisory Planning Committee and the Board of Governors, 1957, 18. The School of Architecture took a similar position, irrespective of enrolment pressures (43).

29 In 1957, the Law Society of Upper Canada authorized the establishment of law schools at Queen's, Western, and Ottawa. Toronto and Osgoode Hall already had legal training programs.

30 This model is described in Blaug, 'Approaches to Educational Planning.' A critique can be found in J. Lennards and E. Harvey, 'The Changing Nature of Post-Secondary Education: Attitudes, Costs and Benefits,' a study done for the Commission on Post-Secondary Education (Toronto, 1970), 22

31 Economic Council of Canada, *Second Annual Review* (Ottawa, 1965), 74–75. See also, G. Bertram, *The Contribution of Education to Economic Growth* (Ottawa: 1966) from which the conclusions of the Economic Council *Review* were derived. Cited in A. Malik, ed., *Social Foundations of Canadian Education* (Toronto: Prentice-Hall, 1969), 101; E. Harvey and J. Lennards, *Key Issues in Higher Education* (Toronto: OISE, 1973), 27

32 *Manpower Forecasting and Educational Policy*, a study prepared for the Commission on Post-Secondary Education in Ontario (Toronto, 1972), 83–4

33 For example, the *Report of the Royal Commission on Health Services* (Ottawa, 1964), defended public investment in education in typically general terms, vol. I, 500

34 Blaug, 'Approaches to Educational Planning,' 262; *Manpower Forecasting and Educational Policy*, 18–19

35 The first comprehensive occupation-by-occupation study done for Ontario was by C. Watson and J.J. Butorac: *Qualified Manpower in Ontario, 1961–86* (Toronto: OISE, 1968). See also N.M. Meltz and G.P. Penz *Canada's Manpower Requirements in 1970* (Ottawa, 1968).

36 *Manpower Forecasting and Educational Policy*, 117

37 M.L. Skolnik, *Skill Substitution, Technology and Supply Conditions: The Case of Engineers and Technicians in Canada* (OISE, Educational Planning, occasional papers 4, 1969), 7, 8

38 *Manpower Forecasting and Educational Policy*, 117–19

39 The three studies cited by Skolnik in his CPUO report, *An Analysis of Projections of the Demand for Engineers in Canada and Ontario* (1970) are: B. Ahamad, *A Projection of Manpower Requirements by Occupation in 1975, Canada and Its Regions* (Ottawa, 1970); Meltz and Penz, *Canada's Manpower Requirements in 1970*; and Watson and Butorac, *Qualified Manpower in Ontario 1961–86*

40 P. Lapp *et al.*, *Ring of Iron*, a report to CPUO (Toronto, 1970),·45

41 B.A. Keys and H.H. Wright, *Manpower Planning in Canada: A Case Study*, prepared for the Economic Council of Canada, staff study 18 (1966), 25

42 *Report*, Royal Commission on Health Services, vol. I (Ottawa, 1964), 141

43 Vol. I, 5–6

44 H.R. Robertson, J.F. Howing, L.F. Michaud, *Health Manpower Output of Canadian Educational Institutions* (Ottawa: AUCC, 1973), 2

45 H. Carver to M. Ross, 27 Sept. 1963. Carver, a well-known planner, was asked by York to investigate this situation, President's Papers, York University Archives

46 J. Miller to H. Best, 4 Dec. 1964, ibid. This contains minutes of a meeting of the Ontario Association of Architects attended by Mr Best of York University.

47 J. Willard to H. Best, 18 Feb. 1965, ibid.

48 Report of the Statistical and Fact Finding Subcommittee, 22–4

49 N. Meltz, 'A Review of Historical Trends and Projections of the Number of Lawyers and Judges in the Ontario Labour Force,' prepared for the Committee of Ontario Law Deans (Toronto, 1974), cited in D. Stager and N. Meltz, 'Manpower Planning in the Professions,' *Canadian Journal of Higher Education*, vol. III (1977), 80. See also B.J. MacKinnon *et al.*,

Report of the Special Committee on Legal Education (Toronto: Law Society of Upper Canada, 1972), 11.

50 ACAP, *Administration, Business and Management Science*, 1974. The report noted that 'assessment of the demand for graduates from MBA programs is difficult if not impossible' since graduates enter public and private fields of business 'with no defineable boundaries,' A-24. See also Max von Zur-Muehlen, *University Business Education and Faculty* (Ottawa: Economic Council of Canada, 1971).

51 Skolnik, *Skill Substitution, Technology and Supply Conditions*

52 In D. Dunton and D. Patterson, eds., *Canadian Universities in a New Age*, proceedings of a conference held by the National Conference of Canadian Universities and Colleges at Ottawa, 13-15 Nov. 1961, 64-81

53 (Ottawa, 1964), 186-7, 194

54 *Report*, Royal Commission on Health Services, vol. 1; and vol. II, 526; McFarlane *et al.*, *Medical Education in Canada*, 200

55 See Dana Porter to William Davis, 22 Sept. 1964 and statement by Premier John Robarts, 29 Oct. 1964, in CUA files, RG-32, Archives of Ontario. Porter's letter included the statistical justifications and normative assertions found in the Royal Commission's report on the need for expanded medical facilities. Despite its many uncertainties, then, the province adopted the reasoning of the Hall Commission's report.

56 University of Western Ontario, *President's Report, 1965; Report*, Royal Commission on Health Services, vol II, 29

57 *Report*, Committee on the Healing Arts, vol. III, 54; vol. I, 178, 182; vol. II, 219, 524, 520, 136-9.

58 Keys and Wright, *Manpower Planning in Canada*, 25

59 *Education and Employment of Arts and Science Graduates: The Last Decade in Ontario*, a study prepared for the Commission on Post-Secondary Education in Ontario (Toronto, 1972)

60 M.L. Chipman, G.G. Clarke, J.W. Steiner, 'Career Choice within Medicine: A Study of One Graduating Class at the University of Toronto,' *Canadian Medical Association Journal*, vol. 101 (29 Nov. 1969)

61 *Report*, Royal Commission on Health Services, vol. I, 82, 294; *Report*, Committee on the Healing Arts, vol. I, 137-43, 153

62 For example, A.N. Bourns, former president of McMaster University and former member of the CUA, claimed: 'McMaster didn't have a chance in the world of getting support for the establishment of another major faculty of any kind after it had committed itself and the Government had committed itself to the establishment of the Faculty of Medicine.' Interview, 3 March 1977

63 *Report of the President*, 16

64 See, for example, Wilson Woodside, *The University Question* (Toronto: Ryerson, 1958), 30

65 Watson and Butorac, *Qualified Manpower in Ontario*, 64, 65-70

66 Memorandum to CUA, 'Trends in Engineering Enrolment,' 30 March 1965. CUA Files, RG-32, Archives of Ontario

67 M.L. Skolnik and W.F. McMullen, 'An Analysis of Projections of the Demand for Engineers in Canada and Ontario,' in D.K. Foot *et al.*, *The Ontario Economy, 1977-87* (Toronto: Ontario Economic Council, 1970), 43

68 University of Toronto, *Report of the President, 1964/65*, 64-6. See also B.D. Bucknall *et al.*, 'Pedants, Practitioners and Prophets: Legal Education at Osgoode Hall to 1957,' *Osgoode Hall Law Journal*, vol. 6 (1968), 142-229; C.A. Wright, 'The Outlook for Legal

Education,' *University of Toronto Law Journal*, vol. 13, (1958); J.A. Corry, 'The Queen's University Faculty of Law,' ibid., vol. 12 (1957); H.W. Arthurs, 'The Affiliation of Osgoode Hall Law School with York University,' ibid., vol. 22 (1967)

69 University of Toronto, Report of the Statistical and Fact Finding Subcommittee, 37

70 Minutes of meeting of CUA, 6–7 March 1967. See also memorandum for the CUA *re* 'The Establishment of Professional Faculties at York University,' 1 Jan. 1965, President's Papers, York University Archives

71 Minutes of CUA meeting, 12 Jan. 1965; also interview with Reva Gerstein (former CUA member), 12 April 1977; minutes, CUA meeting, 6–7 March 1967

72 W. Davis to M. Ross, 30 March 1967, CUA Files, RG–32, Archives of Ontario. Also, according to A.N. Bourns, 'I suppose it would be fair to say that the committee found it very difficult to choose between a new school in southwestern Ontario, and decided it could justify having two schools because Carleton and Waterloo were proposing quite different approaches to architectural education and that influenced the committee.' Interview, 3 March 1977; minutes of CUA meeting, 13 Dec. 1965

73 R.W.B. Jackson, *A Statement of Conditions, Causes, and Issues: Interim Report, the Commission on Declining School Enrolments in Ontario* (Toronto: Ontario Ministry of Education, 1977), 120; W.G. Fleming, 'Estimates of Teacher Supply and Demand in Ontario Secondary Schools for 1957–72,' Toronto: Department of Educational Research, Ontario College of Education, 1956, 18–20; W.G. Fleming, *The Expansion of the Educational System*, vol. I, *Ontario's Educative Society* (Toronto: University of Toronto Press, 1971), 265–9

74 W.G. Fleming, *Supporting Institutions and Services*, vol. V of *Ontario's Educative Society* 94, chaps. 5, 7

75 Interview with Bourns

76 *Report* (to CUA and CPUO), 23

77 Cited in N.L. Nicholson, 'The Evolution of Graduate Studies in the Universities of Ontario, 1841–1971,' unpublished DEd thesis, University of Toronto, 1973, 35. See also the comments of university presidents such as J.W. Hagey from Waterloo who noted, 'Every university and its staff should be able to look forward to the day in which it will be engaged in graduate work.' CUA meeting, 8 Dec. 1964. Murray Ross, president of York, claimed that moving into graduate work was 'a matter of expediency, since several new members of the York staff had indicated that they would only join York if they were able to bring their graduate students with them.' CUA meeting, 12 Jan. 1965

78 Report of the Advisory Committee on University Affairs, 1 Feb. 1964, 5–6

79 'Report on Demand and Supply of University Teachers in the Humanities' (mimeo), 1–10

80 Spinks *Report*, 23–4. In 1964, Bourns and Wright expressed concern that graduate expansion was 'getting out of hand.' Bourns interview

81 Interview with Gerstein, 12 April 1977

82 Interview with Wright, 8 April 1975

83 Material in this section is taken from a variety of sources: R.S. Harris, *A History of Higher Education in Canada, 1663–1960; Report*, Committee on the Healing Arts, esp. vol. II; D.W. Gullett, *A History of Dentistry in Canada* (Toronto: University of Toronto Press, 1971); K.J. Paytner, *Dental Education in Canada* (Ottawa, 1965); B.R. Blishen, *Doctors and Doctrines: The Ideology of Medical Care in Canada* (Toronto: University of Toronto Press, 1969); McFarlane *et al.*, *Medical Education in Canada*; Commission on Pharmaceutical Services, *Pharmacy in a New Age*, (Toronto: Canadian Pharmaceutical Association, 1971); Bucknall *et al.*, 'Pedants, Practitioners and Prophets; Applied Research Associates, *Certification and Post-Secondary Education*, prepared for the Commission on Post-Secondary Education in Ontario (Toronto, 1972).

84 Ontario Council of Deans of Medicine, 'The Role of the Medical School in Health Science Education,' brief to the Commission on Post-Secondary Education in Ontario, 4 Feb. 1971

85 *The Learning Society*, report of the Commission on Post-Secondary Education in Ontario (Toronto, 1972), 65. See also Applied Research Associates, *Professional Education: A Policy Option* (Toronto, 1972), and *Certification and Post Secondary Education*,' 35; *Report*, Committee on the Healing Arts, vol. III, 99

86 ACAP, *Administrative, Business and Management Sciences* (1974), A–12; A–31

87 *Certification and Post-Secondary Education*, 39, 143; interview with Wright. See also J. Scott, *Of Mud and Dreams: University of Waterloo, 1957–67* (Toronto: Ryerson, 1967), 82–97

88 *Certification and Post-Secondary Education*, 35

89 J. Porter, B. Blishen, *et al.*, *Towards 2000: The Future of Post-Secondary Education in Ontario* (Toronto: McClelland and Stewart, 1971), 91. This book constituted the submission of the CPUO to the Commission on Post-Secondary Education.

90 *Report*, Committee on the Healing Arts, vol. III, 93; vol. II, 52, 130, 151

91 Lapp *et al.*, *Ring of Iron*, 11

92 Miriam Hutton, 'Educating for the Social Services,' *Canadian Journal of Higher Education*, vol. 2 (1975), 28

93 Jan de Songh, 'A Retrospective View of Social Work Education,' cited in Hutton, ibid., 24. See also speech by MPP Stephen Lewis in *Debates*, Ontario Legislative Assembly, 6 March 1966, 1,343–54, in which he describes deficiencies of social work education.

94 A. Roman *et al.*, *Legal Education in Ontario*, study prepared for the Commission on Post-Secondary Education (Toronto, 1970), 11

95 MacKinnon *et al.*, *Report of the Special Committee on Legal Education*, 11, 27–30. See also Horace Kreever, 'Professional Education,' in P. Slayton and M.J. Trebilcock eds., *The Professions and Public Policy* (Toronto: University of Toronto Press, 1978).

96 Osgoode Hall Law School, 'Responses to the Recommendations of the Special Committee on Legal Education,' 2 Feb. 1973; M.L. Friedland to S. Robins, 20 Dec. 1972, for the Committee of Ontario Law Deans (in Osgoode Hall Law School Library); S.B. Stein to B.J. MacKinnon, 8 Jan. 1973 (in 'Responses'.)

97 McFarlane *et al.*, *Medical Education in Canada*, 69; *Report*, Committee on the Healing Arts, vol. III, 59–67

98 E.J.M. Campbell, 'The McMaster Medical School at Hamilton, Ontario,' *Lancet*, no. 7676, 10 Oct. 1970, 763; also J.D. Hamilton, 'The Selection of Medical Students at McMaster University,' *Journal of the Royal College of Physicians*, vol. 6, no. 4 (July 1972), 348; and *The McMaster Philosophy: An Approach to Medical Education*, prepared by Faculty of Medicine, McMaster University, educational monograph 5 (1974)

99 John Evans in *Certification and Post-Secondary Education*, 53

100 *Pharmacy in a New Age*: 388

101 Lapp *et al.*, *Ring of Iron*, 34; 'Statement by the Council of Ontario Universities and Responses by Committee of Ontario Deans of Engineering, Ontario Council of Graduate Engineers and Association of Professional Engineers of Province of Ontario to *Ring of Iron: A Study of Engineering Education in Ontario*,' Oct. 1971, 7

102 Brief of the Ontario Region of the Canadian Society for Mechanical Engineering to the Commission on Post-Secondary Education, 1 May 1972 (brief #369). The society was responding to a recommendation contained in the draft report of the commission's work. In the final report, however, the commission modified this proposal and did not specify the number of years before which professionals should be required to requalify. See *The Learn-*

ing Society, 76. The second study referred to is *Certification and Post-Secondary Education*, 49
103 *Report*, vol II, 133
104 David Stager and Noah Meltz, 'Manpower Planning in the Professions,' *Canadian Journal of Higher Education*, vol. III (1977), 80

CHAPTER SIX

1 W.G. Fleming, *The Expansion of the Educational System*, vol. I of *Ontario's Educative Society* (Toronto: University of Toronto Press, 1971), 177, 321, 319
2 See, for example, J.R. Nininger, with F.W.P. Jones, *A Survey of Changing Employment Patterns at Lakehead Cities of Port Arthur and Fort William* (Ontario Economic Council, 1964), which relates economic growth to educational development. See also J.A. Cleworth *et al.*, *The Economic Impact of McMaster University on the City of Hamilton and Surrounding Localities* (McMaster University, Office of Institutional Research, 1973).
3 For E.E. Stewart's comments, see *Globe and Mail*, 14 March 1969. A full page of letters from university professors appeared in response to his comments in ibid., 19 March 1969
4 *Debates*, Ontario Legislative Assembly, 25 Nov. 1969, 8,859
5 *Globe and Mail*, 15 May 1967; Budget Speech, 12 March 1968, 11
6 *Financing Post-Secondary Education in Canada* (1971), 94
7 See L.C. McLaughlin, 'Working Paper, National Student Day,' CUS files, McMaster University Archives
8 *The Learning Society*, Report of the Commission on Post-Secondary Education in Ontario (Toronto, 1972), 222
9 Peitchinis, *Financing Post-Secondary Education in Canada*, 6
10 *Globe and Mail*, 30 Sept. 1969. Patrick Lawlor, NDP education critic, quoted extensively from the initial paper in the Committee of Supply, *Debates*, on the University Affairs Budget, 23 May 1972. The longer study was entitled *Returns to Investment in University Training: The Case of Canadian Accountants, Engineers and Scientists* (Kingston: Queen's University, 1972).
11 *Debates*, Committee of Supply, 23 May 1972, S–668
12 *Globe*, 30 May 1969. See also J.B. Alcombe, 'Some Economic Aspects of Education in Canada,' Economic Council of Canada, Nov. 1973
13 *Returns to Investment*, 111. The discount rate, in simplest terms, is the difference between the present and future value of something, taking into consideration changing interest rates. See E. Harvey and J. Lennards, *Key Issues in Higher Education* (Toronto: OISE, 1973), 24.
14 'Economic Returns to Graduate Study in Science, Engineering and Business,' *Canadian Journal of Economics*, vol. V, no. 2 (May 1972), 195, 198
15 'The Myth of the Well Educated Manager,' *Industrial Canada*, April, May 1971, 24–7
16 *Education and Jobs: The Great Training Robbery* (Penguin, 1970), 154
17 'Educational Planning Models and the Relationship between Education and Occupation,' in S. Ostry, ed., *Canadian Higher Education in the Seventies* (Ottawa, 1971), 59
18 *Design for Decision Making*, Eighth Annual Review, 210, 212. See also comment of Sylvia Ostry of the Economic Council of Canada: 'Education doesn't make you more productive. It just helps convince your boss you're worth more.' *Financial Post*, 23 Feb. 1972
19 Address to the Spring Convocation of McMaster University, 31 May 1968 (Library of Ministry of Colleges and Universities)

20 Address at the University of Windsor, 'Government and the University: Present and Future,' 17 Feb. 1969, ibid.
21 D. Ferguson, 'Student Housing Report,' (CUA files, RG–32, Archives of Ontario), cited *Canadian University*, July–Aug. 1967, 28
22 Canadian Institute of Public Opinion, *Gallup Report*, 3 March 1971; 7 April 1965
23 *Globe and Mail*, 9 May 1970; 'Statement on Operating Support of Provincially Assisted Universities for 1971 / 72 and 1972 / 73,' 27 April 1971 (MCU Library)
24 *Toronto Telegram*, 8 March 1971. See also *Debates*, Ontario Lgislative Assembly, 25 May 1971, 1953
25 *Debates*, Ontario Legislative Assembly, 10 June 1970, 3,846
26 See, for example, J.K. Galbraith, *The New Industrial State* (Boston: Houghton-Mifflin, 1968), 72; James O'Connor, *The Fiscal Crisis of the State* (New York: St Martin's, 1973); J. Porter, B. Blishen, *et al.*, *Towards 2000: The Future of Post-Secondary Education in Ontario* (Toronto: McClelland and Stewart, 1971), chaps. 1 and 2.
27 O'Connor, *The Fiscal Crisis of the State*, 114–15
28 James Laxer, 'Canadian Manufacturing and U.S. Trade Policy,' in R.M. Laxer, ed., *Canada Ltd.: The Political Economy of Dependency* (Toronto: McClelland and Stewart, 1973), 129. Figures are from *Canadian Statistical Review*, published by Statistics Canada.
29 See *Foreign Direct Investment in Canada* (Ottawa, 1972), part 4.
30 Laxer, 'Canadian Manufacturing,' 128
31 *Innovation in a Cold Climate*, Report no. 15 (Oct. 1971), 19
32 Rick Deaton, 'The Fiscal Crisis of the State in Canada,' in D.I. Roussopoulos, ed., *The Political Economy of the State* (Montreal: Black Rose, 1973), 35; Cy Gonick, *Inflation or Depression: An Analysis of the Continuing Crisis of the Canadian Economy* (Toronto: Lorimer, 1975)
33 David Wolfe, 'The State and Economic Policy in Canada, 1968–1975,' in L. Panitch, ed., *The Canadian State: Political Economy and Political Power* (Toronto: University of Toronto Press, 1977)
34 Deaton, 'The Fiscal Crisis,' 40. See also Budgets of Ontario, 1967–73, which indicate that as corporate contributions to taxation revenue fell, individual contributions increased proportionately.
35 *Debates*, Ontario Legislative Assembly, 23 Feb. 1965
36 Wolfe, 'The State and Economic Policy in Canada,' 259, citing Department of Finance, *Economic Review*, 1976; *Financial Post*, 4 April 1970; 23 Jan. 1971; Barbara Frum, 'The Class of '71,' *Maclean's*, June 1971; *Financial Post*, 23 Sept. 1972
37 *Toronto Star*, 17 Nov. 1970; *Globe and Mail*, 26 Jan. and 16 April 1971
38 R. Dyck, 'The Manpower Situation among New Ph.D. Graduates: Preliminary Findings,' Jan. 1971 (Manpower Information and Analysis Branch, Program Development Service, Department of Manpower and Immigration), CUA files, RG–32, Archives of Ontario
39 J. Kushner, I. Masse, R. Blauer, L. Soroka, *The Market Situation for University Graduates in Canada* (Ottawa, 1971), 24–7
40 'Employment of Arts and Science Graduates: The Class of '72' (mimeo, OISE Library)
41 Department of Manpower and Immigration, *Career Outlook* (Ottawa, 1970, 1971); Harvey and Lennards, *Key Issues in Higher Education*, 32
42 *Financing Post-Secondary Education*, a study prepared for the Commission on Post-Secondary Education in Ontario (Toronto 1971), 145
43 *Financial Post*, 5 June 1971
44 Ibid., 23 Sept. 1972. See also his article in Ostry, ed., *Canadian Higher Education in the Seventies*.

45 Committee of Supply, *Debates*, 19 May 1972, 596

46 16 June 1973

47 Ibid., 1 June 1974. For example, Saskatchewan was hiring environmentalists and ecologists; following the election of the NDP government in British Columbia, more social workers were being hired; and in Alberta, job prospects were stronger in the resource sector.

48 Harvey, 'Employment,' 168–9

49 *Key Issues in Higher Education*, 22

50 *Globe and Mail*, 30 Sept. 1969

51 *Design for Decision Making*, 211. See also J. Porter, M. Porter, B. Blishen, *Does Money Matter? Prospects for Higher Education* (Toronto: York University, 1973), 8

52 A capsule summary of most of these schemes can be found in *Does Money Matter?* 25–33. Most entailed some mixture of loan-grant awards to students which would cover up to 50 per cent of a university's operating costs (or all of its 'instructional costs'), and would be repaid by the student on a scale related to his / her future income.

53 *Means Survey*, supervised by Robert Rabinovitch. See CUS, President's Report by Patrick Kenniff, XXXth Congress, 1966 (McMaster University Archives). Aid for the study had come from the federal government, AUCC, and other groups.

54 Resolutions, EA–2, XXXth Congress (ibid.)

55 G. Cook and D. Stager, *Student Financial Assistance Programs*, report to the Ontario Committee on Student Awards (1969), 69, 162, 200

56 The study cited by Cook and Stager (p. 190) is 'Cost and Benefit: Study of Post-Secondary Education in Ontario, School Year, 1968/69,' prepared for the Commission on Post-Secondary Education in Ontario, 1972.

57 Cook and Stager, *Student Financial Assistance Programs*, 264. See also Peitchinis, *Financing Post-Secondary Education in Canada*, and *The Learning Society*, 149

58 *Debates*, 28 March 1972, 711. See conclusion of Dodge, *Returns to Investment*, 111: 'Estimated private returns are much higher than are social returns and hence, private decisions will lead to collective over-investment in university training.' And in 1969, Davis claimed in a convocation speech, 'While higher education clearly benefits society, it can benefit the individual even more.' Address at Lakehead University, 23 Jan. 1969 (MCU Library)

59 See, for example, Alexander DeConda, ed. *Student Activism: Town and Gown in Historical Perspective* (New York: Scribner's, 1971).

60 There is a vast literature on the student movement in the United States, though relatively little about the Canadian experience. See S.M. Lipset, *Rebellion in the University: A History of Student Activism in America* (London: Routledge and Kegan Paul, 1972); Kirkpatrick Sale, *SDS* (New York: Vintage, 1974); Richard Flacks, *Youth and Social Change* (Chicago: Markham, 1971); G.F. McGuigan, ed., *Student Protest* (Toronto: Methuen, 1968); Margaret Daly, *The Revolution Game*, (Toronto: New Press, 1970); Tim and Julyan Reid, *Student Power and the Canadian Campus* (Toronto: Peter Martin, 1968); H. Adelman *et al.*, *The University Game* (Toronto: Anansi, 1968); Jack Quarter, *The Student Movement of the 1960's* (Toronto: OISE, 1973); P. Axelrod, 'Patterns of Student Politics,' *University Affairs*, Oct. 1973; K. Westhues, 'Intergenerational Conflict in the Sixties,' in S. Clark *et al.*, eds., *Prophecy and Protest: Social Movements in Twentieth Century Canada* (Toronto: Gage, 1975).

61 P. Resnick, 'The New Left in Ontario,' in W.E. Mann, ed., *Social and Cultural Change in Canada* vol. 2 (Toronto: Copp-Clark, 1970), 127. For a broad critique of the function of higher education in a capitalist society, see CUS Resolutions, XXXII the Congress, 1968 (McMaster University Archives).

62 See, for example, CUS 'Democracy in the University Community,' 1965 (McMaster University Archives).
63 Between 1966 and 1969, there were reports of frequent demonstrations and student occupations of university campuses in the Canadian press. Some examples: 5 Oct. 1967, students at Ryerson protest the new student awards plan. One week earlier, 2,000 Toronto students had demonstrated on the same issue. In February 1968, students at the Ontario College of Art struck over the firing of several faculty members concerning the nature of education at the college (*Toronto Telegram*, 27 Feb. 1968). In November 1968, 1300 students from Toronto campuses marched on Queen's Park demanding free education for all (*Toronto Star*, 21 Nov. 1968). In February 1969, students at the University of Toronto, who were members of the Toronto Student Movement, prevented Clark Kerr from completing a lecture on the grounds that Kerr (former president of the University of California at Berkeley) was an apologist for the corporate multiversity (*Toronto Telegram*, 7 Feb. 1969). One week later, a fire broke out in the computer centre during a student occupation at Sir George Williams University (*Globe*, 14 Feb. 1969). This was by far the most famous and most sensationalized incident of student unrest during the entire period, though in the Toronto area, the Kerr incident was a close second. One example of a 'sensational' headline: 'The Campus War Heats Up,' *Toronto Telegram*, 15 Jan. 1967.
64 The Canadian Union of Students, in fact, dissolved in 1969 following its failure to secure the support of students from across the country. In the files of the CUS there are many discussions between radical and liberal students. Peter Warrian, president of the organization, was quoted in 1968; 'Our problem is that the student councils have come [to conferences of CUS] and passed radical or reformist policies and done absolutely nothing to implement them.' *Toronto Telegram*, 31 Aug. 1968
65 See Quarter, *The Student Movement of the Sixties*. His survey of Toronto students indicated that, although most opposed the actions of radicals, their attitudes about the university and society had become increasingly critical. Another survey, cited in *Business Quarterly* (winter 1970), recorded the sceptical views that students at the University of Western Ontario held about the activities of corporations ('A Survey of Student Opinion Regarding Business').
66 Canadian Institute of Public Opinion, *The Gallup Poll of Canada*, 27 Aug. 1969, 29 Sept. 1971
67 Letter from Harrison F. Dunning (Scott Paper Co.), *Monetary Times*, Dec. 1965; Robert L. Perry in the *Financial Post*, 23 Sept. 1967; 'Doesn't Anybody Like Business?' *Monetary Times*, Nov. 1966; 'Business and Student: Crisis or Challenge,' *Canadian Business*, Nov. 1968; R.D. Musgjerd (president of International Harvester Company, Canada), 'Is Youth Disenchanted with Business?,' *Business Quarterly*, Dec. 1970; 'Industry–Student Relations: The Need for Bridges,' three-part article in *Industrial Canada*, May–July, 1971. That such attitudes lingered even after university campuses had returned to a state of relative calm was reflected in an article by J. Richard Finlay, 'Don't Be Fooled by the Quiet: Students Mean Trouble for Business,' *Executive*, Oct. 1974
68 Alexander Ross, 'Someday Radicals Might be Picketing Your Plant,' *Financial Post*, 13 Dec. 1969
69 'Who's to Blame?' *Monetary Times*, Nov. 1966
70 *Debates*, Ontario Legislative Assembly, 21 Feb. 1969, 1,431
71 Ibid., 25 Nov. 1969, 8,853 (my emphasis)
72 Ibid., 10 June 1968, 4,181 and 4,193
73 Ibid., 16 March 1970, 685
74 Ibid., 10 June 1970, 3,856–7, 3,871

75 See CPUO, *Campus and Forum*, Third Annual Review, 1968/69, 28; and *Report of the Committee on University Affairs*, 1968/69, 19.

76 Minutes, CUA, 7 Oct. 1969

77 See D. Ferguson, 'Five Year Budget within Tentative Constraints,' May 15, 1970 CUA files, RG–32, Archives of Ontario. See also minutes of a meeting of the CUA, 26 May 1970, where Ferguson, the systems analysis co-ordinator of the Department of University Affairs, explained his memorandum of the 15 May. See also James Cutt, 'Efficiency and Effectiveness in Public Spending: The Programme Budgeting Approach,' *Canadian Public Administration*, vol. XIII, no. 4 (winter 1970); K. Bryden, 'Executive and Legislature in Ontario: A Case Study on Governmental Reform,' ibid., vol. XVIII, no. 2 (summer 1975).

78 Ferguson, 'Five Year Budget;' see also a document prepared by the Treasury Board, 'The Fiscal Outlook and Budgetary Planning, 1968–73,' CUA files, RG–32, Archives of Ontario.

79 Memorandum to the minister of university affairs, re Grant Recommendation for 1970–71 and 1971–72, from D.T. Wright and E.E. Stewart, 8 Jan. 1970, ibid. (where the following correspondence is also lodged)

80 'Forecast Memorandum: Multi-Year Forecast, 1971/72 to 1975/76,' April 1971, ibid.

81 Interview with J.B. Macdonald, former executive director of CPUO, 23 Jan. 1975

82 CPUO, *Participatory Planning*, Fifth Annual Review, 1970/71, 4

83 For announcements of government grants and university responses, see *Globe and Mail*, 26 Nov. 1969; *Windsor Star*, 26 Dec. 1970; *Globe and Mail*, 28 April 1971; *Globe and Mail*, 13 July 1972. See also *Report of the Committee on University Affairs*, 1972/73 and 1973/74, 16–17

84 COU, *Stimulus and Response*, Sixth Annual Review, 1971, 4

85 Ibid., 4, 5. The Treasury Board document is quoted verbatim.

86 *Globe and Mail*, 4 Feb. 1972, where Grosskurth gave her version of the events in a lengthy article

87 Budget Address, *Debates*, March 28, 1972, 711

88 *Report of the Committee on University Affairs*, 1971/72, 13–14

89 Interview with Wright, 8 April 1972

90 *The Learning Society*, 107

91 COU, Brief to the Committee on University Affairs, 11 Dec. 1972, 1.

92 Information taken from briefs by Trent, Brock, Western, and Queen's to CUA, 1972 (MCU Library). See also *Globe and Mail*, 25 Jan. 1973, for additional information on the Brock sit-in, and see also the minutes of CUA meetings at which these briefs were presented.

93 Wright to Stewart, *re* Formula Operating Grant Overruns, 21 Nov. 1969, CUA files, RG–32, Archives of Ontario

94 'Background Information on Enrolment Projections for 1971/72,' 19 Nov. 1971, ibid.

95 To Stewart, 15 April 1971, cited in ibid.

96 Minutes, meeting of CUA, 2 March 1971

97 These figures refer to undergraduate degree enrolment in provincially assisted universities. See *Report of the Minister of University Affairs, 1970/71*, 61, and Statistical Summary (MCU), 1971/72, 3

98 'A Survey Concerning the Short-Fall in Student Attendance at Ontario Colleges and Universities,' prepared by Market Facts of Canada, Toronto, 1972

99 *Report of the Committee on University Affairs*, 1972/73, 1973/74

100 COU, *New Structure, New Environment*: Review 1972/73 to 1974/75, 7

101 Committee of Presidents, *Variations on a Theme*, Fourth Annual Review, 1969/70, 14–16

102 Wright to Stewart, 5 April, 1971; see also 'Suggested Outline for 1971 briefs to the CUA from the Provincially Assisted Universities,' DUA to CUA, 2 April 1971. CUA files, RG–32, Archives of Ontario. The DUA became the Department of Colleges and Universities in late 1971, and finally the Ministry of Colleges and Universities (MCU) in 1972.

103 Macdonald to Wright, 14 June 1971, CUA files, RG–32, Archives of Ontario

104 See the following items on this topic: Stephen Lewis in *Debates*, Ontario Legislative Assembly, 25 Nov. 1969; *CAUT Bulletin*, Oct. 1969 and Jan. 1974; Pauline Jewett in *Maclean's*, March 1969; Mathews and Steele, 'The Universities: The Takeover of the Mind,' in I. Lumsden, ed., *Close the 49th Parallel* (Toronto: University of Toronto Press, 1970); Ellen and Neal Wood, 'Canada and the American Science of Politics,' in ibid., Donald Smiley, 'Must Canadian Political Science Be a Miniature Replica?' *Journal of Canadian Studies*, Feb. 1974; and T.H.B. Symons, *To Know Ourselves: The Report of the Commission on Canadian Studies*, vols. I and II (AUCC, 1975).

105 CPUO, *Campus and Forum*, 34

106 Ibid., 35

107 Sept. 1970; see brief, 'The Graduate Department of English, University of Toronto, A Study of Cringing Colonialism,' by R.D. Mathews and the Subcommittee of Six, the Montreal Committee on the de-Canadianization of the Universities, CUA files, RG–32, Archives of Ontario

108 Minutes, meeting of the CUA, 19 Oct. 1970, ibid.

109 Daniel G. Hill to E.E. Stewart, 16 Oct. 1970, ibid.

110 Excerpts from draft minutes of COU executive meeting held on 15 July 1971. CUA agreed with the presidents that it had erred by initially asking for citizenship of faculty by birth instead of 'current citizenship.' This was redressed in subsequent questionnaires.

111 Submission on Behalf of the Administration to the Select Committee on Economic and Cultural Nationalism of the Legislative Assembly of Ontario, 1973

112 *Debates*, Ontario Legislative Assembly, 5 June 1967, 4,266

113 Interviews with E.E. Stewart, 2 May 1975, and with J.B. Macdonald, 23 Jan. 1975

114 Interviews with Reva Gerstein, 12 April 1977, and James Gibson (former President of Brock University), 25 Aug. 1976

115 See J. Porter, B. Blishen, *et al.*, *Towards 2000: The Future of Post-Secondary Education in Ontario* (Toronto: McClelland and Stewart, 1971)

116 *Draft Report*, Commission on Post-Secondary Education (Toronto, 1972), 35

117 *Stimulus and Response*, 8

118 The presidents proposed a 'double buffer' model, which entailed the structuring of two advisory committees, one closely associated with the government, such as the CUA, and one close to the universities, such as their own organization. See ibid., 10, and COU, *Responses to the Draft Report of the Commission on Post-Secondary Education*, 15–17

119 The final report stressed a prominent role for advisory bodies such as the COU. See *The Learning Society*, 191. With this change, the COU claimed to 'strongly support [the recommendation for an Ontario Council on University Affairs, that is, the new co-ordinating board] on the understanding that it shall seek systematic planning advice from COU and will work closely with COU in the implementation of plans.' *Response to the Report of the Commission on Post-Secondary Education* (1972), 4

120 From a 'preliminary paper' for CPUO circulated confidentially in 1969, cited in Charles Hanly, *Who Pays?* (OCUFA, 1970), 114. A published account by the presidents of earlier proposal can be found in *Campus and Forum*, 64–73.

121 *Participatory Planning*, 10; *Stimulus and Response*, 26 and chart (appendix D) for outline of committee structure.

122 See 'Proposals for Establishing a Council of Universities of Ontario,' *Campus and Forum*, 64. The committee was renamed the Council of Ontario Universities.

123 OCUFA believed that, in presenting itself as a representative of the entire university community, COU was attempting to disguise the fact that in essence it represented 'management'. OCUFA saw itself as the real representative of faculty interests. See *OCUFA Bulletin*, vol. 2, no. 1 (March 1969). OCUFA had not been consulted about the organizational changes within the COU. Also interviews with Greg Bennett, 23 April 1975, and Charles Hanly, 12 April 1977. For an extended discussion of the development of OCUFA and its relations with the COU, see P. Axelrod, 'Higher Education in Transition: The Ontario Case,' unpublished graduate research paper, York University, 1975.

124 COU, *The Ten O'Clock Scholar* (1971)

125 In 1968, OCUFA raised its membership dues from $1.00 to an average of $13.00 per year. The trend to unionization is discussed in the next chapter of this book. OCUFA had warned of this development in its brief to the CUA, Dec. 1971. Also interviews with Bennett, Hanly, and J.S. Kirkaldy, 16 Feb. 1977. On the Ontario Federation of Students, see the next chapter.

126 Ontario Council on Graduate Studies (an affiliate of CPUO) *The First Three Years of Appraisal of Graduate Programmes* (CPUO, 1970), 1, 2

127 COU, *Stimulus and Response*, 19

128 ACAP, *Chemical Engineering*, report no. 11 (1974), 9, A–7; *Planning and Environmental Studies*, report no. 13 (1974), A–16, A–17. This series was called 'Perspectives and Plans for Graduate Studies.'

129 *Education*, report no. 2 (1973), A–17–18

130 *Planning and Environmental Studies*, A–16–21

131 *Chemical Engineering*, 9, A–7. See also reports on Electrical Engineering, Metallurgical Engineering, Mechanical Engineering, Industrial Engineering, and Civil Engineering.

132 *The Learning Society*, 31 and chaps. 3–8

133 'Commission on Post-Secondary Education,' in E. Sheffield, ed., *Agencies for Higher Education in Ontario* (Toronto: OISE, 1974), 75

134 The term was used by E.E. Stewart, former deputy minister, Department of University Affairs, and later assistant to the premier. Interview, 2 May 1975

CHAPTER SEVEN

1 Queen's University, Brief to the CUA, 14 Nov. 1972

2 See the following documents: COU, *An Uncertain Future, Review: 1975/76 to 1977/78*; COU, *Who Pays the Price?* (1979); COU, *Changing Public Priorities: Universities and the Future of Ontario* (1980); COU, *A Future of Lost Opportunities?* (1981); OCUA, *Second Annual Report, 1975/6, Third Annual Report, 1976/77*; OCUA, *System on the Brink: A Financial Analysis of the Ontario University System* (1979), OCUA, *A Financial Analysis of the Ontario University System* (1980)

3 'Towards a Balanced Budget,' Budget Paper C, Ontario Budget, 1977

4 *Globe and Mail*, 18 Oct. 1978; OCUA, *A Financial Analysis of the Ontario University System, 1980*, 9–10; *Changing Public Priorities*, 12–18

5 Statement by H.C. Parrott, minister of colleges and universities, on the establishment of the Ontario Industrial Training Council to the Legislature of Ontario, 20 April 1976

6 *A Future of Lost Opportunities?* 9–15. In December 1981 a new report provided more information on provincial support for universities. In all but one of the eight categories used to measure provincial support, Ontario stood no higher than eighth in the country. See *Interprovincial Comparisons of University Financing*, Third Report of the Tripartite Committee on Interprovincial Comparisons.

7 *Financial Post*, 21 Nov. 1981; *Globe and Mail*, 10 Nov. 1981; *Queen's Journal*, 20 Oct. 1981, McMaster University, *Contact*, 11 Dec. 1981. For a full discussion of the background to the 1977 federal-provincial funding arrangements, see Peter Leslie, *Canadian Universities, 1980 and Beyond: Enrolment, Structural Change and Finance*, (Ottawa: AUCC, 1980), 156–9.

8 Peter Oliver, 'Ontario,' in R.D. Byers and J.T. Saywell, eds., *Canadian Annual Review 1978* (Toronto: University of Toronto Press, 1980) 111–12

9 *Changing Public Priorities*, 13, 61

10 See the following documents: *From the Sixties to the Eighties: A Statistical Portrait of Canadian Higher Education* (prepared for the twelfth Quinquennial Congress of the Universities of the Commonwealth, Vancouver, BC, 19–26 Aug., 1978, by the Education, Science and Culture Division, Statistics Canada), 99–101; OCUA, *The Ontario University System: A Statement of Issues*, Sept. 1978, 9; Linda Moffat, *Room at the Bottom: Job Mobility Opportunities for Ontario Academics in the Mid-Seventies* (MCU, 1980), 13

11 *Corporate Giving in Canada, 1971–1978*, Institute of Donations and Public Affairs Research, Montreal

12 *Corporate Attitudes to Funding Universities*, Institute of Donations and Public Affairs Research (30 March 1978), 7, 10

13 Clearly, there were a variety of conflicting opinions held by individuals from the private sector about the value and importance of Canadian universities, and this short account is by no means intended to simplify or overlook these views. University board chairmen, for example, would in all likelihood be more sensitive to the academic purposes, cultural role, and financial plight of the universities than spokesmen whose opinions are cited here. But it is significant that the views noted reflect a cross-section and consensus identified, not by me, but by Richard Hopkinson. I would like to thank Mr Hopkinson for providing me with information included in this section.

14 Z. Zsigmond, G. Picot, M.S. Devereaux, W. Clark, *Future Trends in Enrolment and Manpower Supply in Ontario* (Ottawa, 1977), 26

15 W. Clark, and Z. Zsigmond, *Job Market Reality for Post-secondary Graduates: Employment Outcome by 1978, Two Years after Graduation* (Ottawa, 1981), 59–70, 128–31

16 *Globe and Mail*, 26 March 1981; *Toronto Star*, 1 Sept. 1980

17 Compare the headlines of stories cited in previous note.

18 Clark and Zsigmond, *Job Market Reality*, 11, 59–70

19 Zsigmond *et al.*, *Future Trends* 26

20 Clark and Zsigmond, *Job Market Reality*, 7

21 Zsigmond *et al.*, *Future Trends*, 27. On school teachers, see R.W.B. Jackson, *A Statement of Effects and Solutions: Final Report of the Commission on Declining School Enrolments in Ontario* (Toronto, 1978), 133, 136.

22 *Two Years After Graduation: Results of a Survey of 1976 Doctoral Recipients in Ontario* (W.B. Wolfe Inc. and MCU, 1979), sec. 4; see also 'Survey of 1976 Doctoral Degree Recipients from Canadian Universities' by Statistics Canada, cited in *University Affairs*, Nov. 1979; and Ministry of Education and MCU, 'Analysis of the Results of the Survey of the 1976 PhD Recipients from Canadian Universities.' The national unemployment rate for PhD graduates of 1976 was 2.18 per cent.

23 Moffat, *Room at the Bottom*, 22; MCU, 'Analysis of the Results of the Survey'
24 Report of Joint COU/OCUFA Committee on the Study of Academic Career Development in Ontario Universities, *The Ivory Tower and the Crystal Ball* (May 1976), 15
25 Moffat, *Room at the Bottom*, 8, 190
26 Wolfe, *Two Years After,* vi; Moffat, *Room at the Bottom*, 55. See also M.S. Devereaux, Edith Rechnitzer, *Higher Education–Hired? Sex Differences in Employment Characteristics of 1976 Post-secondary Graduates* (Ottawa, 1980).
27 Wolfe, *Two Years After*, iii-iv and sec. 2; MCU, 'Analysis of the Results.' See chap. 2 of this book.
28 *Two Years After*, 63
29 Much of the material in this section has been gathered from interviews with some individuals who prefer not to be cited.
30 See, for example, his Graduation Day Address at Fanshawe College, 18 June 1976; Keynote Address on the occasion of Essex County Education Week, 4 April 1976; and Convocation Address at Ryerson Polytechnical Institute, 16 Oct. 1976 (MCU Library)
31 Interview with Dupré, 2 Sept. 1980
32 See, for example, OCUA, *First Annual Report: 1974/75.* In previous years, the CUA did publish minutes of its meetings, but they were frequently heavily edited and sanitized versions.
33 OCUA, *Second Annual Report: 1975/76,* 38–52
34 COU *An Uncertain Future: Review, 1975/76 to 1977/78,* 3
35 S. Dupré, 'The Determination of Tuition Fees,' in Ontario Economic Council, *Emerging Problems in Post-Secondary Education,* 1977. He wrote (p. 38): 'Indeed, in the very year that Government announced its objectives in Global Funding, it was disputed by a group of Weighty Advisors who claimed that what the Government had given was insufficient to meet these objectives. The government did not again enunciate such clear objectives.'
36 COU, *An Uncertain Future,* 3
37 Interview with Winegard, 6 Aug. 1980
38 COU, *An Uncertain Future,* 11
39 Ibid. 15
40 'Aggressive Recruiting: For Some Essential, for others Anathema,' *University Affairs,* March 1980
41 D.G. Sinclair, 'Development Committee – Planning for 1980's,' 22 Oct. 1980
42 Statistics Canada, *From the Sixties to the Eighties,* 35
43 E.E. Stewart to the author, 6 Oct. 1980
44 See *Report of the Interim Committee on Financial Assistance for Students,* Jan. 1977. The author was a member of this committee. On the 'old' student aid plan, see brochure, Ministry of Colleges and Universities, 'Ontario Student Assistance Plan, 1977–78
45 The committee attempted to address this problem by allowing students to deduct annual interest charges a an allowable educational expense.
46 MCU, 'Dr. Parrott Announces Principle of new Student Grant Programmes for 1978/79,' 17 Aug. 1977; and 'Minister Releases Details of new Ontario Student Assistance Program,' 9 March 1978
47 Interview with Winegard, 6 Aug. 1980
48 Ontario Federation of Students, 'From OSAP to OSGP: A Brief History of Student Aid in Ontario,' (1980)
49 'Statement by Harry C. Parrott, Minister of Colleges and Universities, Regarding Fees Charged to Foreign Students by Ontario Post-Secondary Educational Institutions,' to the Legislature, 4 May 1976. See also 'Statement to the Legislature by the Hon. Harry Parrott,

Concerning Operating Funds, Tuition Fees, and Student Assistance in 1977/78,' 26 Nov. 1976.

50 COU, 'Statement on the Principles Which Should Govern the Setting of Tuition Fees,' 3 June 1976

51 According to Statistics Canada, 'The proportion of male undergraduates whose fathers were degree holders rose from 16.4 per cent in 1968/69 to 21.7 per cent in 1974/75. A similar pattern was evident among female students ... However, according to the 1971 Census, only 5.7 per cent of 45–64 year old males had degrees. *From the Sixties to the Eighties*, 54. Over-all participation rates of individuals from the 18–24-year-old range in universities was itself declining in the late 1970s. From a high of 13 per cent in 1975/76, the rate was expected to have dropped to about 11.5 per cent by 1978/79. OCUA, *The Ontario University System: A Statement of Issues* (1978), 30

52 For an examination of the effects of education on social mobility, see Christopher Jencks *et al.*, *Inequality: A Reassessment of the Effect of the Family and Schooling in America* (New York: Basic Books 1972). Another interesting – and self-critical – re-evaluation of the liberal myth can be found in John Porter, *The Measure of Canadian Society: Education, Equality and Opportunity* (Toronto: Gage, 1979), chap. 1.

53 Minutes, Founding Conference, Ontario Federation of Students, Guelph University, March 1972. For a discussion of the demise of the Ontario Union of Students, see P. Axelrod, 'Patterns of Student Politics,' *University Affairs*, Oct. 1973. On the Canadian Union of Students, see Pat Armstrong, 'The Canadian Union of Students,' unpublished paper, 1971

54 Minutes, First Annual Conference, OFS, York University, May 1973

55 'OFS/FEO Referendum, October 10–12, 1972: Total Turnout by Institution'; Craig Heron, 'The Demonstration: A Post Mortem,' 23 Nov. 1972

56 'Report of the Committee to Restructure OFS,' Jan. 1974

57 See, for example, their brief to the OCUA, 18 April 1980

58 OFS, 'From OSAP to OSGP: A Brief History of Student Aid in Ontario,' 1980, 19; and Interview with Jay Drydyck, OFS researcher, 12 Aug. 1980

59 Martin Trow, 'Problems in the Transition from Elite to Mass Higher Education,' from OECD conference on mass higher education, June 1973 (mimeo), 12

60 Donald Savage, 'Professional Societies and Trade Unions,' *CAUT Bulletin*, March 1973. In 1978/79 the median salary for an Ontario professor was $31,000. The national median was $31,800 Statistics Canada, *Teachers in Universities, 1972/3–1979/80* (Ottawa, 1980)

61 Ray La Berge, 'Faculty Members Turn to Collective Bargaining,' *Labour Gazette*, Aug. 1975

62 Roland Penner, 'Faculty Unionization: Background, Development and Impact,' *Interchange*, vol. 9, no. 3 (1978/79), 71. A list of all faculty unions in Canada, the dates of certification, and the numbers involved, can be found in 'Faculty Collective Bargaining at Canadian Universities,' *University Affairs*, May 1980

63 D.D. Carter and B.I. Adell, *Collective Bargaining for University Faculty in Canada* (AUCC, 1972), 5. In its 1971 brief to the CUA, OCUFA warned that unless salary settlements improved, there would be 'increased pressure toward unionization and collective bargaining at the provincial level' (p. 30).

64 See E.C. Ladd and S.M. Lipset, *Professors, Union and American Higher Education* (1973), and Carter and Adell, *Collective Bargaining*, 40

65 Penner, 'Faculty Unionization, 71; Interview with Victor Sim, executive vice-president, CAUT, 18 Aug. 1980

66 Carter and Adell, *Collective Bargaining*, 32–9; Penner, 'Faculty Unionization,' 74
67 See B. Brody, 'Professional Unions and Collective Bargaining: A Few Fundamental Principles,' *CAUT Bulletin* (winter 1972). Other useful materials on the background to unionization among faculty include: W. Lindeman, 'The Five Most Cited Reasons for Faculty Unionization,' *Intellect*, Nov. 1973; M. Thompson, 'The Development of Collective Bargaining in Canadian Universities,' delivered at 28th Annual Meeting of the Industrial Relations Research Association, Dec. 1975; and Terry F. Hercus, 'Unionization and the University,' *Canadian Personnel and Industrial Relations Journal*, Jan. 1978
68 On the changing role of the president, see Clark Kerr, *The Uses of the University* (New York: Harper and Rowe 1972), 29–41. See also Pat Finn, 'Collective Bargaining and Collegiality in the Ontario University System,' unpublished paper, Carleton University, March 1979.
69 *University Government in Canada*, report of a commission sponsored by the CAUT and AUCC (Toronto, 1966)
70 Penner, 'Faculty Unionization,' 72; Donato Savage, 'Collective Bargaining: Where Are We Now?' *CAUT Bulletin*, Feb. 1978; I Cinman, 'Collective Bargaining Sets Tone for CAUT Council Meeting,' *CAUT Bulletin*, June 1974; Donato Savage, 'Report from the Executive Secretary,' *CAUT Bulletin*, June 1974
71 Carter and Addell, *Collective Bargaining*, 31; Carl Garry, 'From Faculty Association to Faculty Union,' *Canadian Personnel and Industrial Relations Journal* (winter 1972)
72 Brody, 'Professional Unions and Collective Bargaining.'
73 Statistics calculated from W.G. Fleming, *The Expansion of the Educational System*, vol. I of *Ontario's Educative Society* (Toronto: University of Toronto Press) 186–9
74 Submission of Carleton University to the CUA, Sept. 1975, cited in Debra Mair, 'Unionization and the Middle Class: The Case of University Faculty,' unpublished MA thesis, Carleton University, 1977, table 14
75 Information about York is drawn from the following sources: *Globe and Mail*, 22 Dec. 1972; B. Richman and R. Farmer, *Leadership Goals and Power in Higher Education* (San Francisco: Jossey-Bass, 1975), chap. 2, an unidentified case study of the York crisis by a former member of the administration; Harry Crowe, 'The York Follies,' *Canadian Forum*, May 1975
76 Interview with J.L. Granatstein (former chairman of the York University Faculty Association), 26 Aug. 1980; see also 'Comment' by William Farr (York vice-president) in *Interchange*, volume 9, no. 3 (1978/79).
77 Mair, 'Unionization and the Middle Class,' 122–5
78 Jill Vickers, President's Report, *CUASA News*, vol. 5, no. 2 (Dec. 1974); Mair, 'Unionization and the Middle Class,' 128
79 Interview with Muni Frumhartz (former president of the Carleton University Academic Staff Association), 19 Aug. 1980
80 Jill Vickers, cited in Mair, 'Unionization and the Middle Class,' 133
81 Only the Faculty of Theology and Canon Law and the Institute of Pastoral Studies and Missiology which were grouped in Saint Paul University (and federated with the University of Ottawa) remained under denominational control and were therefore ineligible for direct aid from the province. See Fleming, *Post-Secondary and Adult Education*, vol. IV of *Ontario's Educative Society*, 134
82 Interview with Cowan, 18 Aug. 1980
83 Carl Garry, 'From Faculty Association to Faculty Union,' *Canadian Personnel and Industrial Relations Journal*, vol. 23, no. 6 (1976)

84 This is supported in Thompson, 'The Development of Collective Bargaining in Canadian Universities.'

85 Mair, 'Unionization and the Middle Class,' 128–32, 150–1

86 Interview with Granatstein

87 Mair, 'Unionization and the Middle Class,' 151

88 'Collective Bargaining by Professionals: Advisability, Practicality and Feasibility,' *CAUT Bulletin*, May 1975 Crispo's article listed the disadvantages *and* advantages of unionization.

89 Ibid.; see also, R. La Berge, 'Faculty Members Turn to Collective Bargaining'; 'Judgement in the Supreme Court of Ontario, Divisional Court in the matter of the Labour Relations Act, R.S.O. 1970, chapter 232 as amended, and in the matter of a purported certificate issued by the Ontario Labour Relations Board to the York University Faculty Association between William A. Jordan et al. and The Ontario Labour Relations Board, York University Faculty Association, York University, and Osgoode Hall Faculty Association; Heard: 13–19 Jan., 1977.' Copy in YUFA files, York University Archives

90 'Faculty Unionization,' 73; see also P. Finn, 'Collective Bargaining and Collegiality in the Ontario University System'; Mair, 'Unionization and the Middle Class,' 143, 165–6

CONCLUSION

1 See, for example, J. Porter, B. Blishen, *et al.*, *Toward 2000: The Future of Post-Secondary Education in Ontario*, (Toronto: McClelland and Stewart, 1971), 25: and C. Bissell, *The Strength of the University: A Selection from the Addresses of Claude T. Bissell* (Toronto: University of Toronto Press, 1968), 153.

2 T.H. McLeod, 'Summary of the Discussions,' in T.H. McLeod, ed., *Post-Secondary Education in a Technological Society* (Montreal: McGill-Queen's University Press, 1973), 212–13.

3 M.L. Handa and M.L. Skolnik, 'Empirical Analysis of the Demand for Education in Canada' in S. Ostry, ed., *Canadian Higher Education in the Seventies* (Ottawa, 1972), 8.

4 See Porter, Blishen, *et al.*, *Towards 2000*, chap. 3.

5 For descriptions of 'planning' in post-secondary education in provinces and countries beyond Ontario, see: McLeod, ed., *Post-Secondary Education in a Technological Society*, esp. chapters on Australia, Germany, Norway, and the United Kingdom; and E.F. Sheffield *et al.*, *Systems of Higher Education: Canada* (New York: International Council for Educational Development, 1978).

6 For the American situation, see E.F. Cheit, *The New Depression in Higher Education* (New York: McGraw Hill, 1971).

7 ACAP *Chemical Engineering*, report no. 11, 1974, A–42–43.

8 Handa and Skolnik, 'Empirical Analysis,' 9, quoting from 'Graduates and Jobs: A Grave New World,' *Time*, Canadian ed. 24 May 1971, 58

9 For a description of educational planning in socialist countries see Abram Bergson, *The Economics of Soviet Planning* (New Haven and London: Yale University Press, 1964); *Soviet Economic Prospects of the Seventies: A Compendium of Papers Submitted to the Joint Economic Committee*, Congress of the United States, 27 June 1973; David Lane, *The Socialist Industrial State: Towards a Political Sociology of State Socialism* (London: Allen and Unwin, 1976); and McLeod, ed., *Post-Secondary Education*, 129–45.

10 See Pierre L. Bourgault, *Innovation and the Structure of Canadian Industry*, background study for the Science Council of Canada (Ottawa 1972); and Science Council of Canada, *Innovation in a Cold Climate*, Report no. 15 (Ottawa 1971).

11 *Responsible Government in Ontario* (Toronto: University of Toronto Press, 1969), 79–80
12 *Globe and Mail*, editorial, 20 Oct. 1980
13 For a discussion of this phenomenon in the United States, see Christopher Lasch, *The Culture of Narcissism* (New York: Warner, 1979), esp. 221–61
14 D.W. Livingstone and D.L. Hart, *Public Attitudes towards Education in Ontario, 1980* (Toronto: OISE 1981), 31. Fifty-eight per cent of those surveyed wanted universities to place more emphasis on job-related instruction.

Note on Sources

The main archival sources used for this study were: RG2-P3, Education Records, 1939–67, and RG-32, Committee on University Affairs Records, 1958–73, Archives of Ontario. Selected materials from the Archives of the University of Toronto, McMaster, Western, York, and Brock were also consulted.

Useful bibliographical sources included the *Business Periodical Index*, the *Canadian Education Index*, the *Canadian Periodical Index*, Ontario Historical Studies Series, *Ontario since 1867: A Bibliography* (Toronto: OHSS, 1973), and R.S. Harris *et al., A Bibliography of Higher Education in Canada, 1960, 1965, 1970, 1982* (Toronto: University of Toronto Press). Collections of newspaper clippings on university affairs were held at the Ministry of Colleges and Universities library and at the Ontario Institute for Studies in Education.

Government documents examined were: *Debates* of the House of Commons and of the Ontario Legislative Assembly, *Budgets* (and *Budget Statements*) of Ontario, speeches of ministers and deputy ministers of Department of University Affairs and Ministry of Colleges and Universities (MCU library), *Annual Reports* of the Ontario Department of Education, Department of University Affairs, and Ministry of Colleges and Universities, and *Statistical Summaries* prepared by the latter. Selected publications of the federal Department of Manpower and Immigration and Department of Labour were also valuable.

Reports from, studies by, and briefs to the following government agencies and commissions were analysed: Dominion Bureau of Statistics, Statistics Canada, Royal Commission on the National Development of Arts, Letters and Sciences (1951), Royal Commission on Canada's Economic Prospects (1957), Royal Commission on Health Services (1964), Ontario Committee on the Healing Arts (1970), Commission on Post-Secondary Education (1972), (Advisory) Committee on University Affairs, and Ontario Council on University Affairs.

The following business, educational, research, and/or professional organizations published reports and journals which were invaluable: Association of Universities and

Colleges of Canada, Canadian Association of University Teachers, Canadian Institute of Public Opinion, Canadian Manufacturers Association, Canadian Medical Association, Canadian Pharmaceutical Association, Canadian Universities Foundation, Canadian Union of Students, Committee of Presidents of the Universities of Ontario, (National Industrial) Conference Board, Council of Ministers of Education in Canada, Council of Ontario Universities, Economic Council of Canada, Humanities Research Council, Industrial Foundation on Education, Institute of Donations and Public Affairs Research, Law Society of Upper Canada, National Conference of Canadian Universities, Ontario Confederation of University Faculty Associations, Ontario Economic Council, Ontario Federation of Students, Ontario Institute for Studies in Education, and Science Council of Canada.

Of particular importance were annual reports of the presidents of Ontario universities and the academic calendars of each institution. Interviews were conducted with some fifty individuals active in university affairs over the last three decades.

Unpublished theses of considerable assistance were: Debra Mair: 'Unionization and the Middle Class: The Case of University Faculty,' MA Carleton University, 1977; Gwendoline Pilkington, 'A History of the National Conference of Canadian Universities, 1911-1961,' DEd University of Toronto, 1974; Robert Stamp, 'The Campaign for Technical Education in Ontario, 1876-1914,' PhD University of Western Ontario, 1970; E.E. Stewart, 'The Role of the Provincial Government in the Development of the Universities of Ontario, 1791-1964,' DEd University of Toronto, 1970.

For more details on primary and secondary sources used, see notes to this book and the bibliography of Paul Axelrod, 'The Economy, Government, and the Universities of Ontario: 1945-1973,' PhD thesis, York University, 1979.

Statistical Appendix

TABLE 1

Enrolment, University Teachers, and Median Salaries in Ontario, 1945-80

Year beginning	Full-time enrolment (graduate[1] and undergraduate)	Full-time university teachers	Full-time university teachers' median salary, Ontario[2] $	Full-time university teachers' median salary, Canada $
1945	21,741	1,336	3,568	3,459
1950	23,207	1,757	4,357	4,203
1955	22,642	1,810	5,643[3]	5,423[3]
1960	32,175	2,555	8,642	8,404
1965	59,274	4,695	10,283	10,250
1970	121,115	9,335	15,514	14,887
1975	159,701	12,078	22,400	22,450
1980	160,241	12,372	34,016	34,062

1 Prior to 1955 graduate enrolment includes part-time students.
2 Prior to 1975 figure includes "central Canada" (Ontario and Quebec).
3 Figure is for 1954/5; unavailable for 1955/6.
SOURCES
Statistics Canada, *Historical Compendium of Education Statistics, from Confederation to 1975* (Ottawa, 1978)
Statistics Canada, *Teachers in Universities*, 1972/3 to 1979/80 (Ottawa, various years)
Dominion Bureau of Statistics, *University Teachers' Salaries, 1937–1960* (Ottawa, 1960); and 1960/61, 1965/66, 1970/71 (Ottawa, various years)
Ministry of Colleges and Universities, Statistics Branch (for unpublished 1980 figures)

TABLE 2

Operating and Capital Expenditures of Universities by Source of Funds, Ontario, 1945–79

OPERATING–thousands of dollars and percentage ( ) of total

Financial year beginning in	Federal	Provincial	Mu-nicipal	Subtotal	Fees	Other[1]	Operating subtotal
1945	988	3,252	49	4,289 (43.2)	3,710 (37.37)	1,583 (15.94)	9,582
1950	744	7,542	151	8,437 (45.25)	5,730 (30.73)	2,330 (12.5)	16,497
1955	5,936	11,449	197	17,582 (52.3)	7,978 (24)	4,790 (14.43)	30,350
1960	17,161	21,984	348	39,493 (40.2)	15,367 (15.64)	7,931 (8.07)	62,791
1965	30,726	69,797	450	100,973 (38)	34,978 (13.17)	16,715 (6.29)	152,666
1970	49,243	361,582	391	411,216 (56.72)	76,526 (10.55)	40,882 (5.63)	528,624
1974	67,792	511,707	513	582,012 (71.62)	118,273 (14.5)	60,638 (7.46)	760,923
1979	113,556	825,955	599	940,110 (76.6)	160,189 (13.05)	98,512 (8.02)	1,198,811

CAPITAL–thousands of dollars and percentage ( ) of total

Federal	Provincial	Mu-nicipal	Subtotal	Other[1]	Capital subtotal	TOTAL (100%) Operating and Capital Expenditures	Financial year beginning in
					345 (3.47)	9,927	1945
					2,145 (11.5)	18,642	1950
6	7,015	450	7,471 (22.5)	–4,622 (–13.9)	2,849	33,199	1955
4,606	15,385	267	20,258 (20.62)	15,164 (15.43)	35,422	98,213	1960
1,705	89,239	573	91,517 (34.45)	21,393 (8.05)	112,910	265,576	1965
2,077	170,659	274	173,010 (23.86)	23,326 (3.21)	196,336	724,960	1970
7,725	6,384	70	14,179 (1.74)	37,541 (4.61)	51,720	812,643	1975
45	15,715	0	15,760 (1.28)	12,699 (1.03)	28,459	1,227,270	1979

1 Includes company contributions, individual donations, income from investments, income from ancillary enterprises, and miscellaneous.

SOURCES

Statistics Canada, *Historical Compendium of Education Statistics, from Confederation to 1975* (Ottawa, 1978); Statistics Canada, *Decade of Education Finance, 1970/71 to 1979/80* (Ottawa, forthcoming, 1982)

TABLE 3

Interprovincial Comparisons of University Grants: Provincial Operating
Grants per Student, 1974–80

Year beginning in	Ontario $	Provincial Rank	Canada (weighted average) $
1974	2,690	7	2,871
1976	3,265	8	3,687
1979	4,140	9	4,851
1980 (e)	4,296	10	5,169

e estimate
SOURCES:
Tripartite Commission on Interprovincial Comparisons, *Interprovincial Comparisons of University Financing* (third report), 1981
Council of Ontario Universities, *Once More With Feeling*, brief to the Ontario Council on University Affairs, 1982

Index

Academic freedom 78, 79
Accessibility to higher education 28–33, 153–6, 160, 196–201; *see also* Student aid
Accountancy 108, 135, 143
Advisory Committee on Academic Planning 173–7
Alberta Department of Education 14
Alberts, E.T. 63
Allenburg Women's Institute 65
Althouse College 127
Althouse, J.G. 84–6, 87, 88
Architecture 116–17, 125–6
Arlt, G.O. 96
Association of Universities and Colleges of Canada 116
Attitudes to university expansion 20–8
Auld, James 188, 189
A.V. Roe Canada Ltd. 42, 43, 63, 123

Bailyn, Bernard 7
Bank of Montreal 36, 38
Bank of Nova Scotia 70
Banking industry 49, 74
Barbour, H.D. 73
Bassett, John 73
Bata, Mrs Thomas 70

Beatty, Samuel 89–90
Bell Telephone Co. 107
Berg, Ivar 145
Bissell, Claude 23, 25, 65, 101n, 109
Blaug, Mark 110
Boards of governors: *see* Business and university boards of governors *and* individual universities
Borden, Henry 48, 68
Bourns, A.N. 127
Brakeley, G.A. and Co. 71–73
Brannan, C.E. 159, 160
Britain 26, 30, 81, 92, 95
Brock University: board of governors 57–8; and business community 56–8; establishment 55, 56–8, 94; Founders Committee 56; fund raising 58; and Laurentian University 57; and McMaster University 56; and Niagara Peninsula Joint Committee on Higher Education 56; and spending restraints 164; and St Catharines 56
Burton, Edgar 66, 69
Business: and establishment of Ontario universities 56, 57, 59, 61, 63–7; and university boards of governors 56–60,

62, 65–76; and university fund raising campaigns 58, 59, 61, 68–76; *see also* Corporate aid to universities

Business administration 117, 134, 144–5

Business attitudes: to curriculum 105–10; to government funding of universities 36–9, 182–3; to professional training 36–7; to tuition fees 31; to university expansion 24, 25, 36–7, 41

Business Quarterly 42

Business Review (Bank of Montreal) 36

Byleveld, H. 41n, 42n, 46n, 49n

Cameron, Donald 25

Canada Council 20

Canada's Crisis in Higher Education (1956 conference) 23, 43

Canadian Annual Review 11

Canadian Association of University Teachers 205, 212

Canadian Business

Canadian Chamber of Commerce 107

Canadian Chartered Accountant 108

Canadian General Electric Co. 61

Canadian Imperial Bank of Commerce 70

Canadian Industries Limited 39

Canadian Labour Congress 27, 30

Canadian Manufacturers Association 10, 60, 106, 110

Canadian Medical Association 133

Canadian Medical Association Journal 122

Canadian Office 27

Canadian Union of Educational Workers 204

Canadian Union of Students 153, 154, 201

Canadian Universities Foundation 128

Canadian University 146

Canadianization of university 168–71

Canon, C.F. 89

Career Outlook 150

Carleton University 23; Architecture 125–6; curriculum 82, 104, 105; Engineering 123, 127; establishment 80; expansion plans 89; fund raising 51; government funding of 80, 83; Journalism 82; unionization of faculty 204, 207, 208–9, 211, 212

Carleton University Academic Staff Association 209

CBC 73

Central Intelligence Agency 24

CFRB 73

CFTO 73

Chemical Industries 48, 49

Chemistry in Canada 39

CHFI 73

Chown, M.A. 56

CHUM 73

CKEY 73

CKFH 73

Clarke, A.A. 63

Clement, Wallace 62

Cody, H.J. 16

Cold war 23–5, 29, 104

College of Physicians and Surgeons in Ontario 133

Columbia University 105

Commission on Post-Secondary Education in Ontario 28, 99, 113, 114, 133, 139, 155, 163, 171, 172, 173, 177–8, 191

Committee on Cultural and Economic Nationalism 170

Committee of Ontario Law Deans 137

Committee of Presidents of the Universities of Ontario: and Commission on Post-Secondary Education 99; and

Committee on University Affairs 93–5, 98, 158–9, 162–3; and economic planning models 110; and Engineering 114; establishment 93; and government funding of universities 158, 162–3; and Pharmacy 120; and professional training 135; and Spinks Commission 96; *see also* Council of Ontario Universities

Committee on University Affairs (*also* Advisory Committee on University Affairs): activities 1958–60, 89–91; and Architecture 126; and Brock University 58; and Canadianization of university 168–71; and Commission on Post-Secondary Education 99; and Committee of Presidents 93–5, 98, 158–9, 162–3; and Council of Ontario Universities 164, 173, 190; and Department of University Affairs 158–65, 190; establishment 89; and formula financing 158; and Engineering 123; and government funding of universities 158–65, 167; and graduate education 127, 128, 130, 162, 174; information gathering 167–8; and Medicine 119; restructuring 1961, 92; under Reva Gerstein 190; and Spinks Commission 96; transition to OCUA 191; and Treasury Board 159–62; and York University 70

Community colleges 77, 94, 136, 166, 180, 183, 184

Cook, G., and Stager, D. 153–5, 178

Cooper, J.L. 73

Corporate aid to universities 37, 43–6, 182–3; to capital expenditures 46, 47–8, 182; by national origin of companies 50–1, 182; to operating expenditures 46; philosophy of giving 38–42; to regions 51–2; to research expenditures 46, 48–9; to scholarships and bursaries 46–7; bv size of company 49–50, 74; to small institutions 52; by type of industry 49, 74–5; *see also* Business and university fund raising campaigns *and* University fund raising campaigns

Cost and Management 108

Cotnam, H.H. 89

Council of Ministers of Education in Canada 142

Council of Ontario Universities 216; and Canadianization 168–71; and Commission on Post-Secondary Education 171–2, 173; and Committee on University Affairs 164, 173, 190; establishment 172; and government funding of universities 181; and graduate education 173–7, 193–4; information gathering 167–8; manpower planning 175; and OCUA 193; and recruitment of students 000; and unemployment, underemployment 183, 186–7; *see also* Committee of Presidents

Cowan, John 210, 212

Crispo, John 212

CTV 26

Cumming, A.A. 36

Curriculum: business attitude to 105–10; graduate 127–31; professional 82, 131–9; undergraduate 101–5; and World War II 17

Curtis, W.A. 63, 65, 66, 67

Dalgleish, Oakley 64, 70

Dare, C.M. 59

Davis, William 28, 96, 97n, 142n, 145–6,

147, 149, 157, 158, 159–60, 163, 188, 191, 196
Dawson, J.W. 131
Deeks, Stanley 31, 43, 56, 57, 63
Defence Training Course 17
Denominational education 12, 55, 59, 210
Dentistry 18, 82, 119–20, 121, 131, 132, 135, 139
Department of Colleges and Universities 166; *see also* Department of University Affairs *and* Ministry of Colleges and Universities
Department of Economics 86, 87, 88
Department of Education 77, 80, 81, 82, 88, 91, 92, 96, 126
Department of Labour 17, 26
Department of Manpower and Immigration 150
Department of University Affairs 95, 96, 146, 158–65, 169; *see also* Ministry of Colleges and Universities
Depression 13, 14, 21, 35, 79
Deutsch, John 28, 152, 179
Deutsch Report 93–94
Dodge, David 143, 152
Drew, George 21, 79
Drop-out rates 29, 30
Drucker, Peter 109
Duff-Berdahl Report 206
Dulles, Allen 24
Duncan, James 24
Dunlop, W.J. 27n, 56, 58, 61, 63, 82, 84
Dupré, Stefan 191–4, 197

Eaton, Mrs John David 66, 67
Economic Council of Canada 26, 107, 112, 115, 121, 145, 152
Economic planning models: manpower planning 39, 110, 113–27, 139–40, 150, 174–7; rate of return 110, 111–13, 150;

social demand 94, 99, 110, 111, 113, 124, 165
Economists' views of educational investment 23, 26, 143–5, 151, 152
Education for citizenship 15
Education for Industrial Purposes 10
Elementary education 8
Ellis, R.G. 118
Engineering 18, 24, 25, 26, 36, 86, 113–15, 123–4, 134–5, 135–6, 139, 143, 176–7, 184
Enrolments 18, 19, 23, 85, 93, 111, 127, 165–7, 176, 195, 207
Environmental studies 125, 176
Equality of opportunity: *see* Accessibility to higher education *and* Student aid
Essex College 91
Established programs financing 3, 181

Farquarson, R.F. 67, 118
Faryon, Reginald R. 61
Federal financing of universities 3, 17, 19, 20, 32, 81, 181
Financial Post 152
Fleming, W.G. 126, 127
Food and beverage industries 49, 74
Food for Thought 15
Foreign investment in Canadian industry 50–1, 182, 187
Forestry 117
Formula financing 81–2, 98–9, 165, 166–7, 192
Fox, Sherwood 16
Fraser, H.J. 36n
Frost, Leslie 19, 31–2, 55, 64, 68, 70, 79, 82, 84, 86, 90, 82, 93, 95, 163
Fund raising by universities 19, 48, 51–2, 58, 59, 61, 68–70; *see also* Corporate aid to universities *and* individual universities

Galbraith, John K. 39n, 148
Gallup polls 21, 22, 23–4, 26, 146, 157
Gathercole, George 86, 87, 89, 92
General education 105, 107–9
Gerstein, Bertrand 66, 67
Gerstein, Reva 130, 190, 191
Glendon College 68
Globe 12
Globe and Mail 17, 64, 70, 73, 81, 154, 218
Gordon, Crawford 42
Gordon, Walter 32
Government funding of universities 12, 14, 19, 20, 25, 33, 46, 70, 75, 83, 98–9, 141, 142, 158–65, 167, 179–81, 192, 207; *see also* Federal financing of universities *and* individual universities
Government spending, philosophy of 14, 21, 22, 35, 149
Graduate Assistants' Association 204
Graduate education 127–31, 162, 173–7, 193–4
Granatstein, Jack 211
Gray, John M. 66
Grube, George 79
Grosskurth, Phyllis 162, 163

Hackett, A.R. 63
Hagey, J.G. 59, 60
Hall Commission: *see* Royal Commission on Health Services
Hall, G.E. 80, 81
Handa, M.L. 217
Hare, F.K. 96
Harris, R.S. 3n, 7n, 19n, 102n
Harris, W.C. 66, 69
Harvard Business Review 39
Harvard Business School 144
Harvard University 105
Harvey, E.B. 122, 150, 151, 152
Health Survey Committee 118
Hepburn, Mitchell 14, 78, 79

Historiography of education 3–5, 7
Honderich, Beland 73
Horsey, J. William 66
Hopkinson, Richard 182
Howe, C.D. 35n
Humanities Research Council 128, 129
Hutchins, Robert 25

Industrial Canada 10, 109, 144
Industrial Education Act (1911) 10
Industrial Foundation on Education 24, 25, 74, 106; attitude to government funding of universities 36; attitude to corporate aid to universities 37; and corporate aid to universities 43–53; establishment 23, 42; membership and sponsors 42, 44–5; publications 43; purposes 42; and student motivation 29–30; and tuition fees 31; and York University 63
Innis, Harold 18
Institute of Chartered Accountants 135
Institute of Donations and Public Affairs Research 182–3
Interim Committee on Financial Assistance for Students 197–9
International Labour Organization 114
International Nickel 57

Jackson, Robert W. 93, 126, 127, 128, 185
James, Cyril F. 17
James, W.F. 67
Johns, Walter H. 107
Jordan, A.R. 63
Journalism 83
Junior colleges 85, 86

Kelly, Frank 151
Kent, Douglas F. 64
Kerr, Clark 97
Kerr, George 151–152, 189

Keynesian economics 21, 77
Kidd, J.R. 64, 65
Kirkconnell, J. Watson 18

Labour 26, 27, 30, 31, 65, 205
Lakehead Technical Institute 61–2, 86
Lakehead University: establishment 55,
61–2; and unionization of faculty 204,
207
Lambert, Allen 66, 69, 70
Lank, Herbert 38
Lapp (Phillip) Report 134, 135, 139, 176
Lascelles, G. Arthur 64
Laurentian University; establishment in
Sudbury 55; and Brock Univer-
sity 57; and unionization of
faculty 204, 207, 210
Law 111, 117, 124–5, 137–8
Law Society of Upper Canada 124–5,
132, 137
Laxer, J. 148n
Leavine, S.F. 59
Lebel, Father E.C. 91
Leitch, John D. 66
Leonard, D'Arcy 67, 92
Lincoln County 56
Little, A.J. 66
Livingston, J. Sterling 144
Loudon, T. 63
Lumbers, L.G. 66
Lutheran Synod of America 60

Mahoney, William 67
Manpower planning: see Economic plan-
ning models
Mansur, David 66, 67
Massachusetts Institute of
Technology 125
Manual training 9, 10
Margison, Arthur 63

Mathews, Robin 168–169
McArthur College 127
McArthur, Duncan 15
McArthy, J.R. 90, 91, 92
McCutcheon, Wallace 58
Macdonald, Ian 208
Macdonald, J.B. 165, 168
McFarlane, J.A. 118
McGill University 71
McKee, A. Douglas 64
McKinnon Commission 137
McKinnon, Neil J. 58
Mackintosh, W.A. 91
McLachlan, W.R. 64
McLean, W.F. 66, 69
Maclean's 13, 25
McMaster University: and Brock Uni-
versity 56; and Canadianization of
university 170; and curriculum 104,
105; and drop-out rate 29; emergence
in Hamilton 55; and Engineering 123;
and expansion plans 89; and fund
raising 71; government funding of 80,
83; and graduate education 128; and
Medicine 82, 119, 138; and seculariza-
tion 80; and World War II 19
McNaughton, Charles 159
McNie, Jack 188, 189
Medical Council of Canada 133
Medical Research Council 118
Medicine 18, 19, 82, 93, 115, 116, 117–20,
121–2, 131, 132, 133, 138–9, 160
Merchandising industries 49
Ministry of Colleges and Universi-
ties 77, 88, 188–92, 195–6, 197; see also
Department of University Affairs
Mitchell, Robert W. 92
Moffat, Linda 186
Monthly Letter, Royal Bank of
Canada 110

National Conference of Canadian Universities 16–17, 23, 25, 52, 60
National Federation of Canadian University Students 30
National Industrial Conference Board 46, 49
National Policy and industrialization 8–9
National Research Council 18
National Selective Service 17
Needles, Ira C. 59, 60, 61
Niagara Peninsula Joint Committee on Higher Education 56
Niagara region 94
Northern Ontario 61, 85, 88, 111
Notre Dame University (BC) 204

O'Connor, J. 148
Oil in Canada 107
Oliver, Michael 208–209
Ontario Association of Architects 116, 126
Ontario Chamber of Commerce 37, 106
Ontario College of Education 126–127; see also Teacher training
Ontario College of Pharmacy 132, 133
Ontario Committee on the Healing Arts 115, 118, 120, 122, 135, 138, 139
Ontario Confederation of University Faculty Associations 95, 99, 173, 186, 187
Ontario Council on University Affairs 181, 191–4, 202, 203
Ontario Dental Association 119
Ontario Economic Council 129
Ontario Farmers Union 27
Ontario Federation of Students 173, 197, 201–3
Ontario Hydro 58
Ontario Industrial Training Council 180

Ontario Medical Association 133
Ontario Student Assistance (Awards) Program 33, 196, 197, 198; see also Accessibility to higher education and Student aid
Ontario Union of Students 201
Orillia Packet and Times 97
Osgoode Hall Law School 124–5, 132, 137

Parker, Ralph 57
Parr, J.G. 189–90
Parrott, Harry 188, 189
Peitchinis, Stephen 142, 178, 155
Penner, Roland 213
Pharmacy 120, 131, 133, 139
Phillips, W.E. (Eric) 66, 81, 89–90
Phillips, Nathan 59
Pitman, Walter 158
Pollard, John A. 39
Pollock, C.A. 59
Polymer Corporation 25
Porter, Dana 24n, 80, 92
Porter, John 62
Post-war baby boom 15, 22, 35
Post-war veterans 19, 22, 28, 82
Prentice, Alison 8
Priestley, F.E.L. 103
Proctor, John S. 66, 69
Professional Engineers of Ontario 134
Professional services industry 49
Professional training 18, 26–7, 36–7, 56, 82–3, 86, 93–4, 113–40, 174–8, 184; see also individual professions

Queen's University 55; Architecture 125–6; curriculum 17, 103, 104, 105; denominational link 12; employment of graduates 151; Engineering 123; expansion plans 89; fund raising 71; government funding of 14, 19, 80, 91, 165; Medicine 17, 82; programming strategy 194–5; Public administration 134; School of Mining 11; and University of Toronto 78; and World War II 16, 17, 18, 19

Recruiting of students 194
Red Cross 16
Reid, Tim 158
Report of the Commission to Study the Development of Graduate Programmes in Ontario Universities: see Spinks Commission
Report on Foreign Direct Investment in Canada (Gray Report) 50
Report of the Special Program Review 197
Resource industries 48, 49, 74
Revisionist educational history 7
Robarts, John 31, 33, 55, 61, 71, 92, 96
Rosenberg, Julius and Ethel 24
Ross, Aileen 55
Ross, Murray 65, 66, 76
Rowntree, Leslie 55
Royal Architectural Institute of Canada 126
Royal College of Dental Surgeons 131, 132
Royal Commission on Canada's Economic Prospects 23, 24, 25, 33, 86, 87, 110
Royal Commission on Health Services (Hall Commission) 115, 118–20, 122, 138
Royal Commission on the National Development of Arts, Letters, and Sciences (Massey Commission) 20, 33, 81
Royal Commission on the University of Toronto 11, 12

Rudolph, Frederick 105
Ryerson, Egerton 8
Ryerson Institute of Technology (Ryerson Polytechnical Institute) 80, 86, 180, 204

St Andrew's conference (1956) 23, 24, 42, 43, 52, 63, 102
St Mary's University 204, 210
Sargent, E. 157
Saturday Night 19, 73
Schindeler, Fred 217
Scott, W.P. 66
Schmon, Arthur 56, 57
Science Council of Canada 148, 217
Scientific research 18, 26, 29, 48, 79–80, 181–2, 187
Seath, John 10
Secondary education 8, 13–14
Sewell, David 145
Sheffield, E.F. 23, 85
Shell Oil 40
Shoemaker, E.J. 59
Sisco, Norman 197
Skolnik, M.L. 217
Smith, Adam 35
Smith, Sidney 42, 86, 106
Snider, A.M. 59
Social work 136–7
Soviet Union 23, 24, 29; see also Cold War
Spinks Commission 96–8, 128, 129, 173–4
Spinks, J.W.T. 96
Sputnik satellite 24, 25, 43
Stager, David 143; see also Cook and Stager
Stamp, Robert 8n, 13n
Steele, James 168
Stephenson, Bette 188, 193, 195, 196
Stevenson, L.Z.G. 118

Stewart, E.E. 78, 95, 142n, 159, 169, 195
Student aid 28–33, 153–5, 163, 196–201;
    see also Accessibility to higher
    education
Student motivation 29
Student movement 14, 30, 105, 156–7,
    164, 201–3
Sweeney, John 181
Symons, Thomas 61

Teacher training: elementary and high
    school 103, 126–7, 185–6; univer-
    sity 127–31, 186–8
Technical and vocational education 8,
    9–11, 13, 27, 37, 80, 94, 180
Technical Education Act (1919) 13
Technical Services Council of
    Canada 150
Tomecko, John 39
Toronto Board of Education 13
Toronto Dominion Bank 67, 69, 70
Toronto Star 73
Toronto Technical School 10
Toronto Telegram 73
Trade and Commerce 36, 38
Treasury Board (Ontario) 159–61, 163–4
Trent University: and business 61; estab-
    lishment 55, 61, 94; and fund rais-
    ing 61; and government funding
    of 61, 164; unionization of
    faculty 204, 207
Tuition fees 13, 30, 31, 142, 155, 159, 162,
    163, 200
Twaits, W.O. 157

Underhill, Frank 79
Unemployment and underemploy-
    ment 28, 147–9, 150–2, 161, 166, 180,
    183–8

Unionization of faculty 203–213; and
    bureaucratization of univer-
    sity 205–207; and Carleton 204, 207,
    208–9, 211, 212; and CAUT 205; criti-
    cisms of 212–213; at Lakehead 204,
    207; at Laurentian 204, 207, 210; in
    Quebec 204; of teaching assist-
    ants 204; at Trent 204, 207; in United
    States 205; and University of
    Ottawa 204, 209–10, 212; and Univer-
    sity of Windsor 204, 207, 210; and
    York 204, 207, 208, 211
United States 8, 23–4, 26, 30, 35, 50–1,
    57, 105, 112, 118, 148, 156, 169, 182, 217
United Steel Workers of America 57, 67
University of Alberta 107
University of British Columbia 19, 71
University of California 96, 97, 156
University of Guelph 55, 194
University of Manitoba 204
University of Ottawa 55; Medicine 82;
    expansion plans 89; Engineering 123;
    government funding of 91; unioniza-
    tion of faculty 204, 209–10, 212
University of Saskatchewan 19
University of Toronto 42, 54, 55; admis-
    sions policy 87; Architecture 125,
    126; board of governors 12, 48, 58;
    Business administration 117, 134; and
    Canadianization of the university 169;
    and city of Toronto 59; and curricu-
    lum 101, 102, 104; and collective bar-
    gaining 204; Dentistry 132; drop-out
    rate 29; employment of gradu-
    ates 102; establishment 12; expansion
    plans 89; Forestry 11, 117; fund rais-
    ing 58, 68, 71, 72; governing struc-
    ture 12, 78–9; government funding
    of 19, 80, 88; Law 124–5; Medi-
    cine 27, 82, 138; professional train-
    ing 82, 122–3; Royal Commission on

the University of Toronto 11, 12; satellite campuses 59, 94; status 78; and World War II 16; and York University 64, 65, 68, 71, 72

University of Waterloo 55; Architecture 125–6; board of governors 59–60; and business 60, 62; and Canadian Manufacturers Association 60; government funding of 59; and Lutheran Synod of America 60; and Waterloo College 59–60

University of Western Ontario 55; curriculum 17, 104; denominational link 12; Dentistry 119–20; Engineering 123; expansion plans 89; fund raising 71; government funding of 19, 80, 164–5; Journalism 83; Medicine 82; and World War II 16, 17; and University of Toronto 78

University of Windsor 55; curriculum 104; fund raising 71; faculty unionization 204, 207, 210; Law 125

Vickers, Jill 209n
Von Zur-Muehlen, Max 151

Walker, E.H. 66, 69
Walker, H.H. 89, 165
Wallace, R.C. 17, 82, 83, 84
Wartime Bureau of Technical Personnel 17
Waterloo College: see University of Waterloo
Watson, J., and Douglas, M. 39n–42n
Welland county 56
Welland District Women's Institute 56
White, John 147, 162, 188
Willmot, D.G. 56, 116n
Wilson 190

Winegard, William 193, 199
Winters, Robert 66, 70, 71
Wolfe, Brian 186, 187
Woodfield, Ray 43
World War I 12
World War II: and Defence Training Course 17; and democratic values 15, 16, 20; and enrolments in universities 18; and humanities' teaching 17–18; and McMaster University 19; and National Conference of Canadian Universities 16–17; and National Research Council 18; and National Selective Service 17; organizing for 16; post-war veterans 19; and primary and secondary education 15; and Queen's University 16, 17, 18, 19; and University of British Columbia 19; and University of Saskatchewan 19; and University of Toronto 16; and University of Western Ontario 17; and Wartime Bureau of Technical Personnel 17
Wright, Douglas 98, 123, 130, 155, 159, 163, 165, 168, 169, 170, 171, 178

YMCA 63, 64
York University: and board of governors 65–76; and business 64, 66; curriculum 68, 105; establishment 55, 63–6; and expansion 76; and fund raising 70–6; government funding of 63, 64, 70, 71; investments 67, 70n; professional training 117, 125–6; and University of Toronto 64, 65, 68, 71, 72; unionization of faculty 204, 207, 208, 211; and YMCA 63, 64
York University Faculty Association 208

THE STATE AND ECONOMIC LIFE
Editors: Mel Watkins, University of Toronto; Leo Panitch, Carleton University

This series, begun in 1978, includes original studies in the general area of Canadian political economy and economic history, with particular emphasis on the part played by the government in shaping the economy. Collections of shorter studies, as well as theoretical or internationally comparative works, may also be included.

1 The State and Enterprise
  Canadian manufacturers and the federal government 1917–1931
  TOM TRAVES

2 Unequal Beginnings
  Agricultural and economic development in Quebec and Ontario until 1870
  JOHN McCALLUM

3 'An Impartial Umpire'
  Industrial relations and the Canadian state 1900–1911
  PAUL CRAVEN

4 Scholars and Dollars
  Politics, economics, and the universities of Ontario 1945–1980
  PAUL AXELROD